5 GED® PRACTICE TESTS

The Staff of The Princeton Review

PrincetonReview.com

Random House, Inc. New York

The Independent Education Consultants Association recognizes The Princeton Review as a valuable resource for high school and college students applying to college and graduate school.

The Princeton Review, Inc.
2315 Broadway
New York, NY 10024
E-mail: editorialsupport@review.com

ISBN: 978-0-375-42956-9
ISSN: 1948-2191

Editor: Rebecca Lessem
Production Editor: Meave Shelton
Production Coordinator: Sheena Paul

Printed in the United States of America on partially recycled paper.

10 9 8 7 6 5 4 3 2 1

Editorial
Rob Franek, VP Test Prep Books, Publisher
Seamus Mullarkey, Associate Publisher
Rebecca Lessem, Senior Editor
Laura Braswell, Senior Editor
Selena Coppock, Editor
Heather Brady, Editor

Production Services
Scott Harris, Executive Director, Production Services
Kim Howie, Senior Graphic Designer

Production Editorial
Meave Shelton, Production Editor
Jennifer Graham, Production Editor

Random House Publishing Team
Tom Russell, Publisher
Nicole Benhabib, Publishing Manager
Ellen L. Reed, Production Manager
Alison Stoltzfus, Associate Managing Editor
Elham Shabahat, Publishing Assistant

ACKNOWLEDGMENTS

The staff of The Princeton Review would like to thank Kim Howie, Rebecca Lessem, Ed Carroll, Mary Kinzel, Colin Fitzpatrick, Mariwyn Curtin, Heather Brady, Selena Coppock, Bill Garrity, Sharon Lauro, Cary Daniel, Peter Hanink, James Matthews, Colleen Platt, and John Moscatiello for their work in bringing this book together.

CONTENTS

Part I
GED Information and Strategies

Chapter 1
About the GED

WHAT IS THE GED?

The General Educational Development test is actually a group of five tests. You can take them in one day or over a few days. It is often referred to as the high school equivalency test, since a passing grade gets you a certificate that most colleges and employers recognize as equal to a high school diploma.

WHERE DOES THE GED COME FROM?

The GED was developed during World War II when about as many people took it to gain employment as to gain opportunities for future study. The test has been revised three times since then, most recently in 2002.

The test is administered by the American Council on Education (ACE). ACE is a council representing the presidents and chancellors of degree-granting institutions. Unlike many makers of standardized tests, ACE only produces one test.

WHO TAKES THE GED?

All sorts of people! Almost 700,000 adults around the world take the GED every year. Some take it because they've been homeschooled; others have left high school before graduation. Some have launched careers that take them away from school.

Here is a list of people who have taken the GED and gone on to tremendous success in their fields.

Celebrities Who Earned a GED	
Augusten Burroughs	Avril Lavigne
Walter Amos	Kelly McGillis
Senator Ben Nighthorse Campbell	Katharine McPhee
Michael Chang	Governor Ruth Ann Miner
Bill Cosby	Tommy Nunez
Governor Jim Florio	Mary Lou Retton
Jerry Garcia	Chris Rock
Michael J. Fox	Jessica Simpson
Paris Hilton	Christian Slater
D. L. Hughley	Dave Thomas
Bishop T. D. Jakes	Mark Wahlberg
Waylon Jennings	Tammy Wynette

WHAT IS THE STRUCTURE OF THE GED?

There are five different tests that comprise the GED:

Language Arts, Writing
Social Studies
Science
Language Arts, Reading
Mathematics

Here's the good news: You don't have to know everything about the moons of Pluto or the fundamental theorem of calculus to pass the GED. The tests are general and not out to get you on the specifics.

Let's take a look at what you should expect from each test.

Language Arts, Writing

Part One: 50 multiple-choice questions; 75 minutes

Each question will consist of a sentence. Most sentences will have something wrong with them, and you will select the answer that fixes the sentence. The errors that you will have to spot include:

Sentence Structure (use of clauses and phrases)	30%
Usage (grammar)	30%
Mechanics (spelling, punctuation, and capitalization)	25%
Organization	15%

Part Two: One essay, 45 minutes

You will be asked to write an essay on a particular topic, such as "The truth is always the best option. Do you agree or disagree?" In this part of the exam, what position you take matters less than how well you express your opinion. There is no right answer, just good writing.

Social Studies

50 multiple-choice questions, 70 minutes

The Social Studies exam contains a mixture of long passages followed by three or four questions each, and shorter passages followed by one question each. Sixty percent of the questions will be based on graphic material (charts, diagrams, graphs and cartoons). **No outside knowledge is tested.** That means that the answer to each question will be contained in the passage or diagram provided. The passages will address the following areas of social studies:

National History	25%
Government and Civics	25%
World History	15%
Economics	20%
Geography	15%

Science

50 multiple-choice questions, 80 minutes

Like the Social Studies exam, the Science exam contains a mixture of long passages followed by up to five questions each, and shorter passages followed by one question each. About fifty percent of the questions will be based on charts and other graphic material. You will need only a **general knowledge** of scientific principles. The answer to each question will be almost always be contained in the passage or diagram provided. The passages will address the following areas of science:

Life Science	45%
Physics and Chemistry	35%
Earth and Space	20%

Language Arts, Reading

40 multiple-choice questions, 65 minutes

You will be given seven total passages: three fiction passages (each from a different time period), one excerpt from a play, and one poem. You will also see two from the following types of passages: a review of a performance, an article about popular culture, or a business-related topic. After each, you will be asked three to five questions designed to test your reading skills and your ability to analyze and apply what you've just read. The passages will be divided into the following sections:

Literary (fiction, play, poem)	80%
Nonfiction (review, workplace document, popular culture)	20%

Mathematics

Part One: *25 multiple-choice questions, 45 minutes; calculator permitted*

Part Two: *25 multiple-choice questions, 45 minutes; calculator NOT permitted*

The emphasis in both parts of the Mathematics exam is on arithmetic problems that are similar to those you may have to do in your daily routine already. Many will be word problems. About half will be based on diagrams or charts. Most will be multiple choice, but approximately ten questions will be short answer. All of the questions will address these general areas of math:

Number Operations/Number Sense	20%–30%
Measurement/Geometry	20%–30%
Data Analysis/Probability/Statistics	20%–30%
Algebra/Functions/Patterns	20%–30%

HOW IS THE GED SCORED?

Each of the five tests is scored from 200 to 800. The essay portion of the Language Arts, Writing test is scored on a scale from 1 to 4. There is no penalty for wrong answers, so make sure you answer every question, even if you are guessing!

WHEN WILL I LEARN MY RESULTS?

You will receive a letter in the mail with your results no more than eight weeks after you take the test. The score report will include your scores on all five sub-tests as well as an overall score. If you need official copies to send to colleges or an employer, you must request those from your state GED office. Some states charge a small fee for sending you the copies.

WHAT IS A PASSING SCORE?

You must get a score of at least 410 on each of the five tests, with an average score of at least 450 overall to pass the GED.

If you get about half the questions correct that will translate to a passing score. There are a few colleges and states that award scholarships for people with very high GED scores, but in general there's no reason to keep studying past the point where you can pass the test.

WHAT IF I DON'T PASS ONE OF THE SECTIONS?

In most states, you need only retake those sections you didn't pass the first time. For example, if you pass Language Arts, Writing; Mathematics; Social Studies; and Language Arts, Reading; but did not pass Science, you would only need to take the Science section over again.

Some states will encourage you to take the whole test again anyway, because only your best scores are kept and you might do even better on the ones you passed the second time around. Regardless, you will be given a different version of the test when you retake it, with completely different questions.

DO I HAVE TO TAKE THE WHOLE TEST AT ONCE?

Each state sets its own rules for how the test is taken. Some require you to take the entire set of tests in one day; others are more flexible. In some states you can take each test when you feel ready for it. Others require that you finish the GED in a two-day period. To find the rules for your state, consult the list of state agencies' numbers below.

HOW DO I REGISTER FOR THE GED?

One of the best ways to register for the GED is to call the information number for your state from the list below. You can also call 800-62 MY GED (800-626-9433) or go to the ACE website:

www.acenet.edu/resources/GED/center_locator.cfm

Here's the specific information about each state's programs:

Alabama
334-353-4885
www.acs.cc.al.us/ged/GED.aspx

Alaska
907-465-4685
www.ajcn.state.ak.us/abe/ged.htm

Arizona
602-258-2410
www.ade.az.gov/adult-ed/ged_home.asp

Arkansas
501-682-1978
www.arkansased.org

California
916-319-0758
916-445-9438
www.cde.ca.gov/ta/tg/gd

Colorado
303-866-6942
www.cde.state.co.us/cdeadult/GEDindex.htm

Connecticut
860-638-4151
www.sde.ct.gov/sde/site/default.asp

Delaware
302-739-3743
www.doe.k12.de.us/services/guide/adulted_pages/ged-centers.shtml

District of Columbia
202-274-7173
www.dcged.org

Florida
850-245-0449
www.fldoe.org/workforce/ged/gedover.asp

Georgia
404-679-1621
www.dtae.tec.ga.us/adultlit/ged.html

Hawaii
808-586-3124
doe.k12.hi.us/communityschools/diplomaged.htm

Idaho
208-332-6980
www.sde.idaho.gov/index.html

Illinois
217-785-0123
www.isbe.net

Indiana
317-232-0523
www.doe.state.in.us/adulted/adultlearner.html#3

Iowa
515-281-3636
www.iowa.gov/educate

Kansas
785-291-3038
www.kansasregents.org/adult_ed/ged.html

Kentucky
502-573-5114, ext. 102
kyae.ky.gov/students/ged.htm

Louisiana
225-342-0444
www.doe.state.la.us/DOE/adulted/ged/ged.asp

Maine
207-624-6754
www.maine.gov/education/aded/dev/hsc.htm

Maryland
401-767-0168
www.marylandpublicschools.org/MSDE/programs/GED

Massachusetts
781-338-6604
www.doe.mass.edu/ged

Michigan
517-373-1692
www.michigan.gov/mdcd

Minnesota
651-582-8437
education.state.mn.us/MDE/Learning_Support/Adult_Basic_Education_GED

Mississippi
601-432-6481
www.mde.k12.ms.us

Missouri
573-751-3504
dese.mo.gov/divcareered/ged_index.htm

Montana
406-444-4438
www.opi.state.mt.us/GED/Index.html

Nebraska
402-471-4807
www.nde.state.ne.us/ADED/home.htm

Nevada
775-687-9167
www.literacynet.org/nvadulted/programs-ged.html

New Hampshire
603-271-6698
www.ed.state.nh.us/education/doe/organization/adultlearning/Adulted/new_hampshire_ged_testing_program.htm

New Jersey
609-984-2420
www.state.nj.us/education/students/ged

New Mexico
505-827-6507
www.ped.state.nm.us

New York
518-474-5906
www.emsc.nysed.gov/ged

North Carolina
919-807-7214
www.ncccs.cc.nc.us/Basic_Skills/ged.htm

North Dakota
701-328-2393
www.dpi.state.nd.us/adulted/index.shtm

Ohio
614-466-1577
www.ode.state.oh.us/GD

Oklahoma
405-521-3321
800-405-0355
www.sde.state.ok.us

Oregon
503-378-8648, ext. 373
www.oregon.gov/CCWD/GED

Pennsylvania
717-783-3373
www.able.state.pa.us/able

Rhode Island
401-222-8950
401-222-8478
401-222-8463
www.ridoe.net/adulteducation

South Carolina
803-734-8348
www.sclrc.org/GED.htm

South Dakota
605-773-3101
www.state.sd.us/dol/abe

Tennessee
615-741-5057
800-531-1515
www.state.tn.us/labor-wfd/AE/aeged.htm

Texas
512-463-9292
www.tea.state.tx.us/ged

Utah
801-538-7870
801-538-7921
www.usoe.K12.ut.us/adulted/ged/index.html

Vermont
802-828-0077
education.vermont.gov/new/html/pgm_adulted/ged/testing.html

Virginia
804-371-2334
www.pen.K12.va.us

Washington
360-704-4321
www.sbctc.ctc.edu/public/y_ged.aspx

West Virginia
304-558-6315
800-642-2670
wvabe.org/ged

Wisconsin
608-267-2275
800-768-8886
dpi.wi.gov/ged_hsed/gedhsed.html

Wyoming
307-777-7885
307-777-7654
307-777-6567 (Fax)
www.k12.wy.us

WHAT IS THE PRINCETON REVIEW?

The Princeton Review is a test-preparation company based in New York City. It has offices in more than 50 cities across the United States and many branches in foreign countries. The Princeton Review's test-taking techniques and review strategies are unique and powerful. We developed them after studying all the real GED tests we could get our hands on, and modeled the tests in this book after real, recent GEDs.

Chapter 2
General Strategies

HOW SHOULD I PREPARE FOR THE GED?

Take one of the practice exams to start. This will give you a baseline score that you can use to measure your progress.

It's probably not practical for you to go through all of the material taught in high school between now and when you take the GED. Fortunately, that's not required. Taking the practice tests in this book will help a lot. Treat them seriously, as you would the real test. Try to replicate the sometimes less-than-comfortable testing environment; don't just sit at home on your couch with a DVD playing. Take the test in silence at a table, and make sure you are not interrupted. Also be sure to use scratch paper and not to write on the test itself, as you will have to do on the real exam.

Once you take an exam, review it thoroughly and go back over the answers and explanations. Ask yourself the following questions:

> Why was the right answer right?
> Why was the wrong answer wrong?
> Why did I pick the wrong answer?
> What can I do differently next time, so I'll pick the right answer?

We also recommend studying with *Cracking the GED* from The Princeton Review. It covers the review material at just the right depth to prepare you for the exam without bogging you down.

MAKE IT REAL

You play the way you practice, so take practice exams as if they were the real thing. In particular this means two things: using scratch paper and using the right calculator.

Calculator

You may think that the first math section (in which you're allowed to use a calculator) would be easier than the second, but there's a catch: You have to use THEIR calculator. You will be provided at the test center with a Casio FX-260.

Like any new calculator, this takes some getting used to. **So beat the system and get a Casio FX-260 *before* the test and practice with it.** It is *essential* that you get used to the calculator ahead of time, so that you can get used to its quirks. Although the testing sites are supposed to show a video about the calculator before the test begins, you don't want to spend valuable time during the exam trying to figure out the buttons. The Casio FX-260 is available in many stores, or you can buy it from ACE for less than ten dollars by calling 1-800-531-5015.

The Weirdness of Calculators

There are three functions on the Casio FX-260 that can be pretty confusing. The first involves using negative numbers. (And, by the way, if you aren't sure what negative numbers are, don't worry. We'll cover them in the next chapter.) To enter a negative number, you first have to enter the number, then hit the "change sign" key located directly above the "7" key. The display now shows the negative number.

The second confusing feature of the FX-260 involves parentheses. (And, again, if you aren't sure how to use parentheses in math, don't worry. We'll cover them in the next chapter.) Parentheses in math usually mean an implied multiplication that you can't actually see on the page. You must remember to multiply to get the right answer. Here's an example: To enter the expression 3(2 + 5), you would enter 3, then the multiplication key, then the left parentheses key, then 2, then the plus key, then the 5 key, then the right parentheses key. To complete the problem, press the "equals" key.

The third confusing feature of the FX-260 involves square roots. (We'll cover them, too, in a later chapter.) There is no dedicated square root key on this calculator—the key for square roots is also the key for squaring. To find the square root of a number, first enter the number (let's say 9), and then locate the square root symbol, which is in smaller letters on the key that says "x^2." If you just pressed this key, it would square the number (9 times 9, or 81), but that's not what we want to do in this case. To find the square root of 9, first enter 9, then press the "shift" key (located at top left), then press the "x^2" key. This will access the second function of the key and give you the square root (in this case, 3).

You can see why we are telling you to get the calculator in advance and become familiar with it.

Scratch Paper

Another annoying part of the GED is that you are not allowed to write in the test booklets. On most other standardized paper-based tests you are allowed to make marks in the book, circling key terms in the reading passages and marking up diagrams. Not so here. Although it may seem like a little thing, using scratch paper can take some getting used to, so start doing it now. Commit to taking the practice tests in this book without writing in the book so you're used to it on test day.

We recommend that you put your scratch paper directly beneath the problem you're working on to minimize distance. Also, be sure to label your work with the problem number. In the heat of battle, you want to be able to tell which calculation belongs to which problem, especially if you start working a problem, skip it and come back. It would be a shame to start over from scratch (haha) because you can't locate the work you previously did. Just as with the calculator, you should start using your scratch paper now!

THE GED'S BIG WEAKNESS

The GED's greatest weakness is that it's a standardized test. Regardless of how we feel about them (and they're sure not fun), standardized tests have certain requirements: They have to be standard. The GED this year has to test the same material in pretty much the same way as the GED last year. This has let us study the test and figure out what they're looking for. We know which grammar rules they test and which they don't; we know what kinds of algebra you'll need and what you won't. And you'll get the benefit of all that research in this book of tests.

Knowing how the test is put together leads us to certain key strategies.

ANSWER EVERY QUESTION!

Q: How many points are deducted for each wrong answer on the GED?

A: Zero!

This leads us to an important strategy on the test—**answer every single question**. Even if you can't eliminate any of the answer choices and guess randomly, you still have a 20 percent chance of being right. That means that for every five questions you answer completely randomly you should pick up one point. Since you get no points for leaving something blank, and you could get points for filling it in, why would you leave a blank?

TAKE OUT THE TRASH

So if you have a one in five chance of getting a question right even if you can't eliminate any of the answer choices, what happens if you can eliminate an answer or three? Take a look at the following question:

Q: How many points are deducted for each wrong answer on the GED?

A:
(1) 5,000,000
(2) 1
(3) 0
(4) Paris
(5) Hassenpfeffer

It's pretty clear that (4) and (5) are wrong; they're not even numbers. And (1) is just too extreme to possibly be true. So even if we didn't know the answer, just by taking out the ones that are clearly wrong we're down to two choices. That's a coin toss—we've got just as good a chance of being right as we have of being wrong. At this point we're sitting pretty because we have a 50 percent chance of getting a point out of this question.

POE

The example above clearly shows the benefit of Process of Elimination, or POE. This is an incredibly powerful tool that you can use on each and every test question on the GED. There are specific strategies for each test, but on every question on the GED you should be looking at which answer choices you can cross off.

Your scratch paper will come in handy here as well. For tougher problems, keep track of which answers you've gotten rid of. Write out 1 through 5 on your paper over and over and cross off the numbers of the answer choices you eliminate for each problem.

DON'T GET BOGGED DOWN

There is another important discovery to be made about how the GED is scored. Since no one question on a particular test is worth more than another, you shouldn't get bogged down and waste time on any particular problem. You can skip around and you have just as good of a chance of getting the last problem in a section right as you do the first problem.

These are basic strategies that apply to the whole test. There are a couple of kinds of questions that show up so prevalently on the GED that we put them in this core strategies section. So let's take a look at Reading Pictures and Reading Answers.

READING PICTURES

The Social Studies, Science, and Math tests all have questions that employ graphics. You'll have to read and glean information from these graphics and then use them in your answers. There are some important key factors that will help you on these kinds of questions no matter which test they show up on.

First Things First

It's tempting to jump into the graphic, but the first thing to look at is always the title. Think of it like a headline for a newspaper story, telling you what it is you're looking at. Let's look at a couple of examples.

The Bar Graph

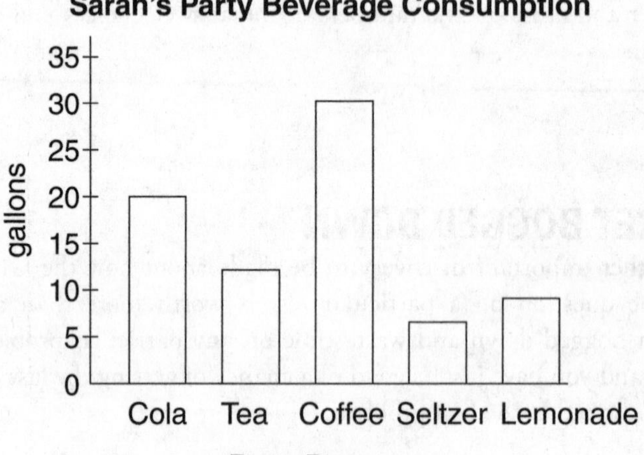

The Vertical Axis and the Horizontal Axis

So the title tells us that this is a graph of Sarah's Party Beverage Consumption. What kind of drinks does she consume? The horizontal axis, running across the bottom of the graph, tells us that she drinks cola, tea, coffee, seltzer, and lemonade. The vertical axis, running along the left side, shows us that she drinks by the gallon.

1. Which beverage did Sarah consume the least of?

(1) Cola
(2) Tea
(3) Coffee
(4) Seltzer
(5) Lemonade

Here's How to Crack It

This would be considered a **comprehension** question, meaning you just need to go back and get the information from the graph. The height of each bar gives you the amount of that beverage sold. If we look for the shortest bar, it would be seltzer, (4).

The Pie Chart

The key thing to remember about a pie chart as opposed to a simple bar graph is that all the pieces have to add up to 100%. That tells you that if you don't know the size of one piece, you can figure it out from the total of the others.

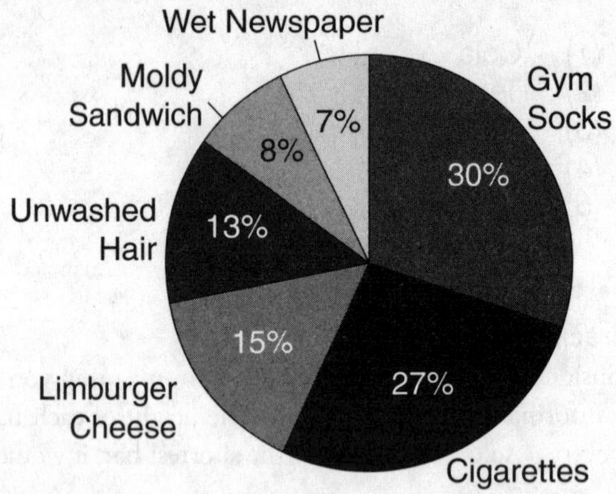

2. Which of the following has a greater percentage than gym socks?

(1) Limburger cheese
(2) Limburger cheese + wet newspaper
(3) unwashed hair + Limburger Cheese
(4) Limburger cheese + moldy sandwich + wet newspaper
(5) cigarettes + wet newspaper

Here's How to Crack It

This is a **number operations** question, looking at comparing a couple of entries on the chart. Gym socks have 30%, while Limburger has 15% of the chart, so that's out. Wet newspaper and Limburger together have 22%, so that's out as well. Unwashed hair + Limburger has 28%, but that's still short. You might think that three segments added together would exceed one segment, but choice (4) only adds up to 30%. That's the same as gym socks, not more. But cigarettes and wet newspaper add up to 34%, so (5) is the answer.

There are more examples of graphics in *Cracking the GED*. If you feel you need more review with these items, that book is an excellent place to start.

READING ANSWERS

Remember what we said earlier about the Social Studies test: There is no outside knowledge required to answer the questions. That's because the answer will be found in the reading passages presented before each question. The same is true in the Language Arts, Reading test. In the Science test a general knowledge of science is required, but again, most always the answers are in the passage.

So if the answer is right there on the page, why do people miss questions on these tests? There are a couple of reasons.

One major reason is boredom. The passages, especially on the Social Studies and Science tests, are usually pretty darn dull. So the key here is to read actively (and take notes) for the information you need to answer the question.

Another reason is vocabulary. Most people use a fairly small number of words in their everyday lives. The GED test writers also have a core set of words that they use, but they aren't the same words the rest of us use.

So how can you get the answers if you don't know all the words?

A Dictionary and a Notebook

One way is to learn the words. As you go through and review these tests, and as you're doing other reading in the course of preparing for the GED, keep a small notebook and a small dictionary with you. Write down any words you don't know and look them up. Reading is the best way to prepare for the vast portions of the GED that are based on reading comprehension.

The Words You Know

The other way to deal with a word you don't know is to focus on the words you do know. Take the following sentence: "The dexterity of the magician's fingers wowed the crowd." Let's say you don't know the word "dexterity." What do you know? You know that it's the magician's fingers that had "dexterity," and that the crowd was impressed. So maybe "dexterity" means something like "excellence." (It actually means "skill," but in this case you'd be close.)

This is the way that focusing on the context can help you get the meaning. When you're reading for the GED, look at the sentence above and the sentence below where you're reading. Those nearby sentences will help you get the meaning.

CLASSIFICATION PASSAGES

There are two main kinds of passages: classification passages and structural passages. You'll see a lot of classification passages in the Social Studies and Science portions of the exam. Here is an example of a classification passage:

> A command economy is one in which the government actively intervenes in economic processes. The government may set prices, nationalize industries, establish quotas or otherwise directly engage in the workings of the economy.
>
> A pure market economy is one in which the government does not directly interfere. Market forces are allowed to act unfettered.
>
> A mixed economy is one in which the government may play some role, but still allows market forces to largely set prices and otherwise move the economic activity.

As you can see, a classification passage is just that. It defines or classifies things. Questions will then largely be about applying that classification to other items. Let's take a look:

---

1. Which of the following groups would most likely benefit from a transition from a command economy to a market economy?

(1) business owners
(2) consumers
(3) retailers
(4) wholesalers
(5) regulators

Here's How to Crack It

Look to the passage to understand the terms of the question. Command economy has the government actively involved; market economy has almost no government involvement. That's going to be best for businesses. Here we don't mention retailers or wholesalers particularly, so cross those off. Regulators have less power under a market economy, so they're out. Consumers aren't necessarily better off from deregulation, so that leaves (1). Again, use POE!

STRUCTURAL PASSAGES

A structural passage looks like less like a list and more like a passage from a book. The key things to look for here are structural words, which are the words that give you a clue as to how the passage is put together.

Look for **Order** words:

First–second–third
Primarily–secondarily
One reason–another reason–finally
For one thing–for another thing

Also look for **Conclusion** words. These tell you when the author is making a particular point:

Therefore
As a result
Thus
Hence
Consequently
In conclusion

Here's an example of a structural passage:

> There are several reasons to hail paperclips as the greatest invention of the twentieth century.
>
> First, paperclips are ubiquitous. They can be found in every office, all around the world.
>
> Second, they are affordable. This makes the paperclip's technology available to everyone of all social strata.
>
> Third, they are elegant. A simple wire with three bends holds together over a dozen sheets of paper.
>
> Consequently one might argue, and perhaps convincingly, that the omnipresence, cost-effectiveness and grace of the paperclip single it out as the pinnacle of human achievement.

There's an important point to make again here. You may not know all the words in the passage (*ubiquitous?*) but you can often figure them out from the rest of the passage ("all around the world"). Focus on the words you know to help you with the others.

Let's look at a question:

2. The primary purpose of the passage is to

(1) show the elegance of paperclips
(2) undermine the argument that paperclips are significant
(3) argue that the paperclip is the greatest creation of the 20th century
(4) emphasize the importance of affordability
(5) show that paperclips can be useful as well as beautiful

Here's How to Crack It

This is an **evaluation** question, basically asking for the main idea of the passage. Look at what is discussed at the beginning and the end of the passage. Did you see the structural words ordering the author's point? Very often the main point will be in the first or last paragraph. Here it's in the first, saying that paperclips are the greatest invention of the twentieth century, which matches (3). Elegance is support for that thesis, not the main point itself so eliminate (1). Always get rid of answers that contradict the passage, like (2). Answers (4) and (5) are again smaller points, not the main point. Always remember to use POE to get rid of answers—the last one standing has to be the right one.

Now that you know how to best use this book and some general strategies on reading graphs and passages, let's go over some more strategies for each test in particular.

Chapter 3
Specific Test Strategies

In this chapter we're going to look at specific strategies for each test.

LANGUAGE ARTS, WRITING, PART ONE

Part One: 50 multiple-choice questions; 75 minutes

Sentence Structure (use of clauses and phrases)	30%
Usage (grammar)	30%
Mechanics (spelling, punctuation and capitalization)	25%
Organization	15%

The first part of the Language Arts, Writing test is focused on sentences. There are a few question types that you need to know how to look at.

Sentence Correction

In a Sentence Correction question, you will be asked how a particular sentence should be fixed. Forty-five percent of the questions will look like this. For example:

(1) Having lost my car to an accidents, I now bicycle to work. (2) A bicycle is greener than a car. (3) In today's environment, one are required to be eco-friendly.

1. Sentence 1: **Having lost my car to an accidents, I now bicycle to work.**

   Which correction should be made to Sentence 1?

   (1) change accidents to accident
   (2) change bicycle to was bicycling
   (3) change Having lost to Losing
   (4) remove the comma after accidents
   (5) no correction is necessary

Here's How to Crack It

If you can spot the errors in the sentence as you're looking at it, that can be useful. If not, plug the answer choice back into the sentence and see if it works. Choice (1) does correct a problem ("an accidents") in the sentence. (2) doesn't solve the problem. There's nothing wrong with "Having lost" so (3) isn't good. Removing the comma would create a run-on, so eliminate (4). That just leaves (1). POE again!

Sentence Revision

Sentence Revision questions will ask you which of five possible rewritings of a portion of the sentence is the best. About 35 percent of the questions will be sentence revision. This is a terrific opportunity to use POE.

2. Sentence 3: **In today's environment, <u>one are required</u> to be eco-friendly.**

   Which of the following is the best way to rewrite the underlined portion of the sentence? If you think the sentence is correct as written choose (1).

   (1) one are required
   (2) one is required
   (3) one has been required
   (4) you used to be required
   (5) you could be required

Here's How to Crack It

In these questions, you know exactly where the error is supposed to be—in the underlined portion of the sentence. Here the problem is with subject/verb agreement (for a more in-depth discussion see *Cracking the GED*). Each of the answer choices contains a slight variation—the change here in the subject and verb is a tipoff that the error might be in their agreement. The correct answer is (2).

Construction Shift

Twenty percent of the questions will be construction shift questions.

3. Sentences 2 and 3: **A bicycle is greener than a car. In today's environment, one are required to be eco-friendly.**

   The most effective combination of sentences 2 and 3 would contain which of the following groups of words?

   (1) which is important in today's environment
   (2) bicycling is greener than a car
   (3) after today's environment
   (4) requiring ecofriendlys
   (5) Despite today's environment

Here's How to Crack It

You are looking for the most effective combination of the two sentences. Again, eliminate answer choices that contain or introduce errors. Some people find construction shift questions challenging, but if you take out the trash you vastly improve your odds. The correct answer is (1).

The Mistake Most People Make

Most people approach the Language Arts, Writing test hoping that inspiration will strike them, that the correct answer will magically waft down from the clouds to hit them on the head.

It probably won't. There are dozens of rules in English. Fortunately the GED doesn't test all of them. *Cracking the GED* has an excellent review of the grammar rules that are covered on the GED. But there are still a number of rules to keep track of. On top of that, many of the wrong answers can sound right, or at least right-ish.

So what should you do?

Remember POE!

The key thing to do on these questions is to use POE to get rid of answers you know are wrong. It's possible that the right answer might not sound good to you; a writer can open the rules of grammar and still write a sentence that sounds awful.

The answer choices contain clues for a careful test-taker. The important thing is to remember to take out the trash. If you spot a grammatical error in a sentence, or if a sentence introduces a grammatical error, then that cannot be the correct answer.

Another useful tool is to look at the answer choices, particularly in Sentence Revision questions, and see what's changing. What's changing in the answer choices can remind you of a grammatical rule, and you can eliminate some answer choices based on that rule.

THE ESSAY

Part Two: One essay, 45 minutes

You will be asked to write an essay on a particular topic, such as "The truth is always the best option. Do you agree or disagree?"

The key thing here is to realize that you can use a standard template for the essay, no matter what the subject is. There are three possible templates:

Template 1

The issue of ________________ is a controversial one.

On the one hand, ____

____.

On the other hand, ____

____.

However, in the final analysis, ______________________________

____.

Template 2

I both agree and disagree with the statement that "[just quote statement word for word]"

On the one hand [list reasons you agree].

On the other hand, [list reasons you disagree].

Both Template 1 and Template 2 are effective for almost all topics, except for one like this:

Technology presents many challenges to our future.

Identify a particular challenge technology poses to our future. Write a composition of about 250 words explaining why you feel this challenge is important.

Provide reasons and examples to support your view.

So how do you deal with a question that asks you to pick a particular topic? Well, you do have to do a little more thinking for this, but there is still a template you can use.

Template 3

Although there are many ______________________ that are

______________________ [good/bad], I think the [best/worst] of all

is ______________________.

A Caution About Templates

Templates are useful organizing your work and thoughts, but the ones we presented are a little simplistic. You can lose points for being too simplistic, so be sure to customize the template to your own writing style and don't copy ours word for word.

SOCIAL STUDIES

50 multiple-choice questions, 70 minutes

There will be a mixture of longer passages, followed by three or four questions, and shorter passages followed by one question. Sixty percent of the questions will be based on graphic material (charts, diagrams, graphs and cartoons). **No outside knowledge is tested.** The answer to each question will be contained in the passage or diagram provided. The passages will address the following areas of social studies:

National History	25%
Government and Civics	25%
World History	15%
Economics	20%
Geography	15%

General Strategy

The key thing to remember here is that **no outside knowledge is tested.** That means that the Social Studies test is basically another big section of reading comprehension.

When you're dealing with this kind of test, the key thing is to **go back to the passage and find the answer.** This is essentially an open-book test, and the answer is somewhere in the passage. Get the answer from the passage if at all possible.

When you find the answer, **put it in your own words.** ACE may change up the wording in the answer choice a bit so it doesn't sound like the wording in the passage. Make sure you know what you want the answer choice to mean and don't just look for the exact words from the passage.

There are four main types of questions. We'll look at each in turn. Let's start with a longer passage and three questions about it.

Immigration has always fueled American innovation and growth. As the United States is poised to have a minority population that exceeds that of the majority Caucasians, some are concerned that American culture will be submerged under the cultures of waves of immigrants from around the world. But a closer examination shows that the idea of "American culture" is actually a patchwork of immigrant contributions.

The all-American hamburger and frankfurter are both named after cities in Germany, Hamburg and Frankfurt respectively. The renowned American political clan the Kennedys are descended from recent Irish immigrants. Even the governor of that most American of states, California, was born in Austria.

With American culture already representing a diversity of influence from around the world, there would seem to be little to fear from the growth of minority populations in the United States.

Comprehension Questions

Comprehensions questions are just asking you something directly from the passage. Go back to the passage and find the right answer.

1. Which of the following observations about American culture is supported by the article?

   (1) All American food comes from Europe
   (2) California requires its governor to be an American citizen.
   (3) The Irish dominate American politics
   (4) Caucasians have not offered any significant contributions to American culture
   (5) Caucasians are currently the majority group in the U.S.

Here's How to Crack It

Go back to the article and see which answer choices actually are true based on the passage. Some of them will be too strongly worded, like choice (1), and you can eliminate them. The correct answer in this case is (5), which is mentioned briefly in the first paragraph. It would be easy to miss that on the first read-through, which is why you always want to go back to the passage to see what's wrong.

And remember to use POE on the answers, and to cross off the things that are wrong. Don't try to talk yourself into a weak answer or one you're not sure of. Look for reasons to eliminate answers because they go against or are not supported by the passage. Then whatever's left has to be the right answer.

Application Questions

An application question asks you to figure out what the passage says about a concept and to apply that understanding to something else.

2. Which of the following would be an example of an immigrant contribution to culture?

   (1) an American citizen opens a coffee shop
   (2) a Native American performs a traditional dance
   (3) the United States government sponsors a play
   (4) an opera company tours rural areas
   (5) a Polish pastry becomes a traditional breakfast in Texas

Here's How to Crack It

First we have to look at what the passage says about immigrant contributions to culture. The contributions to culture listed are the Frankfurter, the Kennedy clan, and Arnold Schwarzenegger's governorship. Of the things listed above, the Polish pastry being adopted in Texas is the closest match, and (5) would be correct.

Analysis Questions

Analysis questions ask you to further break down information from the passage into more specific categories and explore the relationship of those categories.

3. Which of the following would be the most likely explanation of why there should be no concern about the Caucasian American population being no longer the majority?

   (1) They will not actually be outnumbered.
   (2) What is called "American culture" is permanent and unchanging.
   (3) American culture is not simply Caucasian culture.
   (4) German cuisine is superior to Caucasian cuisine.
   (5) Irish political leaders have proved efficient.

Here's How to Crack it

The passage talks about "American culture" as being a patchwork of immigrant cultures. Therefore it's not just Caucasian culture. That would de-emphasize "Caucasian" as meaning "American." We can also use POE here—any answer that contradicts the passage is wrong, so eliminate (1) and (2). Choice (4) draws a comparison that is unsupported in the passage. That leaves us with (3) and (5), and (5) does not relate to the idea of Caucasians no longer being in the majority; eliminate it. Choice (3) is correct.

Evaluation Questions

Evaluation questions ask you to make a prediction or judgment about the information in the passage. Sometimes this may require a little outside knowledge.

4. Concerns about global warming have led the government to consider regulating the coal industry.

   Which of the following might be an action the government could take to achieve its goal?

   (1) subsidize the construction of new coal plants
   (2) cap the amount of greenhouse gases plants are allowed to emit
   (3) encourage consolidation of the holding companies that own power plants
   (4) invest in research to locate new deposits of coal
   (5) fine producers for dumping in rivers

Here's How to Crack It

The key thing to remember in all Social Studies questions is to keep it related to the passage. The passage here is about global warming and the coal industry, so look for answers that relate to the impact coal companies have on global warming, probably via air pollution/greenhouse gases. Choice (1) would probably make the problem worse, as might choice (4), so eliminate them. Neither dumping in rivers nor the ownership of plants would have any direct impact on the amount of global warming, so eliminate (3) and (5). That leaves (2), which would have an impact on the government's goal.

For a more in-depth review of the topics covered in the Social Studies section, see Chapters 14 and 15 of *Cracking the GED.*

SCIENCE

50 multiple-choice questions, 80 minutes

There will be a mixture of longer passages, followed by up to five questions, and shorter passages followed by one question. About fifty percent of the questions will be based on charts and other graphic material. You will need only a ***general knowledge*** of scientific principles. The answer to each question will be almost always be contained in the passage or diagram provided. The passages will address the following areas of social studies:

Life Science	45%
Physics and Chemistry	35%
Earth and Space	20%

There is some general knowledge required for the Science passages, but remember that you can almost always find what you need to know on that page.

Comprehension Questions

As in the Social Studies test, these questions require you to go to the passage and fetch information about whatever the question is asking. Let's look at a passage and then some questions.

Scientists working in the Arctic came across the remarkably well-preserved frozen remains of a baby woolly mammoth. Upon further examination they found neither signs of disease nor wounds on the mammoth when it froze. The scientists hoped to conduct an analysis of the DNA of the animal to confirm their hypothesis that it had no physical defects and had starved to death after becoming separated from its herd.

1. Which statement about the woolly mammoth is best supported by the passage?

   (1) It was unusually strong for its age.
   (2) The scientists had been looking for it for some time.
   (3) The scientists specialized in this type of mammoth.
   (4) Its DNA was damaged by frost.
   (5) It had not yet reached maturity.

Here's How to Crack it

Remember, for comprehension questions like this one you're looking for what the passage said about something. In this case, what the passage said about the mammoth. We don't compare the mammoth to other mammoths its age, so (1) is out; nor do we know that there was DNA damage so (4) is out. We don't know that the scientists are looking for it or that they were specialists in this mammoth, so (2) and (3) are out. Stick to what the passage said. It was a baby, so (5) is correct.

Application Questions

Application questions have you apply a concept from the passage to another situation.

2. A scientist is studying the remains of a chicken. How might he determine the chicken's cause of death?

   (1) Do a DNA analysis to determine the chicken parentage.
   (2) Compare the chicken with other remains of chickens.
   (3) Eliminate predation as a cause through examining the body for wounds.
   (4) Do a statistical analysis of the predominant causes of death in chickens.
   (5) Examine the area where the body was found for additional environmental causes.

Here's How to Crack it

In examining the remains of the mammoth the scientists ruled out illness and injury on their way to developing their hypothesis. Parentage and the deaths of other chickens would not be relevant, so rule out (1), (2) and (4). The area where the body was found is less important than the remains themselves, so rule out (5). Eliminating the possibility of death through injury is what the scientists did with the mammoth; "predation" just means being hunted, so (3) is correct.

Analysis Questions

Analysis questions ask you to break down the information from the passage into more specific categories and then explore the relationship of those categories.

3. Which of the following social behaviors of mammoths is most supported by the passage?

   (1) Mammoths form circles to defend against predators.
   (2) Mammoth mothers care for their young for the first several years of life.
   (3) Mammoths travel in herds, using the earth's magnetic field to guide their migrations.
   (4) Mammoth young have difficulty fending for themselves without the support of other members of the herd.
   (5) Mammoth life expectancy declined towards the end of the last ice age.

Here's How to Crack It

Here we're looking to see what the information about the dead baby mammoth tells us about the social behavior of mammoths. We know that the hypothesis was that the baby mammoth starved when separated; (4) gives us that information slightly restated. None of the other choices are supported by the passage.

Evaluation Questions

Evaluation questions require you to extrapolate from what you know to make a prediction.

4. Which of the following actions would best help the scientists prove their hypothesis?

(1) establishing a database of mammoth DNA sequencing for comparison
(2) attempting to revive the mammoth
(3) researching the prevalent causes of death for mammoths
(4) exploring the DNA of the closest living relations to mammoths
(5) exploring the tissue of the mammoth for signs of sickness

Here's How to Crack it:

The scientists' hypothesis is that the mammoth was separated from the herd and starved. They are hoping to prove this by doing DNA testing to prove that there was nothing physically wrong with the mammoth. Choice (1) would allow them to compare the baby mammoth's DNA to others to see if it was normal; keep it for now. Reviving the mammoth won't help prove the hypothesis. The causes of death for other mammoths and the DNA of living relatives of mammoths won't help show the cause of death for this particular mammoth; keep your eye on the ball! And the scientists have already ruled out sickness. This leaves us with (1) as the best answer.

LANGUAGE ARTS, READING

40 multiple-choice questions, 65 minutes

You will be given three fiction passages (each from a different time period), one excerpt from a play, and one poem. You will also see two from the following types of passages: a review of a performance, an article about popular culture, or a business-related topic. After each, you will be asked three to five questions designed to test your reading ability and your ability to analyze and apply what you've just read. The passages will be divided into the following sections:

Literary (fiction, play, poem) 80%
Nonfiction (review, workplace document, popular culture) 20%

Let's take a look at the varieties of passage that you'll be dealing with, and what to look for in each one.

Fiction

What to Look For:

- *Who's talking?*
  The story might be in the first person ("I") or in the third person (told by an omniscient narrator). If told in the first person, it's important to figure out the point of view of the narrator. Is he or she objective, or does he or she have strong opinions?
- *What's going on?*
  What happens during the passage? Is there a revelation for one of the characters? Is there a choice or decision to make?
- *What is the Mood?*
  Is it silly or serious? If serious, is there anything funny that happens? On the GED, questions about mood tend to be analysis questions.
- *Who are the main characters?*
  Identify the main characters for yourself. Usually there will only be two or three on the GED; they tend to be a little merciful about that.

Not all that Mrs. Bennet, however, with the assistance of her five daughters, could ask on the subject was sufficient to draw from her husband any satisfactory description of Mr. Bingley. They attacked him in various ways; with barefaced questions, ingenious suppositions, and distant surmises; but he eluded the skill of them all; and they were at last obliged to accept the second-hand intelligence of their neighbour

Lady Lucas. Her report was highly favorable. Sir William had been delighted with him. He was quite young, wonderfully handsome, extremely agreeable, and to crown the whole, he meant to be at the next assembly with a large party. Nothing could be more delightful! To be fond of dancing was a certain step towards falling in love; and very lively hopes of Mr. Bingley's heart were entertained.

"If I can but see one of my daughters happily settled at Netherfield, said Mrs. Bennet to her husband, "and all the others equally well married, I shall have nothing to wish for."

Jane Austen, PRIDE AND PREJUDICE

Now go through and answer the "What To Look For" questions in relation to the passage. Who's talking? This is a third-person omniscient (meaning all-knowing, all-seeing) narrator; Mrs. Bennet speaks in the second paragraph. What's going on? Mrs. Bennet and her daughters are trying to get information about Mr. Bingley, an apparently eligible bachelor. What is the mood of the piece? It's rather funny, making fun a bit of how hard they're working to scope this guy out. Who are the main characters? The focus is on Mr. Bingley and on Mrs. Bennets' efforts to find out about him and hopefully marry him to one of her daughters.

Drama

What to Look For:

- *What's Going On?*
  Drama revolves around a pivotal moment when a crisis comes to a head. What is happening between these two characters? What has just happened? What is about to happen?
- *What is the Mood?*
  It might be funny, might be extremely sad. The mood is the general feeling that you get from reading the piece.
- *Who are the Main Characters?*
  The GED isn't going to have a drama excerpt with a million characters. They're going to have two or probably three characters. Identify them. What is their relationship to each other? How does their dialogue differentiate them?
- *Where Does the Action Take Place?*
  The setting could be extremely important or not very relevant. It'll be up to you to figure out which. If a great deal of time is spent on description, then the setting might well be important.

NORA: Yes, I have something to be proud and happy about too I saved Torvald's life, you see.

MRS. LINDE: Saved his life? But how?

NORA: I told you about our trip to Italy. Torvald would never have recovered if it hadn't been for that.

MRS. LINDE: Yes I know—and your father gave you the necessary money.

NORA: That's what everyone thinks—Torvald too—but...

MRS. LINDE: Well--?

NORA: Papa never gave us a penny. I raised the money myself.

MRS. LINDE: All that money! You?

NORA: Twelve hundred dollars. Four thousand eight hundred crowns. What do you think of that?

MRS. LINDE: But, Nora, how on earth did you do it? Did you win the lottery?

NORA: The lottery! Of course not. Any fool could have done that.

MRS. LINDE: Where did you get it then?

NORA: Hmm...tra la lala.

MRS. LINDE: You certainly couldn't have borrowed it.

NORA: Why not?

MRS. LINDE: A wife can't borrow without her husband's consent.

NORA (tossing her head): Oh, I don't know! If a wife has a good head on her shoulders—and has a little sense of business...

Now go through and answer the "What To Look For" questions in relation to the passage. What's going on? Nora is bragging to Mrs. Linde about how she got the money. What is the mood? Nora's quite proud, but Mrs. Linde seems concerned about Nora borrowing the money without her husband's consent. Who are the Main Characters? Clearly Nora and Mrs. Linde in the scene; they also talk about Torvald, although he's not there. Where does the action take place? The passage doesn't really say, so it must not be important.

Poetry

What to Look For:

- *Read it Twice*
  The first thing about poems is to read the poem twice. They're usually pretty short so they don't take long. The first time through don't try to get everything, just read slowly. Then when you're finished immediately go back to the top and start again. You'll be amazed at how much you get the second time.
- *Literal Meaning vs. Figurative Meaning*
  Start—AFTER the second reading—thinking about the poem literally. If it mentions a stream think about a stream. Then maybe you can branch out to the figurative meaning of the poem.
- *Mood*
  Even if you aren't sure what the poem is about, you may be able to get a sense of whether the poem is upbeat or downbeat. That alone may be able to help you with POE, so even if you don't get the whole poem never give up. Remember, with POE and answering all the questions you're still in the hunt even if you're not sure what's going on in the poem.

Ozymandias

I met a traveller from an antique land
Who said: Two vast and trunkless legs of stone
Stand in the desert. Near them, on the sand,
Half sunk, a shattered visage lies, whose frown,
And wrinkled lip, and sneer of cold command,
Tell that its sculptor well those passions read
Which yet survive (stamped on these lifeless things),
The hand that mocked them and the heart that fed;
And on the pedestal these words appear:
'My name is Ozymandias, king of kings;
Look on my works, ye Mighty, and despair!'
Nothing beside remains. Round the decay
Of that colossal wreck, boundless and bare,
The lone and level sands stretch far away.

Percy Bysshe Shelley, "Ozymandias"

Now go through and answer the "What To Look For" questions in relation to the passage. Remember, read the poem TWICE before you start answering the questions. Looking at the literal meaning we see the parts of a sculpture that has broken apart. What might the figurative meaning of that be in a poem that Shelley wrote?

Nonfiction

What to Look For:

- *What is the Main Idea?*
  The nonfiction passages you'll encounter on the GED will always have a point that they're making. Identify it whether the questions ask you to or not. It can be a huge help when you're doing POE.
- *How does the Author Support the Main Idea?*
  Does she give examples or statistics? Does he offer an analogy or comparison? What evidence, reasons or argument does the author provide to back up her main point?
- *What is the Author's Point of View?*
  How does the Author feel about the main point? Is she for it? Is she against? What is the tone of the piece? Tone can vary from mild neutrality to sarcasm. Irony is not uncommon.

I use this example to show that we do not always state explicitly that the patient is actually terminally ill. We attempt to elicit the patient's needs first, try to become aware of their strengths and weaknesses, and look for overt or hidden communications to determine how much a patient wants to face reality at a given moment. This patient, in many ways exceptional, made it clear from the very beginning that denial was essential in order for her to remain sane. Though many staff people regarded her as clearly psychotic, testing showed her sense of reality was intact in spite of the manifestations to the contrary. We learned from it that she was not able to accept her family's need to see her dead "the sooner the better," she was unable to acknowledge her own end when she had just started to enjoy her small children, and she desperately grasped at the reinforcement by the faith healer who assured her of her excellent health.

Elisabeth Kubler-Ross, ON DEATH AND DYING

Now go through and answer the "What To Look For" questions in relation to the passage. What's the main idea? That sometimes they don't tell a terminally ill patient that she's dying, if it would be worse for the patient. How does the author support that? By giving the extended example of the woman whose family was not there for who, and who could not accept the idea of dying just as she was starting to enjoy her children. What is the author's point of view? She has compassion for the woman, even though the nursing staff finds the woman difficult.

READ ACTIVELY

The passages in the Language Arts, Reading test are usually more interesting than the ones in the Social Studies and Science tests. But you want to make sure that you're not just reading through them without pulling out the information you need to answer the questions. Focus on the "What to Look For" questions discussed in this section, and you should be able to handle the Language Arts, Reading passages well.

MATHEMATICS

Part One: *25 multiple-choice questions, 45 minutes; calculator permitted*

Part Two: *25 multiple-choice questions, 45 minutes; calculator NOT permitted*

The emphasis in both parts is on arithmetic problems like those you may be called on to do in your daily routine at work or at home. Many will be word problems. About half will be based on diagrams or charts. Most will be multiple choice, but approximately ten questions will be short answer. The questions will address these general areas of math:

Number Operations/Number Sense	20%–30%
Measurement/Geometry	20%–30%
Data Analysis/Probability/Statistics	20%–30%
Algebra/Functions/Patterns	20%–30%

There is a wide variety of questions on the Math test. For the moment this chapter will confine itself to giving some good general advice that works for the whole Math test. For a more in-depth look at the content of the Math test, please check out Part VIII of *Cracking the GED.*

Calculator

You may think that the first section (in which you're allowed to use a calculator) would be easier than the second, but there's a catch: you have to use THEIR calculator. You will be provided at the test center with a Casio FX-260.

If you haven't yet, go and review the section on the calculator in Chapter 2. Then put this book down and go buy yourself a Casio FX-260. Yes, it's important.

Scratch Paper

We spoke in Chapter 2 of the importance of scratch paper on the GED, but it's worth re-iterating here that you should begin working NOW with scratch paper to get used to it.

We recommend that you put the paper directly beneath the problem you're working on, to minimize distance. Also, be sure to label your work. In the heat of battle you want to be able to tell which calculation belongs to which problem, especially if you start working a problem, skip it and come back. It would be a shame to start over from scratch (sorry) because you can't locate the work you previously did. Just as with the calculator, you want to start using your scratch paper now!

Common Sense

Just because it's math doesn't mean you should abandon your usual good sense. One of the key things to remember on the Math test is to keep your common sense with you at all times. This means a couple of things.

Ballparking

You want to make sure that your answers make logical sense. Check that your answers are in the right ballpark and that no one is getting $15,897.55 in change at the supermarket and no one is eating 0.034 slices of pizza. The numbers that they use in the GED math problems are numbers that would make sense in real life, more like getting $3.22 back from the supermarket and eating 2 slices of pizza.

Partial/Trap Answers

One thing to watch out for is a partial answer. If you're working a problem and come up with a number as part of your solution, but you don't have the answer yet, you can be reasonably sure that that number is not the answer. If you see that partial answer in the answer choices, cross it off and remember that you aren't done yet!

Scale

Here's a helpful hint—the diagrams that you see on the GED are generally drawn to scale. This means that if it looks like a right angle, it probably is; and if one side of the figure is longer than another side in the drawing, then that's what it really is.

Translation

One skill to work on is translating words into math. The GED has plenty of word problems, and if you're going to solve them you want to set them up as math. We may not be able to solve words but we can always solve math.

Let's take a look:

What is 20% of 300?

To translate into math, replace "what" with "x", "is" with "=" and "of" with multiplication. For "%" or "percent" just put that number over 100, giving you:

$$x = \frac{20}{100} \times 300$$

Let's try another one:

What is thirteen more than half of seventy-five?

For "more" just use addition, giving us:

$$x = 13 + (\frac{1}{2} \times 75)$$

So the basic translations from words into math are as follows:

Words	Math
What	x
is	=
of	× (multiply)
more	+ (add)
less	– (subtract)
percent	$\frac{}{100}$

BACKSOLVING

One of the most useful math techniques is what we call backsolving. In backsolving we take the answers that we've been given and plug them back into the problem to see which one comes out right.

This has a couple of advantages. One, you know you're right because the correct answer works and it's the only one that works. But because standardized tests are so predictable, we don't even have to plug in all the answer to see which one works. Let's take a look.

1. If $7x - 14 = 35$, then what is the value of x?

   (1) 3
   (2) 4
   (3) 5
   (4) 6
   (5) 7

Let's try plugging in the middle answer, 5. If we do that we get $7\times5-14=35$, which if we simplify it ends up being $7\times5=49$, which we know is not true. So (3) is out.

But not only is that answer not right, specifically it's too small. Which means that choices (1) and (2) have to be wrong as well, since they're smaller than 5. By testing the middle one we are able to eliminate three answers. If we plug in 6 we get $7\times6-14=35$ which simplifies to $7\times6=49$, but sure enough, choice (5) gives us $7\times7=49$

That's the beauty of backsolving. Since the answers are in order from smallest to largest, if you start in the middle you can either eliminate the first three, eliminate the last three or, if choice (3) works, you've got the answer!

All right! Now that you have some solid techniques behind you, take the practice tests and watch your scores improve!

Part II:
GED
Practice Exams

Practice Test 1

Completely darken bubbles with a No. 2 pencil. If you make a mistake, be sure to erase mark completely. Erase all stray marks.

1

YOUR NAME: (Print) ______ Last ______ First ______ M.I.

SIGNATURE: ______ DATE: ___/___/___

HOME ADDRESS: (Print) ______ Number and Street

______ City ______ State ______ Zip Code

PHONE NO.: (Print) ______

IMPORTANT: Please fill in these boxes exactly as shown on the back cover of your test book.

2. TEST FORM

3. TEST CODE

0	A	0
1	B	1
2	C	2
3	D	3
4	E	4
5	F	5
6	G	6
7		7
8		8
9		9

4. REGISTRATION NUMBER

0	0	0	0	0	0	0	0
1	1	1	1	1	1	1	1
2	2	2	2	2	2	2	2
3	3	3	3	3	3	3	3
4	4	4	4	4	4	4	4
5	5	5	5	5	5	5	5
6	6	6	6	6	6	6	6
7	7	7	7	7	7	7	7
8	8	8	8	8	8	8	8
9	9	9	9	9	9	9	9

5. YOUR NAME

First 4 letters of last name					FIRST INIT	MID INIT
A	A	A	A		A	A
B	B	B	B		B	B
C	C	C	C		C	C
D	D	D	D		D	D
E	E	E	E		E	E
F	F	F	F		F	F
G	G	G	G		G	G
H	H	H	H		H	H
I	I	I	I		I	I
J	J	J	J		J	J
K	K	K	K		K	K
L	L	L	L		L	L
M	M	M	M		M	M
N	N	N	N		N	N
O	O	O	O		O	O
P	P	P	P		P	P
Q	Q	Q	Q		Q	Q
R	R	R	R		R	R
S	S	S	S		S	S
T	T	T	T		T	T
U	U	U	U		U	U
V	V	V	V		V	V
W	W	W	W		W	W
X	X	X	X		X	X
Y	Y	Y	Y		Y	Y
Z	Z	Z	Z		Z	Z

6. DATE OF BIRTH

Month	Day		Year	
JAN				
FEB				
MAR	0	0	0	0
APR	1	1	1	1
MAY	2	2	2	2
JUN	3	3	3	3
JUL		4	4	4
AUG		5	5	5
SEP		6	6	6
OCT		7	7	7
NOV		8	8	8
DEC		9	9	9

7. SEX

MALE

FEMALE

The Princeton Review®

FORM NO. 00001-PR

Start with number 1 for each new section. If a section has fewer questions than answer spaces, leave the extra answer spaces blank. Be sure to erase any errors or stray marks completely.

WRITING

1 Ⓐ Ⓑ Ⓒ Ⓓ Ⓔ	11 Ⓐ Ⓑ Ⓒ Ⓓ Ⓔ	21 Ⓐ Ⓑ Ⓒ Ⓓ Ⓔ	31 Ⓐ Ⓑ Ⓒ Ⓓ Ⓔ
2 Ⓐ Ⓑ Ⓒ Ⓓ Ⓔ	12 Ⓐ Ⓑ Ⓒ Ⓓ Ⓔ	22 Ⓐ Ⓑ Ⓒ Ⓓ Ⓔ	32 Ⓐ Ⓑ Ⓒ Ⓓ Ⓔ
3 Ⓐ Ⓑ Ⓒ Ⓓ Ⓔ	13 Ⓐ Ⓑ Ⓒ Ⓓ Ⓔ	23 Ⓐ Ⓑ Ⓒ Ⓓ Ⓔ	33 Ⓐ Ⓑ Ⓒ Ⓓ Ⓔ
4 Ⓐ Ⓑ Ⓒ Ⓓ Ⓔ	14 Ⓐ Ⓑ Ⓒ Ⓓ Ⓔ	24 Ⓐ Ⓑ Ⓒ Ⓓ Ⓔ	34 Ⓐ Ⓑ Ⓒ Ⓓ Ⓔ
5 Ⓐ Ⓑ Ⓒ Ⓓ Ⓔ	15 Ⓐ Ⓑ Ⓒ Ⓓ Ⓔ	25 Ⓐ Ⓑ Ⓒ Ⓓ Ⓔ	35 Ⓐ Ⓑ Ⓒ Ⓓ Ⓔ
6 Ⓐ Ⓑ Ⓒ Ⓓ Ⓔ	16 Ⓐ Ⓑ Ⓒ Ⓓ Ⓔ	26 Ⓐ Ⓑ Ⓒ Ⓓ Ⓔ	36 Ⓐ Ⓑ Ⓒ Ⓓ Ⓔ
7 Ⓐ Ⓑ Ⓒ Ⓓ Ⓔ	17 Ⓐ Ⓑ Ⓒ Ⓓ Ⓔ	27 Ⓐ Ⓑ Ⓒ Ⓓ Ⓔ	37 Ⓐ Ⓑ Ⓒ Ⓓ Ⓔ
8 Ⓐ Ⓑ Ⓒ Ⓓ Ⓔ	18 Ⓐ Ⓑ Ⓒ Ⓓ Ⓔ	28 Ⓐ Ⓑ Ⓒ Ⓓ Ⓔ	38 Ⓐ Ⓑ Ⓒ Ⓓ Ⓔ
9 Ⓐ Ⓑ Ⓒ Ⓓ Ⓔ	19 Ⓐ Ⓑ Ⓒ Ⓓ Ⓔ	29 Ⓐ Ⓑ Ⓒ Ⓓ Ⓔ	39 Ⓐ Ⓑ Ⓒ Ⓓ Ⓔ
10 Ⓐ Ⓑ Ⓒ Ⓓ Ⓔ	20 Ⓐ Ⓑ Ⓒ Ⓓ Ⓔ	30 Ⓐ Ⓑ Ⓒ Ⓓ Ⓔ	40 Ⓐ Ⓑ Ⓒ Ⓓ Ⓔ

SOCIAL STUDIES

1 Ⓐ Ⓑ Ⓒ Ⓓ Ⓔ	11 Ⓐ Ⓑ Ⓒ Ⓓ Ⓔ	21 Ⓐ Ⓑ Ⓒ Ⓓ Ⓔ	31 Ⓐ Ⓑ Ⓒ Ⓓ Ⓔ
2 Ⓐ Ⓑ Ⓒ Ⓓ Ⓔ	12 Ⓐ Ⓑ Ⓒ Ⓓ Ⓔ	22 Ⓐ Ⓑ Ⓒ Ⓓ Ⓔ	32 Ⓐ Ⓑ Ⓒ Ⓓ Ⓔ
3 Ⓐ Ⓑ Ⓒ Ⓓ Ⓔ	13 Ⓐ Ⓑ Ⓒ Ⓓ Ⓔ	23 Ⓐ Ⓑ Ⓒ Ⓓ Ⓔ	33 Ⓐ Ⓑ Ⓒ Ⓓ Ⓔ
4 Ⓐ Ⓑ Ⓒ Ⓓ Ⓔ	14 Ⓐ Ⓑ Ⓒ Ⓓ Ⓔ	24 Ⓐ Ⓑ Ⓒ Ⓓ Ⓔ	34 Ⓐ Ⓑ Ⓒ Ⓓ Ⓔ
5 Ⓐ Ⓑ Ⓒ Ⓓ Ⓔ	15 Ⓐ Ⓑ Ⓒ Ⓓ Ⓔ	25 Ⓐ Ⓑ Ⓒ Ⓓ Ⓔ	35 Ⓐ Ⓑ Ⓒ Ⓓ Ⓔ
6 Ⓐ Ⓑ Ⓒ Ⓓ Ⓔ	16 Ⓐ Ⓑ Ⓒ Ⓓ Ⓔ	26 Ⓐ Ⓑ Ⓒ Ⓓ Ⓔ	36 Ⓐ Ⓑ Ⓒ Ⓓ Ⓔ
7 Ⓐ Ⓑ Ⓒ Ⓓ Ⓔ	17 Ⓐ Ⓑ Ⓒ Ⓓ Ⓔ	27 Ⓐ Ⓑ Ⓒ Ⓓ Ⓔ	37 Ⓐ Ⓑ Ⓒ Ⓓ Ⓔ
8 Ⓐ Ⓑ Ⓒ Ⓓ Ⓔ	18 Ⓐ Ⓑ Ⓒ Ⓓ Ⓔ	28 Ⓐ Ⓑ Ⓒ Ⓓ Ⓔ	38 Ⓐ Ⓑ Ⓒ Ⓓ Ⓔ
9 Ⓐ Ⓑ Ⓒ Ⓓ Ⓔ	19 Ⓐ Ⓑ Ⓒ Ⓓ Ⓔ	29 Ⓐ Ⓑ Ⓒ Ⓓ Ⓔ	39 Ⓐ Ⓑ Ⓒ Ⓓ Ⓔ
10 Ⓐ Ⓑ Ⓒ Ⓓ Ⓔ	20 Ⓐ Ⓑ Ⓒ Ⓓ Ⓔ	30 Ⓐ Ⓑ Ⓒ Ⓓ Ⓔ	40 Ⓐ Ⓑ Ⓒ Ⓓ Ⓔ

Start with number 1 for each new section. If a section has fewer questions than answer spaces, leave the extra answer spaces blank. Be sure to erase any errors or stray marks completely.

SCIENCE

1 Ⓐ Ⓑ Ⓒ Ⓓ Ⓔ	11 Ⓐ Ⓑ Ⓒ Ⓓ Ⓔ	21 Ⓐ Ⓑ Ⓒ Ⓓ Ⓔ	31 Ⓐ Ⓑ Ⓒ Ⓓ Ⓔ
2 Ⓐ Ⓑ Ⓒ Ⓓ Ⓔ	12 Ⓐ Ⓑ Ⓒ Ⓓ Ⓔ	22 Ⓐ Ⓑ Ⓒ Ⓓ Ⓔ	32 Ⓐ Ⓑ Ⓒ Ⓓ Ⓔ
3 Ⓐ Ⓑ Ⓒ Ⓓ Ⓔ	13 Ⓐ Ⓑ Ⓒ Ⓓ Ⓔ	23 Ⓐ Ⓑ Ⓒ Ⓓ Ⓔ	33 Ⓐ Ⓑ Ⓒ Ⓓ Ⓔ
4 Ⓐ Ⓑ Ⓒ Ⓓ Ⓔ	14 Ⓐ Ⓑ Ⓒ Ⓓ Ⓔ	24 Ⓐ Ⓑ Ⓒ Ⓓ Ⓔ	34 Ⓐ Ⓑ Ⓒ Ⓓ Ⓔ
5 Ⓐ Ⓑ Ⓒ Ⓓ Ⓔ	15 Ⓐ Ⓑ Ⓒ Ⓓ Ⓔ	25 Ⓐ Ⓑ Ⓒ Ⓓ Ⓔ	35 Ⓐ Ⓑ Ⓒ Ⓓ Ⓔ
6 Ⓐ Ⓑ Ⓒ Ⓓ Ⓔ	16 Ⓐ Ⓑ Ⓒ Ⓓ Ⓔ	26 Ⓐ Ⓑ Ⓒ Ⓓ Ⓔ	36 Ⓐ Ⓑ Ⓒ Ⓓ Ⓔ
7 Ⓐ Ⓑ Ⓒ Ⓓ Ⓔ	17 Ⓐ Ⓑ Ⓒ Ⓓ Ⓔ	27 Ⓐ Ⓑ Ⓒ Ⓓ Ⓔ	37 Ⓐ Ⓑ Ⓒ Ⓓ Ⓔ
8 Ⓐ Ⓑ Ⓒ Ⓓ Ⓔ	18 Ⓐ Ⓑ Ⓒ Ⓓ Ⓔ	28 Ⓐ Ⓑ Ⓒ Ⓓ Ⓔ	38 Ⓐ Ⓑ Ⓒ Ⓓ Ⓔ
9 Ⓐ Ⓑ Ⓒ Ⓓ Ⓔ	19 Ⓐ Ⓑ Ⓒ Ⓓ Ⓔ	29 Ⓐ Ⓑ Ⓒ Ⓓ Ⓔ	39 Ⓐ Ⓑ Ⓒ Ⓓ Ⓔ
10 Ⓐ Ⓑ Ⓒ Ⓓ Ⓔ	20 Ⓐ Ⓑ Ⓒ Ⓓ Ⓔ	30 Ⓐ Ⓑ Ⓒ Ⓓ Ⓔ	40 Ⓐ Ⓑ Ⓒ Ⓓ Ⓔ

READING

1 Ⓐ Ⓑ Ⓒ Ⓓ Ⓔ	11 Ⓐ Ⓑ Ⓒ Ⓓ Ⓔ	21 Ⓐ Ⓑ Ⓒ Ⓓ Ⓔ	31 Ⓐ Ⓑ Ⓒ Ⓓ Ⓔ
2 Ⓐ Ⓑ Ⓒ Ⓓ Ⓔ	12 Ⓐ Ⓑ Ⓒ Ⓓ Ⓔ	22 Ⓐ Ⓑ Ⓒ Ⓓ Ⓔ	32 Ⓐ Ⓑ Ⓒ Ⓓ Ⓔ
3 Ⓐ Ⓑ Ⓒ Ⓓ Ⓔ	13 Ⓐ Ⓑ Ⓒ Ⓓ Ⓔ	23 Ⓐ Ⓑ Ⓒ Ⓓ Ⓔ	33 Ⓐ Ⓑ Ⓒ Ⓓ Ⓔ
4 Ⓐ Ⓑ Ⓒ Ⓓ Ⓔ	14 Ⓐ Ⓑ Ⓒ Ⓓ Ⓔ	24 Ⓐ Ⓑ Ⓒ Ⓓ Ⓔ	34 Ⓐ Ⓑ Ⓒ Ⓓ Ⓔ
5 Ⓐ Ⓑ Ⓒ Ⓓ Ⓔ	15 Ⓐ Ⓑ Ⓒ Ⓓ Ⓔ	25 Ⓐ Ⓑ Ⓒ Ⓓ Ⓔ	35 Ⓐ Ⓑ Ⓒ Ⓓ Ⓔ
6 Ⓐ Ⓑ Ⓒ Ⓓ Ⓔ	16 Ⓐ Ⓑ Ⓒ Ⓓ Ⓔ	26 Ⓐ Ⓑ Ⓒ Ⓓ Ⓔ	36 Ⓐ Ⓑ Ⓒ Ⓓ Ⓔ
7 Ⓐ Ⓑ Ⓒ Ⓓ Ⓔ	17 Ⓐ Ⓑ Ⓒ Ⓓ Ⓔ	27 Ⓐ Ⓑ Ⓒ Ⓓ Ⓔ	37 Ⓐ Ⓑ Ⓒ Ⓓ Ⓔ
8 Ⓐ Ⓑ Ⓒ Ⓓ Ⓔ	18 Ⓐ Ⓑ Ⓒ Ⓓ Ⓔ	28 Ⓐ Ⓑ Ⓒ Ⓓ Ⓔ	38 Ⓐ Ⓑ Ⓒ Ⓓ Ⓔ
9 Ⓐ Ⓑ Ⓒ Ⓓ Ⓔ	19 Ⓐ Ⓑ Ⓒ Ⓓ Ⓔ	29 Ⓐ Ⓑ Ⓒ Ⓓ Ⓔ	39 Ⓐ Ⓑ Ⓒ Ⓓ Ⓔ
10 Ⓐ Ⓑ Ⓒ Ⓓ Ⓔ	20 Ⓐ Ⓑ Ⓒ Ⓓ Ⓔ	30 Ⓐ Ⓑ Ⓒ Ⓓ Ⓔ	40 Ⓐ Ⓑ Ⓒ Ⓓ Ⓔ

MATH

1 Ⓐ Ⓑ Ⓒ Ⓓ Ⓔ	11 Ⓐ Ⓑ Ⓒ Ⓓ Ⓔ	21 Ⓐ Ⓑ Ⓒ Ⓓ Ⓔ	31 Ⓐ Ⓑ Ⓒ Ⓓ Ⓔ
2 Ⓐ Ⓑ Ⓒ Ⓓ Ⓔ	12 Ⓐ Ⓑ Ⓒ Ⓓ Ⓔ	22 Ⓐ Ⓑ Ⓒ Ⓓ Ⓔ	32 Ⓐ Ⓑ Ⓒ Ⓓ Ⓔ
3 Ⓐ Ⓑ Ⓒ Ⓓ Ⓔ	13 Ⓐ Ⓑ Ⓒ Ⓓ Ⓔ	23 Ⓐ Ⓑ Ⓒ Ⓓ Ⓔ	33 Ⓐ Ⓑ Ⓒ Ⓓ Ⓔ
4 Ⓐ Ⓑ Ⓒ Ⓓ Ⓔ	14 Ⓐ Ⓑ Ⓒ Ⓓ Ⓔ	24 Ⓐ Ⓑ Ⓒ Ⓓ Ⓔ	34 Ⓐ Ⓑ Ⓒ Ⓓ Ⓔ
5 Ⓐ Ⓑ Ⓒ Ⓓ Ⓔ	15 Ⓐ Ⓑ Ⓒ Ⓓ Ⓔ	25 Ⓐ Ⓑ Ⓒ Ⓓ Ⓔ	35 Ⓐ Ⓑ Ⓒ Ⓓ Ⓔ
6 Ⓐ Ⓑ Ⓒ Ⓓ Ⓔ	16 Ⓐ Ⓑ Ⓒ Ⓓ Ⓔ	26 Ⓐ Ⓑ Ⓒ Ⓓ Ⓔ	36 Ⓐ Ⓑ Ⓒ Ⓓ Ⓔ
7 Ⓐ Ⓑ Ⓒ Ⓓ Ⓔ	17 Ⓐ Ⓑ Ⓒ Ⓓ Ⓔ	27 Ⓐ Ⓑ Ⓒ Ⓓ Ⓔ	37 Ⓐ Ⓑ Ⓒ Ⓓ Ⓔ
8 Ⓐ Ⓑ Ⓒ Ⓓ Ⓔ	18 Ⓐ Ⓑ Ⓒ Ⓓ Ⓔ	28 Ⓐ Ⓑ Ⓒ Ⓓ Ⓔ	38 Ⓐ Ⓑ Ⓒ Ⓓ Ⓔ
9 Ⓐ Ⓑ Ⓒ Ⓓ Ⓔ	19 Ⓐ Ⓑ Ⓒ Ⓓ Ⓔ	29 Ⓐ Ⓑ Ⓒ Ⓓ Ⓔ	39 Ⓐ Ⓑ Ⓒ Ⓓ Ⓔ
10 Ⓐ Ⓑ Ⓒ Ⓓ Ⓔ	20 Ⓐ Ⓑ Ⓒ Ⓓ Ⓔ	30 Ⓐ Ⓑ Ⓒ Ⓓ Ⓔ	40 Ⓐ Ⓑ Ⓒ Ⓓ Ⓔ

CAUTION Use the answer spaces in the grids below for Section 6 or Section 7 only if you are told to do so in your test book.

Student-Produced Responses

ONLY ANSWERS ENTERED IN THE OVALS IN EACH GRID WILL BE SCORED. YOU WILL NOT RECEIVE CREDIT FOR ANYTHING WRITTEN IN THE BOXES ABOVE THE OVALS.

Grids 9, 10, 11, 12, 13 (each grid):

	/	/	
.	.	.	.
	0	0	0
1	1	1	1
2	2	2	2
3	3	3	3
4	4	4	4
5	5	5	5
6	6	6	6
7	7	7	7
8	8	8	8
9	9	9	9

PLEASE DO NOT WRITE IN THIS AREA

SERIAL #

LANGUAGE ARTS, WRITING

Tests of General Educational Development

Directions

The Language Arts, Writing Test is intended to measure your ability to use clear and effective English. This test includes both multiple-choice questions and an essay. These directions apply only to the multiple-choice section; a separate set of directions is given for the essay.

The multiple-choice section consists of paragraphs with lettered paragraphs and numbered sentences. Some of the sentences contain errors in sentence structure, usage, or mechanics (punctuation, and capitalization). After reading the numbered sentences, answer the multiple-choice questions that follow. Some questions refer to sentences that are correct as written. The best answer for these questions is the one that leaves the sentence as originally written. The best answer for some questions is the one that produces a sentence that is consistent with the verb tense and point of view used throughout the text. A document is often repeated in order to allow for additional questions on a second page. The repeated document is the same as the first

You should spend no more than 40 minutes on the multiple-choice questions and 45 minutes on your essay. Work carefully, but do not spend too much time on any one question. Be sure you answer every question. You may begin working on the essay part of this test as soon as you complete the multiple-choice section.

Do not mark in this test booklet. Record your answers on the separate answer sheet provided. Be sure that all requested information is properly recorded on the answer sheet.

To record your answers, mark one numbered space on the answer sheet beside the number that corresponds to the question in the test booklet.

FOR EXAMPLE:
Sentence 1: **We were honored to meet governor Phillips.**

Which correction should be made to sentence 1?

(1) insert a comma after honored
(2) change honored to honer
(3) change governor to Governor
(4) change were to was
(5) no correction is necessary

In this example, the word "governor" should be capitalized; therefore, answer space 3 would be marked on the answer sheet.

Do not rest the point of your pencil on the answer sheet while you are considering your answer. Make no stray or unnecessary marks. If you change an answer, erase your first mark completely. Mark only one answer space for each question; multiple answers will be scored as incorrect. Do not fold or crease your answer sheet. All test materials must be returned to the test administrator.

GO ON TO THE NEXT PAGE

Writing, Part I

Directions: Choose the one best answer to each question.

Questions 1 through 9 refer to the following memorandum.

1421 Pasterne Way
Dubuque, IA 52003
(563) 555-1981

MEMORANDUM

To: Maini Tunica, CFO
From: Jamie Hand, Logistics Manager
Subject: Noise Complaints from the Accounting Department
Date: May 20, 2009

(A)

(1) You know, that the engineering department have been notified about OSHA requirements regarding the accounting department's complaints. (2) Further, we are working to restructure the workday so that the employees have minimal exposure—to excessive noise from aircraft taking off from Dubuque Regional. (3) As that hasn't worked out to our satisfaction, several members of the accounting department in the east wing have written a petition.

(B)

(4) Bob Halladay is aware of the petition and is taking steps to correct the situation but, Engineering has not yet given us an estimate of the cost of installing sufficient levels of soundproofing in the east wing. (5) Without this estimate, we are unable to move forward. (6) Therefore, we are requesting that you hold a meeting with the accounting department in order to address their specific needs. (7) We are hoping for a positive outcome. (8) Regarding this situation, as Accounts Receivable has fallen behind. (9) Please let us know the results of your meeting.

(C)

(10) We understand the scheduling challenges you are currently facing, particularly among the public service announcements that we produced for Clean Coal and Shale. (11) That having been said, please be aware that our situation with the accounting department is far more worse than we had anticipated. (12) Bob expects a resolution to this problem by Monday. (13) If accounts receivable continues to fall behind on its deadlines, our cash flow could be seriously impacted.

(D)

(14) If you have any questions or information to me, please don't hesitate to contact me.

GO ON TO THE NEXT PAGE

Writing, Part I

1. Sentence 1: **<u>You know, that the engineering department have</u> been notified about OSHA requirements regarding the accounting department's complaints.**

   Which is the best way to rewrite the underlined portion of this sentence? If the original is the best way, choose option (1).

   (1) You know, that the engineering department have
   (2) You know that the engineering departments have
   (3) You know that the engineering department has
   (4) You know, that the engineering department has
   (5) You know, the engineering department have

2. Sentence 2: **Further, we are working to restructure the workday so that the employees have minimal exposure—to excessive noise from aircraft taking off from Dubuque Regional.**

   Which correction should be made to sentence 2?

   (1) change to <u>excessive</u> to <u>regarding excessive</u>
   (2) delete the dash
   (3) change <u>Further</u> to <u>Furthermore</u>
   (4) change <u>have</u> to <u>has</u>
   (5) change <u>from aircraft</u> to <u>with aircraft</u>

3. Sentence 4: **Bob Halladay is aware of the petition and is taking steps to <u>correct the situation but, Engineering has not</u> yet given us an estimate of the cost of installing sufficient levels of soundproofing in the east wing.**

   What is the best way to correct the underlined portion of the sentence?

   (1) add a comma after <u>situation</u>
   (2) replace <u>but</u> with <u>however</u>
   (3) change <u>has</u> to <u>have</u>
   (4) add a comma after <u>Engineering</u>
   (5) delete the comma after <u>but</u>

4. Sentences 5 and 6: **Without this estimate, we are unable to <u>move forward. Therefore, we are</u> requesting that you hold a meeting with the accounting department in order to address their specific needs.**

   What is the best way to change the underlined portions to combine these two sentences?

   (1) move forward; therefore, we are
   (2) move forward so that we are
   (3) move forward therefore, we are
   (4) move forward to be
   (5) move forward; because we are

GO ON TO THE NEXT PAGE

The memorandum is repeated for your use in answering the remaining questions.

1421 Pasterne Way
Dubuque, IA 52003
(563) 555-1981

MEMORANDUM

To: Maini Tunica, CFO
From: Jamie Hand, Logistics Manager
Subject: Noise Complaints from the Accounting Department
Date: May 20, 2009

(A)

(1) You know, that the engineering department have been notified about OSHA requirements regarding the accounting department's complaints. (2) Further, we are working to restructure the workday so that the employees have minimal exposure—to excessive noise from aircraft taking off from Dubuque Regional. (3) As that hasn't worked out to our satisfaction, several members of the accounting department in the east wing have written a petition.

(B)

(4) Bob Halladay is aware of the petition and is taking steps to correct the situation but, Engineering has not yet given us an estimate of the cost of installing sufficient levels of soundproofing in the east wing. (5) Without this estimate, we are unable to move forward. (6) Therefore, we are requesting that you hold a meeting with the accounting department in order to address their specific needs. (7) We are hoping for a positive outcome. (8) Regarding this situation, as Accounts Receivable has fallen behind. (9) Please let us know the results of your meeting.

(C)

(10) We understand the scheduling challenges you are currently facing, particularly among the public service announcements that we produced for Clean Coal and Shale. (11) That having been said, please be aware that our situation with the accounting department is far more worse than we had anticipated. (12) Bob expects a resolution to this problem by Monday. (13) If accounts receivable continues to fall behind on its deadlines, our cash flow could be seriously impacted.

(D)

(14) If you have any questions or information to me, please don't hesitate to contact me.

GO ON TO THE NEXT PAGE

5. Sentences 7 and 8: **We are <u>hoping for a positive outcome</u>. <u>Regarding this situation</u>, as Accounts Receivable has fallen behind.**

   How would you change the underlined portions of these sentences in order to combine the two sentences?

   (1) hoping for a positive outcome regarding this situation
   (2) hoping for a positive outcome, regarding this situation
   (3) hoping for a positive outcome, with regards to this situation
   (4) hoping for a positive outcome in regarding this situation
   (5) hoping for a positive outcome, regarding, this situation

6. Sentence 10: **We understand the scheduling challenges you are currently facing, particularly among the public service announcements that we produced for Clean Coal and Shale.**

   How would you correct this sentence?

   (1) delete <u>the</u>
   (2) change <u>produced</u> to <u>producing</u>
   (3) add <u>However,</u> to the beginning of the sentence
   (4) change <u>particularly</u> to <u>most notably</u>
   (5) change <u>among</u> to <u>with</u>

7. Sentence 11: **That having been said, please be aware that our situation with the accounting department is far more worse than we had anticipated.**

   Which correction should be made to sentence 11?

   (1) eliminate the comma
   (2) change <u>with</u> to <u>regarding</u>
   (3) eliminate the word <u>more</u>
   (4) delete <u>we had</u>
   (5) change <u>our situation</u> to <u>the situation</u>

8. Sentence 14: **If you have any questions or information to me, please don't hesitate to contact me.**

   Which is the most effective revision of sentence 14?

   (1) Questions or information to me, if any of which you have, please don't hesitate to contact me.
   (2) If you have questions of any information for me, please don't hesitate to contact me.
   (3) If you have questions or any information to me, please don't hesitate to contact me.
   (4) Questions or information for me, if any of which you have, please don't hesitate to contact me.
   (5) If you have any questions or information for me, please don't hesitate to contact me.

9. Which revision would make the memorandum more effective?

   (1) move sentence 9 to the end of paragraph C
   (2) join paragraphs A and B
   (3) remove paragraph D
   (4) join paragraphs C and D
   (5) delete sentence 2

GO ON TO THE NEXT PAGE

Writing, Part I

Questions 10 through 16 refer to the following informational article.

How to Keep Food From Spoiling (Part 6)

Salmonella

(A)

(1) Nobody want to get food poisoning. (2) And that's obvious. (3) The most important of all the questions are *how do we prevent good food from going bad?*

(4) The answers to this question are usually pretty simplistic. (5) Keep cold food refrigerated, and keep hot food hot. (6) And above all, don't let it sit out all day. (7) Beyond that, there are many other ways food can go bad and there are steps you can take to prevent these thing from happening.

(B)

(8) First of all, did you know that about 10% of the chicken you buy in the store is infected with salmonella? (9) Now this isn't dangerous as long as the chicken is cooked thoroughly.

(C)

(10) But here's something you may not have thought of. (11) If you cut chicken and then cut another food with the same knife, you're transferring the bacteria from the chicken to the other food. (12) Of course, that's often not a problem because very little of the bacteria is transferred. (13) If you cut chicken and then cut vegetables and lettuce for a salad with the same knife, the people eating the salad will usually not become infected with salmonella. (14) But (and this is a big but) if you mix something into the salad that the salmonella bacteria likes to eat, then watch out! (15) Putting dressing on a salad and letting it sit for a few hours is a recipe for food poisoning!

(D)

(16) But knives aren't the only utensil that can spread the salmonella bacterium. (17) Salmonella can live in the grooves of a cutting board. (18) And don't forget to wash your hands! (19) YOU can spread salmonella all over the house if forget to wash your hands after handling chicken.

GO ON TO THE NEXT PAGE

10. Sentence 1: **Nobody want to get food poisoning.**

Which correction should be made to sentence 1?

(1) change get to gets
(2) change want to wants
(3) change poisoning to poisoned
(4) put a hyphen between food and poisoning
(5) change poisoning to poisons

11. Sentence 3: **The most important of all the questions are *how do we prevent good food from going bad*?**

Which correction should be made to sentence 3?

(1) change most important to importantest
(2) delete all
(3) change questions to question
(4) change most to more
(5) change are to is

12. Sentence 4: **The answers to this question are usually pretty simplistic.**

(1) change simplistic to simple
(2) change are to is
(3) delete pretty
(4) change question to questions
(5) insert the word given between answers and to

13. Sentence 5: **Keep cold food refrigerated, and keep hot food hot.**

Which correction should be made to sentence 5?

(1) add the between cold and food
(2) change hot to heated
(3) insert foods that are between Keep and cold
(4) delete the comma
(5) insert foods that are between Keep and cold and between keep and hot

14. Sentence 6: **And above all, don't let it sit out all day.**

Which correction should be made to sentence 6?

(1) Change above all to overall
(2) delete the comma
(3) change And above to Above
(4) delete the word out
(5) change don't to do not

15. Which revision would improve the flow of paragraph C?

(1) put sentence 13 at the beginning of the paragraph
(2) delete sentence 10
(3) put sentence 12 between sentence 10 and 11
(4) change Putting in sentence 15 to put
(5) add For example, to the beginning of sentence 13

16. Sentence 19: **YOU can spread salmonella all over the house if forget to wash your hands after handling chicken.**

Which is the best way to write the underlined portion of this sentence? If the original is the best way, choose option (1).

(1) forget
(2) you forget
(3) one forgets
(4) he or she forgets
(5) you don't forget

GO ON TO THE NEXT PAGE

Questions 17 through 25 refer to the following informational article.

Buy or Lease?

(A)

(1) What's the difference in leasing a car or buying one? (2) It all really depends on what you want out of a car. (3) Knowing these things will help you make your decision. (4) Is it important for you to be in a new car or would you just as soon drive an older model as long as it's reliable? (5) Feeling the need to own a car or are you more concerned with just having a car to drive? (6) Do you take good care of a car or would you be more likely to put scratches in it? (7) Do you drive a lot (over 35 miles per day) or do you put an average number of miles (less than 35 miles per day) on a car?

(B)

(8) The differences with which a lease and a purchase is much the same as between renting and buying a house. (9) Just as mortgage payments are higher than rental payments, so too are monthly payments for a lease lower than a buy. (10) But there are differences, some of them significant. (11) One example, while there is more freedom when one rents a home rather than buying, there is often less freedom when you lease a car than when you buy one.

(C)

(12) When you lease a car, you can't simply trade it in as you would a bought car—most car and finance companies won't allow it. (13) Your alternative is to 'sell' the lease to somebody and have them take over the payments. (14) The problem with this is that leases are almost always non-transferable, so if the person that takes over the car misses payments, the finance company will come after you for the missing payments.

(D)

(15) Leasing is not for everybody, and neither is buying. (16) You need to weigh the pros and cons of each before making an informed decision.

GO ON TO THE NEXT PAGE

Writing, Part I

17. Sentence 1: **What's the difference <u>in leasing a car or</u> buying one?**

Which is the best way to write the underlined portion of this sentence? If the original is the best way, choose option (1).

(1) in leasing a car or
(2) regarding leasing a car or
(3) whether leasing a car or
(4) between leasing a car or
(5) between leasing a car and

18. Sentence 5: **Feeling the need to own a car are you more concerned with just having a car to drive?**

The most effective revision of sentence 5 would begin with which group of words?

(1) Do you feel the need
(2) Does one feel the need
(3) Would needing
(4) If you needed
(5) Does one feel the need

19. Sentence 6: **Do you take good care of a car or <u>would you be more likely</u> to put scratches in it?**

Which is the best way to write the underlined portion of sentence 6? If the original is the best way, choose option (1).

(1) would you be more likely
(2) are you more likely
(3) is it more likely
(4) is one more likely
(5) would one be more likely

20. Which is the most effective way of organizing paragraph (A)?

(1) paragraph (A) is most effective the way it is now
(2) swapping sentences (4) and (7)
(3) moving sentence (3) to the end of the paragraph
(4) deleting sentence (5)
(5) deleting sentence (3)

21. Sentence 8: **The differences <u>with which</u> a lease and a purchase is much the same as between renting and buying a house.**

Which revision should be made to sentence 8? If it is correct as it is now, choose option (1).

(1) as it is now
(2) to which
(3) between
(4) among
(5) is that

22. Sentence 9: **Just as mortgage payments are higher than rental payments, <u>so too</u> are monthly payments for a lease lower than a buy.**

Which revision is the best for sentence 9? If the original is the best way, choose option (1).

(1) so too
(2) so are
(3) just as likely
(4) even still
(5) truly

GO ON TO THE NEXT PAGE

The article is repeated for your use in answering the remaining questions.

Buy or Lease?

(A)

(1) What's the difference in leasing a car or buying one? (2) It all really depends on what you want out of a car. (3) Knowing these things will help you make your decision. (4) Is it important for you to be in a new car or would you just as soon drive an older model as long as it's reliable? (5) Feeling the need to own a car or are you more concerned with just having a car to drive? (6) Do you take good care of a car or would you be more likely to put scratches in it? (7) Do you drive a lot (over 35 miles per day) or do you put an average number of miles (less than 35 miles per day) on a car?

(B)

(8) The differences with which a lease and a purchase is much the same as between renting and buying a house. (9) Just as mortgage payments are higher than rental payments, so too are monthly payments for a lease lower than a buy. (10) But there are differences, some of them significant. (11) One example, while there is more freedom when one rents a home rather than buying, there is often less freedom when you lease a car than when you buy one.

(C)

(12) When you lease a car, you can't simply trade it in as you would a bought car—most car and finance companies won't allow it. (13) Your alternative is to 'sell' the lease to somebody and have them take over the payments. (14) The problem with this is that leases are almost always non-transferable, so if the person that takes over the car misses payments, the finance company will come after you for the missing payments.

(D)

(15) Leasing is not for everybody, and neither is buying. (16) You need to weigh the pros and cons of each before making an informed decision.

GO ON TO THE NEXT PAGE

23. Sentence 11: **One example, while there is more freedom when one rents a home rather than buying, there is often less freedom when you lease a car than when you buy one.**

Which correction should be made to sentence 11?

(1) delete the word while
(2) change One to For
(3) change when you buy to whenever you buy
(4) change the period to a question mark
(5) delete the comma after example

24. Sentence 14: **The problem with this is that leases are almost always non-transferable, so if the person that takes over the car misses payments, the finance company will come after you for the missing payments.**

Which is the best way to write the underlined portion of this sentence? If the sentence is correct as written, choose answer (1).

(1) person that takes over the car misses payments
(2) person who takes over the car misses payments
(3) one that takes over the car misses payments
(4) person which takes over the car misses payments
(5) one which takes over the car misses payments

25. Sentence 16: **You need to weigh these pros and cons of each before making an informed decision.**

Which is the best way to write the underlined portion of sentence 16? If the original is best, choose option (1).

(1) these pros and cons of each
(2) the pros and cons of each
(3) these pro's and con's of each
(4) the pro's and con's of each
(5) pros and cons

GO ON TO LANGUAGE ARTS, WRITING, PART II

DO NOT MARK OR WRITE ON THIS PAGE

LANGUAGE ARTS, WRITING, PART II

Tests of General Educational Development

Essay Directions and Topic

Look at the box on page 70. In the box are your assigned topic and the letter of that topic.

You must write on the assigned topic **ONLY**.

Mark the letter of your assigned topic in the appropriate space on your answer sheet booklet. Be certain that all other requested information is properly recorded in your answer sheet booklet.

You will have 45 minutes to write on your assigned essay topic. You may return to the multiple-choice section after you complete your essay if you have time remaining in this test period. Do not return the Language Arts, Writing booklet until you finish both Parts I and II of the Language Arts, Writing Test.

Two evaluators will score your essay according to its overall effectiveness. Their evaluation will be based on the following features:

- Well-focused main points
- Clear organization
- Specific development of your ideas
- Control of sentence structure, punctuation, grammar, word choice, and spelling

REMEMBER, YOU MUST COMPLETE BOTH THE MULTIPLE-CHOICE QUESTIONS (PART I) and THE ESSAY (PART II) TO RECEIVE A SCORE ON THE LANGUAGE ARTS, WRITING TEST. To avoid having to repeat both parts of the test, be sure to observe the following rules.

- Do not leave the pages blank.
- Write legibly in ink so that the evaluators will be able to read your writing.
- Write on the assigned topic. If you write on a topic other than the one assigned, you will not receive a score for the Language Arts, Writing Test.
- Write your essay on the lined pages of the separate answer sheet booklet. Only the writing on these pages will be scored.

IMPORTANT:
You may return to the multiple-choice section after you complete your essay if you have time remaining in this test period. Do not return the Language Arts, Writing booklet until you finish both Parts I and II of the Language Arts, Writing Test.

GO ON TO THE NEXT PAGE

Topic G

The grass is always greener on the other side.

In your essay, give an example of the grass being greener on the other side of the fence. Explain what this saying means in your view. Use your personal observations, experience, and knowledge to support your essay.

Part II is a test to determine how well you can use written language to explain your ideas.

In preparing your essay, you should take the following steps.

- Read the **DIRECTIONS** and the **TOPIC** carefully.
- Plan your essay before you write. Use the scratch paper provided to make any notes. These notes will be collected but not scored.
- Before you turn in your essay, reread what you have written and make any changes that will improve your essay.

Your essay should be long enough to develop the topic adequately.

END OF EXAMINATION

SOCIAL STUDIES

Tests of General Educational Development

Directions

The Social Studies Test consists of multiple-choice questions intended to measure understanding of general social studies concepts. The questions are based on short readings that often include a map, graph, chart, cartoon, or figure. Study the information given and then answer the question(s) following it. Refer to the information as often as necessary in answering the questions.

You should spend no more than 45 minutes answering the questions in this booklet. Work carefully, but do not spend too much time on any one question. Be sure you answer every question.

Do not mark in this test booklet. Record your answers on the separate answer sheet provided. Be sure that all requested information is properly recorded on the answer sheet.

To record your answers, mark the numbered space on the answer sheet beside the number that corresponds to the question in the test booklet.

FOR EXAMPLE:

Early colonists of North America looked for settlement sites with adequate water supplies and access by ship. For this reason, many early towns were built near

(1) mountains
(2) prairies
(3) rivers
(4) glaciers
(5) plateaus

The correct answer is "rivers"; therefore, answer space 3 would be marked on the answer sheet.

Do not rest the point of your pencil on the answer sheet while you are considering your answer. Make no stray or unnecessary marks. If you change an answer, erase your first mark completely. Mark only one answer space for each question; multiple answers will be scored as incorrect. Do not fold or crease your answer sheet. All test materials must be returned to the test administrator.

GO ON TO THE NEXT PAGE

Questions 1 and 2 refer to the following map.

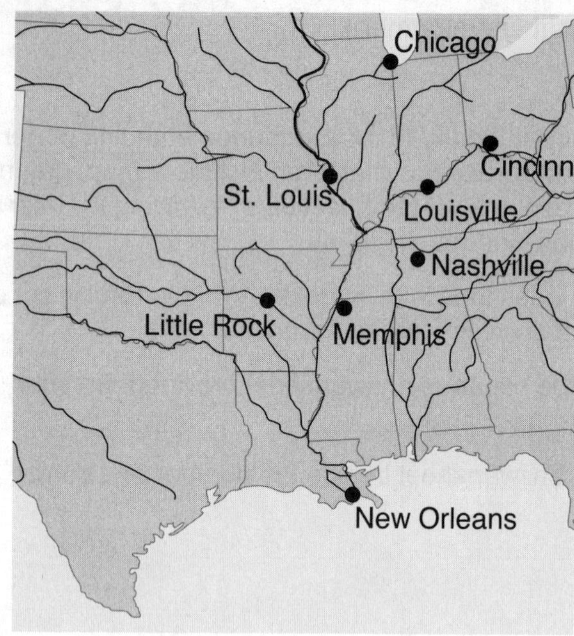

1. Based on the map, which statement is most accurate?

   (1) The American South is home to America's largest cities.
   (2) The smallest states are located in the American West.
   (3) The Atlantic Ocean borders most American states.
   (4) Major cities tend to develop along rivers.
   (5) Urban populations shifted dramatically during the 1950s.

2. Why has the Mississippi River been especially important to the development of the American Midwest?

   The Mississippi River

   (1) has connected the Midwest directly to New England
   (2) has provided an important north-south connection for landlocked Midwestern states
   (3) has provided an important east-west connection across the continental United States
   (4) has supplied many salt-water natural resources
   (5) has not had a measurable impact on the development of the Midwest

3. The signers of the *Declaration of Independence* claimed that "the history of the present King of Great Britain is a history of repeated injuries and usurpations, all having in direct object the establishment of an absolute Tyranny over these States."

   According to this information, which statement about the *Declaration of Independence* is most accurate?

   (1) It sought to portray the King of Great Britain as an unjust and tyrannical ruler.
   (2) It sought to establish a tripartite government without a monarchy.
   (3) It defended the British monarchy from critics in America and in Europe.
   (4) It undermined the Articles of Confederation.
   (5) It was written exclusively by Thomas Jefferson.

GO ON TO THE NEXT PAGE

Questions 4 through 6 refer to the following excerpt from the landmark Supreme Court decision *Brown v. Board of Education of Topeka, Kansas* (1954).

> "To separate them from others of similar age and qualifications solely because of their race generates a feeling of inferiority as to their status in the community that may affect their hearts and minds in a way unlikely ever to be undone.... We conclude that, in the field of public education, the doctrine of 'separate but equal' has no place. Separate educational facilities are inherently unequal."

4. According to the excerpt, what was "the doctrine of 'separate but equal'"?

   The doctrine of "separate but equal"

   (1) allowed for the segregation of American public schools
   (2) separated academic subjects from one another
   (3) undermined the power of the Supreme Court over education
   (4) was enshrined in the Constitution and could not therefore be changed
   (5) was an efficient way to manage education at the level of the federal government

5. What was the impact of *Brown v. Board of Education* on American education?

   (1) It immediately made educational opportunities for all children equal.
   (2) It had little impact on education because it was not enforced until decades after the ruling.
   (3) It impacted private and religious schools only.
   (4) It undermined funding for public education.
   (5) It led to the de-segregation of the American public school system.

6. Which of the following is a statement of **FACT,** rather than an opinion, that best explains the basis of the Court's ruling in this excerpt?

   (1) The Court was biased against the Board of Education of Topeka.
   (2) The Court claimed that segregation was traumatic for African American children.
   (3) The Court was racist against African American children.
   (4) The Court was afraid of violent backlashes from the American public.
   (5) The Court desired to be politically correct.

GO ON TO THE NEXT PAGE

7. After the stock market crash of 1929 and the ensuing economic collapse of the early 1930s, President Franklin Delano Roosevelt issued a series of reforms intended to improve the economy.

   What were these reforms called?

   (1) Reconstruction
   (2) the New Deal
   (3) the Great Society
   (4) the Square Deal
   (5) Fireside Chats

8. A tariff is a tax (or duty) imposed on goods as they move across political boundaries. They are often created by governments to protect their own economic interests against those of foreign countries. They are usually imposed on imported goods.

   Which of the following is a tariff?

   (1) Congress passes legislation that creates a "flat tax" for all income brackets in the federal income tax code.
   (2) The president issues an executive order that establishes a temporary naval blockade with an enemy.
   (3) Congress raises the price of certain goods in supermarkets in order to control the rate of inflation.
   (4) Congress increases the price of French cheese products sold in the United States in order to protect Wisconsin dairy farmers.
   (5) Congress establishes a national sales tax on all goods sold in interstate transactions.

GO ON TO THE NEXT PAGE

Questions 9 through 12 refer to the following excerpt from the First Amendment to the U.S. Constitution.

"Congress shall make no law respecting an establishment of religion, or prohibiting the free exercise thereof; or abridging the freedom of speech, or of the press; or the right of the people peaceably to assemble, and to petition the Government..."

9. Which statement describes the primary purpose of the First Amendment?

The First Amendment

(1) protects the right to bear arms against the government
(2) increases the government's restriction of individual freedoms, such as the freedom of religion, of speech, and of the press
(3) protects essential individual freedoms, such as the freedom of religion, of speech, and of the press
(4) prohibits Congress from making laws
(5) enables Congress to enforce its laws with police power

10. All of the following are guaranteed by the First Amendment EXCEPT:

(1) the freedom of voting
(2) the freedom of petition
(3) the freedom of speech
(4) the freedom of the press
(5) the freedom of religion

11. Which statement best explains the impact of the First Amendment on American law?

The First Amendment

(1) has played a limited role in constitutional law
(2) has been struck down by the Supreme Court on numerous occasions
(3) has been superseded by the Fourteenth Amendment
(4) has been an essential starting point for the protection of individual freedoms
(5) has threatened the power of state governments

12. Which law would be allowed by the First Amendment?

A law that

(1) banned all forms of public protest
(2) placed American newspapers under the direct control of the Supreme Court
(3) banned Internet news websites
(4) created guidelines for petitioning the federal government over the Internet
(5) allocated federal funds for international missions trips from Christian churches

GO ON TO THE NEXT PAGE

<u>Questions 13 and 14</u> refer to the following image and information.

Benjamin Franklin proposed the Albany Plan of Union in 1754 in order to form an alliance among the colonies. The attempt failed quickly. This famous image was made to promote the Albany Plan.

13. Which statement best describes the message of the image?

(1) The colonies must fight together or be destroyed.
(2) The colonies cannot survive in one piece.
(3) The enemy of the colonies was too powerful to be overcome.
(4) Each of the colonies were too small to form a unified whole.
(5) Benjamin Franklin wanted the colonies to be guided by his command.

14. The Albany Plan later served as a template for the writing of the Articles of Confederation. Which statement best describes the Articles of Confederation?

(1) It was an earlier draft of the Declaration of Independence.
(2) It was a strong warning from King George III's government.
(3) It was an early constitution of the newly formed United States of America.
(4) It was the basis for several political parties.
(5) It was written by Thomas Jefferson as a first draft of the Bill of Rights.

GO ON TO THE NEXT PAGE

Questions 15 and 16 refer to the following graph and information.

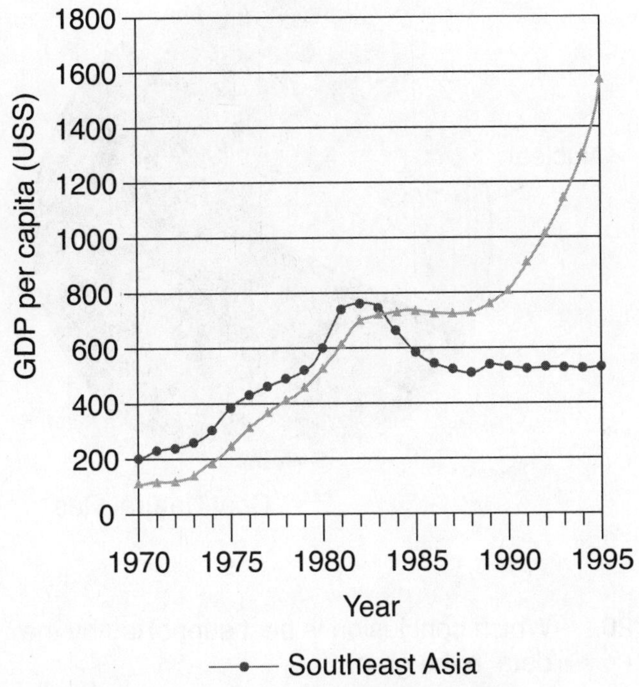

GDP, or Gross Domestic Product, per capita is the average value of the goods and services produced by the citizens of a country in a year. Economists use GDP to compare wealth between individuals and nations.

15. Based on this information, which statement is an **OPINION,** rather than a fact, about the GDP per capita of these nations?

(1) The GDP per capita for Southeast Asia has increased substantially in recent years.
(2) The GDP per capita of Southeast Asia is now higher than that of Sub-Saharan Africa.
(3) Sub-Saharan Africa is in desperate need of foreign aid in order to sustain its economy.
(4) For many years, Southeast Asia and Sub-Saharan Africa had similar patterns of economic growth.
(5) Sub-Saharan Africa has not experienced a dramatic increase in GDP per capita in recent years.

16. Which of these factors have played the most important role in the development of non-Western economies?

(1) language, literature, and culture
(2) climate, geography, and demography
(3) disease, famine, and medicine
(4) race and religion
(5) art, architecture, and engineering

17. The Emancipation Proclamation

(1) ended the Civil War
(2) freed slaves in some states
(3) ended the presidency of Abraham Lincoln
(4) enshrined the rights of African Americans in the Constitution
(5) established the doctrine of "separate but equal"

GO ON TO THE NEXT PAGE

18. President John Quincy Adams wrote that "the whole continent of North America appears to be destined by Divine Providence to be peopled by one nation, speaking one language, professing one general system of religious and political principles, and accustomed to one general tenor of social usages and customs. For the common happiness of them all, for their peace and prosperity, I believe it is indispensable that they should be associated in one federal Union."

The idea that the United States was destined and divinely ordained by God to expand across the entire North American continent is called

(1) Manifest Destiny
(2) capitalism
(3) imperialism
(4) American independence
(5) eminent domain

19. Globalization is the transformation of local or regional phenomena into global ones. Which of the following describes an effect of globalization?

(1) the selling of subsistence farm products in a local market
(2) increased poverty and poor public sanitation
(3) isolationism and xenophobic foreign policy
(4) a decrease in the importation of oil
(5) the easier flow of goods across international borders

Question 20 is based on the following graph.

Power Production in the USA

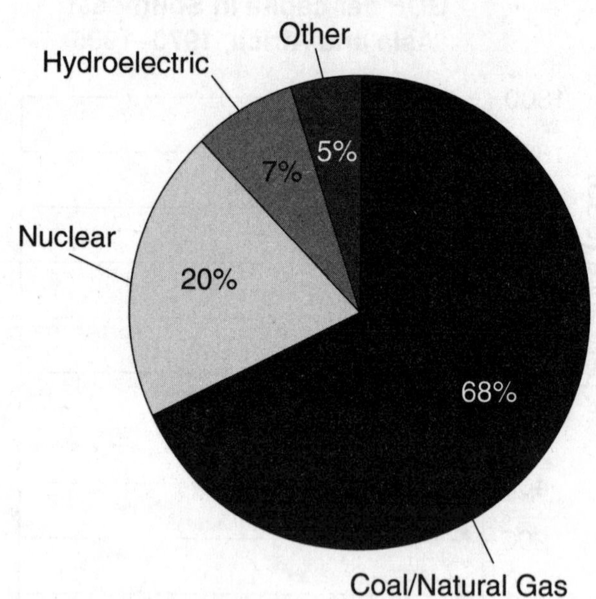

20. Which conclusion is best supported by the data in the graph?

(1) The United States has neglected alternatives to coal and natural gas.
(2) Nuclear power is dangerous and toxic to the environment.
(3) Hydroelectric power is expensive and difficult to produce.
(4) Hydroelectric, wind, and solar power are the way of the future.
(5) The vast majority of American power production is based on coal and natural gas.

GO ON TO THE NEXT PAGE

21. The Nineteenth Amendment, ratified in 1920, was the greatest victory of the women's suffrage movement in the United States. It decreed that "The right of citizens of the United States to vote shall not be denied or abridged by the United States or by any State on account of sex." What was women's suffrage?

Women's suffrage was

(1) the political movement to give women the right to vote
(2) the ideological and legal movement to legalize abortion
(3) the system that allowed women to enter the workforce
(4) the system that helped to prevent women's suffering
(5) the political movement to provide equal pay for men and women

22. Hurricanes are most seriously a threat to cities along the coast of the Atlantic Ocean and the Gulf of Mexico. Which city is **NOT** seriously threatened by hurricanes?

(1) Orlando
(2) New Orleans
(3) Chicago
(4) Washington, DC
(5) San Antonio

23. The modern cotton gin was patented in 1794 by Eli Whitney. It allowed for the easier separation of cotton fibers from their seeds. Why was the cotton gin so revolutionary?

The cotton gin

(1) caused the massive growth of the wool industry in America
(2) caused the economic destruction of rural farmland
(3) ended the need for slavery
(4) caused the expansion of the cotton industry in the American South
(5) ruined the reputation of Eli Whitney

GO ON TO THE NEXT PAGE

Questions 24 and 25 are based on the following graph.

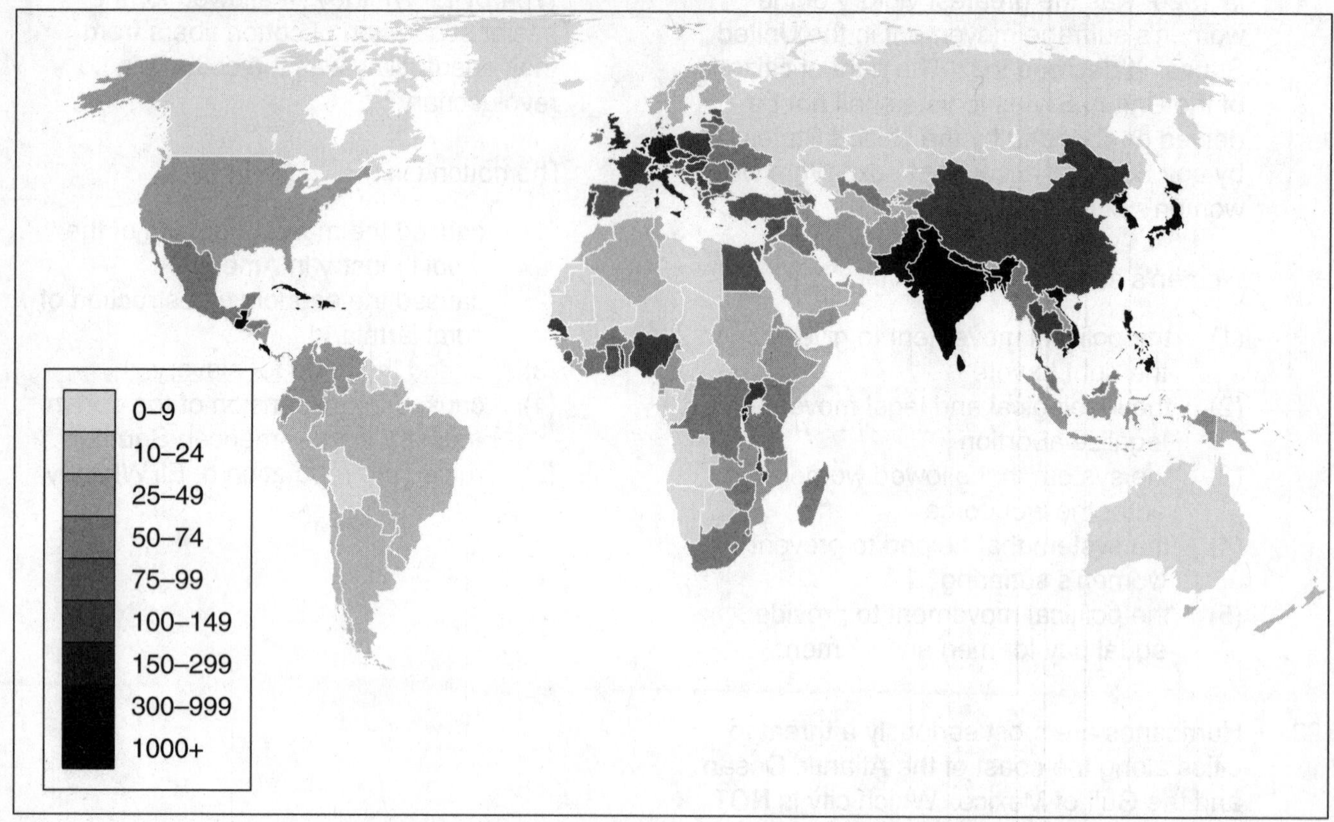

24. According to the graph, what are the most densely populated continents?

    (1) South America and Europe
    (2) Africa and Asia
    (3) Asia and North America
    (4) Europe and Asia
    (5) South America and North America

25. What factors are the most influential in determining population density?

    (1) climate and geography
    (2) race and language
    (3) economic development and globalism
    (4) technology and urbanism
    (5) public sanitation and health

END OF EXAMINATION

SCIENCE

Tests of General Educational Development

Directions

The Science Test consists of multiple-choice questions intended to measure understanding of general concepts in science. The questions are based on short readings that often include a graph, chart, or figure. Study the information given and then answer the question(s) following it. Refer to the information as often as necessary in answering the questions.

You should spend no more than 53 minutes answering the questions in this booklet. Work carefully, but do not spend too much time on any one question. Be sure you answer every question.

Do not mark in this test booklet. Record your answers to the questions on the separate sheet provided. Be sure all requested information is properly recorded on the answer sheet.

To record your answers, mark the numbered space on the answer sheet beside the number that corresponds to the question in the test booklet.

FOR EXAMPLE:

Which of the following is the smallest unit in a living thing?

(1) tissue
(2) organ
(3) cell
(4) muscle
(5) capillary

The correct answer is "cell"; therefore, answer space 3 would be marked on the answer sheet.

Do not rest the point of your pencil on the answer sheet while you are considering your answer. Make no stray or unnecessary marks. If you change an answer, erase your first mark completely. Mark only <u>one</u> answer space for each question; multiple answers will be scored as incorrect. Do not fold or crease your answer sheet. All test materials must be returned to the test administrator.

GO ON TO THE NEXT PAGE

Directions: Choose the one best answer to each question.

1. Carrying capacity is the number of organisms of the same species that an environment can support. Several factors affect the carrying capacity. Density dependant factors are affected by population density, which is the number of organisms occupying a space. Factors that do not depend on the population density are called density independent factors.

   Which of the following is a density independent factor?

   (1) availability of food
   (2) climate of the region
   (3) availability of water
   (4) availability of space
   (5) spread of disease

2. Phineas Gage was a railroad worker who survived an accident in which a large iron rod went through his skull, destroying one of the frontal lobes in his brain. After the accident, Phineas behaved differently and appeared to have a different personality.

   The above information provides support for which of the following statements?

   (1) It is impossible to live with a partially destroyed brain.
   (2) The frontal lobe is a region of a human heart.
   (3) A human skull is too hard to be fractured.
   (4) The frontal lobe is a region of a human brain that plays a role in behavior.
   (5) A man with an iron rod in his head would bleed to death.

3. Below is a table listing the concentrations of chemicals found in human blood and urine.

	Albumin mg/dL	Chloride mg/dL	Glucose mg/dL	Phosphate mg/dL	Urea mg/dL
Blood	4.1	92	95	2.5	4.5
Urine	---	53	---	0.15	1.6

   Based on the table above, which of the following chemicals is not normally found in urine?

   (1) albumin only
   (2) chloride only
   (3) glucose only
   (4) albumin and glucose
   (5) all of the listed chemicals are found in urine

GO ON TO THE NEXT PAGE

4. White light is actually composed of seven colors: red, orange, yellow, green, blue, indigo, and violet. When white light strikes an object, some of the colors are absorbed, while others are reflected. The color an object appears to be is determined by the colors of light that object reflects.

   Based on this information, which of the following statements is true?

   (1) A white shirt absorbs all colors of light.
   (2) A blue shirt absorbs blue light.
   (3) A black shirt reflects all colors of light.
   (4) A yellow shirt reflects all colors except yellow.
   (5) A red shirt reflects red light.

5. A solar eclipse is a celestial event during which the sun appears partially or totally obstructed when viewed from a certain location on earth. The diagram below shows a solar eclipse.

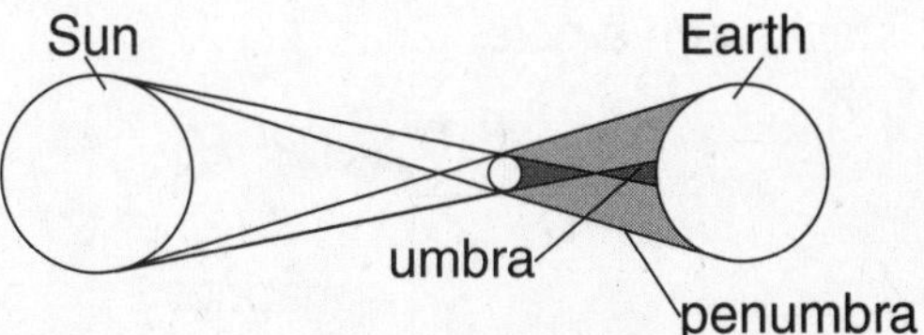

   Based on the information and figure, which of the following is most likely true during a solar eclipse?

   (1) The sun is blocked by clouds.
   (2) The moon is directly between the sun and the earth, blocking the view of the sun.
   (3) Venus casts a shadow on Earth, making everything appear dark.
   (4) Air pollution is so thick that the sun's rays cannot shine through.
   (5) The moon is shining brighter than the sun, making the sun appear dark.

GO ON TO THE NEXT PAGE

6. A magnet has two poles, north and south. Opposite poles attract, while like poles repel.

   Below is a figure of a science experiment in which three ring-shaped magnets were stacked on a pole.

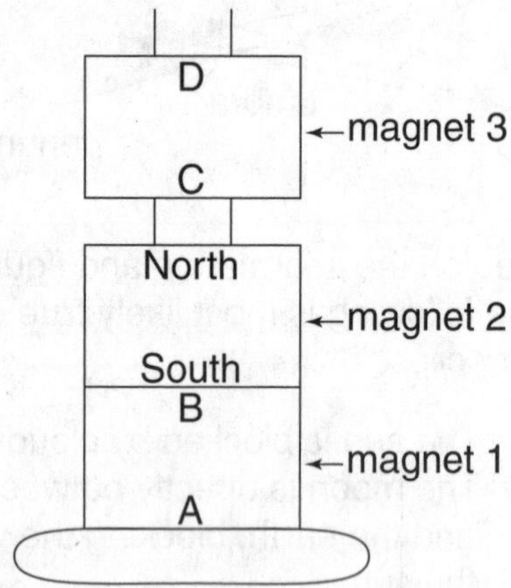

   Based on the information and figure, which of the following represent north poles?

   (1) A only
   (2) B only
   (3) B and C
   (4) A, B, and C
   (5) D only

7. Many illnesses that affect humans are caused by microorganisms, including bacteria, fungi, protists, and viruses. Medical researchers attempt to find treatments for these illnesses by developing pharmaceuticals such as penicillin, which is derived from the spores of a fungus and works by preventing the growth of bacteria. Below is a chart of some common illness and their causes.

Illness	Cause
Common Cold	Rhinovirus
Strep Throat	Streptococcal bacterium
Athlete's Foot	Candida yeast
Malaria	Malaria protist

   Which of the following is most likely treatable with penicillin?

   (1) common cold
   (2) strep throat
   (3) athlete's foot
   (4) malaria
   (5) all of the above can be treated with penicillin

8. Which method can be used to determine whether two brothers are identical twins?

   (1) parents' birth dates
   (2) family history
   (3) saliva analysis
   (4) DNA analysis
   (5) blood glucose levels

GO ON TO THE NEXT PAGE

9. Hereditary traits are coded for by genes, which are located on chromosomes. Chromosomes come in pairs, and the pair of genes for a particular feature determines the characteristics of that trait. In many cases, genes exhibit a pattern called classical dominance. In such cases, the gene for a dominant trait is always expressed when present. An individual can be pure for the dominant gene and have two copies, or the individual can be hybrid and have one dominant gene and one recessive gene. In hybrids, the dominant gene hides the expression of the recessive gene. A recessive gene is only expressed when both copies of the gene are recessive. Dominant genes are represented by capital letters, while recessive genes are represented by lowercase letters.

In pea plants, pea color is a hereditary trait. Green color is dominant and yellow color is recessive, so if a plant has one gene for green color and one gene for yellow color, the plant will produce green peas.

Below is a Punnett Square showing the results when two hybrid green pea plants produce new plants. Punnett Squares predict the likelihood of specific gene combinations occurring. Approximately 75% of the offspring are green, and the rest are yellow.

Punnett Square-Color in Pea Plants

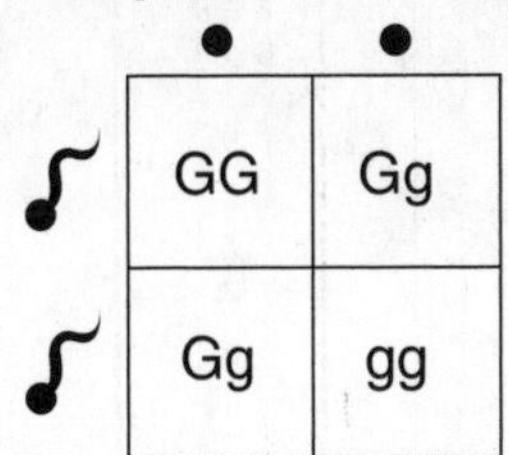

ʃ	sperm cell of male parent
•	egg cell of female parent
G	dominant green color gene
g	recessive yellow color gene

Which is the best explanation for the results in this Punnett Square?

(1) One parent plant was pure for the yellow color gene.
(2) One parent plant was pure for the dominant gene.
(3) Both parents were pure for the green color gene.
(4) Neither parent had the hidden gene for yellow color.
(5) Both parents were hybrid and carried the hidden gene for yellow color.

10. If Deanna stood on a scale in an elevator and the elevator began to move up, which of the following would occur?

(1) Her weight reading would increase.
(2) Her weight reading would decrease.
(3) Her weight reading would stay the same.
(4) The scale would display her weight as 0.
(5) The scale would become demagnetized by the elevator and would never work again.

11. A cook forgets that he is boiling salt water and leaves the kitchen. When he returns later, he finds that there is no water left in the pot but that there is a white residue left on the bottom.

What is the best explanation of the cause of this white residue?

(1) The cook used a dirty pot to boil the water.
(2) The water burned and left ashes in the pot.
(3) The salt never dissolved in the water and was at the bottom of the pot the whole time.
(4) The metal pot rusted from the water.
(5) The water evaporated and left the salt behind in the bottom of the pot.

GO ON TO THE NEXT PAGE

12. In a certain forest, foxes prey on rabbits. A virus that only infects rabbits spreads through the forest, killing many rabbits.

    Which of the following is most likely to occur to the fox population?

    (1) It will decrease, since the foxes will not have enough food.
    (2) It will decrease, since the foxes will get sick from the virus.
    (3) It will stay the same, since the rabbit population does not affect the fox population.
    (4) It will increase, since the foxes will no longer have to compete with the rabbits for food.
    (5) It will increase, since the foxes will evolve to resist disease.

13. Animal trainers often use operant conditioning to teach animals how to behave. In this type of conditioning, the animal learns to behave through a system of punishments and rewards. Positive reinforcement is when good behaviors are rewarded, and negative reinforcement is when bad behaviors are punished.

    Based on the information, what action should an animal trainer take to use positive reinforcement to teach a cat to use a litter box?

    (1) change the litter regularly
    (2) punish the cat if it does not use the litter box
    (3) have the cat watch another cat who is already trained to use a litter box
    (4) give the cat a treat when it uses the litter box
    (5) take no action and allow the cat to learn on its own

GO ON TO THE NEXT PAGE

Questions 14 through 15 refer to the information and graph below.

The graph below shows a science experiment in which a sample of ice at –20 degrees C is heated to 120 degrees C. During the experiment, the ice melted into water and then the water boiled and turned into steam.

Heat and Temperature of Water

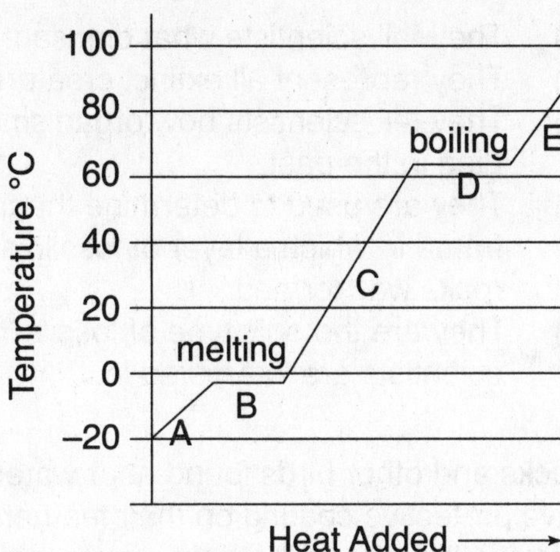

14. Based on the graph and information, which statement is most accurate?

    (1) The sample increased in temperature at the same rate throughout the experiment.
    (2) The sample spent the most time as ice.
    (3) The sample increased in temperature, then melted, then increased in temperature, then boiled, then increased in temperature.
    (4) The sample melted and increased in temperature at the same time.
    (5) The sample increased in mass throughout the experiment.

15. Which letter represents a part in the experiment during which the entire sample consisted of liquid water?

    (1) A
    (2) B
    (3) C
    (4) D
    (5) E

16. Which of the following is an example of an organism?

    (1) rock
    (2) air
    (3) sun
    (4) flower
    (5) river

17. Bees are insects that play an important role in any ecosystem that has flowering plants. Bees serve as the primary pollinators, and enable flowering plants to reproduce. It is estimated that nearly one third of human food supply consists of plants that depend on bees for pollination.

    Based on the information above, which characteristic of bees is most important to an ecosystem?

    (1) Bees create honey for human consumption.
    (2) Bees serve as pollinators.
    (3) Bees sting harmful insects that would otherwise eat and destroy plants.
    (4) Bees transfer their genes to plants.
    (5) Bees gather nectar.

18. Which of the following is a characteristic of gases?

    (1) Gases are more dense than solids.
    (2) All gases are identical.
    (3) Gases take up space and have mass.
    (4) All gases are clear and odorless.
    (5) Gases are weightless.

GO ON TO THE NEXT PAGE

19. The figure below shows a weather system approaching a mountain range.

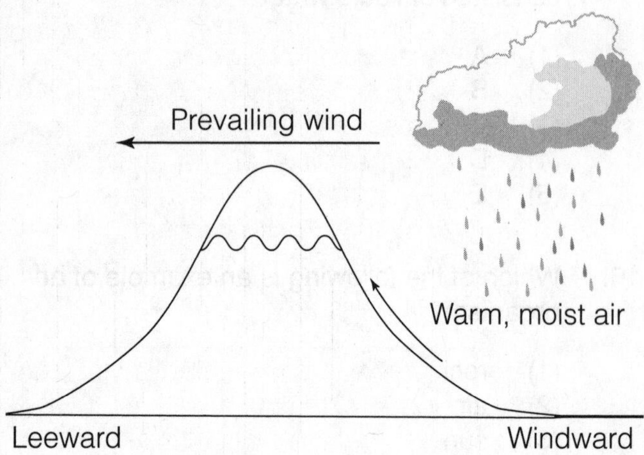

Which statement is best supported by the figure?

(1) The climate is the same on both sides of the mountain.
(2) Precipitation is occurring on the windward side only.
(3) Precipitation is occurring on the leeward side only.
(4) The wind is blowing in both directions.
(5) Warm, moist air is moving towards the ground.

20. An index fossil is a fossil that is known to have come from a certain time period. Scientists can easily recognize many index fossils and use them as time markers when examining layers of fossilized rocks deep underground. If an unknown fossil is found near an index fossil, the scientist can estimate the age of the unknown fossil.

Based on the information, why are index fossils useful to scientists?

(1) They tell scientists what dinosaurs ate.
(2) They represent all extinct creatures.
(3) They tell scientists how organisms died in the past.
(4) They are used to determine the time frame in which a layer of fossilized rocks was formed.
(5) They are the only type of fossils scientists are interested in.

21. Ducks and other birds found near water have protective coating on their feathers. This coating makes feathers waterproof and helps the bird maintain a warm body temperature. Commercial oil has been shown to break down this natural coating, leading to decreased ability for a bird to swim, fly, and keep warm.

This information answers which of the following questions?

(1) Why do many birds fly south in the winter?
(2) Why are oil spills harmful to birds?
(3) What do ducks eat?
(4) How many feathers does a bird have?
(5) Why do birds fly?

GO ON TO THE NEXT PAGE

Questions 22–23

The bar graph below shows data collected by a scientist studying different moth characteristics in two different ecosystems.

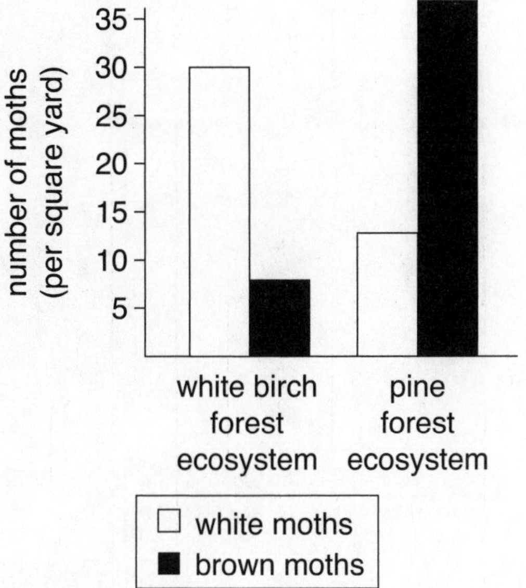

22. Which type of scientist most likely performed this study?

(1) astronomer
(2) chemist
(3) marine biologist
(4) medical researcher
(5) ecologist

23. Which statement provides the most likely explanation for the results in the graph?

(1) In the white birch ecosystem, white moths eat the brown moths, while in the pine forest ecosystem brown moths eat the white moths.
(2) In the white birch ecosystem, white moths are better able to blend into their surroundings while in the pine forest ecosystem, brown moths are better able to blend in.
(3) White moths are allergic to pine trees and brown moths are allergic to birch trees.
(4) The environment has no affect on moth coloration.
(5) Brown moths survive best in white birch ecosystems and white moths survive best in pine forest ecosystems.

24. A year is the approximate length of time required for Earth to make one full orbit around the sun. It takes 365.25 days for the Earth to orbit, but most calendar years have 365 days.

For which fact does this information provide a reason?

(1) Every fourth year is a "leap year" with 366 days.
(2) Each year has four seasons.
(3) Winter is usually colder than summer.
(4) A day has 24 hours.
(5) The sun appears to rise in the east.

25. Which of the following pairs represents types of collisions?

(1) kinetic and potential
(2) solar and lunar
(3) elastic and inelastic
(4) inertial and non inertial
(5) magnetic and electrical

END OF EXAMINATION

DO NOT MARK OR WRITE ON THIS PAGE

LANGUAGE ARTS, READING

Tests of General Educational Development

Directions

The Language Arts, Reading Test consists of excerpts from fiction and nonfiction. Each excerpt is followed by multiple-choice questions about the reading material.

Read each excerpt first and then answer the questions following it. Refer back to the reading material as often as necessary in answering the questions.

Each excerpt is preceded by a "purpose question." The purpose question gives a reason for reading the material. Use these purpose questions to help focus your reading. You are not required to answer these purpose questions. They are given only to help you concentrate on the ideas presented in the reading material.

You should spend no more than 35 minutes answering the questions in this booklet. Work carefully, but do not spend too much time on any one question. Be sure you answer every question.

Do not mark in this test booklet. Record your answers on the separate answer sheet provided. Be sure that all requested information is properly recorded on the answer sheet.

To record your answers, mark the numbered space on the answer sheet beside the number that corresponds to the question in the test booklet.

FOR EXAMPLE:

It was Susan's dream machine. The metallic blue paint gleamed, and the sporty wheels were highly polished. Under the hood, the engine was no less carefully cleaned. Inside, flashy lights illuminated the instruments on the dashboard, and the seats were covered by rich leather upholstery.

The subject ("It") of this excerpt is most likely

(1) an airplane
(2) a stereo system
(3) an automobile
(4) a boat
(5) a motorcycle

The correct answer is "an automobile"; therefore, answer space 3 would be marked on the answer sheet.

Do not rest the point of your pencil on the answer sheet while you are considering your answer. Make no stray or unnecessary marks. If you change an answer, erase your first mark completely. Mark only <u>one</u> answer space for each question; multiple answers will be scored as incorrect. Do not fold or crease your answer sheet. All test materials must be returned to the test administrator.

GO ON TO THE NEXT PAGE

Directions: Choose the one best answer to each question.

Questions 1 through 4 refer to the following excerpt.

WHAT DOES THE COMPANY PRESIDENT BELIEVE ABOUT HOW EMPLOYEES WORK BEST?

Letter from the Company President

All our employees are our product.

Changing the perception in the marketplace of customers, vendors and business partners about what we do and what we sell is quickly becoming the primary focus of our campaign to improve our profitability. Without such change, it will be largely impossible to achieve the two largest goals of our marketing plans—increasing the quality of the actual products we sell and closing the sales gap between us and our marketplace leaders.

Gregory Schoenfeld of Digital Partners Inc., our new marketing consultant in this endeavor, has helped to formulate our two new directives in this area and he believes our recent decisions are already leading us toward greater success. You may already be aware that Mr. Schoenfeld's previous work has included leading several *Fortune* 500 companies through similar rebranding and reworked production initiatives, work that led to his bestselling novel *Employ Your Employees*.

He has found that "employees who, throughout every aspect of their job experience, are treated as if they are true developers of product, actually become so." In his book, he refers to this as "habits of the working mind" in which employees are encouraged to be decision-makers and to become more responsible for quality by taking a personal stake in the final product.

The book also explains, "If employees are given challenges and goals set at a high, but reasonable, level, they naturally begin to assume greater roles of leadership and ownership in final results. They think of themselves as not merely assemblers of product but instead see themselves as part of the success of that product." We expect the recent changes made company-wide will begin to give evidence that this is happening throughout our workforce.

Respectfully,

Cindy S. Price

Cindy S. Price, President

Amalgamated Software Games

GO ON TO THE NEXT PAGE

Reading

1. What does the president of the company believe is the challenge hindering the company from achieving its current goals?

   (1) employees' lack of effort
   (2) managers' poor organization
   (3) shortage of available products
   (4) marketplace's perception of the product
   (5) owners' missing marketing plan

2. The president says that one of the goals of the company is "closing the sales gap between us and our marketplace leaders" (line 7). What does the president mean by this phrase?

   She means that the company as a whole must

   (1) treat competitors with less concern
   (2) begin to sell as much as the competitors do
   (3) reconsider the difference between the companies' products
   (4) end the promotion of competing businesses
   (5) imitate the business practices of the competition

3. Why does the president quote the consultant Gregory Schoenfeld in her letter?

   She quotes Schoenfeld in order to

   (1) make the letter longer
   (2) provide a conflicting point of view
   (3) confuse the audience with extra information
   (4) promote Schoenfeld's book
   (5) give support to her claims

4. Based on the president's beliefs about what is best for the company's future as expressed in this letter, what kind of employees would she most likely want to hire?

   Employees whose main focus is

   (1) working overtime hours
   (2) preparing for competitors' criticisms
   (3) participating in development of product quality
   (4) reintroducing out-of-date products
   (5) preserving the current systems and products

GO ON TO THE NEXT PAGE

Questions 5 through 10 refer to the following excerpt from a novel.

WHAT IS UPSETTING THE SPEAKER IN THE STORY?

"What will become of us if and when we do get back?" wondered Müller, and even he is anxious.

Kropp shrugs. "I don't know. Let's just get there first and then see what happens."

None of us really has any ideas. "What could we possibly do?" I ask.

"There isn't anything I fancy doing," Kropp answers wearily. "One day you'll be dead anyway and what have you got then? In any case, I don't think we'll ever get home."

"If I think about it, Albert," I say after a little while, rolling over on my back, "when I hear the word 'peace', and if peace really came, what comes into my head is that I'd like to do something, well, unimaginable. Something—you know what I mean—that would make it all worthwhile, being out here under fire and all the rest. But I just can't picture what it could be. The only possibilities there are—all this business with a job, studying, earning money and so on—they all make me sick, because they were always there and they put me off. I can't think of anything, Albert, I can't think of anything."

All at once everything seems to be pointless and desperate.

Kropp takes it further along the same line. "It will be just as difficult for all of us. I wonder whether the people back at home don't worry about it themselves occasionally? Two years of rifle fire and hand grenades—you can't just take it all of like a pair of socks afterwards—

We all agree that it is the same for everyone; not only for us here, but for everyone in the same boat, some to a greater, others to a lesser extent. It is the common fate of our generation.

Albert put it into words. "The war has ruined us for everything."

He is right. We're no longer young men. We've lost any desire to conquer the world. We are refugees. We are fleeing from ourselves. We were eighteen years old, and we had just begun to love the world and to love being in it; but we had to shoot at it. The first shell to land went straight for our hearts. We've been cut off from the real action, from getting on, from progress. We don't believe in those things anymore; we believe in the war.

Erich Maria Remarque, ALL QUIET ON THE WESTERN FRONT, 1929.

GO ON TO THE NEXT PAGE

5. Why do the soldiers have trouble thinking of things they will want to do when the war ends?

   (1) They do not expect to remain friends once the war is over.
   (2) They will likely re-enlist in the army when the fighting ends.
   (3) The war has damaged so much that no longer have homes to go back to.
   (4) The war is so overwhelming that it is the only thing they can think about.
   (5) None of the soldiers has a reason to start a new career if the war ends.

6. The main character in this story is Paul Baumer. He says that after the war, the idea of "a job, studying, earning money, and so on" makes him sick. Why does he say this?

   (1) He does not have the skills to succeed in business.
   (2) He does not appreciate the value of a good education.
   (3) He has enough money at this point in his life.
   (4) These things are not spectacular enough.
   (5) Those goals do not agree with the expectations of his friends.

7. Which of the following statements are most in agreement with the opinion of Kropp as he states it in the story?

   (1) No one fighting in the war will survive.
   (2) It will be difficult to transition into civilian life.
   (3) Making money should be everyone's goal following the war.
   (4) People at home will not accept returning soldiers if they lose.
   (5) Returning to school will be beneficial to all soldiers.

8. Erich Maria Remarque, the author this novel, also fought in World War I as a young man. This experience most likely helped Remarque in the writing of this novel to

   (1) accurately depict the real conversations of soldiers
   (2) completely explain the reasons for the war's end
   (3) contradict the political forces that led to the war
   (4) predict the likely winner of the conflict
   (5) thoroughly investigate advances in military technology

9. Albert's comment that "the war has ruined us for everything" could be translated as which of the following?

   (1) There is no hope to survive such a brutal conflict.
   (2) We are likely to lose the war and embarrass our country.
   (3) The war has ended our youth and hope for a future.
   (4) We will not live to see all our friends again.
   (5) If we return home, we will not want to see our loved ones.

10. The speaker in the story states, "We're no longer young men." He says this because

   (1) they have aged many years since the start of the war
   (2) only the youngest soldiers fight at the front
   (3) compared to their companions they are much older
   (4) they are now too old to continue fighting
   (5) they experience of war has matured them quickly

GO ON TO THE NEXT PAGE

Questions 11 through 15 refer to the following excerpt from a play.

WHY DOES JEAN WANT VERA TO LEAVE?

[The living room in a small flat. Two women, one of them in mourning after her husband's death, sit beside the remains of tea.]

VERA: But Jean, where are you going, when you pack up here?

JEAN: I'm not leaving here. I'm staying on.

VERA: Oh. But I thought that now… you were talking about being free for your own work at last....

JEAN: If I have any work to do, I can do it here. You don't understand, quite. All these years have been living from whirlpool to whirlpool, never settled. The thought of getting accustomed to another place makes me shudder.

VERA: I can imagine, now, how it has been, Jean. But can you find any peace here? With all these things about? You are so sensitive—lamps, and pictures, and rugs—these aren't just furniture to you, they are images of the past. Won't they be, too—real? Too personal? Won't you feel more at liberty with yourself if you create your own atmosphere?

JEAN: Ah, they are real enough! That table is a winter in Munich; the samovar is Warsaw one night in May; the lucerna is Rome… and all that those places mean to me. I never realized how things could be alive—be personal—until I was left all alone in the midst of these.

VERA: There, don't you see? They're so dominating. I knew you before all this.... I wish you would get away—be yourself.

JEAN: No. I shall stay here. As close as possible.

VERA: But really, Jean! I'm thinking of your work. Perhaps you don't appreciate what an insidious drug memory can be. Especially the memory of unhappiness. Let's be frank, Jean, for the sake of your future. You have been unhappy.

JEAN: Unhappy? Yes, I have been outrageously unhappy! Years of it! Sharp arrows and poisoned wine. I wanted to die....

VERA: Jean!

JEAN: You read a play by Strindberg, and you say it's very strong, very artistic, but all the while you believe it is only the nightmare of a diseased mind. It's just a play—you shut the book and return to "real" life, thankfully. Well, the Strindberg play has been my real life, and real life my play, my impossible dream. You can't imagine how terrifying it is to feel the situation develop around you. Two bodies caught naked in an endless wilderness of thorns. Every movement one makes to free the other only wounds him the more. Two souls, each innocent and aspiring, bound together by serpents.... It is one of those things that are absolutely impossible… and yet true.

VERA: I'll help you pack. Now. You must!

JEAN: We had the deepest respect and admiration for one another, but somehow we never walked in step. His emotion repressed mine, my emotion repressed his. Sometimes one was

GO ON TO THE NEXT PAGE

the slave, sometimes the other. We couldn't both be free at the same time. There was always something to hide, to be afraid of.... Not words nor acts, but moods. It passed over from one soul to the other like invisible rays. And we couldn't separate. That was part of it. We just went on and on....

VERA: People wondered. The first time I met Paul... he seemed to impress me like a powerful motor car stalled in a muddy road.

JEAN: Ah. I know!

VERA: Poor child.

Horace Holley, HIS LUCK, 1916

11. What major difference between the two characters is discovered in the first several lines?

Vera assumes that Jean

(1) will be happier if she remains at home with memories
(2) does not truly know how to love
(3) cannot possibly make a rational decision
(4) must want to leave her home
(5) has lost the ability to be happy

12. Vera says that Jean is sensitive to images of the past and asks "Won't they be, too—real?" (line 24). What does this reveal about Vera's ideas about possession?

Vera likely believes that

(1) reminders are frequently painful reminders
(2) memories only exist in the home
(3) images are more important than feelings
(4) memories should be forgotten once someone dies
(5) real memories are more complicated than imagined ones

13. When Jean describes her memories and comments on things she sees in her home she says, "that table is a winter in Munich." She also describes other items in a similar way. What is the likely explanation for what Jean believes about these things?

(1) Some items are so closely related to memories that they nearly become the memory themselves.
(2) Material possessions that come from foreign countries are the best mementos one can have.
(3) Traveling through foreign countries is the best way to collect memories.
(4) No one other than the owner of an object can appreciate the beauty that it possesses.
(5) When traveling, it is best to purchase items that best reflect the country that they come from.

GO ON TO THE NEXT PAGE

14. Though Jean's husband is not a character in the play, some information about him is revealed through the conversation of his mourning wife and her friend. What is most likely true about him?

    Jean's deceased husband most likely

    (1) was sick for a very long time before dying
    (2) did not love her
    (3) disapproved of her friendship with Vera
    (4) was a powerful but frustrated man
    (5) was an accomplished car mechanic

15. This play ends without a clear resolution as to whether or not Jean will stay because much is revealed about her relationship with her dead husband. From the information in the passage, what can be guessed about Jean's relationship with her husband?

    Their marriage was likely

    (1) happy, with only small differences between them
    (2) indifferent, without much emotion or feeling
    (3) full of poison, danger, and violence
    (4) thoroughly sad and without hope
    (5) respectful, but without balance or harmony

GO ON TO THE NEXT PAGE

Questions 16 through 20 refer to the following poem.

WHAT DOES THIS SPEAKER HAVE TO SAY ABOUT PAIN?

After Great Pain

After great pain, a formal feeling comes—
The nerves sit ceremonious like tombs—
The stiff heart questions—was it he that bore,
And yesterday, and centuries before?
The feet, mechanical, go round—
Of ground, or air, or ought*—
A wooden way
Regardless grown
A quartz contentment like a stone
This is the hour of lead—
Remembered if outlived
As freezing persons recollect the snow—
First chill—then stupor—then the letting go—

*nothing

Emily Dickinson, "After Great Pain"

16. Emily Dickinson, the author of this poem, is known for her many poems that are highly personal and reveal very simple emotions common to all people. What aspect of this poem is consistent with this information and may help to explain its meaning?

(1) the use of many dashes
(2) the reference to snow
(3) the poem's lack of rhyme
(4) the image of a questioning heart
(5) the description of quartz and stone

17. The speaker in the poem states that "nerves sit ceremonious like tombs" (line 2) in order to convey a feeling that could best be described as

(1) frightened
(2) confused
(3) numb
(4) angry
(5) supernatural

GO ON TO THE NEXT PAGE

18. The speaker in the poem is describing what happens after

(1) the birth of a child
(2) a marriage
(3) a visit to the hospital
(4) a car accident
(5) a loved one's death

19. The speaker in the poem uses the phrase "remembered if outlived" (line 11) in order to convey which of the following ideas?

(1) It is possible to remember many things in a lifetime.
(2) People do not remember events if they do not live through them.
(3) Difficult things should be forgotten.
(4) Some painful things are difficult to overcome.
(5) All memories are painful.

20. Which of the following images is NOT used to convey the theme of grief

(1) uncontrollable crying
(2) walking aimlessly
(3) heavy objects
(4) thawing snow
(5) internal questions

END OF EXAMINATION

MATHEMATICS, PART I

Tests of General Educational Development

Directions

The Mathematics Test consists of questions intended to measure general mathematics skills and problem-solving ability. The questions are based on short readings that often include a graph, chart, or figure.

You should spend no more than 45 minutes answering the questions in this booklet. Work carefully, but do not spend too much time on any one question. Be sure you answer every question.

Formulas you may need are given on page 102. Only some of the questions will require you to use a formula. Not all the formulas given will be needed.

Some questions contain more information than you will need to solve the problem; other questions do not give enough information. If the question does not give enough information to solve the problem, the correct answer choice is "Not enough information is given."

The use of calculators is allowed only in Part I.

Do not mark in this test booklet. The test administrator will give you blank paper for your calculations. Record your answers on the separate answer sheet provided. Be sure that all requested information is properly recorded on the answer sheet.

To record your answers, fill in the numbered circle on the answer sheet beside the number that corresponds to the question in the test booklet.

FOR EXAMPLE:

If a grocery bill totaling $15.75 is paid with a $20.00 bill, how much change should be returned?

(1) $5.25
(2) $4.75
(3) $4.25
(4) $3.75
(5) $3.25

The correct answer is $4.25; therefore, answer space (3) would be marked on the answer sheet.

Do not rest the point of your pencil on the answer sheet while you are considering your answer. Make no stray or unnecessary marks. If you change an answer, erase your first mark completely. Mark only <u>one</u> answer space for each question; multiple answers will be scored as incorrect. Do not fold or crease your answer sheet. All test materials must be returned to the test administrator.

GO ON TO THE NEXT PAGE

Mathematics, Part I

FORMULAS

AREA (*A*) of a:

square	$A = s^2$; where s = side
rectangle	$A = lw$; where l = length, w = width
parallelogram	$A = bh$; where b = base, h = height
trapezoid	$A = \frac{1}{2}(b_1 + b_2)h$; where b = base, h = height
triangle	$A = \frac{1}{2}bh$; where b = base, h = height
circle	$A = \pi r^2$; where $\pi = 3.14$, r = radius

PERIMETER (*P*) of a:

square	$P = 4s$; where s = side
rectangle	$P = 2l + 2w$; where l = length, w = width
triangle	$P = a + b + c$; where a, b, and c are the sides

CIRCUMFERENCE (*C*) of a circle: $C = \pi d$; where $\pi = 3.14$, d = diameter

VOLUME (*V*) of a:

cube	$V = s^3$; where s = side
rectangular container	$V = lwh$; where l = length, w = width, h = height
square pyramid	$V = \frac{1}{3}(\text{base edge})^2 h$
cone	$V = \frac{1}{3}\pi r^2 h$
cylinder	$V = \pi r^2 h$; where $\pi = 3.14$, r = radius, h = height

PYTHAGOREAN RELATIONSHIP	$c^2 = a^2 + b^2$; where c = hypotenuse, a and b are legs of a right triangle
DISTANCE (*d*) BETWEEN TWO POINTS ON A PLANE	$d = \sqrt{(x_2 - x_1)^2 + (y_2 - y_1)^2}$; where (x_1, y_1) and (x_2, y_2) are two points in a plane
SLOPE OF A LINE (*m*)	$m = \frac{y_2 - y_1}{x_2 - x_1}$; where (x_1, y_1) and (x_2, y_2) are two points in a plane
MEAN	**mean** $= \frac{x_1 + x_2 + \ldots x_n}{n}$; where the x's = the values for which a mean is desired, and n = number of values in the series
MEDIAN	**median** = the point in an ordered set of numbers at which half of the numbers are above and half of the numbers are below this value
SIMPLE INTEREST (*i*)	$i = prt$; where p = principal, r = rate, t = time
DISTANCE (*d*) as function of rate and time	$d = rt$; where r = rate, t = time
TOTAL COST (*c*)	$c = nr$; where n = number of units, r = cost per unit

Mathematics, Part I

Directions: You will have 22 minutes to complete questions 1–13. You may use your calculator with these questions only. Choose the one best answer to each question.

1. The Great Pyramid in Egypt has a height of approximately 150 meters and a base of approximate area 50,000 square meters. In cubic meters, what is its approximate internal volume?

   (1) 7,500,000

   (2) 5,000,000

   (3) 3,750,000

   (4) 2,500,000

   (5) 750,000

2. A bus driver is restricted by law to 10 hours or less driving per day, and buses have a speed limit of 55 miles per hour. If a driver is on the road for 3 days, what is the maximum distance (in miles) that can be traveled?

   (1) 11,000

   (2) 5,500

   (3) 1,650

   (4) 550

   (5) 165

3. A ski run must not exceed a slope of $-\frac{3}{5}$ due to safety concerns. What is the maximum elevation drop (in yards) if the run is to be 4000 yards long?

   (1) 24,000

   (2) 12,000

   (3) 4,800

   (4) 4,000

   (5) 2,400

4. Artificial turf costs $15 per square yard. What is the cost of covering a field that is 75 yards long by 60 yards wide?

   (Disregard the dollar sign when gridding in your answer.)

	/	/	/	
.	.	.	.	.
0	0	0	0	0
1	1	1	1	1
2	2	2	2	2
3	3	3	3	3
4	4	4	4	4
5	5	5	5	5
6	6	6	6	6
7	7	7	7	7
8	8	8	8	8
9	9	9	9	9

PLEASE DO NOT WRITE IN THIS TEST BOOKLET.

Mark your answer in the circles in the grid on your answer sheet.

GO ON TO THE NEXT PAGE

5. What is the length of the shortest path to connect points *A, B,* and *C*?

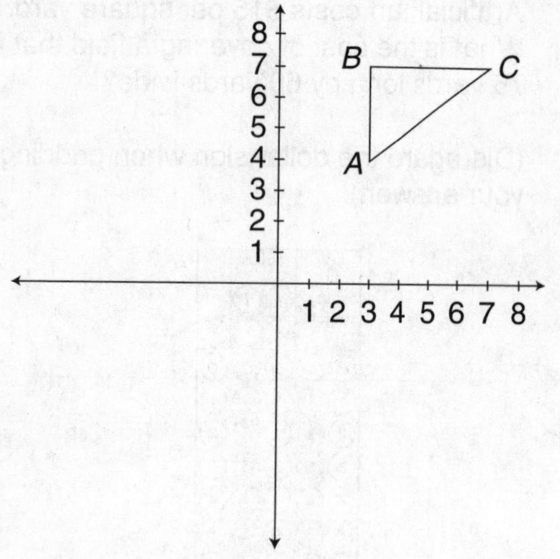

(1) 3

(2) 4

(3) 6

(4) 7

(5) 12

6. If 2 out of 5 of drivers are exceeding the speed limit at any given time on a highway, what is the percent chance that an automated speed camera will capture a speeder if it photographs a car at random?

(1) 20%

(2) 40%

(3) 50%

(4) 60%

(5) 80%

7. If a man spends 16 hours per day awake and works for half of his waking hours, approximately what percentage of the total day is this man working?

(1) 10%

(2) 25%

(3) 33%

(4) 50%

(5) 66%

8. What is the minimum perimeter of these two shapes if they are allowed to touch without overlapping?

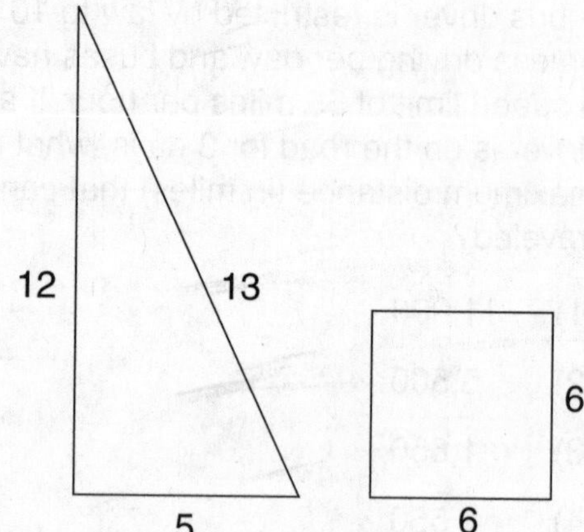

(1) 60

(2) 42

(3) 30

(4) 24

(5) 6

GO ON TO THE NEXT PAGE

9. Sales of surfboards and the number of shark sightings at a beach are inversely related. If 4 boards are sold on a day with 2 sightings, how many will be sold if there are 8 shark sightings?

(1) 1

(2) 4

(3) 6

(4) 8

(5) 16

10. An electrical contractor spends $10,000 a week on supplies and another $20,000 on employee wages. If sales tax is 10% and payroll tax is 5%, then the contractor's weekly cost will be

(1) $30,000
(2) $31,500
(3) $32,000
(4) $33,000
(5) $34,500

11. A class with 12 students has an average test score of 76 points. If more students scored above the average than below, what is a possible value of the median score?

(1) 70

(2) 72

(3) 74

(4) 76

(5) 78

12. A triangular sail has two sides of the same length and its largest angle is 90°. What is the value of the smallest angle (in degrees)?

(1) 0

(2) 30

(3) 45

(4) 50

(5) 90

13. Zarbini's gourmet grocery buys pickles in barrels that are 4 ft tall and measure 24 inches in diameter. What is the approximate volume (in cubic feet) of pickles that will fill a barrel with these dimensions?

(1) 4

(2) 12.5

(3) 23

(4) 46

(5) 96

END OF MATHEMATICS, PART I

Directions: You will have 22 minutes to complete questions 14–25. You may NOT use a calculator with these questions. Choose the one best answer to each question.

14. The scale on a pirate's map is 1 inch = 200 feet. If the treasure is buried 2.5 inches from the pirate's current position on the map, what is the distance (in feet) to his treasure?

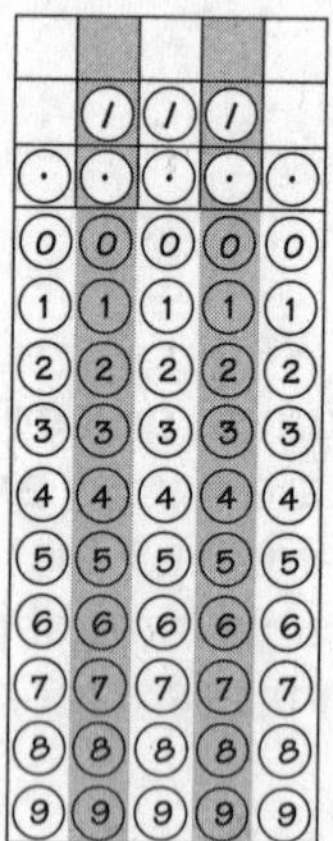

PLEASE DO NOT WRITE IN THIS TEST BOOKLET.

Mark your answer in the circles in the grid on your answer sheet.

15. The graph below shows the average revenue per hour from a shaved ice stand, based on the outside temperature.

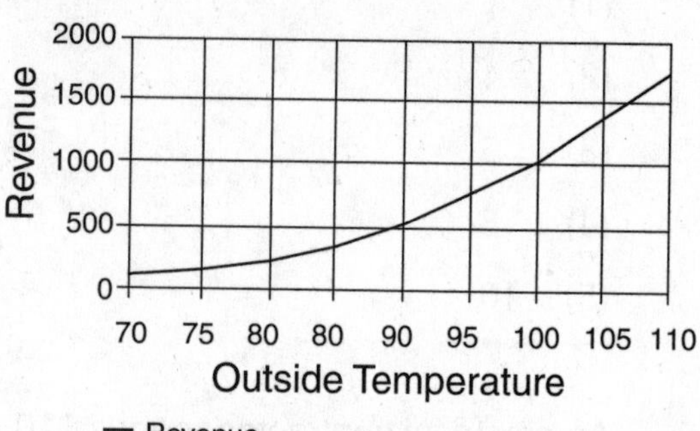

Based on the graph, approximately how much revenue is expected after 3 hours at a constant 90° F?

(1) 95

(2) 100

(3) 500

(4) 1500

(5) 3000

GO ON TO THE NEXT PAGE

16. A moving company charges \$50 per hour for each person working, plus an additional \$.50 per mile driven. If Fritz hires 3 movers for 2 hours of work apiece and the total distance driven is 40 miles, what will his total cost be?

(1) \$460
(2) \$320
(3) \$300
(4) \$166
(5) \$66

17. For the triangle shown in the diagram below, both angle A and angle C measure 60°. If side AB has a length of 4 inches, what is the sum (in inches) of sides AC and BC?

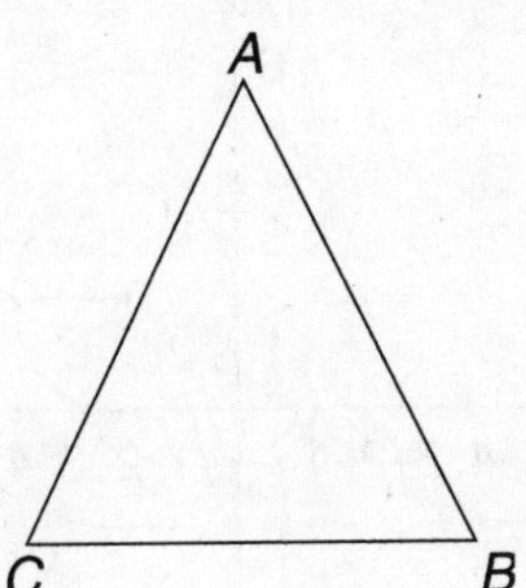

(1) 8
(2) 6
(3) 4
(4) 2
(5) 1

18. A triangular loading ramp has the dimensions shown in the figure below. Side c is the length. If a new ramp is made for a dock that is twice as high off of the ground as the one with length c but with the same incline, what will the new ramp's length be (in feet)?

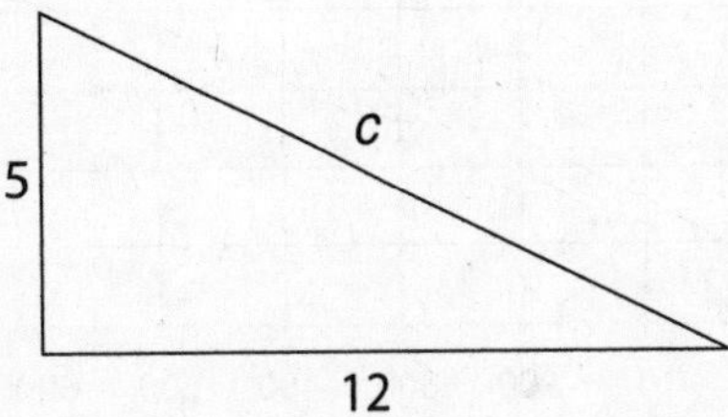

(1) 12
(2) 13
(3) 24
(4) 26
(5) 30

19. To rent a convention hall costs a \$400 base fee, plus an additional \$5 per attendee. If x legionnaires are attending an event, which equation can be used to find the total cost T, of renting the hall (in dollars)?

(1) $T = 400 + 5x$
(2) $T = 400 + x$
(3) $T = (400 + 5)x$
(4) $T = 400x + 5x$
(5) $T = 400(5x)$

GO ON TO THE NEXT PAGE

Questions 20 and 21 refer to the graph below.

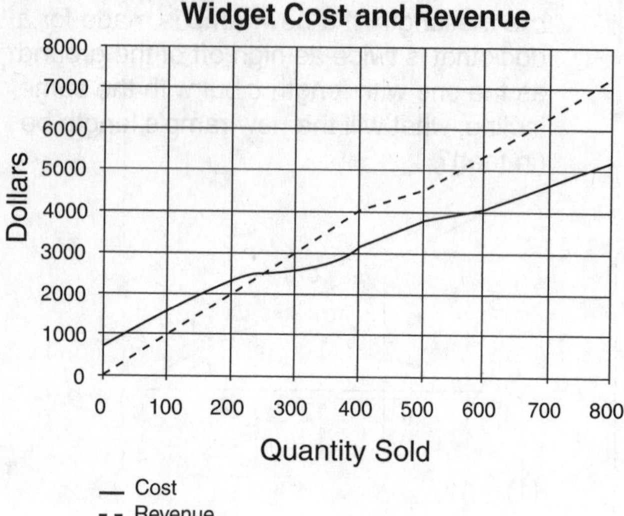

20. What is the minimum number of widgets that must be sold in order to avoid losing money?

(1) 50
(2) 100
(3) 250
(4) 550
(5) 800

21. Although the revenue is zero when there have been no sales made, the manufacturing cost is still approximately $750. What is a possible explanation for this fact?

(1) Sprocket sales are currently outpacing those of widgets.
(2) The economy is in a recession.
(3) Money must be spent to produce widgets whether or not they are sold.
(4) The widget-makers union has gone on strike.
(5) Revenue is proportional to the amount sold.

22. A graph of two circles is shown on the grid below.

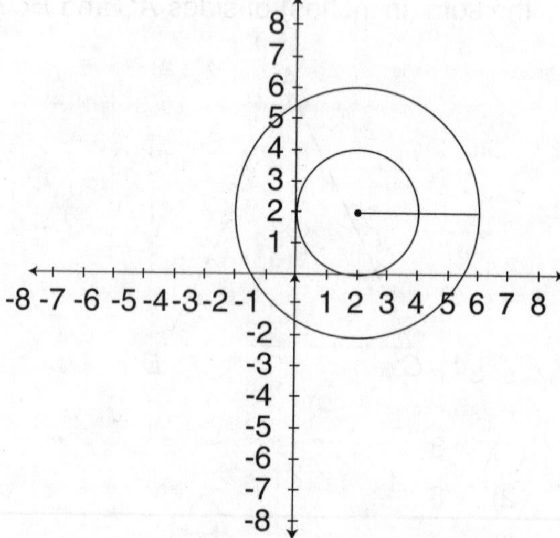

Which one of the following statements is true?

(1) The larger circle has twice the diameter and twice the area of the smaller one.
(2) The larger circle has twice the diameter and four times the area of the smaller one.
(3) The larger circle's circumference is 2π.
(4) The smaller circle has a radius of 4.
(5) The larger circle's circumference is 2π times that of the smaller one.

GO ON TO THE NEXT PAGE

23. Mindy invested \$500 in a savings account. After one year, her account balance was \$515. What percent of yearly interest did her bank pay?

(Leave off the % sign when gridding your answer.)

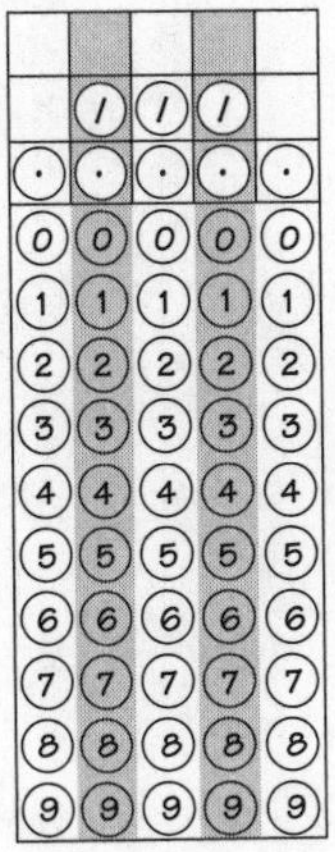

PLEASE DO NOT WRITE IN THIS TEST BOOKLET.

Mark your answer in the circles in the grid on your answer sheet.

24. On a certain job site, carpenters make an average of \$600 per week, while electricians earn \$750 per week. Let x represent the number of carpenters and y be the number of electricians.

Which of the following functions will correctly calculate the weekly payroll (P) for all of these types of workers on the site?

(1) $P = 600y + 750x$

(2) $P = 600 + x + 750 + y$

(3) $P = (600x)(750y)$

(4) $P = (x + y)(600 + 750)$

(5) $P = (150)(4x + 5y)$

25. A contractor charges \$450 to lay tile in a 10 x 15 room. If the cost (c) of tiling a room is proportional to the area of its floor, which of the following expressions correctly determines the cost (c), in dollars, of tiling a larger 25 x 30 room?

(1) $\frac{1}{3} = \frac{750}{c}$

(2) $\frac{3}{1} = \frac{750}{c}$

(3) $c = \frac{750}{450}$

(4) $c = \frac{750}{150}$

(5) $\frac{750}{450} = \frac{150}{c}$

END OF EXAMINATION

DO NOT MARK OR WRITE ON THIS PAGE

Answers and Explanations for Practice Test 1

WRITING

1. 3
2. 2
3. 5
4. 1
5. 1
6. 5
7. 3
8. 5
9. 2
10. 2
11. 5
12. 1
13. 4
14. 3
15. 5
16. 2
17. 5
18. 1
19. 2
20. 3
21. 3
22. 1
23. 2
24. 2
25. 2

SOCIAL STUDIES

1. 4
2. 2
3. 1
4. 1
5. 5
6. 2
7. 2
8. 4
9. 3
10. 1
11. 4
12. 4
13. 1
14. 3
15. 3
16. 2
17. 2
18. 1
19. 5
20. 5
21. 1
22. 3
23. 4
24. 4
25. 1

SCIENCE

1. 2
2. 4
3. 4
4. 5
5. 2
6. 3
7. 2
8. 4
9. 5
10. 1
11. 5
12. 1
13. 4
14. 3
15. 3
16. 4
17. 2
18. 3
19. 2
20. 4
21. 2
22. 5
23. 2
24. 1
25. 3

READING

1. 4
2. 2
3. 5
4. 3
5. 4
6. 4
7. 2
8. 1
9. 3
10. 5
11. 4
12. 1
13. 1
14. 4
15. 5
16. 4
17. 3
18. 5
19. 2
20. 1

MATH

1. 4
2. 3
3. 5
4. 67,500
5. 4
6. 2
7. 3
8. 1
9. 1
10. 3
11. 5
12. 3
13. 2
14. 500
15. 4
16. 2
17. 1
18. 4
19. 1
20. 3
21. 3
22. 2
23. 3
24. 1
25. 1

EXPLANATIONS

Writing

1. **3** No comma is necessary in the underlined portion of the sentence. A comma generally separates elements of a sentence, but there are no elements to separate here. For example, you wouldn't write, "He, hit the ball." You would write, "He hit the ball." This eliminates choices 1, 4 and 5. Choice 2 changes the meaning of the sentence—we go from having an engineering department to having more than one engineering department. This also doesn't make much sense. That leaves answer 3 as the correct choice.

2. **2** As with the comma in question 1, a dash sets off elements in a sentence. The phrase *exposure to excessive noise* needs no separation. Choice 1 makes the sentence redundant, since *to* and *regarding* have roughly the same meaning. Choice 3 doesn't change the sentence at all. Choice 4—*have* refers to the plural pronoun *employees*, so that doesn't need to be changed. The phrase, "noise from aircraft" is correct, so that leaves us with choice 2 as the correct choice.

3. **5** There are no discrete elements of this sentence that need to be separated by a comma. Also, a comma is never used after the word *but*. Answer 5 is correct.

4. **1** Choices 2, 4 and 5 change the intended meaning of the sentence, so they're out. Answer 3 has a comma after *therefore* which is correct, but the first part of the sentence still needs to be separated from the rest. This leaves you with answer 1.

5. **1** The underlined portion of the sentence doesn't contain elements that need to be separated, so no comma is necessary. That leaves us with choices 1 and 4. Number 1 is straightforward while number 4 is awkward at best. Choice 1 is your answer.

6. **5** In this sentence, the word *among* implies that there are scheduling challenges thrown in with the public service announcements. This is where the sentence needs to be corrected. Choice 5 is the only one that addresses this.

7. **3** The phrase *more worse* is redundant and needs to be changed. Answer choice 3 addresses this error.

8. **5** You can *give* information *to* someone and you can *have* information *for* someone, but you can't *have* information *to* someone. Choices 4 and 5 address this, but choice 4 is hopelessly awkward and confusing. Choice 5 is your answer.

9. **2** Paragraph C has nothing to do with a meeting, so sentence 9 doesn't belong there. Eliminate choice 1. Paragraph D (choices 3 and 4) concludes the memo. It needs to be there and separated from the paragraph before. Sentence 3 refers to sentence 2 (choice 5), and while the memo *could* work without sentence 2, choice 2 is the better answer because since sentences 3 and 4 both talk about the petition, they would work better joined in the same paragraph. Answer 2 is correct.

10. 2 The word *nobody* is singular, so *want* needs to be changed to *wants*. Answer 2 takes care of that problem.

11. 5 Whenever you see a prepositional phrase, take it out and see how the sentence reads. In this case, it reads, "The most important are *how do we prevent food from going bad*?" While it's usually easy to see if you should use a singular or plural by using this technique, it's not so easy in this case. Does *The most important* refer to something singular or plural? Well, it refers to **the question** *how do we prevent food from going bad?* which is singular. This means you need to change the word *are* to *is.* Answer choice 5 is the only one that fixes this problem.

12. 1 If you use the technique we just used in question 11 here, it reads, "The answers are usually pretty simplistic," so the word *are* stays. This eliminates choice 2. Choice 3 doesn't really change the sentence and doesn't correct an error, so that one's out. You can't say *this questions*, so answer 4 is out. Choice 5 changes the meaning of the sentence in that it refers to answers that aren't listed. The word *simplistic* has a slightly negative connotation meaning *oversimplified*, and that's not what the author is trying to convey. The word the author means to use is *simple*, which is given in choice 1.

13. 4 You don't need a comma when you use the word *and.* This is addressed in answer 4.

14. 3 The main reason answer 3 is the best choice is that all the others are wrong. Answers 1 and 4 change the intended meaning, answer 5 doesn't change anything, and answer 2 is incorrect (the comma here is appropriate). While it is becoming more and more acceptable to begin a sentence with a conjunction (in this case, *And*), it's better to start without one.

15. 5 Choice 5 is correct because sentence 13 gives an example of the statement made in sentence 12.

16. 2 This is a simple grammatical error in which the word *you* was left out of the sentence—and you know it's *you* as opposed to *one* or *he or she* because the sentence begins with the word *You* (see parallelism, question 19). Choice 5 reverses the meaning of the sentence. Answer 2 is correct.

17. 5 This sentence is asking what the difference is ***between** one thing **and** another*. Answer choice 5 is the correct wording for this sentence.

18. 1 As with question 16, the phrase *are **you** more concerned* tells you that the most effective revision would have the pronoun *you* as opposed to *one* or *he or she*, etc. This eliminates answers 2 and 5. Choice 3 makes the sentence passive, so that choice is out. Of the two remaining choices, 1 is better because 4 is more hypothetical and changes the meaning of the sentence.

19. 2 The error in this sentence has to do with what's called parallelism, which means all things in a list must be in the same form. For example, you can say, "Are you playing, writing, swimming or jumping?" but you can't say, "Are you playing, writing, swimming or will you jump?" The word *jump* should be *jumping* so that it can be in the same form as the other words in the list. In sentence 6, the list is *do you* do this or *would you be more likely to.* Since none of the choices give you a straight "do you or do you" parallelism, you have to go for the next best thing, which is *are you,* which satisfies the rule of parallelism and is in the same tense (present).

20. 3 Answer choice 3 is correct because it is a concluding sentence that summarizes what's said in the paragraph.

21. 3 Just as in question 17, sentence 8 is talking about the difference between one thing and another. There's also a parallelism issue as in question 19—*the difference between this and that is the same as the difference between that and the other thing.* Answer choice 3, *between,* solves both problems.

22. 1 While this sentence is awkward, the only thing you can change is the underlined portion, and that is correct as is. Answer 1 is correct.

23. 2 There are plenty of things wrong with this sentence, but only one of the answer choices is correct. *One example* should be *For example.* That's taken care of in choice 2. If you delete the word *while,* as choice 1 suggests, you get a run-on sentence. There are all kinds of problems with the rest of the sentence, but none of them are addressed in choices 3, 4 or 5. Choice 2 is your only correct answer.

24. 2 *Things* are always referred to as *that,* while *people* are always referred to as *who.* The sentence should read, "the person *who...*" This is addressed in answer 2.

25. 2 You can say, "weigh the pros and cons of blah, blah blah" or "weigh these pros and cons," but you can't say "weigh these pros and cons of blah, blah, blah." Answer choice 2 offers the correct option of "the pros and cons of each."

Social Studies

1. 4 The map indicates that major American cities in the Midwest have developed along rivers. Therefore, answer choice 4 is correct.

2. 2 The Mississippi River has played a major role in the economic and cultural development of the American Midwest. Answer choice 5 is therefore incorrect. The river is freshwater, so choice 4 is also incorrect. The river flows north from its river delta in Louisiana, so choices 1 and 3 are incorrect, while 2 is correct.

3. 1 It was the Constitution, not the Declaration of Independence, that sought to establish a tripartite (three-branch) government, so answer choice 2 is incorrect. The Articles of Confederation was written after the Declaration of Independence, so choice 4 is impossible. Choice 5 is both untrue and irrelevant to this topic. The quote indicates that the Declaration of Independence criticized the King of England for leading a tyrannical government, so choice 3 is incorrect, and choice 1 is correct.

4. 1 Because the quote says "to separate them from others... because of their race," the doctrine of separate but equal is best described by answer choice 1. In the Supreme Court decision *Plessy v. Ferguson* (1896), the doctrine of separate but equal was created and allowed for racial segregation in the United States. Thus, choice 4 is incorrect. Choices 2 and 5 are irrelevant to the quote.

5. 5 *Brown v. Board of Education* has had an enormous impact on public education in the United States. Many states, however, were reluctant to enforce the orders of the Supreme Court, which led to dramatic standoffs between state leaders and the federal government, most notably in Little Rock, Arkansas. Therefore, choice 1 is incorrect. Choice 2 exaggerates the problem and is also incorrect.

6. 2 The Supreme Court reasoned that racial segregation was traumatic for African American children (choice 2): "[it] generates a feeling of inferiority... that may affect their hearts and minds in a way unlikely ever to be undone..." The other choices express opinions (mostly incorrect opinions) about the Court's reasoning, assuming that fear or bias colored the Court's argument.

7. 2 The New Deal was Franklin Delano Roosevelt's plan of economic and social reforms. Reconstruction (choice 1) was the period immediately following the end of the Civil War. The Great Society (3) was President Lyndon Johnson's series of social reforms during the 1960s. The Square Deal (4) was Theodore Roosevelt's domestic policy intended to help middle class citizens, while the Fireside Chats (5) were Franklin Delano Roosevelt's radio addresses during the Great Depression.

8. 4 Only answer choice 4 describes a situation that satisfies the definition offered by the question. The other choices address different topics: income tax (choice 1), naval blockades (2), inflation (3), and interstate trade and sales taxes (5).

9. 3 The First Amendment protects five essential freedoms, three of which are listed in choice 3, the correct answer. The Second Amendment protects the right to bear arms (choice 1), but not *against* the government. Choice 4 is obviously wrong: the primary role of Congress is to make laws. Choice 5 is irrelevant to this topic.

10. 1 The First Amendment does not guarantee the right to vote. Rather it makes five guarantees: those listed in answer choices 2 through 5 and also the freedom of assembly.

11. 4 Choice 4 best describes the impact of the First Amendment on American law. The Supreme Court cannot 'strike down' amendments to the Constitution, so choice 2 is incorrect. Remember to read the quote closely in order to avoid off-topic answer choices, such as choice 5.

12. 4 The extreme language in choice 1 ("all forms") should raise a red flag: the First Amendment protects the right to petition and assemble in protest of the government. The freedom of the press makes choices 2 and 3 impossible. The freedom of religion and the separation of church state make choice 5 unlikely.

13. 1 The famous caption of the image, "Join, or Die" encouraged the colonies to band together or else be destroyed, so answer choice 1 is correct. The Albany Plan of Union was not an attempt to unite the colonies against Great Britain, but against the French and Indian threat from the north and west. The extreme pessimism of choices 2, 3, and 4 is not accurate and choice 5 sounds too conspiratorial to be likely.

14. 3 The Articles of Confederation was written by the colonists in order to organize the newly formed United States of America. So it cannot have been an earlier draft of the Declaration of Independence (choice 1) and was not issued from George III's government (2). Choices 4 and 5 are also inaccurate.

15. 3 Do not let the academic language of the prompt throw you off. While it may sound intimidating, GDP is just a measure of wealth. For this question, the definition does not even matter because it asks you to select the *opinion* from among the facts. Each of the choices 1, 2, 4, and 5 can be verified from the data in the graph. They do not express personal opinions. So long as the data from the graph is accurate, they cannot be disputed. Choice 3, however, expresses a political opinion, not a fact.

16. 2 Of the choices listed here, economic development is most directly affected by climate, geography, and demography (the dynamics of population change). While many of the other factors listed among the choices, especially those in choice 3, are important, they exert less of an impact than those of choice 2. Consider, for example, the role that climate and geography play in the development of agriculture and manufacturing. A desert area rich in gold and iron will encourage the development of mining, rather than agriculture.

17. 2 The Emancipation Proclamation of 1863 was President Lincoln's famous decree that ended slavery in Southern states, so choice 2 is correct. It was his assassination in 1865 that led to the end of his presidency (choice 3). Equal rights for African Americans were guaranteed in Amendments 13, 14, and 15 ("The Civil War Amendments") to the Constitution. The doctrine of "separate but equal," which allowed for racial segregation, was established in the 1896 Supreme Court decision *Plessy v. Ferguson.*

18. 1 Manifest Destiny was the idea that it was the destiny of the United States to expand across North America. Choice 1 is therefore the right answer. Capitalism (choice 2) is a system in which wealth and wealth production are privately owned. Imperialism (3) is a general term describing the rule of empires. Eminent domain (5) is the right of the government to seize private property (with monetary compensation) in the interest of the state.

19. 5 One of the major effects of globalization has been "the easier flow of goods across international borders" (choice 5). The other choices do not describe a major effect of globalization.

20. 5 Some of these choices are more obviously incorrect than the others. Choices 1, 2, and 4 are not supported by the *data,* but are merely opinions about energy production in general. Choice 5 is clearly a fact supported by the data.

21. 1 Use the information in the question to help you determine that the women's suffrage movement was focused on equal voting rights. The legalization of abortion (choice 2) occurred in 1973 when the Supreme Court struck down abortion laws in *Roe v. Wade* and *Doe v. Bolton.* Women have always participated in the workforce (3) in one form or another. Choice 4 is a trap: suffering is different from suffrage.

22. 3 Chicago is located in Illinois, along Lake Michigan and not near the Atlantic Ocean or the Gulf of Mexico. Therefore, choice 3 is correct.

23. 4 The cotton gin "caused the expansion of the cotton industry in the American South" (choice 4) by making the production of cotton much more efficient. None of the other answers address this impact.

24. 4 This question requires you to pay attention to the information in the graph. The most densely populated continents are, in fact, Europe and Asia (choice 4). Two of the world's most populous nations, China and India, are found in Asia. They contain nearly 2.5 billion of the Earth's 6.5 billion inhabitants between them.

25. 1 Population density is determined most importantly by climate and geography. Deserts, extreme arctic environments, highly mountainous regions, have few human inhabitants. Therefore choice 1 is correct.

Science

1. 2 The question states that density independent factors are not related to the number of organisms in an environment. Answer 2 is correct because climate is not affected by the number of organisms in a location.

2. 4 Answer 4 is correct because the passage states that Phineas Gage injured his frontal lobe and afterward underwent a change in personality. Answers 1 and 5 are incorrect because the passage states that Gage lived after the accident. Answer 2 is incorrect because the passage states the frontal lobe is part of the brain, and answer 3 is incorrect because if the rod went through Gage's skull, the skull must have been fractured.

3. 4 On the chart provided, no values are given for urine concentration of albumin and glucose, so these chemicals are not normally found in urine. Therefore, answer 4 is correct.

4. 5 The passage states that the color of an object is determined by the colors of light reflected. Answer 5 is correct because based on the information, if a shirt is red, it must reflect red light.

5. 2 The figure given shows the moon between the sun and the Earth, and the passage states that during an eclipse the view of the sun is obstructed from Earth. Thus, answer 2 is the most logical since it suggests the moon is the object obstructing the view of the sun.

6. 3 The passage states that opposite poles attract and like poles repel. B is attracted to a south pole, so B is north and A is south. C is repelled by a north pole, so C is north and D is south. Thus, the north poles are B and C, so answer 3 is correct.

7. 2 The passage states that penicillin works by preventing the growth of bacteria. According to the chart, only strep throat is caused by bacteria, so answer 2 is correct.

8. 4 Answer 4 is correct because only identical twins would have identical DNA. Parents' birth dates and family history would be the same for any siblings, so answers 1 and 2 are incorrect. Blood glucose levels and saliva content are determined by several factors, including food that was recently eaten, answers 3 and 5 are not the best methods.

9. 5 The passage states that both plants were green and hybrid, so answers 1, 2, 3, and 4 can be eliminated, leaving only answer 5. If both parents carry a hidden yellow gene, then some of the offspring may be yellow, so answer 5 supports the results.

10. 1 Weight is determined by mass and acceleration due to gravity or vertical movement. If Deanna is moving upwards, her weight would increase since the elevator is accelerating and exerting a force on her against the direction of gravity. Thus, answer 1 is correct.

11. 5 Salt dissolves in water, so answer 3 is wrong, and water does not burn and turn to ash, so answer 2 is wrong. Rust is not white, so 4 is wrong, and while it is possible that the pot was dirty, boiling water should clean the pot so 1 is not the best explanation. Answer 5 is correct because when water boils, any salt in the water is left behind.

12. 1 Answer 1 is the best answer because if the rabbits all die, some foxes will likely starve to death so the fox population will decrease as well.

13. 4 The passage states that operant condition is a system of punishments and rewards. Answer 4 mentions giving the cat a treat, which is a reward, so this describes operant conditioning and is the correct answer.

14. 3 The graph shows the temperature increasing, then staying constant while the sample melts, then increasing, then staying constant while the sample boils, than increasing. Answer 3 supports this. Note that a horizontal line means that the variable on the y axis, in this case temperature, is not changing.

15. 3 C represents the sample between melting and boiling. Such a sample would be liquid, so answer 3 is correct. During melting, some of the sample would be solid and some liquid, so answer 2 is incorrect. During boiling, some of the sample would be liquid and some gas, so answer 4 is incorrect.

16. 4 An organism is a living thing. Answer 4 is correct because a flower is a living thing, while rocks, air, the sun, and rivers are not living.

17. 2 The passage states that bees are important because they pollinate flowering plants, so answer 2 is best. While answers 1 and 5 describe other roles of bees, they are not mentioned in the passage. Answers 3 and 4 do not describe bees.

18. 3 This question requires knowledge of the properties of gases. Answer 3 is correct because gases are a form of matter and all matter takes up space and has mass. Gases have weight so answer 5 is wrong. Solids are denser than gases, so answer 1 is incorrect, and not all gases are identical nor are they all clear and odorless, so 2 and 4 are incorrect.

19. 2 The figure labels the windward side and shows a thunderstorm on that side. No precipitation is shown on the leeward side, so answer 2 is correct.

20. 4 The passage states that index fossils are known to have come from a specific time frame, so they are useful because they allow scientists to determine the age of nearby fossils. Therefore, choice 4 is correct.

21. 2 This passage discusses how oil can break down a natural coating of birds, decreasing their ability to survive. This information provides an answer to the question in answer 2.

22. 5 This study examined ecosystems. An ecologist is most likely to study ecosystems, so answer 5 is correct.

23. 2 The graphs show that there are more white moths in a white birch ecosystem and more brown moths in a pine forest ecosystem. The most logical explanation is answer 2, that the moths blend in better with trees the same color as the moths.

24. 1 The passage states that most years have 365 days, even though it takes 365.25 days for Earth to orbit the sun. Thus, it makes sense that every 4 years a leap year with 366 days is required, so answer 1 is correct.

25. 3 Answer 3 is correct because elastic and inelastic represent all possible types of collisions. Answer 1 represents types of energy, answer 2 represents types of eclipses, answer 4 does not represent anything, and answer 5 represents types of forces.

Reading

1. 4 The answer is 4 because the president states that "changing the perception in the marketplace…is quickly becoming the primary focus" and that "without such change" it will be "largely impossible to achieve the two largest goals." Employees effort and managers' organization are not mentioned, as in 1 and 2. The passage does not indicate there is a shortage of products, as in 3 and it is not clearly stated that the owners are missing a marketing plan, as in 5.

2. 2 The answer is 2 because a sales gap must refer to the difference in sales between the company and its competitors. Answer 1 cannot be true since the president is concerned about competitors. Answer 3 incorrectly focuses only on the competition, not both companies. Answer 4 suggests that competing companies have been promoted, which is not evident. Answer 5 might be logical, but is not stated and is not as good an answer as 2.

3. 5 The Answer is 5 because the quote follows the main plan of the president, to organize the product around the employees. The quote serves as support for this plan. This is how most quotes are employed, as supporting evidence. Answer 2 is flawed since the quote gives a point of view in agreement with the letter overall. There is no reason to make the letter longer, as in 1 or to confuse the letter's audience, as in 3. Answer 4 is not supported by the passage.

4. 3 The answer is 3 because the president quotes the book in which employees are "encouraged to be decision-makers and to become more responsible for quality by taking a personal stake." Answer 5 contradicts the main goals of the letter and organization. None of the other answers are supported by information in the passage.

5. 4 The answer is 4 because the speaker says, "I can't think of anything" twice, showing his fear and frustration with the idea all at once. The passage also states, "everything seems to be pointless and desperate," indicating that the war has a heavy influence on them. The passage does not comment on their future as friends, as in 1. No evidence is in the passage about their homes, answer 3. None of the soldiers discuss re-enlisting. Answer 5 talks about future careers, but is too extreme and not as good and answer as 4.

6. 4 The answer is 4 because he has been so affected by the war that he cannot consider doing regular things such as "job, studying, earning money" because they were always part of life. But following life in the war, he needs "something, well, unimaginable." He desires a great change from the world he has known, and normal things will not do for him. His skills, education and money are unknown in this passage excerpt, answers 1, 2, and 3. Answer 5 mentions the expectations of his friends which are not clearly expressed.

7. 2 The answer is 2 because Kropp states, "It will be as difficult for all of us." He refers to all of the war fighting by saying that "you can't just take it off like a pair of socks." Kropp is concerned just about getting home and living, but he believes that it will be hard to readjust and begin living a normal life again after the war. Answer 1 is extreme and uncertain. Kropp does not mention money or school as his priority, answers 3 and 5. Answer 4 cannot be concluded based on information in the passage.

8. 1 The answer is 1 because the passage at its basic presentation is a conversation among soldiers. It reveals their very simple and real worries about life during and after the war. These personal conversations are most likely to be familiar to an author who experienced them firsthand. Answers 2 and 5 are extreme. Answer 3 attempts to discuss political forces for war which is not mentioned. Answer 4 suggests the author could predict the future, when in fact, he only relates the experience of the war in the past.

9. 3 The answer is 3 because Albert is summarizing the different comments of his fellow soldiers who are concerned with doing something new and spectacular after the war, yet can't think of anything else and may not be able to transition easily anyway. He is commenting on their potential future lives if they survive the war. Answer 1 addresses the anger of war, but does not summarize Albert's comment. The winner of the war is never at issue in this conversation, so answer 2 is incorrect. Answer 4 predicts the future which Albert does not do. Answer 5 is never stated.

10. 5 The answer is 5 because they have all realized that the war has given them tough experiences that they cannot escape or forget. Yet, they began the war as young men, so the statement does not literally mean that they are not young. Instead, it comments on the age and maturity that they feel as a result of the war. So, answer 1 and 4 are too literal and incorrect. Answer 2 is extreme and unsupported. Answer 3 is incorrect since no soldiers age is actually given.

11. 4 The answer is 4 because Vera asks Jean where she is going and is surprised to hear that Jean is not leaving. Answer 1 contradicts what Vera actually expects. Answer 2, 3, and 5 are extreme and not clearly indicated in the passage.

12. 1 The answer is 1 because it is clear that each item mentioned is directly tied to a memory. Answer 2 is similar to Vera's comment, but is too extreme. Answer 3 and 4 are not stated or supported by the passage. Answer 5 may be true but does not reflect Vera's stated opinion.

13. 1 The answer is 1 because each item in her home is connected to a specific time and place. Clearly Jean thinks of places she has been with each item she discusses with Vera. Answer 1 paraphrases this idea. Answer 2 falsely focuses on where the items come from rather than their memory connection. Answer 3 focuses on the travel incorrectly. Answer 4 is extreme. Answer 5 may be true but does not answer the question.

14. 4 The answer is 4 because Vera describes him as a man who was "like a powerful motor car stalled in a muddy road." This, combined with Jean's description of her husband reveals that they shared a marriage of tumultuous emotions. These descriptions show the man to likely be strong in some ways but without an entirely successful marriage and perhaps "stuck" in other ways. There is no evidence to say how sick he was, answer 1, or what his opinion of Vera was, answer 3. Answer 5 is never mentioned. His love for Vera and their marriage is in question, but it is never stated that he did not love her, answer 2.

15. 5 The answer is 5 because Jean directly describes herself as "outrageously happy." Her emotions were very strong, but she couldn't understand her own life while using phrases like "terrifying" and "endless wilderness" and "bound together by serpents." This combined with the "deepest respect and admiration for one another" shows that their marriage was uneven, both good and bad. Answer 5 captures this best. All other answers are at best, only half-right.

16. 4 The answer is 4 because it is the only answer of the five given that directly references something personal. A questioning heart is an image of personal search for answers. The other answers all reference a part of the poem or language contained in it, but none of them are of a personal nature.

17. 3 The answer is 3 because nerves that "sit" are obviously not moving and the image of a "tomb" is also quite still. Other imagery in the poem leads to the conclusion that these reference stillness or, in the instance of emotions, numbness. Only answer 3 is supported. The other answers reference emotions that are extreme and unmentioned.

To Do...

17. **1** The 3 angles of a triangle total 180°. If two of the angles are 60° each (60° + 60° = 120°), the third angle must also be 60° (180° – 120° = 60°). If all 3 angles are equal, then all 3 sides must be equal. Since side *AB* is 4 inches, the other two sides, *AC* and *BC*, are also 4 inches each. *AC* + *BC* = 8.

18. **4** Use the Pythagorean theorem to find side c: $a^2 + b^2 = c^2$. So $(5)^2 + (12)^2 = c^2$. $25 + 144 = c^2$. $169 = c^2$. $13 = c$. Since the new ramp is going to be twice as high off the ground, but the angles will be the same, each side of the triangle will be twice as long. The new ramp will be $13 \times 2 = 26$.

19. **1** The number of attendees is x. Each must pay \$5, so multiply x by 5, to get $5x$. Add the base fee of \$400. Total cost is \$400 + $5x$.

20. **3** When 250 widgets are sold, that is the point where the cost of producing them crosses the point where there is revenue from their sale. After that point, the company will begin to receive more revenue than it has to spend to produce them.

21. **3** Money must be spent to produce widgets whether or not they are sold.

22. **2** The smaller circle has a radius of 2 and a diameter of 4. The larger circle has a radius of 4 and a diameter of 8, which is twice the diameter of the smaller circle. The area of smaller circle is $\pi r^2 = \pi(2)^2 = 4\pi$. The area of larger circle is $\pi(4)^2 = 16\pi$. This is four times larger than the area of the smaller circle.

23. **3** She earned \$15 in interest on \$500. Percent interest is based on 100. So she earned \$3 for every \$100 she invested = 3%.

24. **1** Multiply the number of carpenters (x) by their weekly pay, \$600. Multiply the number of electricians (y) by their weekly pay, \$750. Add the two together to get the weekly Payroll (P) = $600x + 750y$

25. **1** Set up a proportion: 150/450 = 750/c. The 150/450 reduces to 1/3. $\frac{1}{3} = \frac{750}{c}$. Cross multiply to find c.

17. 1 The 3 angles of a triangle total 180°. If two of the angles are 60° each (60 + 60 = 120), the third angle must also be 60 (180 − 120 = 60). If all 3 angles are equal, then the triangle is equilateral. Since side AB is 4 inches, the other two sides, AC and BC, are also 4 inches each.

18. 4 Use the Pythagorean theorem: [illegible] So [illegible] 25 [illegible] 16 [illegible] 18 [illegible]. Since the new ratio is going to be twice as great as the original [illegible] will be the same; each side of the triangle will be twice as long [illegible].

19. 1 The number of attendees is 8. Each [illegible] so [illegible]. Add the [illegible] cost [illegible] totals $400 [illegible].

20. 3 When 250 sweaters are sold, that is the point where [illegible] where there is no [illegible]. From this [illegible] point [illegible] revenue than [illegible].

21. 3 Money must be spent on [illegible] was [illegible] as follows.

22. 2 The smaller circle has a radius of 2 and a diameter of 4. The larger circle has a radius of 4 and a diameter of 8, which is twice the diameter of the smaller circle. [illegible] the area of the larger circle [illegible] is four times larger than the area of the smaller circle.

23. 3 She earned $15 in interest on $500 [illegible] 100 she invested [illegible].

24. 1 Multiply the number of [illegible] by their weekly pay [illegible] pay $750. Add the [illegible].

25. 3 Set up a proportion: [illegible] 15 [illegible].

Practice Test 2

Completely darken bubbles with a No. 2 pencil. If you make a mistake, be sure to erase mark completely. Erase all stray marks.

1

YOUR NAME: (Print) ______ Last ______ First ______ M.I.

SIGNATURE: ______ DATE: ___/___/___

HOME ADDRESS: (Print) ______ Number and Street

______ City ______ State ______ Zip Code

PHONE NO.: (Print) ______

IMPORTANT: Please fill in these boxes exactly as shown on the back cover of your test book.

2. TEST FORM

3. TEST CODE

0	A	0	0	0
1	B	1	1	1
2	C	2	2	2
3	D	3	3	3
4	E	4	4	4
5	F	5	5	5
6	G	6	6	6
7		7	7	7
8		8	8	8
9		9	9	9

4. REGISTRATION NUMBER

0	0	0	0	0	0
1	1	1	1	1	1
2	2	2	2	2	2
3	3	3	3	3	3
4	4	4	4	4	4
5	5	5	5	5	5
6	6	6	6	6	6
7	7	7	7	7	7
8	8	8	8	8	8
9	9	9	9	9	9

6. DATE OF BIRTH

Month	Day		Year	
JAN				
FEB				
MAR	0	0	0	0
APR	1	1	1	1
MAY	2	2	2	2
JUN	3	3	3	3
JUL		4	4	4
AUG		5	5	5
SEP		6	6	6
OCT		7	7	7
NOV		8	8	8
DEC		9	9	9

7. SEX

MALE

FEMALE

The Princeton Review®

FORM NO. 00001-PR

5. YOUR NAME

First 4 letters of last name				FIRST INIT	MID INIT
A	A	A	A	A	A
B	B	B	B	B	B
C	C	C	C	C	C
D	D	D	D	D	D
E	E	E	E	E	E
F	F	F	F	F	F
G	G	G	G	G	G
H	H	H	H	H	H
I	I	I	I	I	I
J	J	J	J	J	J
K	K	K	K	K	K
L	L	L	L	L	L
M	M	M	M	M	M
N	N	N	N	N	N
O	O	O	O	O	O
P	P	P	P	P	P
Q	Q	Q	Q	Q	Q
R	R	R	R	R	R
S	S	S	S	S	S
T	T	T	T	T	T
U	U	U	U	U	U
V	V	V	V	V	V
W	W	W	W	W	W
X	X	X	X	X	X
Y	Y	Y	Y	Y	Y
Z	Z	Z	Z	Z	Z

Start with number 1 for each new section. If a section has fewer questions than answer spaces, leave the extra answer spaces blank. Be sure to erase any errors or stray marks completely.

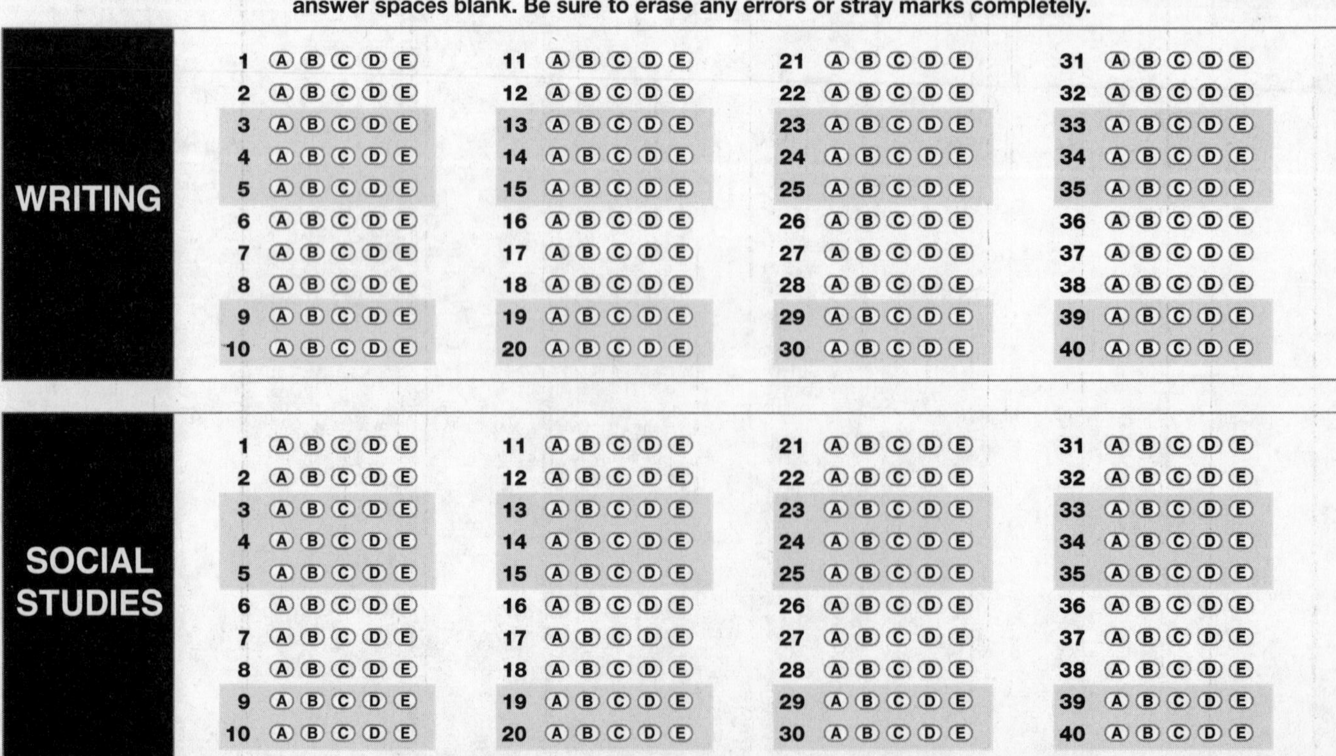

WRITING

1 Ⓐ Ⓑ Ⓒ Ⓓ Ⓔ	11 Ⓐ Ⓑ Ⓒ Ⓓ Ⓔ	21 Ⓐ Ⓑ Ⓒ Ⓓ Ⓔ	31 Ⓐ Ⓑ Ⓒ Ⓓ Ⓔ
2 Ⓐ Ⓑ Ⓒ Ⓓ Ⓔ	12 Ⓐ Ⓑ Ⓒ Ⓓ Ⓔ	22 Ⓐ Ⓑ Ⓒ Ⓓ Ⓔ	32 Ⓐ Ⓑ Ⓒ Ⓓ Ⓔ
3 Ⓐ Ⓑ Ⓒ Ⓓ Ⓔ	13 Ⓐ Ⓑ Ⓒ Ⓓ Ⓔ	23 Ⓐ Ⓑ Ⓒ Ⓓ Ⓔ	33 Ⓐ Ⓑ Ⓒ Ⓓ Ⓔ
4 Ⓐ Ⓑ Ⓒ Ⓓ Ⓔ	14 Ⓐ Ⓑ Ⓒ Ⓓ Ⓔ	24 Ⓐ Ⓑ Ⓒ Ⓓ Ⓔ	34 Ⓐ Ⓑ Ⓒ Ⓓ Ⓔ
5 Ⓐ Ⓑ Ⓒ Ⓓ Ⓔ	15 Ⓐ Ⓑ Ⓒ Ⓓ Ⓔ	25 Ⓐ Ⓑ Ⓒ Ⓓ Ⓔ	35 Ⓐ Ⓑ Ⓒ Ⓓ Ⓔ
6 Ⓐ Ⓑ Ⓒ Ⓓ Ⓔ	16 Ⓐ Ⓑ Ⓒ Ⓓ Ⓔ	26 Ⓐ Ⓑ Ⓒ Ⓓ Ⓔ	36 Ⓐ Ⓑ Ⓒ Ⓓ Ⓔ
7 Ⓐ Ⓑ Ⓒ Ⓓ Ⓔ	17 Ⓐ Ⓑ Ⓒ Ⓓ Ⓔ	27 Ⓐ Ⓑ Ⓒ Ⓓ Ⓔ	37 Ⓐ Ⓑ Ⓒ Ⓓ Ⓔ
8 Ⓐ Ⓑ Ⓒ Ⓓ Ⓔ	18 Ⓐ Ⓑ Ⓒ Ⓓ Ⓔ	28 Ⓐ Ⓑ Ⓒ Ⓓ Ⓔ	38 Ⓐ Ⓑ Ⓒ Ⓓ Ⓔ
9 Ⓐ Ⓑ Ⓒ Ⓓ Ⓔ	19 Ⓐ Ⓑ Ⓒ Ⓓ Ⓔ	29 Ⓐ Ⓑ Ⓒ Ⓓ Ⓔ	39 Ⓐ Ⓑ Ⓒ Ⓓ Ⓔ
10 Ⓐ Ⓑ Ⓒ Ⓓ Ⓔ	20 Ⓐ Ⓑ Ⓒ Ⓓ Ⓔ	30 Ⓐ Ⓑ Ⓒ Ⓓ Ⓔ	40 Ⓐ Ⓑ Ⓒ Ⓓ Ⓔ

SOCIAL STUDIES

1 Ⓐ Ⓑ Ⓒ Ⓓ Ⓔ	11 Ⓐ Ⓑ Ⓒ Ⓓ Ⓔ	21 Ⓐ Ⓑ Ⓒ Ⓓ Ⓔ	31 Ⓐ Ⓑ Ⓒ Ⓓ Ⓔ
2 Ⓐ Ⓑ Ⓒ Ⓓ Ⓔ	12 Ⓐ Ⓑ Ⓒ Ⓓ Ⓔ	22 Ⓐ Ⓑ Ⓒ Ⓓ Ⓔ	32 Ⓐ Ⓑ Ⓒ Ⓓ Ⓔ
3 Ⓐ Ⓑ Ⓒ Ⓓ Ⓔ	13 Ⓐ Ⓑ Ⓒ Ⓓ Ⓔ	23 Ⓐ Ⓑ Ⓒ Ⓓ Ⓔ	33 Ⓐ Ⓑ Ⓒ Ⓓ Ⓔ
4 Ⓐ Ⓑ Ⓒ Ⓓ Ⓔ	14 Ⓐ Ⓑ Ⓒ Ⓓ Ⓔ	24 Ⓐ Ⓑ Ⓒ Ⓓ Ⓔ	34 Ⓐ Ⓑ Ⓒ Ⓓ Ⓔ
5 Ⓐ Ⓑ Ⓒ Ⓓ Ⓔ	15 Ⓐ Ⓑ Ⓒ Ⓓ Ⓔ	25 Ⓐ Ⓑ Ⓒ Ⓓ Ⓔ	35 Ⓐ Ⓑ Ⓒ Ⓓ Ⓔ
6 Ⓐ Ⓑ Ⓒ Ⓓ Ⓔ	16 Ⓐ Ⓑ Ⓒ Ⓓ Ⓔ	26 Ⓐ Ⓑ Ⓒ Ⓓ Ⓔ	36 Ⓐ Ⓑ Ⓒ Ⓓ Ⓔ
7 Ⓐ Ⓑ Ⓒ Ⓓ Ⓔ	17 Ⓐ Ⓑ Ⓒ Ⓓ Ⓔ	27 Ⓐ Ⓑ Ⓒ Ⓓ Ⓔ	37 Ⓐ Ⓑ Ⓒ Ⓓ Ⓔ
8 Ⓐ Ⓑ Ⓒ Ⓓ Ⓔ	18 Ⓐ Ⓑ Ⓒ Ⓓ Ⓔ	28 Ⓐ Ⓑ Ⓒ Ⓓ Ⓔ	38 Ⓐ Ⓑ Ⓒ Ⓓ Ⓔ
9 Ⓐ Ⓑ Ⓒ Ⓓ Ⓔ	19 Ⓐ Ⓑ Ⓒ Ⓓ Ⓔ	29 Ⓐ Ⓑ Ⓒ Ⓓ Ⓔ	39 Ⓐ Ⓑ Ⓒ Ⓓ Ⓔ
10 Ⓐ Ⓑ Ⓒ Ⓓ Ⓔ	20 Ⓐ Ⓑ Ⓒ Ⓓ Ⓔ	30 Ⓐ Ⓑ Ⓒ Ⓓ Ⓔ	40 Ⓐ Ⓑ Ⓒ Ⓓ Ⓔ

Start with number 1 for each new section. If a section has fewer questions than answer spaces, leave the extra answer spaces blank. Be sure to erase any errors or stray marks completely.

SCIENCE

1 Ⓐ Ⓑ Ⓒ Ⓓ Ⓔ	11 Ⓐ Ⓑ Ⓒ Ⓓ Ⓔ	21 Ⓐ Ⓑ Ⓒ Ⓓ Ⓔ	31 Ⓐ Ⓑ Ⓒ Ⓓ Ⓔ
2 Ⓐ Ⓑ Ⓒ Ⓓ Ⓔ	12 Ⓐ Ⓑ Ⓒ Ⓓ Ⓔ	22 Ⓐ Ⓑ Ⓒ Ⓓ Ⓔ	32 Ⓐ Ⓑ Ⓒ Ⓓ Ⓔ
3 Ⓐ Ⓑ Ⓒ Ⓓ Ⓔ	13 Ⓐ Ⓑ Ⓒ Ⓓ Ⓔ	23 Ⓐ Ⓑ Ⓒ Ⓓ Ⓔ	33 Ⓐ Ⓑ Ⓒ Ⓓ Ⓔ
4 Ⓐ Ⓑ Ⓒ Ⓓ Ⓔ	14 Ⓐ Ⓑ Ⓒ Ⓓ Ⓔ	24 Ⓐ Ⓑ Ⓒ Ⓓ Ⓔ	34 Ⓐ Ⓑ Ⓒ Ⓓ Ⓔ
5 Ⓐ Ⓑ Ⓒ Ⓓ Ⓔ	15 Ⓐ Ⓑ Ⓒ Ⓓ Ⓔ	25 Ⓐ Ⓑ Ⓒ Ⓓ Ⓔ	35 Ⓐ Ⓑ Ⓒ Ⓓ Ⓔ
6 Ⓐ Ⓑ Ⓒ Ⓓ Ⓔ	16 Ⓐ Ⓑ Ⓒ Ⓓ Ⓔ	26 Ⓐ Ⓑ Ⓒ Ⓓ Ⓔ	36 Ⓐ Ⓑ Ⓒ Ⓓ Ⓔ
7 Ⓐ Ⓑ Ⓒ Ⓓ Ⓔ	17 Ⓐ Ⓑ Ⓒ Ⓓ Ⓔ	27 Ⓐ Ⓑ Ⓒ Ⓓ Ⓔ	37 Ⓐ Ⓑ Ⓒ Ⓓ Ⓔ
8 Ⓐ Ⓑ Ⓒ Ⓓ Ⓔ	18 Ⓐ Ⓑ Ⓒ Ⓓ Ⓔ	28 Ⓐ Ⓑ Ⓒ Ⓓ Ⓔ	38 Ⓐ Ⓑ Ⓒ Ⓓ Ⓔ
9 Ⓐ Ⓑ Ⓒ Ⓓ Ⓔ	19 Ⓐ Ⓑ Ⓒ Ⓓ Ⓔ	29 Ⓐ Ⓑ Ⓒ Ⓓ Ⓔ	39 Ⓐ Ⓑ Ⓒ Ⓓ Ⓔ
10 Ⓐ Ⓑ Ⓒ Ⓓ Ⓔ	20 Ⓐ Ⓑ Ⓒ Ⓓ Ⓔ	30 Ⓐ Ⓑ Ⓒ Ⓓ Ⓔ	40 Ⓐ Ⓑ Ⓒ Ⓓ Ⓔ

READING

1 Ⓐ Ⓑ Ⓒ Ⓓ Ⓔ	11 Ⓐ Ⓑ Ⓒ Ⓓ Ⓔ	21 Ⓐ Ⓑ Ⓒ Ⓓ Ⓔ	31 Ⓐ Ⓑ Ⓒ Ⓓ Ⓔ
2 Ⓐ Ⓑ Ⓒ Ⓓ Ⓔ	12 Ⓐ Ⓑ Ⓒ Ⓓ Ⓔ	22 Ⓐ Ⓑ Ⓒ Ⓓ Ⓔ	32 Ⓐ Ⓑ Ⓒ Ⓓ Ⓔ
3 Ⓐ Ⓑ Ⓒ Ⓓ Ⓔ	13 Ⓐ Ⓑ Ⓒ Ⓓ Ⓔ	23 Ⓐ Ⓑ Ⓒ Ⓓ Ⓔ	33 Ⓐ Ⓑ Ⓒ Ⓓ Ⓔ
4 Ⓐ Ⓑ Ⓒ Ⓓ Ⓔ	14 Ⓐ Ⓑ Ⓒ Ⓓ Ⓔ	24 Ⓐ Ⓑ Ⓒ Ⓓ Ⓔ	34 Ⓐ Ⓑ Ⓒ Ⓓ Ⓔ
5 Ⓐ Ⓑ Ⓒ Ⓓ Ⓔ	15 Ⓐ Ⓑ Ⓒ Ⓓ Ⓔ	25 Ⓐ Ⓑ Ⓒ Ⓓ Ⓔ	35 Ⓐ Ⓑ Ⓒ Ⓓ Ⓔ
6 Ⓐ Ⓑ Ⓒ Ⓓ Ⓔ	16 Ⓐ Ⓑ Ⓒ Ⓓ Ⓔ	26 Ⓐ Ⓑ Ⓒ Ⓓ Ⓔ	36 Ⓐ Ⓑ Ⓒ Ⓓ Ⓔ
7 Ⓐ Ⓑ Ⓒ Ⓓ Ⓔ	17 Ⓐ Ⓑ Ⓒ Ⓓ Ⓔ	27 Ⓐ Ⓑ Ⓒ Ⓓ Ⓔ	37 Ⓐ Ⓑ Ⓒ Ⓓ Ⓔ
8 Ⓐ Ⓑ Ⓒ Ⓓ Ⓔ	18 Ⓐ Ⓑ Ⓒ Ⓓ Ⓔ	28 Ⓐ Ⓑ Ⓒ Ⓓ Ⓔ	38 Ⓐ Ⓑ Ⓒ Ⓓ Ⓔ
9 Ⓐ Ⓑ Ⓒ Ⓓ Ⓔ	19 Ⓐ Ⓑ Ⓒ Ⓓ Ⓔ	29 Ⓐ Ⓑ Ⓒ Ⓓ Ⓔ	39 Ⓐ Ⓑ Ⓒ Ⓓ Ⓔ
10 Ⓐ Ⓑ Ⓒ Ⓓ Ⓔ	20 Ⓐ Ⓑ Ⓒ Ⓓ Ⓔ	30 Ⓐ Ⓑ Ⓒ Ⓓ Ⓔ	40 Ⓐ Ⓑ Ⓒ Ⓓ Ⓔ

MATH

1 Ⓐ Ⓑ Ⓒ Ⓓ Ⓔ	11 Ⓐ Ⓑ Ⓒ Ⓓ Ⓔ	21 Ⓐ Ⓑ Ⓒ Ⓓ Ⓔ	31 Ⓐ Ⓑ Ⓒ Ⓓ Ⓔ
2 Ⓐ Ⓑ Ⓒ Ⓓ Ⓔ	12 Ⓐ Ⓑ Ⓒ Ⓓ Ⓔ	22 Ⓐ Ⓑ Ⓒ Ⓓ Ⓔ	32 Ⓐ Ⓑ Ⓒ Ⓓ Ⓔ
3 Ⓐ Ⓑ Ⓒ Ⓓ Ⓔ	13 Ⓐ Ⓑ Ⓒ Ⓓ Ⓔ	23 Ⓐ Ⓑ Ⓒ Ⓓ Ⓔ	33 Ⓐ Ⓑ Ⓒ Ⓓ Ⓔ
4 Ⓐ Ⓑ Ⓒ Ⓓ Ⓔ	14 Ⓐ Ⓑ Ⓒ Ⓓ Ⓔ	24 Ⓐ Ⓑ Ⓒ Ⓓ Ⓔ	34 Ⓐ Ⓑ Ⓒ Ⓓ Ⓔ
5 Ⓐ Ⓑ Ⓒ Ⓓ Ⓔ	15 Ⓐ Ⓑ Ⓒ Ⓓ Ⓔ	25 Ⓐ Ⓑ Ⓒ Ⓓ Ⓔ	35 Ⓐ Ⓑ Ⓒ Ⓓ Ⓔ
6 Ⓐ Ⓑ Ⓒ Ⓓ Ⓔ	16 Ⓐ Ⓑ Ⓒ Ⓓ Ⓔ	26 Ⓐ Ⓑ Ⓒ Ⓓ Ⓔ	36 Ⓐ Ⓑ Ⓒ Ⓓ Ⓔ
7 Ⓐ Ⓑ Ⓒ Ⓓ Ⓔ	17 Ⓐ Ⓑ Ⓒ Ⓓ Ⓔ	27 Ⓐ Ⓑ Ⓒ Ⓓ Ⓔ	37 Ⓐ Ⓑ Ⓒ Ⓓ Ⓔ
8 Ⓐ Ⓑ Ⓒ Ⓓ Ⓔ	18 Ⓐ Ⓑ Ⓒ Ⓓ Ⓔ	28 Ⓐ Ⓑ Ⓒ Ⓓ Ⓔ	38 Ⓐ Ⓑ Ⓒ Ⓓ Ⓔ
9 Ⓐ Ⓑ Ⓒ Ⓓ Ⓔ	19 Ⓐ Ⓑ Ⓒ Ⓓ Ⓔ	29 Ⓐ Ⓑ Ⓒ Ⓓ Ⓔ	39 Ⓐ Ⓑ Ⓒ Ⓓ Ⓔ
10 Ⓐ Ⓑ Ⓒ Ⓓ Ⓔ	20 Ⓐ Ⓑ Ⓒ Ⓓ Ⓔ	30 Ⓐ Ⓑ Ⓒ Ⓓ Ⓔ	40 Ⓐ Ⓑ Ⓒ Ⓓ Ⓔ

CAUTION Use the answer spaces in the grids below for Section 6 or Section 7 only if you are told to do so in your test book.

Student-Produced Responses

ONLY ANSWERS ENTERED IN THE OVALS IN EACH GRID WILL BE SCORED. YOU WILL NOT RECEIVE CREDIT FOR ANYTHING WRITTEN IN THE BOXES ABOVE THE OVALS.

Grids 9, 10, 11, 12, 13 (each grid):

	/	/	
.	.	.	.
	0	0	0
1	1	1	1
2	2	2	2
3	3	3	3
4	4	4	4
5	5	5	5
6	6	6	6
7	7	7	7
8	8	8	8
9	9	9	9

PLEASE DO NOT WRITE IN THIS AREA

SERIAL #

LANGUAGE ARTS, WRITING PART I

Tests of General Educational Development

Directions

The Language Arts, Writing Test is intended to measure your ability to use clear and effective English. This test includes both multiple-choice questions and an essay. These directions apply only to the multiple-choice section; a separate set of directions is given for the essay.

The multiple-choice section consists of paragraphs with lettered paragraphs and numbered sentences. Some of the sentences contain errors in sentence structure, usage, or mechanics (punctuation, and capitalization). After reading the numbered sentences, answer the multiple-choice questions that follow. Some questions refer to sentences that are correct as written. The best answer for these questions is the one that leaves the sentence as originally written. The best answer for some questions is the one that produces a sentence that is consistent with the verb tense and point of view used throughout the text. A document is often repeated in order to allow for additional questions on a second page. The repeated document is the same as the first

You should spend no more than 40 minutes on the multiple-choice questions and 45 minutes on your essay. Work carefully, but do not spend too much time on any one question. Be sure you answer every question. You may begin working on the essay part of this test as soon as you complete the multiple-choice section.

Do not mark in this test booklet. Record your answers on the separate answer sheet provided. Be sure that all requested information is properly recorded on the answer sheet.

To record your answers, mark one numbered space on the answer sheet beside the number that corresponds to the question in the test booklet.

FOR EXAMPLE:

Sentence 1: **We were honored to meet governor Phillips.**

Which correction should be made to sentence 1?

(1) insert a comma after honored
(2) change honored to honer
(3) change governor to Governor
(4) change were to was
(5) no correction is necessary

In this example, the word "governor" should be capitalized; therefore, answer space 3 would be marked on the answer sheet.

Do not rest the point of your pencil on the answer sheet while you are considering your answer. Make no stray or unnecessary marks. If you change an answer, erase your first mark completely. Mark only one answer space for each question; multiple answers will be scored as incorrect. Do not fold or crease your answer sheet. All test materials must be returned to the test administrator.

GO ON TO THE NEXT PAGE

Writing, Part I

Directions: Choose the one best answer to each question.

Questions 1 through 9 refer to the following memorandum.

Montgomery Wells
Bank & Trust Company
501 Industrial Hwy
East York, PA 17405
(717) 555-7511

MEMORANDUM

To: James Blanchard, Senior VP, Operations
From: Jessica Danderfield, Manager, Computer Operations
Subject: Unauthorized Phone Calls
Date: July 17, 2009

(A)

(1) It has come to my attention, that employees have been making unauthorized phone calls from the Computer Operations Department. (2) Not only have there been $38,000 worth of calls to 900 numbers, but also very much calls to 911. (3) Apparently as some sort of hazing ritual, where new employees were told to call their supervisor at extension "9911". (4) Of course, '9' gets the call out of the building, then 911 goes to the police.

(B)

(5) It goes without saying that this is cause for concern. (6) What is equally disturbing to me, however, is that I seem to have been the last to find out about it. (7) I was made aware of the situation on Monday by one of the shift supervisors in the IT Department. (8) Further investigation revealed that employees in at least half of the departments. (9) Were aware of this situation. (10) Given the gravity of the circumstances, I feel that I should have apprised the situation. (11) The fact that disciplinary action is already being considered is particularly alarming, since given the fact that I have been kept out of the loop.

(C)

(11) Regarding managerial responsibility, we have no idea if the 900 calls were made by members of my department. (13) This is under investigation. (14) I don't know whether or not you are aware of this situation. (15) I would like to have a meeting with you ASAP. (16) I also feel that a meeting with all of the VPs and department managers is in order.

(D)

(17) Thanking you in advance for your prompt attention to this matter.

GO ON TO THE NEXT PAGE

Writing, Part I

1. Sentence 1: **It has come to my attention, that employees have been making unauthorized phone calls from the Computer Operations Department.**

   Which is the best way to write the underlined portion of this sentence? If the original is the best way, choose option (1).

   (1) attention, that employees have been
   (2) attention, the employees have been
   (3) attention, that employees had been
   (4) attention that employees have been
   (5) attention, that employees were

2. Sentence 2: **Not only have there been $38,000 worth of calls to 900 numbers, but also very much calls to 911.**

   Which correction should be made to sentence 2?

   (1) change Not to Nor
   (2) change $38,000 worth of to $38,000 in
   (3) change very much to numerous
   (4) change have to had
   (5) change the period to a question mark

3. Sentence 3: **Apparently as some sort of hazing ritual, where new employees were told to call their supervisor at extension "9911".**

   Which correction should be made to the sentence?

   (1) add a comma after Apparently
   (2) remove the comma after ritual
   (3) delete where
   (4) add a comma after supervisor
   (5) change where to in which

4. Sentences 7: **I was made aware of the situation on Monday by one of the shift supervisors in the IT Department.**

   If you were to rewrite sentence 7 beginning with

   One of the shift supervisors from IT

   the next words should be

   (1) increased my awareness
   (2) enabled me to become aware
   (3) were aware
   (4) made me wary
   (5) made me aware

GO ON TO THE NEXT PAGE

The memorandum is repeated for your use in answering the remaining questions.

Montgomery Wells
Bank & Trust Company
501 Industrial Hwy
East York, PA 17405
(717) 555-7511

MEMORANDUM

To: James Blanchard, Senior VP, Operations
From: Jessica Danderfield, Manager, Computer Operations
Subject: Unauthorized Phone Calls
Date: July 17, 2009

(A)

(1) It has come to my attention, that employees have been making unauthorized phone calls from the Computer Operations Department. (2) Not only have there been $38,000 worth of calls to 900 numbers, but also very much calls to 911. (3) Apparently as some sort of hazing ritual, where new employees were told to call their supervisor at extension "9911". (4) Of course, '9' gets the call out of the building, then 911 goes to the police.

(B)

(5) It goes without saying that this is cause for concern. (6) What is equally disturbing to me, however, is that I seem to have been the last to find out about it. (7) I was made aware of the situation on Monday by one of the shift supervisors in the IT Department. (8) Further investigation revealed that employees in at least half of the departments. (9) Were aware of this situation. (10) Given the gravity of the circumstances, I feel that I should have apprised the situation. (11) The fact that disciplinary action is already being considered is particularly alarming, since given the fact that I have been kept out of the loop.

(C)

(11) Regarding managerial responsibility, we have no idea if the 900 calls were made by members of my department. (13) This is under investigation. (14) I don't know whether or not you are aware of this situation. (15) I would like to have a meeting with you ASAP. (16) I also feel that a meeting with all of the VPs and department managers is in order.

(D)

(17) Thanking you in advance for your prompt attention to this matter.

GO ON TO THE NEXT PAGE

5. Sentences 8 and 9: **Further investigation revealed that employees in at least half of the departments. Were aware of this situation.**

   How would you change the underlined portions of these sentences in order to combine the two sentences?

   (1) departments. Moreover, knew
   (2) departments' awareness
   (3) departments who were aware
   (4) departments were aware
   (5) department was aware

6. Sentence 10: **Given the gravity of the circumstances, I feel that I should have apprised the situation.**

   How would you correct this sentence?

   (1) change apprised to been apprised of
   (2) change I should to you should
   (3) put a comma after that I
   (4) change apprised to appraised
   (5) change apprised to been apprised in

7. Sentence 11: **The fact that disciplinary action is already being considered is particularly alarming, since given the fact that I have been kept out of the loop.**

   Which is the most effective revision of sentence 11?

   (1) change already being to being
   (2) change been kept to was kept
   (3) change particularly alarming to particularly alarmed
   (4) change been kept out of to kept out of
   (5) delete since

8. Sentence 16: **I also feel that a meeting with all of the VPs and department managers is in order.**

   Which is the best way to write the underlined portion of the sentence? If the original is the best way, choose option (1).

   (1) managers is in order
   (2) manager is in order
   (3) managers are in order
   (4) managers in order
   (5) manager in order

9. Sentence 17: **Thanking you in advance for your prompt attention to this matter.**

   Which correction should be made to sentence 17?

   (1) change Thanking to I thank
   (2) change to this matter to of this matter
   (3) put a comma after advance
   (4) change this matter to the matter
   (5) change prompt to swift

GO ON TO THE NEXT PAGE

Questions 10 through 16 refer to the following informational article.

Did We Evolve From Neanderthals?

(A)

(1) This question have been debated since humanlike remains were found in the Neander Valley in Germany in 1856. (2) The fossils were different than any found before. (3) The bones were so thick and strong that the construction workers that found them thought they were from a bear. (4) Upon examination, the bones appeared human, but unlike those of any humans alive at the time. (5) They appeared very apelike. (6) It was like they were from an animal that was half ape and half human. (7) Most of us have seen the series of pictures that depicts the evolution of humans. (8) This series of pictures shows a chimpanzee on the left and a modern human on the right. (9) In between the two are about a half dozen or so pictures that create a progression or 'links' between apes and modern humans.

(B)

(10) This illustration was abandoned after key discoveries were found by Louis Leakey and his family. (11) These discoveries suggested that human evolution was far more complicated than previously believed.

(C)

(12) One discovery led scientists to conclude that humans were not descended from Neanderthals. (13) This was the fact that the two species lived side by side for tens of thousands of years. (14) From as early as 100,000 years ago to as late as 25,000 years ago, humans and Neanderthals coexisted in Europe and Asia.

(D)

(15) Just because chimpanzees and gorillas descended from a common ancestor, so too did humans and Neanderthals. (16) But are Neanderthals and humans actually separate species or are they subspecies or races of the same species? (17) This is unclear and we'll leave that for another discussion. (18) One thing is for certain, though—we were not descended from Neanderthals.

GO ON TO THE NEXT PAGE

10. Sentence 1: **This question have been debated since humanlike remains were found in the Neander Valley in Germany in 1856.**

Which correction should be made to sentence 1?

(1) change question to questions
(2) change have to has
(3) change since to because
(4) change humanlike to human-like
(5) no correction is necessary

11. Sentence 2: **The fossils were different than any found before.**

Which correction should be made to sentence 2?

(1) change fossils to fossil
(2) change were to was
(3) change than to from
(4) change any to any others
(5) change any to any ever

12. Sentence 3: **The bones were so thick and strong that the construction workers that found them thought they were from a bear.**

Which correction should be made to sentence 3?

(1) change bones were to bone was
(2) change and to or
(3) change that found to who found
(4) change thought to thinking
(5) no correction is necessary

13. Sentence 6: **It was like they were from an animal that was half ape and half human.**

Which is the best way to write the underlined portion of this sentence? If the original is the best way, choose option (1).

(1) like they were
(2) like it was
(3) as if they was
(4) like they were
(5) as though they were

14. Sentence 10: **This illustration was abandoned after key discoveries were found by Louis Leakey and his family.**

Which correction should be made to sentence 10?

(1) change were found to were made
(2) change were found to were discovered
(3) delete were found
(4) change abandoned to deleted
(5) change key to bone

15. Sentence 15: **Just because chimpanzees and gorillas descended from a common ancestor, so too did humans and Neanderthals.**

Which correction should be made to sentence 10?

(1) change because to as
(2) change and to or
(3) change ancestor to descendent
(4) delete too
(5) change humans to Human

16. Which revision would make the article more effective?

(1) delete paragraph B
(2) combine paragraphs A and B
(3) let paragraph B begin at sentence 7
(4) switch paragraphs B and C
(5) delete sentence 18

GO ON TO THE NEXT PAGE

Questions 17 through 25 refer to the following informational article.

How to Plant Bulbs

(A)

(1) I been asked this question many times. (2) The answer is pretty simple. (3) What is a bulb? (4) A bulb is a rootlike structure. (5) That certain plants such as onions and tulips have. (6) It is used to store food and enable the plant to survive the winter. (7) Therefore, bulbs are very durable. (8) But don't forget, they won't survive the winter on your shelf.

(B)

(9) The best time to plant bulbs is a few weeks before the first frost, but they can actually be planted by you any time of year. (10) How do you plant them? (11) There's another easy question. (12) Dig a hole, put the bulb in, cover it up. (13) That's all you need to do in order to have a reasonable chance of getting beautiful flowers from your bulbs. (14) But there are a few things that are good to know in order to get the best out of your bulbs.

(C)

(15) Here are some tips to give your bulbs and even better chance. (16) Dig a hole that's about three times the width of the thickest part of the bulb. (17) Basically that's the same as going just deep enough to cover the bulb. (18) Next, make sure that the stem is pointing up. (19) Again, you can put them in any way, but this way will give them a better chance. (20) When they're in the ground, give the bulbs a little water. (21) After that, you only need to water them if the weather gets really dry.

(D)

(22) Once you've done that, just sit and wait for the flowers to come up in the spring. (23) Don't forget that most bulbs like sunny areas, but don't worry too much about that. (24) They'll almost grow anywhere. (25) They also don't like it too wet, so don't plant them at the bottom of a hill or in front of a drainage area. (26) One way you can enhance the look of your flowerbed is to plant the bulbs in clumps. (27) This is a much more appealing to the eye than seeing the flowers in a row or scattered throughout the garden or yard. (28) Enjoy your flowers and don't think too much about how to plant the bulbs!

GO ON TO THE NEXT PAGE

17. Sentence 1: **<u>I been</u> asked this question many times.**

Which is the best way to write the underlined portion of this sentence? If the original is the best way, choose option (1).

(1) I been
(2) I was
(3) I am
(4) I've been
(5) I'm

18. Sentence 3: **What is a bulb?**

Which revision should be made to the placement of sentence 3?

(1) remove sentence 3
(2) move sentence 3 to the beginning of paragraph A
(3) move sentence 3 to follow sentence 1
(4) move sentence 3 to follow sentence 5
(5) move sentence 3 to the beginning of paragraph B

19. Sentences 4 and 5: **A bulb is a rootlike structure. That certain plants such as onions and tulips have.**

Which is the best way to combine these two sentences? If the original is the best way, choose option (1).

(1) structure. That
(2) structure of
(3) structure, that
(4) structure, which
(5) structure that

20. Sentence 9: **The best time to plant bulbs is a few weeks before the first frost, but <u>they can actually be planted by you</u> any time of year.**

Which is the best way to write the underlined portion of this sentence? If the original is the best way, choose option (1).

(1) they can actually be planted by you
(2) the planting of them can be
(3) it would be good
(4) you can actually plant them
(5) but it would be done

21. Sentence 13: **That's all you need to do in order to have a <u>reasonable chance</u> of getting beautiful flowers from your bulbs.**

Which revision should be made to the underlined portion of this sentence? If it is correct as it is now, choose option (1).

(1) reasonable chance
(2) reasoned chance
(3) reason for a chance
(4) reasoning chance
(5) reason and a chance

GO ON TO THE NEXT PAGE

The article is repeated for your use in answering the remaining questions.

How to Plant Bulbs

(A)

(1) I been asked this question many times. (2) The answer is pretty simple. (3) What is a bulb? (4) A bulb is a rootlike structure. (5) That certain plants such as onions and tulips have. (6) It is used to store food and enable the plant to survive the winter. (7) Therefore, bulbs are very durable. (8) But don't forget, they won't survive the winter on your shelf.

(B)

(9) The best time to plant bulbs is a few weeks before the first frost, but they can actually be planted by you any time of year. (10) How do you plant them? (11) There's another easy question. (12) Dig a hole, put the bulb in, cover it up. (13) That's all you need to do in order to have a reasonable chance of getting beautiful flowers from your bulbs. (14) But there are a few things that are good to know in order to get the best out of your bulbs.

(C)

(15) Here are some tips to give your bulbs and even better chance. (16) Dig a hole that's about three times the width of the thickest part of the bulb. (17) Basically that's the same as going just deep enough to cover the bulb. (18) Next, make sure that the stem is pointing up. (19) Again, you can put them in any way, but this way will give them a better chance. (20) When they're in the ground, give the bulbs a little water. (21) After that, you only need to water them if the weather gets really dry.

(D)

(22) Once you've done that, just sit and wait for the flowers to come up in the spring. (23) Don't forget that most bulbs like sunny areas, but don't worry too much about that. (24) They'll grow almost anywhere. (25) They also don't like it too wet, so don't plant them at the bottom of a hill or in front of a drainage area. (26) One way you can enhance the look of your flowerbed is to plant the bulbs in clumps. (27) This is much more appealing to the eye than seeing the flowers in a row or scattered throughout the garden or yard. (28) Enjoy your flowers and don't think too much about how to plant the bulbs!

GO ON TO THE NEXT PAGE

22. Sentence 15: **Here are some tips to give your bulbs and even better chance.**

Which correction should be made to sentence 15?

(1) change Here are to Here's
(2) change give to get
(3) change and to an
(4) change even better to even greater
(5) change chance to change

23. Sentence 21: **After that, you only need to water them if the weather gets really dry.**

Which is the best way to rewrite this sentence? If the sentence is correct as written, choose answer (1).

(1) After that, you only need to water them if the weather gets really dry.
(2) After that, you need to water them only if the weather gets really dry.
(3) After that, you need to water only them if the weather gets really dry.
(4) After that, you need only to water them if the weather gets really dry.
(5) After that, you need to water them if the weather only gets really dry.

24. Sentence 24: **They'll almost grow anywhere.**

Which is the best way to rewrite sentence 24? If the sentence is correct as it is now, choose option (1).

(1) no rewrite is necessary
(2) They'll nearly grow anywhere.
(3) They'll almost grow everywhere.
(4) They'll nearly grow anywhere.
(5) They'll grow almost anywhere.

25. Sentence 27: **This is a much more appealing to the eye than seeing the flowers in a row or scattered throughout the garden or yard.**

Which is the best way to write the underlined portion of sentence 27? If the original is best, choose option (1).

(1) a much more
(2) much more
(3) a very much more
(4) an increasingly more
(5) a greater

GO ON TO LANGUAGE ARTS, WRITING, PART II

DO NOT MARK OR WRITE ON THIS PAGE

LANGUAGE ARTS, WRITING, PART II

Tests of General Educational Development

Essay Directions and Topic

Look at the box on page 144. In the box are your assigned topic and the letter of that topic.

You must write on the assigned topic **ONLY**.

Mark the letter of your assigned topic in the appropriate space on your answer sheet booklet. Be certain that all other requested information is properly recorded in your answer sheet booklet.

You will have 45 minutes to write on your assigned essay topic. You may return to the multiple-choice section after you complete your essay if you have time remaining in this test period. Do not return the Language Arts, Writing booklet until you finish both Parts I and II of the Language Arts, Writing Test.

Two evaluators will score your essay according to its overall effectiveness. Their evaluation will be based on the following features:

- Well-focused main points
- Clear organization
- Specific development of your ideas
- Control of sentence structure, punctuation, grammar, word choice, and spelling

REMEMBER, YOU MUST COMPLETE BOTH THE MULTIPLE-CHOICE QUESTIONS (PART I) and THE ESSAY (PART II) TO RECEIVE A SCORE ON THE LANGUAGE ARTS, WRITING TEST. To avoid having to repeat both parts of the test, be sure to observe the following rules.

- Do not leave the pages blank.
- Write legibly in ink so that the evaluators will be able to read your writing.
- Write on the assigned topic. If you write on a topic other than the one assigned, you will not receive a score for the Language Arts, Writing Test.
- Write your essay on the lined pages of the separate answer sheet booklet. Only the writing on theses pages will be scored.

IMPORTANT:
You may return to the multiple-choice section after you complete your essay if you have time remaining in this test period. Do not return the Language Arts, Writing booklet until you finish both Parts I and II of the Language Arts, Writing Test.

GO ON TO THE NEXT PAGE

Writing, Part II

Topic E

The suit makes the man.

In your essay, give an example of the suit making the man. Explain what this saying means in your view. Use your personal observations, experience, and knowledge to support your essay.

Part II is a test to determine how well you can use written language to explain your ideas.

In preparing your essay, you should take the following steps.

- Read the **DIRECTIONS** and the **TOPIC** carefully.
- Plan your essay before you write. Use the scratch paper provided to make any notes. These notes will be collected but not scored.
- Before you turn in your essay, reread what you have written and make any changes that will improve your essay.

Your essay should be long enough to develop the topic adequately.

END OF EXAMINATION

SOCIAL STUDIES

Tests of General Educational Development

Directions

The Social Studies Test consists of multiple-choice questions intended to measure general understanding of social studies concepts. The questions are based on short readings that often include a map, graph, chart, cartoon, or figure. Study the information given and then answer the question(s) following it. Refer to the information as often as necessary in answering the questions.

You should spend no more than 45 minutes answering the questions in this booklet. Work carefully, but do not spend too much time on any one question. Be sure you answer every question.

Do not mark in this test booklet. Record your answers on the separate answer sheet provided. Be sure that all requested information is properly recorded on the answer sheet.

To record your answers, mark the numbered space on the answer sheet beside the number that corresponds to the question in the test booklet.

FOR EXAMPLE:

Early colonists of North America looked for settlement sites with adequate water supplies and access by ship. For this reason, many early towns were built near

(1) mountains
(2) prairies
(3) rivers
(4) glaciers
(5) plateaus

The correct answer is "rivers"; therefore, answer space 3 would be marked on the answer sheet.

Do not rest the point of your pencil on the answer sheet while you are considering your answer. Make no stray or unnecessary marks. If you change an answer, erase your first mark completely. Mark only one answer space for each question; multiple answers will be scored as incorrect. Do not fold or crease your answer sheet. All test materials must be returned to the test administrator.

GO ON TO THE NEXT PAGE

Directions: Choose the one best answer to each question.

Questions 1 through 3 refer to the following graphs.

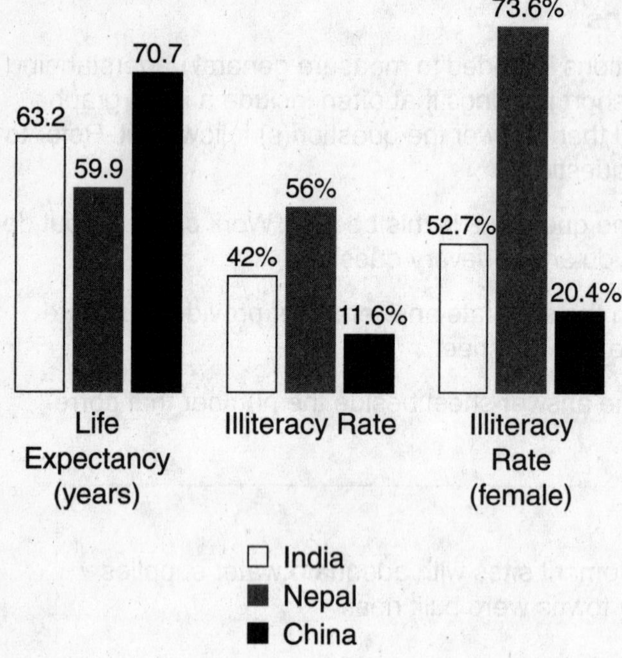

1. According to the graphs, which statement is true?

   (1) All three countries have communist systems of government and economy.
   (2) The illiteracy rate is directly proportional to life expectancy.
   (3) The life expectancy of women is lower than that of men in all three countries.
   (4) All three countries are under the rule of repressive regimes.
   (5) The illiteracy rate for women is higher than the illiteracy rate of men in all three countries.

2. According to the graphs, approximately how many more years does the typical Chinese person live than the typical Nepalese person?

   (1) 5 years
   (2) 10 years
   (3) 15 years
   (4) 20 years
   (5) 25 years

3. Which statement best helps to explain why Nepal's illiteracy rate is so much higher than China's illiteracy rate?

   (1) Chinese is much easier to read than Nepali.
   (2) China is a much poorer country than Nepal.
   (3) Nepal is constantly afflicted by famine and plague.
   (4) The economy and education system are less developed in Nepal.
   (5) Chinese people like reading more than most people.

GO ON TO THE NEXT PAGE

4. Eminent domain is the right of the government to seize property from American citizens without their consent. The government is required to provide fair monetary compensation for the property.

Which is an example of eminent domain?

(1) The establishment of the Department of the Interior in 1849.
(2) The government purchases a farm in order to build a national railroad.
(3) The annexation of Texas in 1845.
(4) The government prohibits the selling of real estate property across state boundaries.
(5) The government sells land at low prices to encourage Westward expansion.

5. The armed conflict between Mexico and the United States gave the United States control of Texas and other southwestern territories. What is the name of this war?

(1) the French and Indian War
(2) the Spanish-American War
(3) the Civil War
(4) the Mexican-American War
(5) the Cold War

6. Which statement is true of the Bill of Rights?

The Bill of Rights

(1) was added to the Constitution before ratification
(2) guaranteed women the right to vote
(3) replaced the legal authority of the Constitution
(4) nullified many of the clauses of the Declaration of Independence
(5) abolished slavery in northern states

7. Capitalism is an economic system in which wealth, and the means of producing wealth, are owned and controlled by individuals rather than by a state or by all individuals equally.

Which statement describes capitalism in the twentieth century?

During the twentieth century

(1) no countries practiced capitalism
(2) most countries in the world abandoned capitalist practices
(3) some countries abandoned capitalistic practices and embraced a form of communism
(4) the United States experimented with alternative forms of economy and government
(5) capitalism was invented as a new system of economy and government

GO ON TO THE NEXT PAGE

Questions 8 and 9 refer to the following image.

8. This image is Paul Revere's famous depiction of the Boston Massacre. Which statement best describes the Boston Massacre?

The Boston Massacre

(1) increased American colonists' resentment of the British Empire and helped ignite the American Revolution
(2) effectively ended the American Revolution
(3) ended in the deaths of hundreds of thousands of American colonists
(4) helped ease tensions between the colonists and the British Empire
(5) had no effect on the American Revolution

9. Which statement best describes the primary purpose of the image?

The image was intended to

(1) justify the actions of the British soldiers
(2) discredit the colonists
(3) emphasize the brutality of the British soldiers
(4) show that the massacre was unintentional
(5) indicate that the massacre did not take place in Boston

10. "Outsourcing" is often used to describe the movement of factories, service centers, or jobs from one location to another in order to cut costs.

Which of the following is an example of this type of "outsourcing"?

(1) A company fires half of its employees to lower costs.
(2) Two companies merge into a single major corporation.
(3) A company's board of directors decides to open a new product line.
(4) A newspaper decides to print only an online edition.
(5) A company stops manufacturing automobiles in the United States, moving its factories to Canada.

GO ON TO THE NEXT PAGE

11. The system of checks and balances was created by the framers of the Constitution in order to prevent one branch of the government from becoming too powerful. Which of the following was a provision created as part of the system of checks and balances?

(1) Only the President can declare war on other nations.
(2) The Supreme Court has no authority to determine which laws are unconstitutional.
(3) The President cannot be removed from office under any circumstances.
(4) Members of the Supreme Court are appointed by the President and confirmed by the Senate.
(5) The decisions of the Supreme Court must be approved by the President.

Questions 12 and 13 refer to the following excerpt from the Fourth Amendment to the U.S. Constitution.

> "The right of the people to be secure in their persons, houses, papers, and effects, against unreasonable searches and seizures, shall not be violated, and no Warrants shall issue, but upon probable cause..."

12. Which statement describes the primary purpose of the Fourth Amendment?

The Fourth Amendment

(1) creates the Department of Homeland Security to protect individual security
(2) prevents the government from issuing warrants under any circumstances
(3) prevents the government from searching private homes or confiscating goods without a warrant
(4) protects the freedom of speech
(5) abolishes the ownership of private property

13. In which circumstance would the Fourth Amendment be violated?

(1) The police enter an individual's home with a search warrant.
(2) The FBI investigates corruption at a local police station.
(3) Police officers believe that a man is storing illegal drugs in his home and enter without a search warrant.
(4) A police officer arrests an individual with the use of force.
(5) A man spies on his neighbor's home.

GO ON TO THE NEXT PAGE

Questions 14 through 16 refer to the following map of global exploration from 1492 to 1522.

Voyages of Early European Explorers (1492–1522)

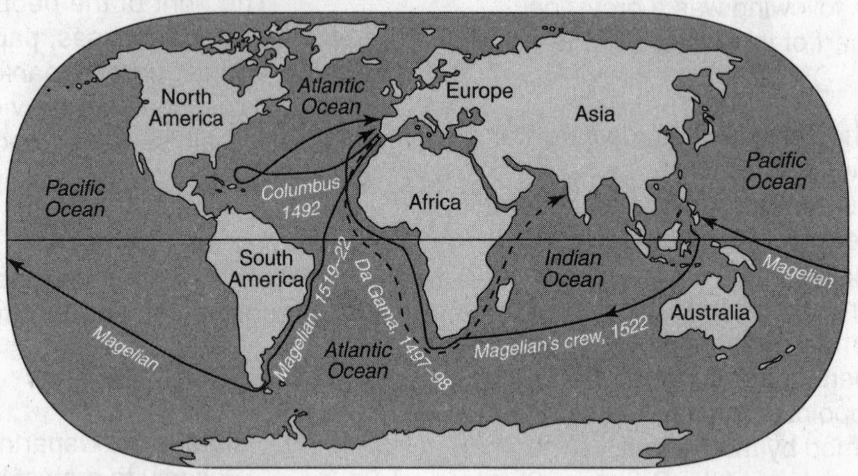

14. According to the map, Christopher Columbus

    (1) did not reach the mainland of the United States in 1492
    (2) circumnavigated the entire globe in less than a year
    (3) sailed south along the coast of Africa
    (4) never reached the Western Hemisphere on his journey
    (5) sailed after major discoveries by da Gama and Magellan in the Indian Ocean

15. Which statement describes Magellan's exploration through 1522?

    Magellan's exploration

    (1) went south along the coast of Africa
    (2) headed west toward the New World and then crossed the Pacific Ocean
    (3) landed in North America at least twice
    (4) departed from Asia and arrived in Europe
    (5) followed the path of da Gama's exploration

16. Explorers travelled around the world for a number of reasons. Which statement best describes their motives?

    The explorers intended to

    (1) undermine the political power of non-European nations
    (2) sell English goods overseas
    (3) find a shorter route to the East Indies
    (4) win a world-wide exploration contest held in 1499
    (5) undermine the authority of the Spanish king

GO ON TO THE NEXT PAGE

<u>Questions 17 through 19</u> refer to the following excerpt of President Woodrow Wilson's address to Congress in 1917.

"It is a fearful thing to lead this great peaceful people into war, into the most terrible and disastrous of all wars, civilization itself seeming to be in the balance. But the right is more precious than peace, and we shall fight for the things which we have always carried nearest our hearts—for democracy, for the right of those who submit to authority to have a voice in their own governments, for the rights and liberties of small nations, for a universal dominion of right by such a concert of free peoples as shall bring peace and safety to all nations and make the world itself at last free."

17. President Wilson made the argument for America to enter World War I. Which statement describes his reasoning?

President Wilson

(1) was not convinced that World War I posed a serious threat to Western civilization
(2) believed that the United States should fight for principles such as democracy, universal rights, and freedom
(3) believed that Germany posed little threat to the United States
(4) disagreed with the prevailing public opinion about the morality of warfare and armed conflict
(5) recognized that universal freedom is not a reasonable goal

18. Which statement most accurately describes World War I?

World War I

(1) was a truly global war involving many nations from South America, Asia, and Africa
(2) was one of the largest wars in history, involving all of the world's major superpowers at the time
(3) came only five years before the beginning of World War II
(4) was resolved quickly and without much bloodshed or destruction
(5) never involved the United States

19. According to the information presented in the excerpt, President Wilson supported all of the following **EXCEPT**

(1) tyrannical government
(2) democracy
(3) universal rights
(4) world peace
(5) voting rights for individuals

GO ON TO THE NEXT PAGE

Questions 20 and 21 refer to the following graph.

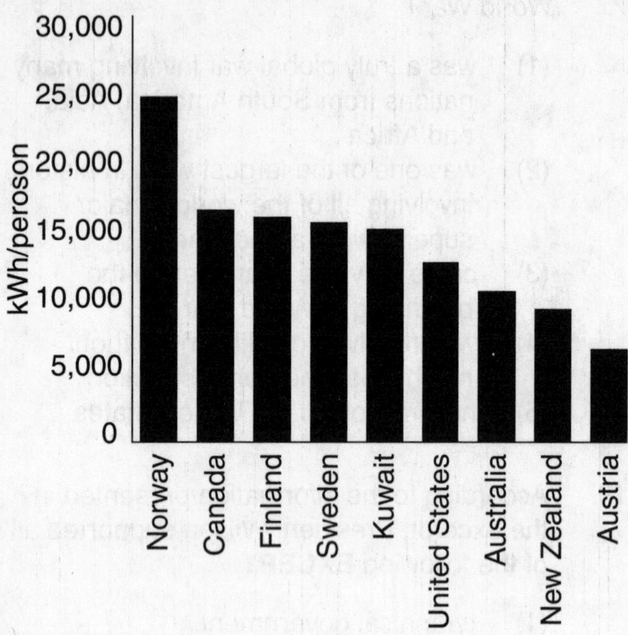

20. Based on the information in the graph, which statement is most accurate?

(1) Political pressures have reduced the consumption of electricity in Norway.
(2) Citizens in Canada, Finland, and Sweden consume very similar amounts of electricity.
(3) Electricity is the most important form of consumption in every country.
(4) The consumption of electricity is extremely costly for national governments.
(5) The United States consumes half as much electricity as Kuwait.

21. Which of the following explanations accounts for the high consumption of electricity in Norway, Canada, Finland, and Sweden?

(1) These countries have poor diplomatic relations with many other countries.
(2) These countries do not have access to oil.
(3) These countries have primitive economic systems.
(4) These countries tax their citizens highly and have many government-funded programs.
(5) These countries have substantially colder climates than many other countries.

GO ON TO THE NEXT PAGE

Questions 22 and 23 refer to the following excerpt from the Supreme Court decision *Korematsu v. United States* (1944) about the internment of Japanese Americans during World War II.

> "[Fred] Korematsu was not excluded from the Military Area because of hostility to him or his race. He was excluded because we are at war with the Japanese Empire, because the properly constituted military authorities feared an invasion of our West Coast and felt constrained to take proper security measures, because they decided that the military urgency of the situation demanded that all citizens of Japanese ancestry be segregated from the West Coast temporarily, and, finally, because Congress, reposing its confidence in this time of war in our military people—as inevitably it must—determined that they should have the power to do just this."

22. Based on the excerpt, which statement most accurately describes the Court's reasoning for the internment of many Japanese Americans?

(1) Japanese Americans were members of an inferior race and had to be segregated from the rest of the population.
(2) Japanese Americans were guilty of many war crimes against the United States.
(3) Congress needed to raise funds for American military efforts.
(4) Japanese Americans posed a threat to the military security of the United States during World War II.
(5) The West Coast of the United States was subject to an environmental catastrophe.

23. Which of the following expresses an **OPINION**, rather than a fact, about the ruling?

The Supreme Court

(1) believed that Congress had the right to move Japanese Americans from the West Coast
(2) claimed that times of war create special military and legal circumstances
(3) did not believe that its support of the internment was racist
(4) followed the claims of military authorities, who believed that Japanese citizens posed a threat to the United States
(5) was afraid of Japanese Americans and racist against all Asian people

GO ON TO THE NEXT PAGE

24. The Stamp Act of 1765 was imposed on the colonists by the British government. Why did the colonists' react so negatively to the Stamp Act?

(1) They felt that the British government had abandoned them during the French and Indian War.
(2) They believed that King George III desired to impose military rule on the colonists.
(3) They believed they could not be taxed without their consent through legislative representation.
(4) They were afraid that it would destroy American agriculture.
(5) They opposed all forms of taxation.

25. The United Nations, an international organization dedicated to international law and global peace, was founded after the end of World War II. Which statement expresses a **FACT,** rather than an opinion, about the United Nations?

The United Nations

(1) includes most of the world's nations
(2) has destroyed independence of the United States
(3) is ineffective at preventing war
(4) was created for the wrong reasons
(5) should be abolished immediately

END OF EXAMINATION

SCIENCE

Tests of General Educational Development

Directions

The Science Test consists of multiple-choice questions intended to measure understanding of general concepts in science. The questions are based on short readings that often include a graph, chart, or figure. Study the information given and then answer the question(s) following it. Refer to the information as often as necessary in answering the questions.

You should spend no more than 53 minutes answering the questions in this booklet. Work carefully, but do not spend too much time on any one question. Be sure you answer every question.

Do not mark in this test booklet. Record your answers to the questions on the separate sheet provided. Be sure all requested information is properly recorded on the answer sheet.

To record your answers, mark the numbered space on the answer sheet beside the number that corresponds to the question in the test booklet.

FOR EXAMPLE:

Which of the following is the smallest unit in a living thing?

(1) tissue
(2) organ
(3) cell
(4) muscle
(5) capillary

The correct answer is "cell"; therefore, answer space 3 would be marked on the answer sheet.

Do not rest the point of your pencil on the answer sheet while you are considering your answer. Make no stray or unnecessary marks. If you change an answer, erase your first mark completely. Mark only <u>one</u> answer space for each question; multiple answers will be scored as incorrect. Do not fold or crease your answer sheet. All test materials must be returned to the test administrator.

GO ON TO THE NEXT PAGE

Directions: Choose the one best answer to each question.

1. An ecosystem consists of all the living and nonliving factors occupying the same habitat. The biotic factors are the living organisms, while the abiotic factors are the nonliving components of the environment.

   Which of the following is a biotic factor?

   (1) water
   (2) grass
   (3) air
   (4) rocks
   (5) soil

Questions 2–3

The table below lists the normal ranges of various chemicals found in human blood.

Substance	Normal Range
total cholesterol	125–200 mg/dL
HDL cholesterol	under 40 mg/dL
LDL cholesterol	under 130 mg/dL
triglycerides	under 150 mg/dL

2. Which of the following health care professionals would probably be the most familiar with the information presented in the table?

   (1) physician
   (2) optometrist
   (3) home health aide
   (4) veterinarian
   (5) dentist

3. Which of the following statements is accurate based on the table above?

   (1) A total cholesterol level of 100 is normal.
   (2) A triglycerides level of 180 is normal.
   (3) A triglycerides level of 100 is abnormal.
   (4) An LDL cholesterol level of 110 is above the normal range.
   (5) A total cholesterol level of 150 is normal.

GO ON TO THE NEXT PAGE

Questions 4–5

Cardiac output is the amount of blood a human heart pumps out per minute. Increases in heart rate, blood pressure, and cardiac muscle strength all lead to higher cardiac output. Below is a graph that shows the effects of blood pressure on cardiac output.

Cardiac Output and Blood Pressure

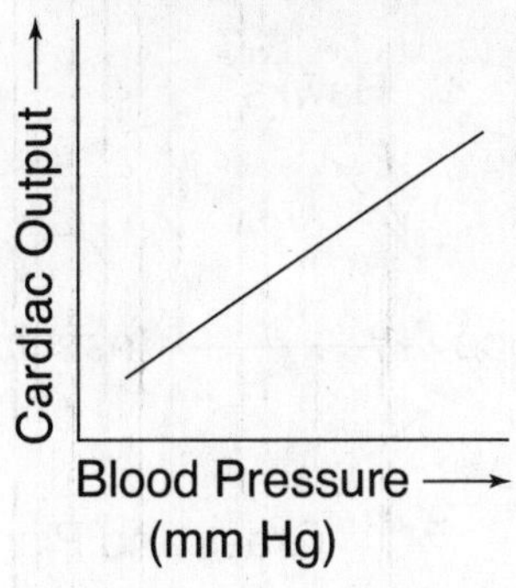

4. Which conclusion is best supported by the graph?

(1) As blood pressure increases, cardiac output increases.
(2) As blood pressure increases, cardiac output decreases.
(3) As blood pressure increases, cardiac output remains constant.
(4) Cardiac output is measured in mm HG.
(5) Cardiac output increases and decreases irregularly as blood pressure changes.

5. Under which of the following conditions is cardiac output increased?

(1) after death
(2) as heart rate drops during sleep
(3) as heart rate increases during exercise
(4) after heart muscle is damaged by a heart attack
(5) as blood pressure drops due to dehydration.

6. When most winged insects feel threatened, they respond by flying away from the source of the threat. However, most winged insects can only process one threat at a time. If one of these insects perceives more than one threat, that insect will become immobilized.

Based on the information, which is the best way to capture most winged insects?

(1) approach it from the top
(2) approach it from the front
(3) approach it from behind
(4) approach it both from the front and from behind
(5) approach it from one side

GO ON TO THE NEXT PAGE

7. Which of the following is the molecule by which genes are passed from a parent to a child?

(1) hormone
(2) DNA
(3) protein
(4) embryo
(5) glucose

8. The figures below show two possible arrangements of gas molecules. Which of these is more likely to occur in the universe?

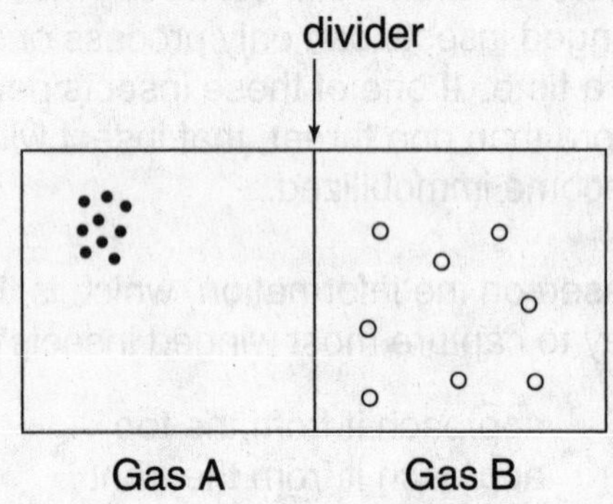

(1) A, because the universe favors order.
(2) B, because the universe favors order.
(3) A, because the universe favors disorder.
(4) B, because the universe favors disorder.
(5) Both A and B are equally favorable.

9. A food web is a diagram that shows which organisms feed on which other organisms in a community. The arrow points from the food source to the consumer. Some animals are herbivores, meaning they eat only plants, some are carnivores, meaning they eat only animals, and some are omnivores, meaning they eat both plants and animals. Below is a food web for a grassland ecosystem.

Food Web

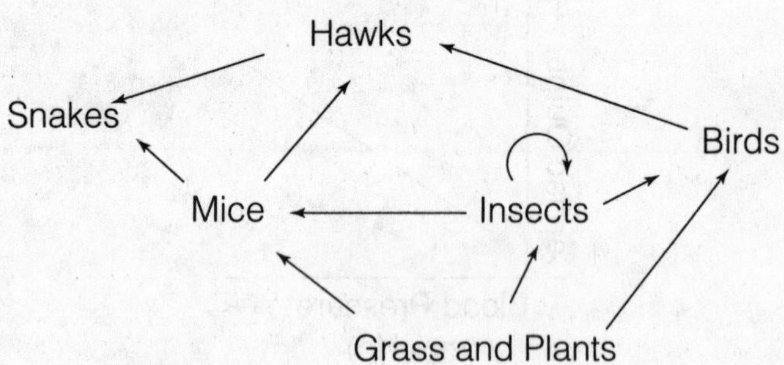

Which organisms in this food web are carnivores only?

(1) hawks only
(2) snakes only
(3) both snakes and hawks
(4) insects only
(5) grass and plants only

GO ON TO THE NEXT PAGE

10. If a suitcase were placed on a scale inside a plane in the air, its weight reading would decrease as the plane began to fly closer to the ground.

Which of the following factors would most affect the decrease in the suitcase's weight reading?

(1) the size of the plane
(2) the weight of the suitcase on land
(3) the speed at which the plane approaches the ground
(4) the accuracy of the scale
(5) the initial height of the plane

11. A steam iron is a device that boils water and releases the water as steam. Only the water boils and leaves the iron, so any other substances present in the water will stay in the appliance. Over time, these substances create a solid buildup in the iron.

Based on the above information, which of the following is the best type of water to use in a steam iron?

(1) well
(2) hard
(3) spring
(4) distilled
(5) tap

12. A medical student is researching the rate of growth of a certain population of bacteria. She cultures the bacteria on a petri dish and observes the bacteria under a microscope at regular time intervals. Below is a graph of her results.

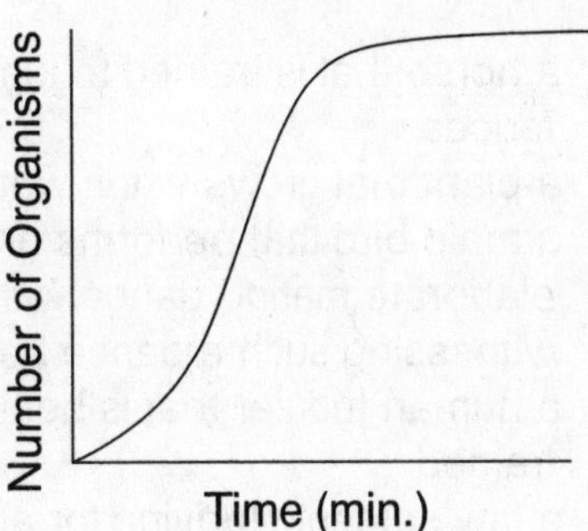

Which of the following best described the results shown in the graph?

(1) The bacterial population started small, then increased quickly, and then all of the bacteria died.
(2) The bacterial population started small, then increased quickly, and then became constant.
(3) The bacterial population increased at a steady rate.
(4) The bacterial population was constant at first and then increased quickly.
(5) The bacterial population started small, then increased, and then decreased.

GO ON TO THE NEXT PAGE

13. Some animals exhibit complex rituals or behaviors that they were never taught but instead seem to know by instinct. Such behaviors are known as fixed action patterns.

Based on the information, which of the following could be a fixed action pattern?

(1) a horse that is trained to jump over fences
(2) a plant that grows when watered
(3) a male bird that performs an elaborate mating dance without witnessing such a dance before
(4) a human toddler that is being toilet trained
(5) a law student studying for an exam

14. Whether a substance is classified as acidic, basic, or neutral is determined by its pH. A pH below 7 is acidic, a pH of 7 is neutral, and a pH above 7 is basic. Below is a table of common substances and their pH's.

Substance	ph
lemon juice	2
water	7
vinegar	2.2
baking soda solution	8.3

Based on the information and the table, which of the following is acidic?

(1) lemon juice only
(2) vinegar only
(3) water only
(4) baking soda solution only
(5) both vinegar and lemon juice

15. Dr. Patel studies cells in a lab. Below is a table describing characteristics of three types of cells.

Characteristics of Cells

Characteristic	Type of Cell: Bacteria	Plant	Animal
Nucleus	Absent	Present	Present
Cell Wall	Present	Present	Absent
Chromosomes	1 circular chromosomes	several linear chromosomes	several linear chromosomes
Organelles	Absent	Present	Present

Below are three cells that Dr. Patel wants to classify.

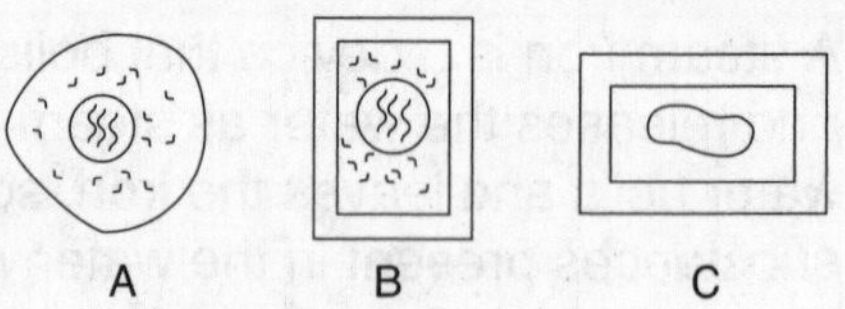

Which statement gives an accurate classification of a cell?

(1) Cell A is a bacterial cell.
(2) Cell A is an animal cell.
(3) Cell A is a plant cell.
(4) Cell B is an animal cell.
(5) Cell C is a plant cell.

GO ON TO THE NEXT PAGE

16. Magnets are often made of polarized metal bars, especially bars made of iron. Magnets are only attracted to certain types of metal. Typically, metals that make good magnets are also attracted to magnets. Based on this information, which of the following is a magnet most likely attracted to?

(1) copper penny
(2) aluminum can
(3) plastic wrap
(4) wooden block
(5) iron fillings

17. Tamika makes and cans fruit jelly in her kitchen. She uses a pressure cooker as part of this process. If she follows the correct procedures, the jelly will be properly sterilized.

Why does Tamika use a pressure cooker?

(1) to enhance the flavor of the jelly
(2) to maintain the color of the jelly
(3) to kill bacteria
(4) to prevent unpleasant odors
(5) to preserve the vitamin content of the jelly

18. Boyle's law explains some aspects of the behavior of gases, such as those in our atmosphere. The law states that if temperature remains constant, volume decreases as pressure increases. The graph below illustrates Boyle's law for one gas.

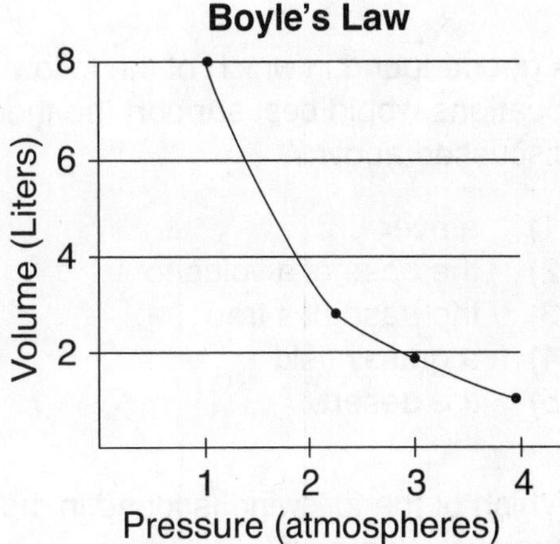

Which statement best describes the behavior of the gas in the graph?

(1) Pressure and volume increase at the same rate.
(2) As the pressure rises from 1 to 3 atmospheres, the volume rises from 2 to 8 liters.
(3) As the pressure rises from 1 to 2 atmospheres, the volume drops from 8 to 2 liters.
(4) Atmospheres measure volume of gas.
(5) If the trend in the graph continues, as the pressure reaches 5 atmospheres the volume will near 1 liter.

GO ON TO THE NEXT PAGE

19. A geode is a rock that appears dull on the outside but is filled with crystals inside. Many scientists theorize that some round geodes are formed when lava bubbles as it cools after a volcanic eruption. Minerals and water seep into the bubbles, and after the water evaporates the minerals form crystals.

    A geode found in which of the following locations would best support the theory discussed above?

    (1) a river
    (2) the base of a volcano
    (3) the base of a tree
    (4) a grassy field
    (5) the desert

20. Which of the following is found in the nucleus of an atom?

    (1) neutron
    (2) electron
    (3) positron
    (4) cell
    (5) battery

21. When a human becomes overheated, there are several ways to bring down the temperature. These include sweating, dilation of blood vessels, removing layers of clothing, and drinking cold water.

    Which of the responses to heat mentioned above are under conscious control?

    (1) all of the mentioned responses
    (2) none of the mentioned responses
    (3) removing layers of clothing and drinking cold water
    (4) sweating only
    (5) sweating and dilation of blood vessels

GO ON TO THE NEXT PAGE

Questions 22–23

Melinda wanted to determine whether compost and fertilizer helped plants grow, so she set up an experiment to determine the effects of several factors on plant growth. Below is a graph showing some of her results.

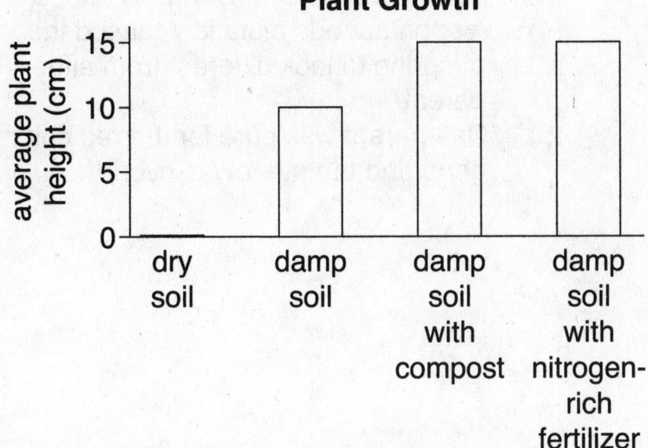

22. Which conclusion best supports the analysis of her data?

(1) Plants grow the same in all conditions.
(2) Compost and nitrogen-rich fertilizer slowed the growth of plants.
(3) Compost was more effective at increasing plant growth than was nitrogen-rich fertilizer.
(4) Soil must be damp for plants to grow.
(5) Plants grow fastest in dry soil.

23. Which of the following state fits best with the data?

(1) A person wishing to grow tall plants must use commercial nitrogen-rich fertilizer.
(2) A person wishing to grow tall plants must use organic compost.
(3) Compost and fertilizer appear to equally improve the growth rate of plants.
(4) Watering plants does not affect their growth.
(5) Compost is dangerous to plants.

Questions 24–25

Hereditary traits are coded for by genes, which are located on chromosomes. Chromosomes come in pairs, and the pair of genes for a particular feature determines the characteristics of that trait. Often, there are several varieties of genes for a trait. Sometimes, the different genes exhibit a pattern called incomplete dominance. In such cases, a gene is expressed when it is pure, meaning both genes in a pair are alike. A hybrid is when the two genes in the pair are different, and in cases of incomplete dominance the two traits will blend together to make a new trait.

Flower color in carnations follows an incomplete dominance pattern. When both genes in a pair are for red color, the plant produces red flowers. When both genes in the pair are for yellow color, the plant produces yellow flowers. When the plant is hybrid and has one gene for red color and one for yellow color, the two traits blend to produce orange flowers.

Below is a Punnett Square showing the results when a carnation with yellow flowers and a carnation with red flowers are crossed to produce offspring. Punnett Squares predict the likelihood of specific gene combinations occurring.

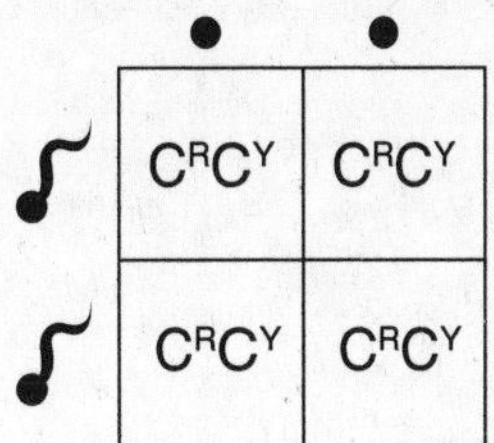

●	egg cell of female parent
ʃ	sperm cell of male parent
C^R	gene for red color
C^Y	gene for yellow color

GO ON TO THE NEXT PAGE

24. What color are the flowers of the offspring shown in the Punnett Square?

(1) all red
(2) all yellow
(3) all orange
(4) half are red and half are yellow
(5) all red and yellow striped

25. Which statement provides the best explanation for the results in the Punnett Square?

(1) One parent was pure for the yellow color gene and one parent was pure for the red color gene, and the offspring inherited one of each gene.
(2) Both parents carried a hidden gene for orange color.
(3) Both parents were hybrid.
(4) A spontaneous mutation caused the offspring to look different from either parent.
(5) One parent was pure for the red color gene and the other was hybrid.

END OF EXAMINATION

LANGUAGE ARTS, READING

Tests of General Educational Development

Directions

The Language Arts, Reading Test consists of excerpts from fiction and nonfiction. Each excerpt is followed by multiple-choice questions about the reading material.

Read each excerpt first and then answer the questions following it. Refer back to the reading material as often as necessary in answering the questions.

Each excerpt is preceded by a "purpose question." The purpose question gives a reason for reading the material. Use these purpose questions to help focus your reading. You are not required to answer these purpose questions. They are given only to help you concentrate on the ideas presented in the reading material.

You should spend no more than 35 minutes answering the questions in this booklet. Work carefully, but do not spend too much time on any one question. Be sure you answer every question.

Do not mark in this test booklet. Record your answers on the separate answer sheet provided. Be sure that all requested information is properly recorded on the answer sheet.

To record your answers, mark the numbered space on the answer sheet beside the number that corresponds to the question in the test booklet.

FOR EXAMPLE:

It was Susan's dream machine. The metallic blue paint gleamed, and the sporty wheels were highly polished. Under the hood, the engine was no less carefully cleaned. Inside, flashy lights illuminated the instruments on the dashboard, and the seats were covered by rich leather upholstery.

The subject ("It") of this excerpt is most likely

(1) an airplane
(2) a stereo system
(3) an automobile
(4) a boat
(5) a motorcycle

The correct answer is "an automobile"; therefore, answer space 3 would be marked on the answer sheet.

Do not rest the point of your pencil on the answer sheet while you are considering your answer. Make no stray or unnecessary marks. If you change an answer, erase your first mark completely. Mark only <u>one</u> answer space for each question; multiple answers will be scored as incorrect. Do not fold or crease your answer sheet. All test materials must be returned to the test administrator.

GO ON TO THE NEXT PAGE

Directions: Choose the one best answer to each question.

Questions 1 through 4 refer to the following excerpt.

WHAT DOES THE LETTER WRITER BELIEVE ABOUT WHAT IS BEST FOR THE COMMUNITY FAIR?

Community Fair is for the Community

By now, everyone in the local area is familiar with the unfortunate incident that took place last Friday night at the Digger County Community Fair. Because of the turmoil stirred up that night, some people are now suggesting that the entire event should be reconsidered with some going far as to recommend that we entirely forgo the event next summer. This would be a massive mistake.

First, the revenue generated for the Digger County Community Center is crucial to the continued success of all the DCCC programs. Too many resident rely on such programs (continuing education, vocational classes, daycare, healthclub) for them to be denied this important source of funding. We simply cannot remove the Fair from the calendar without significantly affecting the budget of the DCCC.

Secondly, though the difficulties experienced this year need to be addressed and rectified, this is the first time in its 12-year history that there has been any kind of problem of any kind. The Fair has a track record of safety and success that cannot be ignored despite the results this year. We can obviously expect a greater focus on safety in the future and the entire enterprise will continue to operate efficiently and safely.

Lastly, though we may look at the Fair as merely a local county event, it has actually continued to grow at such a rate that it now is nearly half the size of the better-known State Fair, which itself has occasionally had some operational challenges. So, we can recognize that such things are part of running such a large public event. But we can meet this challenge and we should. The Digger County Community Fair is something all residents should be very proud of and we should support its continued presence every summer. It is a great reflection of the kind of solid people we have in our area and our renewed dedication to it will reflect that to all who visit us.

Sincerely,

Mrs. Leslie O. Dunn
Digger County Resident

GO ON TO THE NEXT PAGE

1. It can be inferred from the previous letter that something negative happened recently at a local fair. Because of this event, there is now some controversy. Some people are advocating the

(1) suspension of responsible officials
(2) prosecution of perpetrators
(3) firing fair managers
(4) cancellation of the next fair event
(5) dismissal of all fair workers

2. The writer of this letter believes what about the problem at the fair?

She believes the reported problem was

(1) exaggerated and limited
(2) deadly and unacceptable
(3) an unusual occurrence
(4) a chronic historical issue
(5) a sensational story

3. Based solely on the information given in the passage, which of the following is the best reflection of the writer's attitude toward the Digger County Community Center?

(1) Too many people utilize it.
(2) Continuing education is the foremost program at the center.
(3) The DCCC relies heavily on funding for its programs.
(4) The DCCC requires new safety regulations.
(5) The DCCC will likely be forced to close next year.

4. Which of the following results would be most agreeable to the writer of this letter? Next year, the community fair should

(1) continue, but with increased security and safety
(2) terminate all fair activities
(3) move the fair to a nearby, safer county
(4) continue with no change in the organization or operations
(5) continue but with a change in the admission price

GO ON TO THE NEXT PAGE

Questions 5 through 10 refer to the following excerpt.

WHAT DOES THE SPEAKER OF THE STORY BELIEVE ABOUT THE PEOPLE?

The People, Yes

And go back to the nourishing earth for rootholds,
The people so peculiar in renewal and comeback,
You can't laugh off their capacity to take it.
The mammoth rests between his cyclonic dramas.

The people so often sleepy, weary, enigmatic,
is a vast huddle with many units saying:
"I earn my living.
I make enough to get by
and it takes all my time.
If I had more time I could do more for myself
and maybe for others.
I could read and study and talk things over
and find out about things.
It takes time.
I wish I had the time."

The people is a tragic and comic two-face:
hero and hoodlum: phantom and gorilla
twisting to moan with a gargoyle mouth:

"They buy me and sell me . . . it's a game . . .
sometime I'll break loose . . ."

The people know the salt of the sea
and the strength of the winds
lashing the corners of the earth.
The people take the earth
as a tomb of rest and a cradle of hope.
Who else speaks for the Family of Man?
They are in tune and step
with constellations and universal law.

Man is a long time coming.
Man will yet win.
Brother may yet line up with brother.

This old anvil laughs at many broken hammers.
There are men who can't be bought.
The fireborn are home in fire.
The stars make no noise.

GO ON TO THE NEXT PAGE

You can't hinder the wind from blowing.
Time is a great teacher.
Who can live without hope?

In the darkness with a great bundle of grief the people march.
In the night, and overhead a shovel of stars for keeps, the people march:

"Where to? what next?"

Carl Sandburg, "The People, Yes," 1936.

5. The speaker of the poem says that "you can't laugh off their capacity to take it" (line 3). Which of the following best summarizes the meaning of this line?

(1) The ability of common people to often start over is impressive.
(2) People who have been tricked should not be laughed at.
(3) Once people are tricked, they go back to their prior work.
(4) Most people don't laugh when they witness a blunder.
(5) Mockery of common people only happens when they make a mistake.

6. The word "units" (line 6) could best be replaced by which of the following without changing the meaning of the sentence?

(1) sleepers
(2) compartments
(3) integers
(4) individuals
(5) buildings

7. The author of this passage continually writes, "The people is" instead of "The people are." Why did the author intentionally make this obvious grammatical mistake?

The author wrote of the people in this way in order to

(1) show his disregard for grammar rules
(2) reveal his inefficient knowledge of grammar
(3) emphasize the main idea that all people are unified
(4) break the monotony of the passage's writing
(5) show the difference between two groups of people

8. "Hero and hoodlum" (line 17) are referred to in the passage in order to give an example of the fact that "the people"

(1) frequently use violence
(2) always find enemies in society
(3) contain both good and bad elements
(4) achieve great results at the expense of the less fortunate
(5) should consider how the extremes in society exist

GO ON TO THE NEXT PAGE

9. The line in the passage, "This old anvil laughs at many broken hammers." (line 32) may seem out of place, but it repeats an idea about people within the same paragraph. This theme could be summarized as

(1) Mankind cannot be defeated, though many have tried.
(2) Humans cannot stop the wind from blowing.
(3) People have always worked with tools throughout history.
(4) Laughter is the strongest human emotion.
(5) No one can be persuaded by money to pursue certain goals.

10. This excerpt is from a book by Carl Sandburg titled "The People, Yes" that contains many passages similar to the one above. Based on what you know of this representative passage, which of the following groups is likely to be a major focus in the other passages in this book?

(1) infant children
(2) foreign kings
(3) famous scientists
(4) common workmen
(5) religious leaders

GO ON TO THE NEXT PAGE

Questions 11 through 15 refer to the following excerpt.

WHAT DOES THE MANUFACTURER WANT PIERROT TO LEARN?

MANUFACTURER: Well, friend Pierrot, so business is not very brisk.

PIERROT: Brisk! If laughter meant business, it would be brisk enough, but there's no money.

MANUFACTURER: Pierrot, if you had all the money in the world you wouldn't be happy.

PIERROT: Wouldn't I? Give me all the money in the world and I'll risk it. To start with, I'd build schools to educate the people up to high-class things.

MANUFACTURER: You dream of fame and wealth and empty ideals, and you miss all the best things there are. You are discontented. Why? Because you don't know how to be happy.

PIERROT: That's not true. I am happy. I write songs.

MANUFACTURER: Why don't you write a song without any end, one that goes on for ever?

PIERROT: I say, that's rather silly, isn't it?

MANUFACTURER: It all depends. For a song of that sort the singer must be always happy.

PIERROT: That wants a bit of doing in my line.

MANUFACTURER: Pierrot, you don't know who I am.

PIERROT: That makes no difference. All are welcome, and we thank you for your courteous attention.

MANUFACTURER: I am a maker of dreams. I make all the dreams that float about this musty world.

PIERROT: Say, you'd better have a rest for a bit. I expect you're a trifle done up.

MANUFACTURER: Pierrot, Pierrot, your superior mind can't tumble to my calling. A child or one of the "people" would in a moment. I am a maker of dreams, little things that glide about into people's hearts and make them glad.

PIERROT: Oh, I say, you can't expect me to believe that.

MANUFACTURER: When flowers fade, have you never wondered where their colours go to, or what becomes of all the butterflies in the winter? There isn't much winter about my workshop. It's a kind of lost property office, where every beautiful thing that the world has neglected finds its way. And there I make my celebrated dream, the dream that is called "love."

PIERROT: Ho ho! Now we're talking.

MANUFACTURER: You don't believe in it?

PIERROT: Yes, in a way. But it doesn't last. Oh, I've tried hard enough to believe it, but after the first wash, the colours run.

Oliphant Down, MAKER OF DREAMS, 1913

GO ON TO THE NEXT PAGE

11. The Manufacturer in the story recognizes Pierrot's qualities, but wants him to try to be more

(1) focused on business
(2) practical and serious
(3) silly and imaginative
(4) responsible and prepared
(5) excitable and hard-working

12. Pierrot says that the Manufacturer is "a trifle done up" (lines 34–35). Another way that he could have said this is

(1) "You're overdressed."
(2) "You don't have enough money."
(3) "You seem to be in love."
(4) "You aren't making sense."
(5) "You are a dishonest person."

13. The Manufacturer suggests that Pierrot should write a song that does not end. Why?

The Manufacturer wants Pierrot to

(1) improve his own poor song-writing skills
(2) remove the need to write a new song every day
(3) demonstrate that true love songs are always long
(4) understand a new, different kind of happiness for himself
(5) create an opportunity for other people to be happy

14. Pierrot's initially reaction to the Manufacturer's claims is

(1) anger
(2) disbelief
(3) fear
(4) confusion
(5) immobilization

15. Pierrot claims that he has tried hard to believe in love, but that "after the first wash, the colors run" (line 60–61). What is Pierrot's opinion of love?

Pierrot believes that love

(1) exists but doesn't last
(2) is real but is not truly colorful
(3) takes time and requires patience
(4) is not made of dreams
(5) requires more than one person to contribute

GO ON TO THE NEXT PAGE

Questions 16 through 20 refer to the following excerpt.

WHY IS MINIVER CHEEVY UNHAPPY?

Miniver Cheevy

Miniver Cheevy, child of scorn,
Grew lean while he assailed the seasons
He wept that he was ever born,
And he had reasons.

Miniver loved the days of old
When swords were bright and steeds were prancing;
The vision of a warrior bold
Would send him dancing.

Miniver sighed for what was not,
And dreamed, and rested from his labors;
He dreamed of Thebes and Camelot,
And Priam's neighbors.

Miniver mourned the ripe renown
That made so many a name so fragrant;
He mourned Romance, now on the town,
And Art, a vagrant.

Miniver loved the Medici,
Albeit he had never seen one;
He would have sinned incessantly
Could he have been one.

Miniver cursed the commonplace
And eyed a khaki suit with loathing:
He missed the medieval grace
Of iron clothing.

Miniver scorned the gold he sought,
But sore annoyed was he without it;
Miniver thought, and thought, and thought,
And thought about it.

Miniver Cheevy, born too late,
Scratched his head and kept on thinking;
Miniver coughed, and called it fate,
And kept on drinking.

"Miniver Cheevy" by Edwin Arlington Robinson

GO ON TO THE NEXT PAGE

16. In the second stanza, it is stated that Miniver "dreamed, and rested from his labors" (line 10). What does this reveal about Miniver's character?

Miniver is likely

(1) independent
(2) industrious
(3) lazy
(4) intelligent
(5) creative

17. In line 27–28, "Miniver thought, and thought, and thought, And thought about it." This is a redundant, but interesting way to highlight what a likely element of Miniver's life?

(1) He is intelligent, but poor.
(2) He thinks, but does not act on his ideas.
(3) He is annoyed by the possession of gold.
(4) He is creative and insightful.
(5) He works, but cannot save any money for himself.

18. What is Miniver's primary reason for weeping "that he was ever born" (line 3)?

Miniver wishes that he

(1) had been born at another time in history
(2) had never found gold
(3) knew more information about history
(4) could speak to famous people
(5) had been able to meet a romantic artist

19. In many poems, there is a difference between the character in the story and the speaker of the poem. Miniver regrets many things, but how would the speaker likely describe Miniver?

The speaker in the poem would likely say that Miniver is

(1) unemotional
(2) uninformed
(3) unrealistic
(4) unprepared
(5) unartistic

20. What is likely to happen next, following the information in the last stanza?

Miniver will likely

(1) find out how to become one of the Medici
(2) work hard to get the gold he desires
(3) finally act on his need for new clothing
(4) change his passions and hobbies
(5) continue to live with regret and inaction

END OF EXAMINATION

MATHEMATICS

Tests of General Educational Development

Directions

The Mathematics Test consists of questions intended to measure general mathematics skills and problem-solving ability. The questions are based on short readings that often include a graph, chart, or figure.

You should spend no more than 45 minutes answering the questions in this booklet. Work carefully, but do not spend too much time on any one question. Be sure you answer every question.

Formulas you may need are given on page 176. Only some of the questions will require you to use a formula. Not all the formulas given will be needed.

Some questions contain more information than you will need to solve the problem; other questions do not give enough information. If the question does not give enough information to solve the problem, the correct answer choice is "Not enough information is given."

The use of calculators is allowed only in Part I.

Do not mark in this test booklet. The test administrator will give you blank paper for your calculations. Record your answers on the separate answer sheet provided. Be sure that all requested information is properly recorded on the answer sheet.

To record your answers, fill in the numbered circle on the answer sheet beside the number that corresponds to the question in the test booklet.

FOR EXAMPLE:

If a grocery bill totaling $15.75 is paid with a $20.00 bill, how much change should be returned?

(1) $5.25

(2) $4.75

(3) $4.25

(4) $3.75

(5) $3.25

The correct answer is $4.25; therefore, answer space 3 would be marked on the answer sheet.

Do not rest the point of your pencil on the answer sheet while you are considering your answer. Make no stray or unnecessary marks. If you change an answer, erase your first mark completely. Mark only <u>one</u> answer space for each question; multiple answers will be scored as incorrect. Do not fold or crease your answer sheet. All test materials must be returned to the test administrator.

GO ON TO THE NEXT PAGE

Mathematics, Part I

FORMULAS

AREA (A) of a:

square	$A = s^2$; where s = side
rectangle	$A = lw$; where l = length, w = width
parallelogram	$A = bh$; where b = base, h = height
trapezoid	$A = \frac{1}{2}(b_1 + b_2)h$; where b = base, h = height
triangle	$A = \frac{1}{2}bh$; where b = base, h = height
circle	$A = \pi r^2$; where $\pi = 3.14$, r = radius

PERIMETER (P) of a:

square	$P = 4s$; where s = side
rectangle	$P = 2l + 2w$; where l = length, w = width
triangle	$P = a + b + c$; where a, b, and c are the sides

CIRCUMFERENCE (C) of a circle: $C = \pi d$; where $\pi = 3.14$, d = diameter

VOLUME (V) of a:

cube	$V = s^3$; where s = side
rectangular container	$V = lwh$; where l = length, w = width, h = height
square pyramid	$V = \frac{1}{3}(\text{base edge})^2 h$
cone	$V = \frac{1}{3}\pi r^2 h$
cylinder	$V = \pi r^2 h$; where $\pi = 3.14$, r = radius, h = height

PYTHAGOREAN RELATIONSHIP — $c^2 = a^2 + b^2$; where c = hypotenuse, a and b are legs of a right triangle

DISTANCE (d) BETWEEN TWO POINTS ON A PLANE — $d = \sqrt{(x_2 - x_1)^2 + (y_2 - y_1)^2}$; where (x_1,y_1) and (x_2,y_2) are two points in a plane

SLOPE OF A LINE (m) — $m = \frac{y_2 - y_1}{x_2 - x_1}$; where (x_1,y_1) and (x_2,y_2) are two points in a plane

MEAN — **mean** $= \frac{x_1 + x_2 + \ldots x_n}{n}$; where the x's = the values for which a mean is desired, and n = number of values in the series

MEDIAN — **median** = the point in an ordered set of numbers at which half of the numbers are above and half of the numbers are below this value

SIMPLE INTEREST (i) — $i = prt$; where p = principal, r = rate, t = time

DISTANCE (d) as function of rate and time — $d = rt$; where r = rate, t = time

TOTAL COST (c) — $c = nr$; where n = number of units, r = cost per unit

Mathematics, Part I

Directions: You will have 22 minutes to complete questions 1–13. You may use your calculator with these questions only. Choose the one best answer to each question.

1. If a plane travels at 300 miles per hour, how many miles does it travel in 20 minutes?

(1) 6
(2) 100
(3) 200
(4) 900
(5) 6,000

2. A can of fruit weighs w ounces. The fruit itself, without the can, weighs f ounces. Which equation can be used to find C, the weight of the empty can?

(1) $C = w$
(2) $C = w + f$
(3) $C = w - f$
(4) $C = f - w$
(5) $C = f$

3. In the figure below, the larger square is made of four equal smaller squares. If each side of the larger square has a length of 2, what is the AREA of one of the smaller squares?

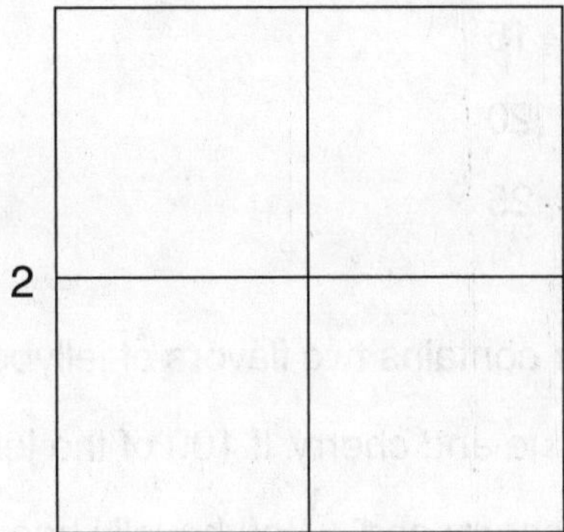

(1) 8
(2) 4
(3) 2
(4) 1
(5) $\frac{1}{4}$

4. If $\frac{1}{5}$ of $x = 15$, what is $\frac{2}{5}$ of x?

(1) 30
(2) 45
(3) 60
(4) 75
(5) 125

GO ON TO THE NEXT PAGE

5. The total cost C, in dollars, to order n copies of a textbook is given by the equation $C = 90n + 15$. If the total cost of the textbooks is $1815, how many textbooks were ordered?

   (1) 5
   (2) 8
   (3) 15
   (4) 20
   (5) 25

6. A jar contains two flavors of jellybeans: orange and cherry. If 100 of the jellybeans are cherry and $\frac{3}{5}$ of the jelly beans are orange, how many jellybeans are in the jar?

   (1) 250
   (2) 300
   (3) 450
   (4) 500
   (5) 600

7. A wire fence marks the perimeter of a rectangular pen that measures 30 ft by 40 ft. How long, in feet, is the wire fence?

   (1) 35
   (2) 70
   (3) 140
   (4) 400
   (5) 1,200

8. If $3x + 2y = 23$ and $3x = 21$, then $y =$

PLEASE DO NOT WRITE IN THIS TEST BOOKLET.

Mark your answer in the circles in the grid on your answer sheet.

9. John earned $40,000 each year for 2 consecutive years. For the each of the next two years he earned $50,000. For this four-year period, what is John's average yearly earnings, in dollars?

   (1) 48,000
   (2) 45,000
   (3) 44,000
   (4) 42,000
   (5) 41,000

GO ON TO THE NEXT PAGE

10. In the figure below, if the perimeter of triangle *ABC* is 48, what is the value of *x*?

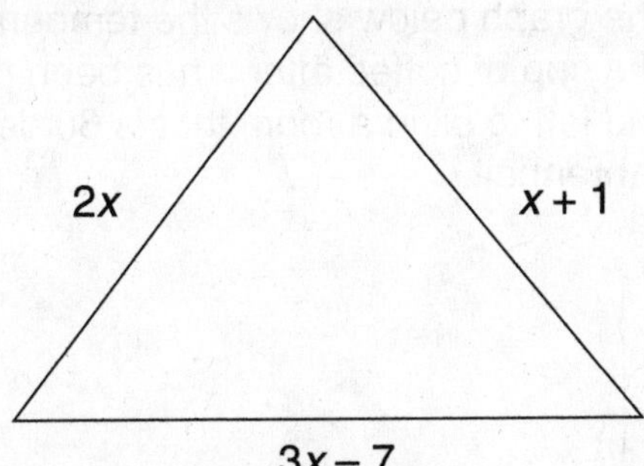

PLEASE DO NOT WRITE IN THIS TEST BOOKLET.

Mark your answer in the circles in the grid on your answer sheet.

11. In the figure below, what are the coordinates of point *a*?

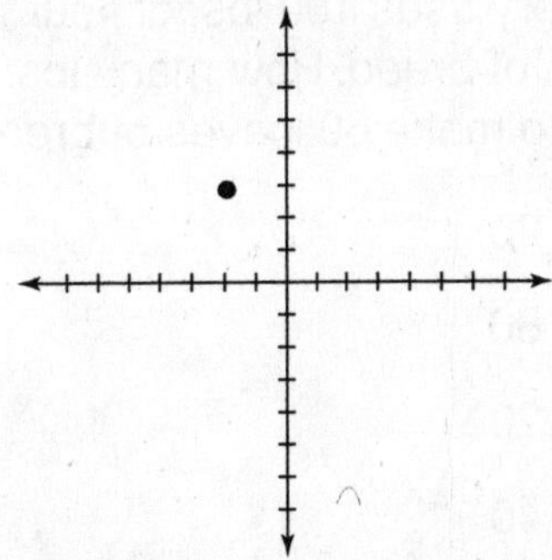

(1) (3, 2)
(2) (2, 3)
(3) (–3, –2)
(4) (–3, 2)
(5) (–2, 3)

12. A certain number is added to 5 and this sum is multiplied by 2. If the final product is 16, what is the number?

(1) 16
(2) 10
(3) 7
(4) 6
(5) 3

13. In the figure below, what is the measure, in degrees, of the OBTUSE angle?

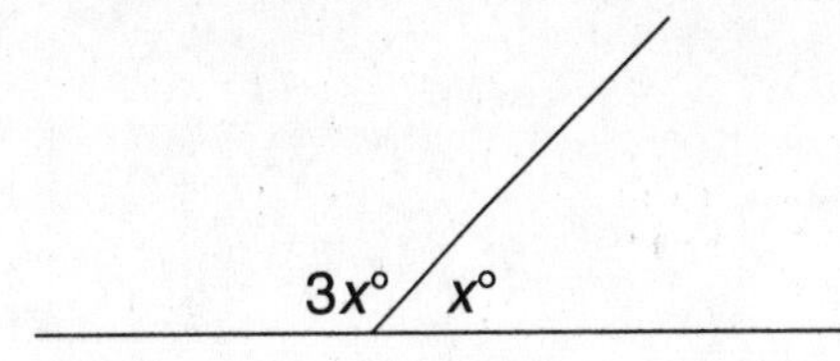

(1) 180
(2) 135
(3) 120
(4) 90
(5) 45

END OF MATHEMATICS, PART I

Directions: You will have 22 minutes to complete questions 14–25. You may NOT use a calculator with these questions. Choose the one best answer to each question.

14. A bakery uses 100 lbs. of flour to make 40 loaves of bread. How many lbs. of flour they need to make 60 loaves of bread?

(1) 20

(2) 80

(3) 120

(4) 140

(5) 150

15. The graph below shows the temperature of a cup of coffee after it has been poured and left to sit in a room that is 60 degrees Fahrenheit.

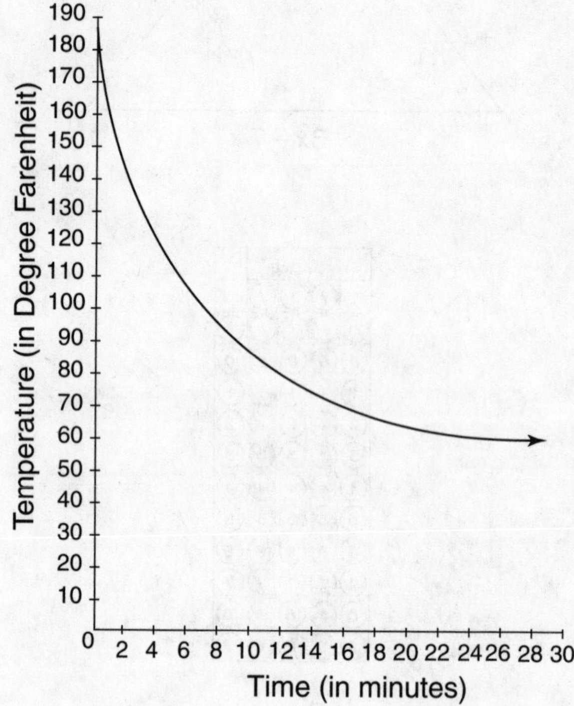

Based on the graph, what would be the approximate temperature of the cup of coffee, in degrees, after 9 minutes?

(1) 1,855

(2) 110

(3) 90

(4) 75

(5) 60

GO ON TO THE NEXT PAGE

Mathematics, Part II

16. A company rents moving vans for a rental fee of \$60.00 per day with an additional charge of \$.40 per mile that the van is driven. If Mario rents a van for two days and drives it 110 miles, what will the company charge?

(1) \$120
(2) \$124
(3) \$164
(4) \$180
(5) \$184

17. The figure below shows quadrilateral *WXYZ*. What is the measure of angle *Y*, in degrees?

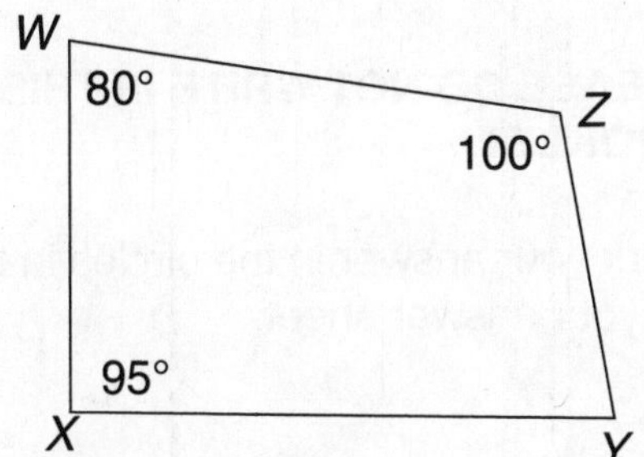

(1) 85
(2) 95
(3) 105
(4) 115
(5) 120

18. In the two triangles below, the area of triangle *ABC* is twice that of triangle *PQR*. What is the height of triangle *ABC*?

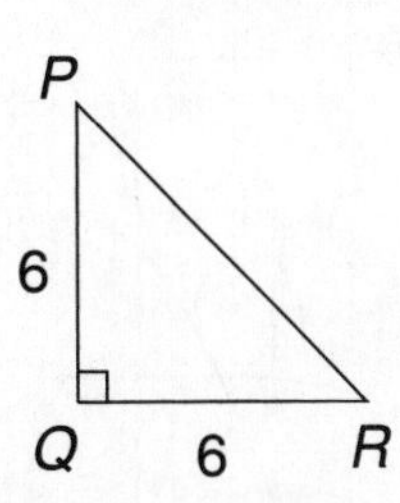

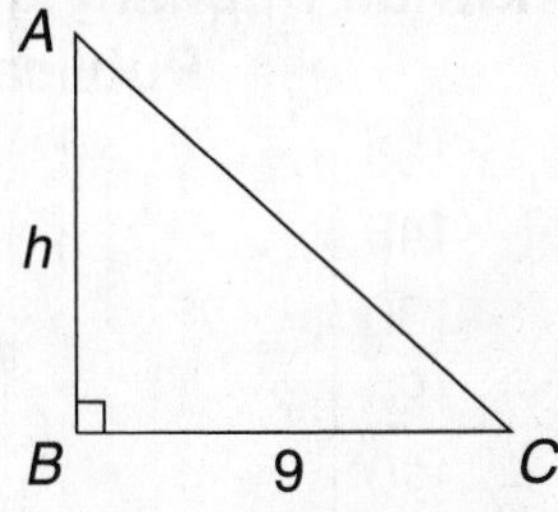

(1) 12
(2) 9
(3) 8
(4) 6
(5) 4

19. To rent a ballroom for an event costs a base fee of \$400 and an additional fee of \$3 per person. If *x* persons are expected to attend the event, which equation can be used to find *C*, the cost of renting the ballroom?

(1) $C = 3x + 400$
(2) $C = 400x + 3$
(3) $C = (400 + 3)x$
(4) $C = \dfrac{400}{3x}$
(5) $C = (400)(3x)$

GO ON TO THE NEXT PAGE

Questions 20 and 21 refer to the graph below

Projected Cost and Revenue Functions for Worldwide Publishing's Latest Hardcover Publication

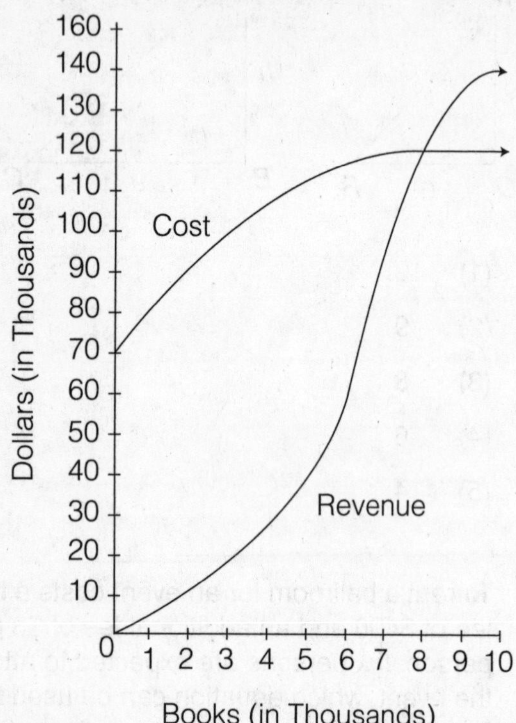

20. Based on the graph, before any books are sold, there will be no revenue generated. At the same time, however, the cost of production will be approximately $70,000. Why might this be true?

    (1) Hardcover books are always expensive.
    (2) The book might not sell as well as the publisher expects.
    (3) The book will sell faster at a reduced price.
    (4) There are start-up costs to publish the book.
    (5) Books sell better at the end of the year.

21. Based on the graph, approximately how many books must be sold before the revenue from sales exceeds the cost of publishing the book?

PLEASE DO NOT WRITE IN THIS TEST BOOKLET.

Mark your answer in the circles in the grid on your answer sheet.

GO ON TO THE NEXT PAGE

22. What are the coordinates of the midpoint of the two points shown on the grid below?

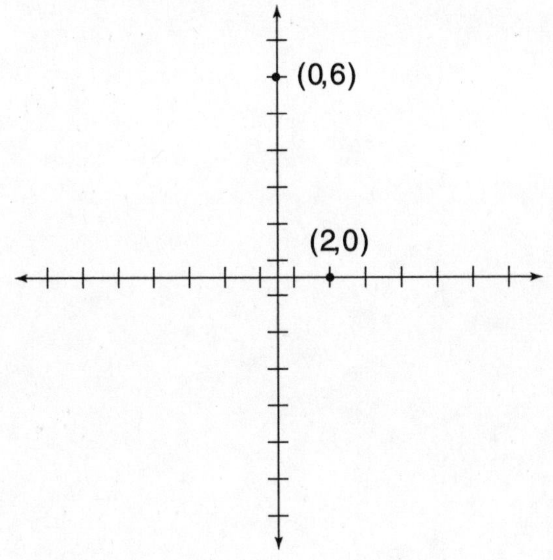

(1) (0, 3)
(2) (3, 1)
(3) (1, 3)
(4) (4, 0)
(5) (0, 5)

23. Julia invested a certain amount of money for one year at 4%. At the end of that year she was paid $60.00 above her original investment. How much was Julia's investment, in dollars?

(1) 1,500
(2) 1,200
(3) 1,000
(4) 800
(5) 150

24. At an accounting firm, accountants earn an average of $1400 more per month than associates do. If the firm employs 4 accountants and 12 associates, and x represents the average monthly pay of an accountant, which of the following can be used to express the monthly pay (M) of these sixteen employees?

(1) $M = 4x + 12(x–1400)$
(2) $M = 12x + 4(x–1400)$
(3) $M = 16x$
(4) $M = 16(x–1400) + x$
(5) $M = 12(x + 1400) + 16x$

25. A store that sells posters charges $60 for a poster that is 3 ft. by 4 ft. If the price (p) of any poster is proportional to its size, which of the following equations correctly express the cost of a poster that is 4 ft by 5 ft?

(1) $\frac{12}{60} = \frac{p}{20}$
(2) $\frac{60}{20} = \frac{p}{12}$
(3) $\frac{7}{p} = \frac{60}{9}$
(4) $\frac{7}{9} = \frac{60}{9}$
(5) $\frac{12}{20} = \frac{60}{p}$

END OF EXAMINATION

DO NOT MARK OR WRITE ON THIS PAGE

Answers and Explanations for Practice Test 2

WRITING

1. 4
2. 3
3. 3
4. 5
5. 4
6. 1
7. 5
8. 1
9. 1
10. 2
11. 3
12. 3
13. 5
14. 1
15. 1
16. 3
17. 4
18. 2
19. 5
20. 4
21. 1
22. 3
23. 2
24. 5
25. 2

SOCIAL STUDIES

1. 5
2. 2
3. 4
4. 2
5. 4
6. 1
7. 3
8. 1
9. 3
10. 5
11. 4
12. 3
13. 3
14. 1
15. 2
16. 3
17. 2
18. 2
19. 1
20. 2
21. 5
22. 4
23. 5
24. 3
25. 1

SCIENCE

1. 2
2. 1
3. 5
4. 1
5. 3
6. 4
7. 2
8. 4
9. 3
10. 3
11. 4
12. 2
13. 3
14. 5
15. 2
16. 5
17. 3
18. 5
19. 2
20. 1
21. 3
22. 4
23. 3
24. 3
25. 1

READING

1. 4
2. 3
3. 3
4. 1
5. 1
6. 4
7. 3
8. 3
9. 1
10. 4
11. 3
12. 4
13. 4
14. 2
15. 1
16. 3
17. 2
18. 1
19. 3
20. 5

MATH

1. 2
2. 3
3. 4
4. 1
5. 4
6. 1
7. 3
8. 1
9. 2
10. 9
11. 5
12. 5
13. 2
14. 5
15. 3
16. 3
17. 1
18. 3
19. 1
20. 4
21. 8,000
22. 3
23. 1
24. 1
25. 1

EXPLANATIONS

Writing

1. 4 Answer 4 is correct because you don't need a comma before *that* when it separates two parts of a sentence. Since all other choices contain a comma before *that*, they're eliminated.

2. 3 The word *much* is a problem here. You use *much* when you're talking about an amount that you can measure but can't count, as in "so much sand." When you're talking about something you can count, you would use the word *many*. For example, you can say "so much sand" and you can say "so many grains of sand," but you can't say "so many sand" or "so much grains." Choice 3 is the only answer that addresses this issue.

3. 3 Answer 3 is correct because *where* turns the sentence into a fragment. Choices 1, 2 and 4 do not address the issue, so they are eliminated. Answer choice 5 addresses the issue, but doesn't fix it. The phrase in which also makes the sentence a fragment. If *where* is simply deleted, the sentence is okay.

4. 5 The phrase *I was made aware* is passive and therefore could be written better. Choices 3 and 4 change the original meaning of the sentence and should be eliminated. Choices 1 and 2, although technically correct (as is the original sentence) are awkward. Answer 5 is the best choice.

5. 4 Sentences 8 and 9 clearly need to be combined, so that eliminates choice 1. Choices 2 and 3 each create a sentence fragment. Choice 5 is technically correct, but choice 4 makes much more sense.

6. 1 A person can be *apprised*, but a situation cannot, so clearly the sentence needs to be corrected. Choices 2 and 3 don't address this, so they need to be eliminated. Choice 4 changes the original meaning. You can't be *apprised* in a situation—this eliminates number 5. You're left with 1 as the correct choice.

7. 5 The word *since* creates a sentence fragment and has to go. Answer choice 5 is the only one that addresses this issue.

8. 1 Whenever you see a prepositional phrase, read the sentence without it to see how it looks. In this case, the prepositional phrase is *with all the VPs and department managers*. Take that out and the sentence reads, "I also feel that a meeting is in order." There's nothing wrong with that sentence, so the correct choice is 1.

9. 1 The word *Thanking* creates a fragment. Choice 1 is the only answer that addresses this issue.

10. 2 The sentence must read either *This question has* or *These questions have* in order to be correct. Since the title asks only one question, the choice has to be *This question*. Answer 2 is the only answer that addresses the issue.

11. 3 Something can be greater than or less than something else, but they can't be different *than*; they must be different *from*. Choice 3 is the only answer that addresses this.

12. 3 The word *that* can be used in reference to something that is not human. For example, you can say "the chair that was over there" or "the mouse that ran by" but you can't say "the boy that is standing here." The word *who* must always be used when referring to a person. Answer choice 3 is the only one that addresses this.

13. 5 This is a tough one because it addresses *like* versus *as*. These two words are often used interchangeably in casual conversation, but they are not technically interchangeable. Both are used to make comparisons, but *like* comes before a noun, while *as* comes before a noun and a verb. For example, you can say "he looks like a chicken" but you have to say "he walks as though he were a chicken." This eliminates answers 1, 2, and 4. The difference between choices 3 and 5 is more subtle. *As if* and *as though* are actually virtually interchangeable, but as if is most often used in less likely or wishful scenarios such as "as if I could fly." This leaves answer choice 5 as the correct one.

14. 1 Choice 1 is correct because *found* is the same as *discovered*, making the sentence redundant.

15. 1 The word *because* is the problem in this sentence because it implies that humans and Neanderthals descended from a common ancestor because chimps and gorillas did. Since this is not the case (the evolutionary paths were independent of each other), choice 1 is correct.

16. 3 Choice 3 is correct because paragraph B begins in the middle of an idea (the evolution picture series) that begins with sentence 7. Therefore, paragraph B should begin at sentence 7.

17. 4 The word *been* is always associated with either *has, have, have not* or *has not* or any contraction of these. This makes 4 the correct choice.

18. 2 Sentence 1 refers to a question that hasn't been asked yet. Where is that question? It's in sentence 3, so this sentence must be moved to a place before sentence 1.

19. 5 Sentence 4 is fine on its own, but sentence 5 is a fragment. Putting these two sentences together without additional punctuation is correct. This eliminates answer choices 1, 3 and 4. Choice 2 works only if you eliminate *have*. That leaves choice 5.

20. 4 The underlined portion of the sentence is passive. This eliminates choices 1 and 2. The pronoun *it* in choice 3 is ambiguous. The same goes for choice 5, which is also vague. The sentence can be improved by making the word *you* the subject of the sentence. Choice 4 is your answer.

21. 1 Reasoned means "thought out." You can have a reasoned reply or a reasoned decision but you can't have a reasoned chance. A chance is the likelihood of something happening and can't be thought out. This eliminates choice 2. Choices 3, 4, and 5 change the meaning of the sentence, which is that your bulbs will likely grow. The sentence is correct the way it is—choice 1.

22. 3 This is a simple spelling error. The sentence should read, "Here are some tips to give your bulbs an even better chance." Choice 3 fixes the error.

23. 2 This question is tough because it sounds exactly the way people talk. Clearly, the question is saying that the bulbs don't need anything more than a little water. But what the sentence is actually saying is that the bulbs "only need," implying that "needs" are not important when the opposite is the case. Since the bulbs need "only water," choice 2 fits the bill. Choice 5, like choice 1 changes the intended meaning of the sentence. While choice 4 is technically correct, it's awkward. Choice 2 works best.

24. 5 Sentence 24 implies that the bulbs won't grow—they'll *almost grow*. The same problem lies with choices 2 through 4. Choice 5 is the only answer that conveys the intended meaning of the sentence.

25. 2 This is a simple grammatical error with an extra *a* thrown into the sentence. Delete that and the sentence is correct. Answer choice 2 is the correct answer.

Social Studies

1. 5 The graphs indicate that women have higher illiteracy rates in these countries, so choice 5 is correct. The information indicated in choices 1 and 4 has nothing to do with the graphs, while choices 2 and 3 misrepresent the data altogether.

2. 2 The life expectancy for the typical Chinese citizen is 70.7 years, whereas the typical Nepalese person's is 59.9 years. This represents a difference of about 10 years, so choice 2 is correct.

3. 4 The difference between the illiteracy rates is not the result of intrinsic cultural differences. Therefore, choices 1 and 5 are incorrect. Choice 4 most accurately describes a plausible explanation for the difference.

4. 2 The only example that precisely satisfies the definition is choice 2. In none of the four other choices is the government seizing individual property.

5. 4 The Mexican-American War, which lasted from 1846 to 1848, helped the United States secure territories in the American Southwest. Therefore, choice 4 is correct. The French and Indian War (choice 1), was fought before the American Revolution. The Spanish-American War of 1898 (2) led to U.S. control of Puerto Rico and other territories and commonwealths.

6. 1 Some of the Founding Fathers were concerned that the Constitution did not include enough protections of individual rights. Thus the Bill of Rights "was added to the Constitution before ratification" (choice 1). Women were not guaranteed the right to vote (2) until the Nineteenth Amendment was ratified in 1920. Nothing has "replaced the legal authority of the Constitution" (3) and the Declaration of Independence has not been "nullified," so choice 4 is also incorrect.

7. 3 Several countries, most notably Russia (later the Soviet Union), China, Cuba, and Vietnam embraced communist forms of government. Therefore, choice 3 is the correct answer. Choice 2 overstates the number of countries that embraced Communism.

8. 1 The Boston Massacre did, in fact, increase resentment toward the British empire, so choices 4 and 5 are incorrect and choice 1 is correct. Because it took place *before* the Revolutionary War, choice 2 is also incorrect. Choice 3 overstates the number of people killed in the "massacre" because only five civilians were killed.

9. 3 The image emphasizes the innocence of the protestors (on the left) and the deliberate cruelty of the soldiers (on the right). Therefore, answer choice 3 is correct and choices 1, 2, and 4 are incorrect.

10. 5 Based on the definition provided in the question, choice 5 best describes "the movement of factories, service centers, or jobs from one location to another." While choice 1 does lower costs, it does not involve this transfer. Choices 2, 3, and 4 are typical business decisions, but have nothing to do with "outsourcing" per se.

11. 4 Answering this question requires that you understand the division of powers among the different branches of the government. It is Congress, not the president, that can declare war (choice 1). The most important power of the Supreme Court is that to determine whether laws are unconstitutional, so choice 2 is also incorrect. This power is called *judicial review* and was established in the decision *Marbury v. Madison* (1803). Presidents can be impeached (3) and have no power to strike down Supreme Court decisions (5). Choice 4 is the only one that accurately describes an example of checks and balances.

12. 3 The Fourth Amendment protects American citizens from "unreasonable searches and seizures" by the government without a warrant based on "probable cause." Choice 3 is therefore the only correct answer. Choices 2 and 5 are extreme and 4 is irrelevant to this topic.

13. 3 Choices 1, 2, and 4 are constitutionally permissible and therefore incorrect. Choice 3 describes a situation in which the Fourth Amendment would be violated because law enforcement officers are required to acquire a search warrant if they believe an individual is hiding illegal weapons in his home.

14. 1 Christopher Columbus did not discover the land that would become the United States of America in 1492. Therefore, choice 1 most accurately represents the information presented on the map. Choices 2 through 5 each distort the factual information presented in the map in one way or another.

15. 2 Be sure to read the information in the map carefully. Magellan's exploration through 1522 did travel westward to the New World and passed through the Pacific Ocean. Therefore, choice 2 is correct. Magellan did not land in North America, so choice 3 is incorrect. He did not travel south along the African coast and did not, therefore, follow da Gama's route, so choices 1 and 5 are also incorrect.

16. 3 One classic way to remember why the explorers travelled is "God, Gold, and Glory." In other words, many explorers were motivated by a desire to spread Christianity, to acquire resources (such as gold and spices), and to achieve personal glory. Choice 3 relates to "Gold" in that the explorers wanted to have access to wealthy goods in the East Indies. The other four choices are either factually incorrect or irrelevant.

17. 2 Do not be intimidated by a long quote like this. Just read through the quote and try to understand the general point. Then read the question and carefully eliminate wrong answers. Choices 1 and 3, for example, ignore the first sentence of the quote, which emphasizes that "civilization itself seeming to be in the balance." Equally problematic is choice 5 because it ignores the obvious optimism of the final clause: "peace and safety to all nations... the world itself at last free." The best answer choice is therefore choice 2 because it describes the major point of the excerpt.

18. 2 World War I, which lasted from 1914 to 1918, involved the major European superpowers and global empires at the time, so choice 2 is correct. Choices 1, 3, 4, and 5 are all factually incorrect.

19. 1 President Wilson did not support tyrannical governments (choice 1), so it is the correct answer. Wilson lists choices 2 through 5 throughout the passage as reasons for the United States' entry into World War I.

20. 2 Eliminate answers that are clearly incorrect. Choice 5 is clearly wrong from the data in the graph. Choices 1, 3, and 4 all make claims that have no basis in the graph itself, so choice 2 is correct.

21. 5 This question requires you to go beyond the information presented in the graph to determine which answer choice makes the most sense. What would diplomatic relations (choice 1) or "primitive" economic systems (3) have to do with high consumption of electricity? Choices 2 and 4 are likewise incorrect or irrelevant. Therefore, choice 5 makes the most sense because it does require a lot of electricity to heat buildings in cold climates.

22. 4 Be careful that you do not select answers that make sweeping claims about the court's motives. However much we may disagree with the court's decision today, the authors of the *Korematsu* decision did not believe they were being racist. Therefore, choice 1 is a trap answer. Choices 2, 3, and 5 all raise topics that are irrelevant to the excerpt. Only choice 4 directly addresses the court's reasoning as described in the excerpt.

23. 5 Choice 5 is obviously an opinion about what the Supreme Court believed. Notice that *opinions* often claim that people were "afraid" and that opinions make judgments that go beyond mere factual evidence. Each of the other five choices represents a fact that can be verified from the passage.

24. 3 The Stamp Act of 1765 set off a firestorm of controversy among the colonists. Many famously decried "no taxation without representation," which is the point of choice 3. The language of choice 5 is extreme: the colonists did not condemn all forms of taxation. Choice 1 is inaccurate because the British Empire rushed to defend its colonies during the French and Indian War.

25. 1 Too many of the choices express points of view too opinionated to be considered facts. Each of choices 2 through 5 makes some sort of judgment against the United Nations, whereas choice 1 makes a simple, factually accurate claim. It is therefore the correct answer.

Science

1. 2 The passage states that biotic factors are living. Choice 2, grass, is the only living factor.

2. 1 The table provides information about cholesterol levels. Optometrists specialize in eye care, home health aides assist with basic health needs, veterinarians work with animals, and dentists specialize in teeth, so choices 2, 3, 4, and 5 are incorrect. A physician, also known as a doctor, is likely to be familiar with cholesterol levels, so choice 1 is correct.

3. 5 According to the table, normal total cholesterol range is between 125 and 200 mg/dl. Choice 5 is correct because a level of 150 fits into this normal range.

4. 1 The graph shows a straight line moving up and to the right. Such a line shows a constant increase of both factors being compared, in this case blood pressure and cardiac output. Therefore, as the cardiac output increases, so too does blood pressure, so choice 1 is correct.

5. 3 The passage states causes of increased cardiac output are increased heart rate, blood pressure, and cardiac muscle strength. Choice 3 describes an increase in heart rate, so it is the correct answer. Choices 2 and 5 describe drops in heart rate and blood pressure, respectively, so they are incorrect. After death or heart attack, cardiac muscles would not pump blood normally, so choices 1 and 4 are incorrect.

6. 4 The passage states that most winged insects can respond to only one threat at a time. Approaching such an insect from the front and from behind would subject the insect to two threats at once and cause the insect to become immobilized, so 4 is correct.

7. 2 This question requires the knowledge that DNA is the molecule through which genes are passed from parent to child, so 2 is correct.

8. 4 Figure A shows all the gas molecules clumped together, while figure B shows them spread out. B is more likely to occur, because gas molecules spread out to fill a space. This question also requires the knowledge that the universe favors disorder, so answer 4 is correct.

9. 3 The passage defines that a carnivore is an animal that eats other animals. Hawks are carnivores because they eat snakes and mice, and snakes are carnivores because they eat mice, so 3 is correct. Note that since insects eat both plants and other insects, they are omnivores, not carnivores, and 4 is wrong.

10. 3 Weight is determined by the mass of an object and by acceleration of the object. Since the mass of the suitcase cannot change, the correct answer must involve acceleration of the suitcase. Choice 3, the speed at which the plane approaches the ground, is the only answer dealing with the acceleration.

11. 4 Since the passage states that solids from the water can build up in a steam iron, the best water to use would have the least dissolved solids. Choice 4, distilled water, has little to no dissolved solids and so it is the correct answer.

12. 2 The graphs show that the bacteria population started small. The curved part of the graph shows a rapid increase. Then, the graph becomes level. However, this does not mean the bacteria all died. The level area is high up on the graph, meaning the population is high when it levels off. Choice 2 best describes this graph.

13. 3 The passage describes a fixed action pattern as an animal behavior that was never taught. Choices 1, 4, and 5 involve training and learning, so they are incorrect. Answer 2 involves a plant, so it is incorrect. The correct answer is 3, since the bird performs a ritual without being taught.

14. 5 The passage states that acids have a pH below 7. In the table, lemon juice and vinegar both have pH below 7, so they are both acidic and 5 is correct.

15. 2 Cell A has a nucleus, organelles, several linear chromosomes, and no cell wall, so it is an animal cell and 2 is correct while 1 and 3 are incorrect. Cell B has a cell wall and a nucleus, so it is a plant cell and 4 is incorrect. Cell C has no nucleus so it is a bacterial cell and 5 is incorrect.

16. 5 The passage states that magnets are often made of iron and that the materials that make magnets are also attracted to magnets, so it can be inferred that magnets and iron attract. Therefore, 5, iron fillings, is correct.

17. 3 The passage states that if Tamika follows the correct procedures, the jelly will be sterilized. Sterilization involves killing bacteria; therefore, 3 is correct.

18. 5 The figure shows a curve going down quickly at first and then leveling off slightly. Choice 1 is incorrect because as the pressure increases the volume decreases. Choice 2 is incorrect because as the pressure rises the volume drops. Choice 3 is incorrect because as the pressure rises from 1 to 2 atm the pressure drops from 8 to 3 L, not 8 to 2 liters. Choice 4 is incorrect because atmospheres measure pressure. Choice 5 is correct because the volume is still decreasing slightly so as the pressure reaches 5 atm the volume will be around 1 L.

19. 2 The theory for how geodes develop involves rock cooling after a volcanic eruption. Only choice (2) mentions a volcano. The settings mentioned in the other choices are not mentioned in the passage.

20. 1 This problem requires the knowledge that the nucleus of an atom includes neutrons and protons, so 1 is correct. Electrons are in an atom but not in the nucleus, so 2 is wrong, and positrons deal with radioactivity, so 3 is wrong. Cells and batteries are made up of atoms, so 4 and 5 are wrong.

21. 3 The problem asks which ways of regulating body temperature are under conscious control, meaning which responses are voluntary. People cannot consciously make themselves sweat, or dilate blood vessels, but they can decide to drink cold water or remove clothing. Thus, 3 is correct.

22. 4 According to the bar graph, the plants in dry soil did not grow, those in plain damp soil grew to be 10 cm, and those in both damp composted soil and damp fertilized soil grew to be 15 cm. Choice 4 is correct because only the plants in some type of damp soil grew. Choice 1 is wrong because the plants grew at different rates, answer 2 is wrong because compost and fertilizer made the plants grow taller, choice 3 is wrong because compost and fertilizer were equally effective, and 5 is wrong because the plants in dry soil did not grow.

23. 3 Choice 3 is correct and answers 1 and 2 are incorrect because compost and fertilizer appear to equally help plants grow. Plants in damp soil grew and those in dry soil did not, so watering was a factor and 4 is incorrect. Choice 5 is incorrect because compost helped the plants grow and there is no evidence that compost is dangerous.

24. 3 The passage states that a flower with one yellow gene and one red gene have orange flowers. All of the offspring have one red gene and one yellow gene, so all of the offspring must have orange flowers and 3 is correct.

25. 1 The passage states that one parent is yellow and one is red. According to the passage, a yellow flower is pure for the yellow gene and a red flower is pure for the red gene. Therefore, answer 1 is correct and 2, 3, and 5 are incorrect. A yellow flower and a red flower would be expected to have orange offspring, so there is no reason to suspect that a mutation caused the orange offspring, so 4 is not the best explanation.

Reading

1. 4 The answer is 4 because the first paragraph indicates that "some people" are considering the event as a whole and some are recommending that "we entirely forgo the event." That is a clear call to end the fair. All other answers discuss placing blame or repercussions with officials, perpetrators, managers or fair workers. But no specific blame is placed anywhere in the letter.

2. 3 The answer is 3 because ending the fair is called a "massive mistake" and the history of safety is mentioned. Furthermore, a "greater focus on safety in the future" is expected. So, the letter writer obviously anticipates another fair in the future. Thus the problem this year was real, but understandable and can be dealt with. Choice 1 is incorrect since the writer agrees that the problem occurred and is not exaggerated. Choice 2 is extreme and false. Answer 4 contradicts the passage. Choice 5 is not clearly stated and is not as good as 3.

3. 3 The answer is 3 because the second paragraph clearly states that "revenue generated for the DCCC is crucial" for future programs, and that many residents use the services that need "this important source of funding." Choice 1 is not stated and too literal. Choice 2 mentions one program of many

and none are stated as most important. Safety is not mentioned as an issue at the DCCC, as in 4. Choice 5 is logically possible, but not supported by the details in the passage.

4. 1 The answer is 1 because ending the fair is called a mistake, the future fair is discussed, and additional safety measures are mentioned and expected. Choice 1 encompasses all of this the best. Choice 2 is not in agreement with the theme of the letter. Choice 3 is not mentioned. Choice 4 is incorrect since the recent must be addressed and are discussed in the letter. Choice 5 is wrong because admission price is never mentioned.

5. 1 The answer is 1 because the preceding line describes "the people so particular in renewal and comeback." Thus an ability to "take it" must refer to renewal and a return to strength after hardship. Choice 1 restates this idea best. Choice 2 does not address the quote in context. Nothing is in the passage to support answers 3 or 4. Choice 5 is extreme and off-topic.

6. 4 The answer is 4 because the line suggests that "many units" actually speak. This means that it must be a person, or, in other words, a part of the great group called "the people." Only 4 fits this description as a part of the larger group.

7. 3 The answer is 3 because the passage speaks constantly about "people" as one solid group representing all things. It is clearly a grammar mistake, but if the author does it intentionally, it must be for emphasis. Choices 1 and 2 are too literally focused on the grammar. Choice 4 is incorrect since it assumes the passage is monotonous which would not be the author's intent. Choice 5 is incorrect since there is only one group of people, called "the people," with many parts.

8. 3 The answer is 3 because the people are described as "a tragic and comic two-face." This includes "hero and hoodlum" as well as "phantom and gorilla." This represents two different, opposed sides of personality representing the extremes that a group of people can represent, the extremes that any human person can represent. Choice 1 is somewhat true but only addresses half the question. Choice 2 is extreme and not supported. Choice 4 is half-right in reference to achievement, but half-wrong in saying it comes at the expense of the less-fortunate. There is no support in the passage for answer 5.

9. 1 The answer is 1 because this reference follows the statement that "Man is a long time coming. Man will yet win," which states that mankind is a slow, irresistible force and will eventually triumph. The anvil is an example of another thing, like mankind, that is hard and strong and will not break under pressure. Choice 1 summarizes this idea best. Choice 2 is too specific and irrelevant. Choice 3 may be true, but does not address the meaning and importance of the reference to laughing at "broken hammers." Laughter may be a strong emotion, answer 4, but this answer misses the connection to the concept of defeat and triumph. Choice 5 references money which is not on topic and extreme.

10. 4 The answer is 4 because the passage excerpt talks about a group of people by describing the group's characteristics. All the characteristics are about common worries, common experiences, and common struggles. Choice 4 best captures this idea of regular, working people. The other four answers

are not as good as 4. Children, kings, scientists, and religious leaders are all also part of the people of the world, but the passage does not provide evidence to highlight any of them. The subject here is common people.

11. 3 The answer is 3 because the Manufacturer tells Pierrot he would still be unhappy with money. He also states that Pierrot should "write a song without any end" because he would have to always be happy to do so. Thus, the Manufacturer is discouraging pursuit of money and encouraging silly things like endless songs. Choices 1 and 2 contradict the passage and are not what the Manufacturer is suggesting. Choices 4 and 5 focus on work and responsibilities which are nothing like writing endless songs and dreaming which the Manufacturer emphasizes.

12. 4 The answer is 4 because Pierrot makes his comment immediately after the Manufacturer states that he is "a maker of dreams" that "float about this musty world." Obviously, this is an unusual claim and Pierrot doesn't quite believe it. Thus, his comment is another way of stating that he does not believe such silliness. Only 4 paraphrases this idea. There is no evidence to support details about dress, as in 1, or love, as in 3, or dishonesty, as in 5. The reference to money, as in 4, is out of place and does not answer this question.

13. 4 The answer is 4 because a song that does not end would force Pierrot to be happy. The Manufacturer believes that writing an endless song is a better pursuit, though silly, than money for Pierrot because it is more likely to show him how to be happy. Choices 1 and 2 incorrectly focus on the literal song-writing instead of happiness. Choice 3 improperly references love songs which are not discussed. Choice 5 introduces the idea of other people's happiness, which is not the Manufacturer's focus.

14. 2 The answer is 2 because Pierrot resists and argues with the Manufacturer's comments about songs. He then does not believe the Manufacturer's claims about making dreams when he calls him "a trifle done up." This attitude is one of disbelief. Only 2 is an accurate tone.

15. 1 The answer is 1 because Pierrot is discussing love and says that he believes in it, but that "it doesn't last." He further states that he has "tried hard to believe," so the reference to colors that run after a wash compares love to clothing that fades. Pierrot's opinion is that love doesn't last, as in 1. Choice 2 is half-right in that love is real, but the reference to colors is too literal. Choices 3, 4 and 5 are not discussed by Pierrot and do not reference Pierrot's comments or opinion.

16. 3 The answer is 3 because dreaming is not a difficult or hard-working activity. To say that Miniver then "rested from his labors" is to suggest that he rests even when he has not worked hard. That means that Miniver is likely lazy, as in 3. Nothing is known about Miniver's intelligence or creativity, as in 4 and 5. Choices 1 and 2 miss the point of the poem and Miniver's regret and inaction.

17. 2 The answer is 2 because this quote and several others in the poem show how much Miniver thinks about his life, but nothing in the poem describes what Miniver does. He takes no action; he only thinks and regrets. Choice 1 falsely references intelligence. Choice 3 contradicts the passage since Miniver desires gold. There is no support in the passage regarding Miniver's creativity or his savings, as in 4 and 5.

18. 1 The answer is 1 because the poem discusses all of Miniver's desires and they all come from the past. He wishes that he could have witnessed or participated in events before his time. So, his life is one primarily of regret. Choice 1 summarizes this idea best. Choice 2 is not stated, so it cannot be considered correct. Choice 3 is not supported by the passage and Miniver already knows several things from history. There is no evidence in the passage's details to support 4 or 5.

19. 3 The answer is 3 because the speaker describes Miniver as if watching him from a close viewpoint. The speaker also comments on Miniver's desires and inaction in regards to those desires. By choosing to highlight Miniver's many regrets, sighing and weeping, the speaker shows that Miniver is unrealistic about his own life. Only 3 completely captures Miniver's condition.

20. 5 The answer is 5 because Miniver has shown no evidence that he will ever do anything specific to make his desires come true. He only sits and regrets. The entire poem shows that he is most likely to continue as before when he "thought and thought and thought and thought about it." The poem ends with Miniver continuing to drink, but not making any claims about his future or taking an action to make anything happen. Choice 5 states this most clearly. Answer 1 incorrectly focuses on only one of Miniver's many regrets. Choices 2, 3 and 4 all contradict the main theme of the passage regarding Miniver's inaction. He does not take action; he only regrets.

Math

1. 2 The plane travels 300 miles in one hour. 20 minutes is one-third of an hour, so divide 300 miles by 3. 300/3 = 100

2. 3 The weight of the empty can (C) is equal to the weight of the full can (w) minus the contents of the can (f). If we express the sentence as an equation, we get $C = w - f$.

3. 4 Because the four smaller squares are equal, the sides of two small squares equal the side of the large square. Therefore the side of a small square equals 1. Since the area of a square is equal to the length of one side squared, the area of one of the smaller squares equals 1 squared, which is one.

4. 1 2/5 is 1/5 times 2. Therefore, if 1/5 of x equals 15, 2/5 of x will be twice as much or 2 times 15 which equals 30.

5. 4 Plug the total cost of the textbooks in for C in the equation: $1815 = 90n + 15$. Subtract 15 from both sides to get: $1800 = 90n$. Divide both sides by 90 to find $n = 20$.

6. 1 If 3/5 of the jelly beans are orange, then the remaining 2/5 must be cherry. Because 2/5 of the jellybeans are cherry, 2/5 of the jellybeans equals 100. If we let J equal the total number of jellybeans, we can write the equation: 2/5J = 100. Multiply both sides of the equation by 5/2 to isolate J and we get J = 250.

7. 3 Because the pen is rectangular, two of the sides are 30 feet and two of the sides are 40 feet. Multiply the sides by two and add the resulting products: $2(30) + 2(40) = 140$.

8. 1 Use the second equation first to plug in to the first one. You know that $3x = 21$, so the new equation could read $21 + 2y = 23$. Subtract 21 from both sides and you get $2y = 1$, so $y = 1$.

9. 2 For the first two years he worked John earned 2 times $40,000 or $80,000. For the next two years he earned 2 times $50,000 or $100,000. For the four years he earned $80,000 + $100,000 = $180,000. Divide that total by 4 to find the average of the four years: $180,000/4 = $45,000.

10. 9 The perimeter of a triangle is the sum of the lengths of its sides. Add the sides to find that the perimeter equals $6x - 6$. Therefore $6x - 6 = 48$ and solving for x yields $x = 9$.

11. 5 The point is in the second quadrant where x is negative and y is positive. Line up the marks on the axes with the point to find that the point is at $(-2,3)$

12. 5 Let the number be n. The number added to 5 is $n + 5$. That sum multiplied by two is $2(n + 5)$. Therefore $2(n + 5) = 16$. Divide both sides by two: $n + 5 = 8$. Subtract both sides by 5 to find $n = 3$.

13. 2 Angles that form a straight line add up to 180, so $3x + x = 180$. $4x = 180$ and $x = 45$

14. 5 Set up a proportion for the pounds of flour to the loaves of bread: 100 lbs/ 40 loaves. Write an equation with the proportion we are given on one side and the quantity we are looking for on the other, making sure to keep the pounds of flour in the numerator and the number of loaves in the denominator: $100/40 = x/60$. Multiply both sides by 60 to find $x = 150$.

15. 3 The x-axis gives the time and the y-axis gives the temperature. Look for the point on the x-axis where $x = 9$. Move your pencil directly up to the curve. Now move your pencil directly to the left, to the y-axis. The corresponding y value is 90.

16. 3 To rent the van for two days at $60.00 per day costs 2($60) or $120. If Mario drives 110 miles at $.40 per mile, the mileage cost is 110($.40) or $44. Add the daily cost and the mileage cost: $120 + $44 = $164.

17. 1 The sum of the angles in a quadrilateral is 360 degrees. The sum of the given angles is 275 degrees. To find the missing angle, subtract 275 from 360: $360 - 275 = 85$.

18. 3 The area of a triangle is given by the formula Area= ½(base)(height). Plugging into the formula, the area of the smaller triangle is $½(6)(6) = 18$. The larger triangle must have an area of 36. Plug that information into the formula again to find the height of the larger triangle: $½\,(9n)(h) = 36$. Solve for h which equals 8.

19. 1 The total cost must be $400 plus $3 times the number of people expected to attend. Translate the sentence into an equation: $C = 400 + 3x$ which is a rearranged version of $C = 3x + 400$.

20. **4** The question asks why production costs might be $70,000 before any books are sold. The answer must be that there are costs associated with publishing a book that must be paid before a book is sold and any revenue is generated. These costs are the start-up costs, which, according to the graph, are $70,000.

21. **8,000** Follow the curves to reach the point at which the revenue curve meets the cost curve. Just to the right of that point, the revenue curve goes higher than the cost curve. That is the point at which revenue from sales exceeds the cost of publishing the book. Move your pencil straight down to find the value on the x-axis that corresponds to that point. The x value is approximately 8,000.

22. **3** The formula for the midpoint is: $((x_1 + x_2)/2 , (y_1 + y_2)/2)$. Plugging into the formula we get: $((0 + 2)/2 , (6 + 0)/2)$. The coordinates of the midpoint are (1,3)

23. **1** If Julia received $60 at the end of the year, then 4% of the investment must equal $60. If we let A equal the amount invested and write 4% as 4/100, then we can write the equation: 4/100(A) = 60. Solve for A to get find that the investment was $1500.

24. **1** The total pay for the 4 accountants is $4x$. The monthly pay for each associate is $x - 1400$, so the total pay for the associates is $12(x - 1400)$. Add the total pay for the accountants and the associates to find the monthly pay for all sixteen employees: $M = 4x + 12(x\text{-}1400)$

25. **5** A poster that is 3-ft. by 4-ft. is 12 square ft. A poster that is 4-ft. by 5-ft. is 20 square ft. Because the price is proportional to the size of the poster, set up a proportion with the size of the posters on one side of the equation and the price on the other: $12/20 = 60/p$. Make sure that the correct size is matched up to the correct price.

[illegible] The question asks why [illegible] cost [illegible] $1,000 for any [illegible]. The answer [illegible] that there are [illegible] compared with [illegible]. [illegible] that [illegible] a [illegible] and [illegible] is [illegible], according to the graph.

[illegible] $6,000 [illegible] the curve [illegible] the point [illegible] that [illegible]. [illegible] the [illegible] higher than the [illegible] curve. This is the point [illegible] revenue [illegible] exceeds the cost [illegible]. [illegible] the value on the x-axis that corresponds to that point. The value is approximately $6,000.

[illegible] The formula for the [illegible] is [illegible]. [illegible] the [illegible] of the [illegible] are [illegible].

[illegible] [illegible] $500 at the end of the year [illegible] interest [illegible] the amount invested [illegible] $100. [illegible] we can write the equation [illegible] solve for A to get [illegible] the amount is $500 [illegible].

[illegible] The total pay for the [illegible] accountant [illegible] for each [illegible] total pay for the [illegible] is [illegible]. For the accountant, [illegible] and the monthly pay for [illegible] employees [illegible].

[illegible] that [illegible] the [illegible] the [illegible] They are [illegible] proportional to the size of the [illegible] a proportion with [illegible] of the equation and the [illegible] (20) [illegible] 20% [illegible] that the correct answer [illegible].

Practice Test 3

Completely darken bubbles with a No. 2 pencil. If you make a mistake, be sure to erase mark completely. Erase all stray marks.

1

YOUR NAME: (Print) ______ Last ______ First ______ M.I.

SIGNATURE: ______ DATE: / /

HOME ADDRESS: (Print) ______ Number and Street

______ City ______ State ______ Zip Code

PHONE NO.: (Print) ______

IMPORTANT: Please fill in these boxes exactly as shown on the back cover of your test book.

2. TEST FORM

3. TEST CODE

4. REGISTRATION NUMBER

3. TEST CODE		4. REGISTRATION NUMBER								
0	A	0	0	0	0	0	0	0	0	0
1	B	1	1	1	1	1	1	1	1	1
2	C	2	2	2	2	2	2	2	2	2
3	D	3	3	3	3	3	3	3	3	3
4	E	4	4	4	4	4	4	4	4	4
5	F	5	5	5	5	5	5	5	5	5
6	G	6	6	6	6	6	6	6	6	6
7		7	7	7	7	7	7	7	7	7
8		8	8	8	8	8	8	8	8	8
9		9	9	9	9	9	9	9	9	9

6. DATE OF BIRTH

Month	Day		Year	
JAN				
FEB				
MAR	0	0	0	0
APR	1	1	1	1
MAY	2	2	2	2
JUN	3	3	3	3
JUL		4	4	4
AUG		5	5	5
SEP		6	6	6
OCT		7	7	7
NOV		8	8	8
DEC		9	9	9

7. SEX

MALE

FEMALE

The Princeton Review®

FORM NO. 00001-PR

5. YOUR NAME

First 4 letters of last name				FIRST INIT	MID INIT
A	A	A	A	A	A
B	B	B	B	B	B
C	C	C	C	C	C
D	D	D	D	D	D
E	E	E	E	E	E
F	F	F	F	F	F
G	G	G	G	G	G
H	H	H	H	H	H
I	I	I	I	I	I
J	J	J	J	J	J
K	K	K	K	K	K
L	L	L	L	L	L
M	M	M	M	M	M
N	N	N	N	N	N
O	O	O	O	O	O
P	P	P	P	P	P
Q	Q	Q	Q	Q	Q
R	R	R	R	R	R
S	S	S	S	S	S
T	T	T	T	T	T
U	U	U	U	U	U
V	V	V	V	V	V
W	W	W	W	W	W
X	X	X	X	X	X
Y	Y	Y	Y	Y	Y
Z	Z	Z	Z	Z	Z

Start with number 1 for each new section. If a section has fewer questions than answer spaces, leave the extra answer spaces blank. Be sure to erase any errors or stray marks completely.

WRITING

1 A B C D E	11 A B C D E	21 A B C D E	31 A B C D E
2 A B C D E	12 A B C D E	22 A B C D E	32 A B C D E
3 A B C D E	13 A B C D E	23 A B C D E	33 A B C D E
4 A B C D E	14 A B C D E	24 A B C D E	34 A B C D E
5 A B C D E	15 A B C D E	25 A B C D E	35 A B C D E
6 A B C D E	16 A B C D E	26 A B C D E	36 A B C D E
7 A B C D E	17 A B C D E	27 A B C D E	37 A B C D E
8 A B C D E	18 A B C D E	28 A B C D E	38 A B C D E
9 A B C D E	19 A B C D E	29 A B C D E	39 A B C D E
10 A B C D E	20 A B C D E	30 A B C D E	40 A B C D E

SOCIAL STUDIES

1 A B C D E	11 A B C D E	21 A B C D E	31 A B C D E
2 A B C D E	12 A B C D E	22 A B C D E	32 A B C D E
3 A B C D E	13 A B C D E	23 A B C D E	33 A B C D E
4 A B C D E	14 A B C D E	24 A B C D E	34 A B C D E
5 A B C D E	15 A B C D E	25 A B C D E	35 A B C D E
6 A B C D E	16 A B C D E	26 A B C D E	36 A B C D E
7 A B C D E	17 A B C D E	27 A B C D E	37 A B C D E
8 A B C D E	18 A B C D E	28 A B C D E	38 A B C D E
9 A B C D E	19 A B C D E	29 A B C D E	39 A B C D E
10 A B C D E	20 A B C D E	30 A B C D E	40 A B C D E

Start with number 1 for each new section. If a section has fewer questions than answer spaces, leave the extra answer spaces blank. Be sure to erase any errors or stray marks completely.

SCIENCE

1 Ⓐ Ⓑ Ⓒ Ⓓ Ⓔ	11 Ⓐ Ⓑ Ⓒ Ⓓ Ⓔ	21 Ⓐ Ⓑ Ⓒ Ⓓ Ⓔ	31 Ⓐ Ⓑ Ⓒ Ⓓ Ⓔ
2 Ⓐ Ⓑ Ⓒ Ⓓ Ⓔ	12 Ⓐ Ⓑ Ⓒ Ⓓ Ⓔ	22 Ⓐ Ⓑ Ⓒ Ⓓ Ⓔ	32 Ⓐ Ⓑ Ⓒ Ⓓ Ⓔ
3 Ⓐ Ⓑ Ⓒ Ⓓ Ⓔ	13 Ⓐ Ⓑ Ⓒ Ⓓ Ⓔ	23 Ⓐ Ⓑ Ⓒ Ⓓ Ⓔ	33 Ⓐ Ⓑ Ⓒ Ⓓ Ⓔ
4 Ⓐ Ⓑ Ⓒ Ⓓ Ⓔ	14 Ⓐ Ⓑ Ⓒ Ⓓ Ⓔ	24 Ⓐ Ⓑ Ⓒ Ⓓ Ⓔ	34 Ⓐ Ⓑ Ⓒ Ⓓ Ⓔ
5 Ⓐ Ⓑ Ⓒ Ⓓ Ⓔ	15 Ⓐ Ⓑ Ⓒ Ⓓ Ⓔ	25 Ⓐ Ⓑ Ⓒ Ⓓ Ⓔ	35 Ⓐ Ⓑ Ⓒ Ⓓ Ⓔ
6 Ⓐ Ⓑ Ⓒ Ⓓ Ⓔ	16 Ⓐ Ⓑ Ⓒ Ⓓ Ⓔ	26 Ⓐ Ⓑ Ⓒ Ⓓ Ⓔ	36 Ⓐ Ⓑ Ⓒ Ⓓ Ⓔ
7 Ⓐ Ⓑ Ⓒ Ⓓ Ⓔ	17 Ⓐ Ⓑ Ⓒ Ⓓ Ⓔ	27 Ⓐ Ⓑ Ⓒ Ⓓ Ⓔ	37 Ⓐ Ⓑ Ⓒ Ⓓ Ⓔ
8 Ⓐ Ⓑ Ⓒ Ⓓ Ⓔ	18 Ⓐ Ⓑ Ⓒ Ⓓ Ⓔ	28 Ⓐ Ⓑ Ⓒ Ⓓ Ⓔ	38 Ⓐ Ⓑ Ⓒ Ⓓ Ⓔ
9 Ⓐ Ⓑ Ⓒ Ⓓ Ⓔ	19 Ⓐ Ⓑ Ⓒ Ⓓ Ⓔ	29 Ⓐ Ⓑ Ⓒ Ⓓ Ⓔ	39 Ⓐ Ⓑ Ⓒ Ⓓ Ⓔ
10 Ⓐ Ⓑ Ⓒ Ⓓ Ⓔ	20 Ⓐ Ⓑ Ⓒ Ⓓ Ⓔ	30 Ⓐ Ⓑ Ⓒ Ⓓ Ⓔ	40 Ⓐ Ⓑ Ⓒ Ⓓ Ⓔ

READING

1 Ⓐ Ⓑ Ⓒ Ⓓ Ⓔ	11 Ⓐ Ⓑ Ⓒ Ⓓ Ⓔ	21 Ⓐ Ⓑ Ⓒ Ⓓ Ⓔ	31 Ⓐ Ⓑ Ⓒ Ⓓ Ⓔ
2 Ⓐ Ⓑ Ⓒ Ⓓ Ⓔ	12 Ⓐ Ⓑ Ⓒ Ⓓ Ⓔ	22 Ⓐ Ⓑ Ⓒ Ⓓ Ⓔ	32 Ⓐ Ⓑ Ⓒ Ⓓ Ⓔ
3 Ⓐ Ⓑ Ⓒ Ⓓ Ⓔ	13 Ⓐ Ⓑ Ⓒ Ⓓ Ⓔ	23 Ⓐ Ⓑ Ⓒ Ⓓ Ⓔ	33 Ⓐ Ⓑ Ⓒ Ⓓ Ⓔ
4 Ⓐ Ⓑ Ⓒ Ⓓ Ⓔ	14 Ⓐ Ⓑ Ⓒ Ⓓ Ⓔ	24 Ⓐ Ⓑ Ⓒ Ⓓ Ⓔ	34 Ⓐ Ⓑ Ⓒ Ⓓ Ⓔ
5 Ⓐ Ⓑ Ⓒ Ⓓ Ⓔ	15 Ⓐ Ⓑ Ⓒ Ⓓ Ⓔ	25 Ⓐ Ⓑ Ⓒ Ⓓ Ⓔ	35 Ⓐ Ⓑ Ⓒ Ⓓ Ⓔ
6 Ⓐ Ⓑ Ⓒ Ⓓ Ⓔ	16 Ⓐ Ⓑ Ⓒ Ⓓ Ⓔ	26 Ⓐ Ⓑ Ⓒ Ⓓ Ⓔ	36 Ⓐ Ⓑ Ⓒ Ⓓ Ⓔ
7 Ⓐ Ⓑ Ⓒ Ⓓ Ⓔ	17 Ⓐ Ⓑ Ⓒ Ⓓ Ⓔ	27 Ⓐ Ⓑ Ⓒ Ⓓ Ⓔ	37 Ⓐ Ⓑ Ⓒ Ⓓ Ⓔ
8 Ⓐ Ⓑ Ⓒ Ⓓ Ⓔ	18 Ⓐ Ⓑ Ⓒ Ⓓ Ⓔ	28 Ⓐ Ⓑ Ⓒ Ⓓ Ⓔ	38 Ⓐ Ⓑ Ⓒ Ⓓ Ⓔ
9 Ⓐ Ⓑ Ⓒ Ⓓ Ⓔ	19 Ⓐ Ⓑ Ⓒ Ⓓ Ⓔ	29 Ⓐ Ⓑ Ⓒ Ⓓ Ⓔ	39 Ⓐ Ⓑ Ⓒ Ⓓ Ⓔ
10 Ⓐ Ⓑ Ⓒ Ⓓ Ⓔ	20 Ⓐ Ⓑ Ⓒ Ⓓ Ⓔ	30 Ⓐ Ⓑ Ⓒ Ⓓ Ⓔ	40 Ⓐ Ⓑ Ⓒ Ⓓ Ⓔ

MATH

1 Ⓐ Ⓑ Ⓒ Ⓓ Ⓔ	11 Ⓐ Ⓑ Ⓒ Ⓓ Ⓔ	21 Ⓐ Ⓑ Ⓒ Ⓓ Ⓔ	31 Ⓐ Ⓑ Ⓒ Ⓓ Ⓔ
2 Ⓐ Ⓑ Ⓒ Ⓓ Ⓔ	12 Ⓐ Ⓑ Ⓒ Ⓓ Ⓔ	22 Ⓐ Ⓑ Ⓒ Ⓓ Ⓔ	32 Ⓐ Ⓑ Ⓒ Ⓓ Ⓔ
3 Ⓐ Ⓑ Ⓒ Ⓓ Ⓔ	13 Ⓐ Ⓑ Ⓒ Ⓓ Ⓔ	23 Ⓐ Ⓑ Ⓒ Ⓓ Ⓔ	33 Ⓐ Ⓑ Ⓒ Ⓓ Ⓔ
4 Ⓐ Ⓑ Ⓒ Ⓓ Ⓔ	14 Ⓐ Ⓑ Ⓒ Ⓓ Ⓔ	24 Ⓐ Ⓑ Ⓒ Ⓓ Ⓔ	34 Ⓐ Ⓑ Ⓒ Ⓓ Ⓔ
5 Ⓐ Ⓑ Ⓒ Ⓓ Ⓔ	15 Ⓐ Ⓑ Ⓒ Ⓓ Ⓔ	25 Ⓐ Ⓑ Ⓒ Ⓓ Ⓔ	35 Ⓐ Ⓑ Ⓒ Ⓓ Ⓔ
6 Ⓐ Ⓑ Ⓒ Ⓓ Ⓔ	16 Ⓐ Ⓑ Ⓒ Ⓓ Ⓔ	26 Ⓐ Ⓑ Ⓒ Ⓓ Ⓔ	36 Ⓐ Ⓑ Ⓒ Ⓓ Ⓔ
7 Ⓐ Ⓑ Ⓒ Ⓓ Ⓔ	17 Ⓐ Ⓑ Ⓒ Ⓓ Ⓔ	27 Ⓐ Ⓑ Ⓒ Ⓓ Ⓔ	37 Ⓐ Ⓑ Ⓒ Ⓓ Ⓔ
8 Ⓐ Ⓑ Ⓒ Ⓓ Ⓔ	18 Ⓐ Ⓑ Ⓒ Ⓓ Ⓔ	28 Ⓐ Ⓑ Ⓒ Ⓓ Ⓔ	38 Ⓐ Ⓑ Ⓒ Ⓓ Ⓔ
9 Ⓐ Ⓑ Ⓒ Ⓓ Ⓔ	19 Ⓐ Ⓑ Ⓒ Ⓓ Ⓔ	29 Ⓐ Ⓑ Ⓒ Ⓓ Ⓔ	39 Ⓐ Ⓑ Ⓒ Ⓓ Ⓔ
10 Ⓐ Ⓑ Ⓒ Ⓓ Ⓔ	20 Ⓐ Ⓑ Ⓒ Ⓓ Ⓔ	30 Ⓐ Ⓑ Ⓒ Ⓓ Ⓔ	40 Ⓐ Ⓑ Ⓒ Ⓓ Ⓔ

CAUTION Use the answer spaces in the grids below for Section 6 or Section 7 only if you are told to do so in your test book.

Student-Produced Responses ONLY ANSWERS ENTERED IN THE OVALS IN EACH GRID WILL BE SCORED. YOU WILL NOT RECEIVE CREDIT FOR ANYTHING WRITTEN IN THE BOXES ABOVE THE OVALS.

Grids 9, 10, 11, 12, 13 (each four columns):

/		/	/	
.	.	.	.	.
0		0	0	0
1	1	1	1	1
2	2	2	2	2
3	3	3	3	3
4	4	4	4	4
5	5	5	5	5
6	6	6	6	6
7	7	7	7	7
8	8	8	8	8
9	9	9	9	9

PLEASE DO NOT WRITE IN THIS AREA

SERIAL #

LANGUAGE ARTS, WRITING

Tests of General Educational Development

Directions

The Language Arts, Writing Test is intended to measure your ability to use clear and effective English. This test includes both multiple-choice questions and an essay. These directions apply only to the multiple-choice section; a separate set of directions is given for the essay.

The multiple-choice section consists of paragraphs with lettered paragraphs and numbered sentences. Some of the sentences contain errors in sentence structure, usage, or mechanics (punctuation, and capitalization). After reading the numbered sentences, answer the multiple-choice questions that follow. Some questions refer to sentences that are correct as written. The best answer for these questions is the one that leaves the sentence as originally written. The best answer for some questions is the one that produces a sentence that is consistent with the verb tense and point of view used throughout the text. A document is often repeated in order to allow for additional questions on a second page. The repeated document is the same as the first

You should spend no more than 40 minutes on the multiple-choice questions and 45 minutes on your essay. Work carefully, but do not spend too much time on any one question. Be sure you answer every question. You may begin working on the essay part of this test as soon as you complete the multiple-choice section.

Do not mark in this test booklet. Record your answers on the separate answer sheet provided. Be sure that all requested information is properly recorded on the answer sheet.

To record your answers, mark one numbered space on the answer sheet beside the number that corresponds to the question in the test booklet.

FOR EXAMPLE:

Sentence 1: **We were honored to meet governor Phillips.**

Which correction should be made to sentence 1?

(1) insert a comma after honored
(2) change honored to honer
(3) change governor to Governor
(4) change were to was
(5) no correction is necessary

In this example, the word "governor" should be capitalized; therefore, answer space 3 would be marked on the answer sheet.

Do not rest the point of your pencil on the answer sheet while you are considering your answer. Make no stray or unnecessary marks. If you change an answer, erase your first mark completely. Mark only one answer space for each question; multiple answers will be scored as incorrect. Do not fold or crease your answer sheet. All test materials must be returned to the test administrator.

GO ON TO THE NEXT PAGE

Directions: Choose the one best answer to each question.

Questions 1 through 9 refer to the following memorandum.

Emory Distribution, LLC
26500 Plymouth Rd.
Livonia, MI 48150
313-555-6700

MEMORANDUM

From: Janet Margarito, Senior Manager, Human Resources
To: Vero Massitti, President, Warehousing Division
Subject: Theft of Vacation Time
Date: September 29, 2009

(A)

(1) On August 11, Jeff Hannahan, discovered that Kevin Sable had erroneously marked leave-earlies on the first shift logsheet as "1" instead of "3" for forklift operators Gonzales and Reed. (2) This resulted in deposits into the selector's V-time bank accounts of 150 minutes and 120 minutes respectively. (3) Further investigation discovered that Gonzales and Reed had been given more than 18,000 minutes of unauthorized V-time between them. (4) It was also discovered by Human Resources that each of them had withdrawn all of that time out of their accounts. (5) That adds up to nearly 2 weeks of stolen vacation time.

(B)

(6) There is no doubt that Gonzales and Reed been aware that they were being awarded unauthorized V-time every time they took a leave-early. (7) Termination hearings were quickly scheduled, but it was then discovered that other employees had been erroneously awarded V-time as well. (8) Between January 2 and August 8, 2009, twenty-three warehousemen on the first shift had been given more than 125,000 minutes in unearned V-time. (9) The termination hearings have been postponed definitely until a course of action can be determined.

(C)

(10) Clearly, disciplinary action needs to be taken, but Charlie Sanderson has failed to pursue the matter from a punitive standpoint. (11) Seven of the warehousemen are not selectors and therefore have very little opportunity to work-off their debt. (12) His decision to require the warehousemen to repay the V-time at their own pace is flawed at best. (13) The only way they can do this is to select on overtime, and if they choose to walk, they will never have to repay their debt according to Charlie's decision.

(D)

(14) Please be advised as to how we can compel the warehousemen to put the illegally-awarded V-time back into their accounts in a timely manner.

GO ON TO THE NEXT PAGE

Writing, Part I

1. Sentence 1: **On August 11, Jeff Hannahan, discovered that Kevin Sable had erroneously marked leave-earlies on the first shift logsheet as "1" instead of "3" for forklift operators Gonzales and Reed.**

Which is the best way to write the underlined portion of this sentence? If the original is the best way, choose option (1).

(1) Hannahan, discovered that
(2) Hannahan, discovers that
(3) Hannahan discovered that
(4) Hannahan, discovering that
(5) Hannahan discovers that

2. Sentence 2: **This resulted in deposits into the selector's V-time bank accounts of 150 minutes and 120 minutes respectively.**

Which correction should be made to sentence 2?

(1) change resulted to results
(2) change the to their
(3) delete respectively
(4) change into to among
(5) change selector's to selectors'

3. Sentence 3: **Further investigation discovered that Gonzales and Reed had been given more than 18,000 minutes of unauthorized V-time between them.**

Which is the best way to write the underlined portion of this sentence? If the original is the best way, choose option (1).

(1) Further investigation discovered
(2) Farther investigation discovered
(3) Further investigation revealed
(4) Further investigations discover
(5) Furthermore, investigation discovered

4. Sentence 4: **It was also discovered by Human Resources that each of them had withdrawn all of that time out of their accounts.**

If you rewrote sentence 4 beginning with Human Resources the next words should be

(1) also have been finding
(2) as well discovered
(3) was discovered to have
(4) later discovers
(5) also discovered

5. Sentence 6: **There is no doubt that Gonzales and Reed been aware that they were being awarded unauthorized V-time every time they took a leave-early.**

Which is the best way to write the underlined portion of this sentence? If the original is the best way, choose option (1).

(1) been aware
(2) were aware
(3) had awareness
(4) were being aware
(5) being aware

6. Sentence 9: **The termination hearings have been postponed definitely until a course of action can be determined.**

Which correction should be made to sentence 9?

(1) replace have been to were
(2) change definitely to indefinitely
(3) change hearings to hearing
(4) replace postponed to delayed
(5) change postponed to postpone

GO ON TO THE NEXT PAGE

The memorandum is repeated for your use in answering the remaining questions.

Emory Distribution, LLC
26500 Plymouth Rd.
Livonia, MI 48150
313-555-6700

MEMORANDUM

From: Janet Margarito, Senior Manager, Human Resources
To: Vero Massitti, President, Warehousing Division
Subject: Theft of Vacation Time
Date: September 29, 2009

(A)

(1) On August 11, Jeff Hannahan, discovered that Kevin Sable had erroneously marked leave-earlies on the first shift logsheet as "1" instead of "3" for forklift operators Gonzales and Reed. (2) This resulted in deposits into the selector's V-time bank accounts of 150 minutes and 120 minutes respectively. (3) Further investigation discovered that Gonzales and Reed had been given more than 18,000 minutes of unauthorized V-time between them. (4) It was also discovered by Human Resources that each of them had withdrawn all of that time out of their accounts. (5) That adds up to nearly 2 weeks of stolen vacation time.

(B)

(6) There is no doubt that Gonzales and Reed been aware that they were being awarded unauthorized V-time every time they took a leave-early. (7) Termination hearings were quickly scheduled, but it was then discovered that other employees had been erroneously awarded V-time as well. (8) Between January 2 and August 8, 2009, twenty-three warehousemen on the first shift had been given more than 125,000 minutes in unearned V-time. (9) The termination hearings have been postponed definitely until a course of action can be determined.

(C)

(10) Clearly, disciplinary action needs to be taken, but Charlie Sanderson has failed to pursue the matter from a punitive standpoint. (11) Seven of the warehousemen are not selectors and therefore have very little opportunity to work-off their debt. (12) His decision to require the warehousemen to repay the V-time at their own pace is flawed at best. (13) The only way they can do this is to select on overtime, and if they choose to walk, they will never have to repay their debt according to Charlie's decision.

(D)

(14) Please be advised as to how we can compel the warehousemen to put the illegally-awarded V-time back into their accounts in a timely manner.

GO ON TO THE NEXT PAGE

7. Sentence 11: **Seven of the warehousemen are not selectors and therefore have very little opportunity to work-off their debt.**

   Which revision should be made to sentence 11?

   (1) change are not to aren't
   (2) replace little with few
   (3) change opportunity to opportunities
   (4) change work-off to work off
   (5) no correction is necessary

8. Sentence 14: **Please be advised as to how we can compel the warehousemen to put the illegally-awarded V-time back into their accounts in a timely manner.**

   Which correction should be made to sentence 14?

   (1) change illegally awarded to legally awarding
   (2) change their accounts to they're accounts
   (3) change be advised to advise
   (4) change illegally-awarded to illegally award
   (5) change be advised to advice

9. Which revision would improve the effectiveness of the memorandum?

   (1) switch sentences 11 and 12
   (2) put sentence 6 at the end of the memorandum
   (3) join paragraphs A and B
   (4) put sentence 14 at the beginning of the memorandum
   (5) delete sentence 14

GO ON TO THE NEXT PAGE

Questions 10 through 17 refer to the following informational article.

Was There an Adam and Eve?

(A)

(1) Is there scientific evidence that humans are descended from single man and woman? (2) There is evidence, that points to that possibility. (3) First, geneticists have uncovered evidence in mitochondrial DNA that suggests a population bottleneck that occurred approximately 75,000 years ago. (4) According to the DNA studies, there may have been less than 2,000 humans alive at that time. (5) This evidence dovetails with discoveries made by geologists showing that a massive supervolcano, or caldera, erupted approximately 75,000 years ago, likely causing mass extinctions.

(B)

(6) While evidence of a population bottleneck is strong, it does not prove that there was an Adam and Eve as is told in the story of Genesis in the Judeo-Christian Bible. (7) For farther compelling evidence, we go back to the DNA drawing board.

(C)

(8) All great apes—the orangutan, the chimpanzee, the bonobo and the gorilla—all have 24 pairs of chromosomes. (9) Humans have 23. (10) If apes and humans were descended from a common ancestor as is currently accepted theory in the scientific community. (11) How then, did the chromosome count go from 24 to 23? (12) The answer lies in human chromosome #2. (13) This may have been the event that brought humans to the brink of extinction.

(D)

(14) Ape chromosomes 12 and 13 match band-for-band with human chromosome 2. (15) This points to a single event in which ape chromosomes 12 and 13 fused to form human chromosome 2. (16) If true, the implication is that two apes gave birth to the first human. (17) While this theory is still in its infancy and more research needs to be done, it is fascinating to learn that Adam and Eve may have been apes.

GO ON TO THE NEXT PAGE

10. Sentence 1: **Is there scientific evidence that humans are descended from single man and woman?**

Which correction should be made to sentence 1?

(1) change descended to descend
(2) change Is there to There is
(3) change single to a single
(4) change man and woman to men and women
(5) no correction is necessary

11. Sentence 2: **There is evidence, that points to that possibility.**

Which correction should be made to sentence 2?

(1) change evidence, that points to evidence points
(2) change points to leads
(3) change that points to than points
(4) delete the comma
(5) no change is necessary

12. Sentence 4: **According to the DNA studies, there may have been less than 2,000 humans alive at that time.**

Which correction should be made to sentence 4?

(1) change studies to study
(2) change less to fewer
(3) delete the comma after studies
(4) change that to the
(5) no correction is necessary

13. Sentence 7: **For farther compelling evidence, we go back to the DNA drawing board.**

Which is the best way to write the underlined portion of this sentence? If the original is the best way, choose option 1.

(1) farther compelling evidence
(2) even compelling evidence
(3) farther compelling evidences
(4) better compelling evidence
(5) more compelling evidence

14. Sentence 8: **All great apes—the orangutan, the chimpanzee, the bonobo and the gorilla—all have 24 pairs of chromosomes.**

Which correction should be made to the sentence?

(1) no correction is necessary
(2) change all have to have
(3) delete the last comma
(4) change pairs to pair
(5) change apes to ape

15. Sentence 10: **If apes and humans were descended from a common ancestor as is currently accepted theory in the scientific community.**

Sentence 10 is

(1) a fragment
(2) a run-on
(3) a prepositional phrase
(4) an alliteration
(5) correct as written

GO ON TO THE NEXT PAGE

The informational article is repeated for your use in answering the remaining questions.

Was There an Adam and Eve?

(A)

(1) Is there scientific evidence that humans are descended from single man and woman? (2) There is evidence, that points to that possibility. (3) First, geneticists have uncovered evidence in mitochondrial DNA that suggests a population bottleneck that occurred approximately 75,000 years ago. (4) According to the DNA studies, there may have been less than 2,000 humans alive at that time. (5) This evidence dovetails with discoveries made by geologists showing that a massive supervolcano, or caldera, erupted approximately 75,000 years ago, likely causing mass extinctions.

(B)

(6) While evidence of a population bottleneck is strong, it does not prove that there was an Adam and Eve as is told in the story of Genesis in the Judeo-Christian Bible. (7) For farther compelling evidence, we go back to the DNA drawing board.

(C)

(8) All great apes—the orangutan, the chimpanzee, the bonobo and the gorilla—all have 24 pairs of chromosomes. (9) Humans have 23. (10) If apes and humans were descended from a common ancestor as is currently accepted theory in the scientific community. (11) How then, did the chromosome count go from 24 to 23? (12) The answer lies in human chromosome #2. (13) This may have been the event that brought humans to the brink of extinction.

(D)

(14) Ape chromosomes 12 and 13 match band-for-band with human chromosome 2. (15) This points to a single event in which ape chromosomes 12 and 13 fused to form human chromosome 2. (16) If true, the implication is that two apes gave birth to the first human. (17) While this theory is still in its infancy and more research needs to be done, it is fascinating to learn that Adam and Eve may have been apes.

GO ON TO THE NEXT PAGE

16. Sentence 13: **This may have been the event that brought humans to the brink of extinction.**

Which revision should be made to the placement of sentence 13?

(1) delete sentence 13
(2) move sentence 13 to the beginning of paragraph A
(3) move sentence 13 to the end of paragraph A
(4) move sentence 13 to follow sentence 4
(5) move sentence 13 to the beginning of paragraph B

17. Sentence 14: **Ape chromosomes 12 and 13 <u>match band-for-band with</u> human chromosome 2.**

Which is the best way to write the underlined portion of this sentence? If the original is the best way, choose option (1).

(1) match band-for-band with
(2) match band for band with
(3) match band for band-width
(4) match band-for-band on
(5) match band for band in

GO ON TO THE NEXT PAGE

Questions 18 through 25 refer to the following informational article.

A Simple Look at Compound Interest

A

(1) Have you ever seen those bank advertisements who say "interest compounded daily"? (2) Ever wonder what it means? (3) Well here's a quick look at what compound interest is and what it means to you and your wallet.

B

(4) The definition of compound interest is really quiet simple. (5) It's interest on interest. (6) Here's how it works. (7) At 5% interest, $100 put in the bank by you will gain 5%, or $5. (8) But when do you get that $5? (9) Well, interest is always computed on a per-year basis, so your interest would come in at the end of one year. (10) What if you take your money out after 6 months? (11) Will you get $2.50? (12) Not if the interest is compounded daily.

C

(13) When banks compound interest daily they take the percentage and divide it by 365 days. (14) In this scenario, 5% on $100 comes out to about 01.37¢ per day. (15) You might ask, "how can I get one-third of a penny?" (16) Well you can't, and that's why interest compounded daily doesn't work well for the consumer. (17) It's just something the banks put in their ads to make their deals looking good. (18) That money can go a long way for a dozen corporate executives whose bonuses are based on that daily compounding.

D

(19) But interest compounded daily works great for credit card companies (which owned the same banks that "give" you interest compounded daily). (20) If you multiply that one-third of a penny by 10 billion dollars you get—let's do the math—33 MILLION DOLLARS!

GO ON TO THE NEXT PAGE

Writing, Part I

18. Question 1: **Have you ever seen those bank advertisements <u>who say</u> "interest compounded daily"?**

    Which is the best way to write the underlined portion of this sentence? If the original is the best way, choose option (1).

    (1) who say
    (2) who said
    (3) that said
    (4) that say
    (5) that says

19. Sentence 4: **The definition of compound interest is <u>really quiet simple</u>.**

    Which is the best way to write the underlined portion of sentence 4? If the original is the best way, choose option (1).

    (1) really quiet simple
    (2) really quiet and simple
    (3) really quite simple
    (4) really simply
    (5) quiet simple

20. Sentence 7: **At 5% interest, $100 put in the bank by you will gain 5%, or $5.**

    The most effective revision of sentence 7 would begin with which group of words?

    (1) If you put $100
    (2) If in the bank
    (3) With 5% gaining
    (4) Out of 5%
    (5) If 5% was interested in

21. Sentence 16: **Well you can't, and that's why interest compounded daily <u>doesn't work well</u> for the consumer.**

    Which is the best way to write the underlined portion of this sentence? If the original is the best way, choose option (1).

    (1) doesn't work well
    (2) don't work well
    (3) works well
    (4) works not well
    (5) doesn't work poorly

22. Sentence 17: **It's just something the banks put in their ads to make their deals looking good.**

    Which correction should be made to sentence 17?

    (1) change <u>something</u> to <u>some things</u>
    (2) change <u>put</u> to <u>putting</u>
    (3) change <u>make</u> to <u>making</u>
    (4) delete <u>their</u>
    (5) change <u>looking</u> to <u>look</u>

23. Sentence 18: **That money can go a long way for a dozen corporate executives whose bonuses are based on that daily compounding.**

    Which revision should be made to the placement of sentence 18?

    (1) move sentence 18 to follow sentence 16
    (2) move sentence 18 to the end of paragraph D
    (3) remove sentence 18
    (4) move sentence 18 to follow sentence 13
    (5) move sentence 18 to follow sentence 19

GO ON TO THE NEXT PAGE

The informational article is repeated for your use in answering the remaining questions.

A Simple Look at Compound Interest

A

(1) Have you ever seen those bank advertisements who say "interest compounded daily"? (2) Ever wonder what it means? (3) Well here's a quick look at what compound interest is and what it means to you and your wallet.

B

(4) The definition of compound interest is really quiet simple. (5) It's interest on interest. (6) Here's how it works. (7) At 5% interest, $100 put in the bank by you will gain 5%, or $5. (8) But when do you get that $5? (9) Well, interest is always computed on a per-year basis, so your interest would come in at the end of one year. (10) What if you take your money out after 6 months? (11) Will you get $2.50? (12) Not if the interest is compounded daily.

C

(13) When banks compound interest daily they take the percentage and divide it by 365 days. (14) In this scenario, 5% on $100 comes out to about 01.37¢ per day. (15) You might ask, "how can I get one-third of a penny?" (16) Well you can't, and that's why interest compounded daily doesn't work well for the consumer. (17) It's just something the banks put in their ads to make their deals looking good. (18) That money can go a long way for a dozen corporate executives whose bonuses are based on that daily compounding.

D

(19) But interest compounded daily works great for credit card companies (which owned the same banks that "give" you interest compounded daily). (20) If you multiply that one-third of a penny by 10 billion dollars you get—let's do the math—33 MILLION DOLLARS!

GO ON TO THE NEXT PAGE

24. Sentence 19: **But interest compounded daily works great for credit card companies (which owned the same banks that "give" you interest compounded daily).**

Which correction should be made to sentence 19?

(1) change compounded to compounds (in both instances)
(2) change great to greatly
(3) change the same to some
(4) change owned to are owned by
(5) delete card

25. Sentence 20: **If you multiply that one-third by 10 billion dollars you get—let's do the math—33 MILLION DOLLARS!**

Which revision should be made to this sentence? If the original is the best way, choose option (1).

(1) no revision necessary
(2) change multiply to multiplies
(3) replace one-third with percentages
(4) change billion to billions
(5) change multiply to multiplying

GO ON TO LANGUAGE ARTS, WRITING, PART II

DO NOT MARK OR WRITE ON THIS PAGE

LANGUAGE ARTS, WRITING, PART II

Tests of General Educational Development

Essay Directions and Topic

Look at the box on page 220. In the box are your assigned topic and the letter of that topic.

You must write on the assigned topic **ONLY**.

Mark the letter of your assigned topic in the appropriate space on your answer sheet booklet. Be certain that all other requested information is properly recorded in your answer sheet booklet.

You will have 45 minutes to write on your assigned essay topic. You may return to the multiple-choice section after you complete your essay if you have time remaining in this test period. Do not return the Language Arts, Writing booklet until you finish both Parts I and II of the Language Arts, Writing Test.

Two evaluators will score your essay according to its overall effectiveness. Their evaluation will be based on the following features:

- Well-focused main points
- Clear organization
- Specific development of your ideas
- Control of sentence structure, punctuation, grammar, word choice, and spelling

REMEMBER, YOU MUST COMPLETE BOTH THE MULTIPLE-CHOICE QUESTIONS (PART I) and THE ESSAY (PART II) TO RECEIVE A SCORE ON THE LANGUAGE ARTS, WRITING TEST. To avoid having to repeat both parts of the test, be sure to observe the following rules.

- Do not leave the pages blank.
- Write legibly in ink so that the evaluators will be able to read your writing.
- Write on the assigned topic. If you write on a topic other than the one assigned, you will not receive a score for the Language Arts, Writing Test.
- Write your essay on the lined pages of the separate answer sheet booklet. Only the writing on these pages will be scored.

IMPORTANT:
You may return to the multiple-choice section after you complete your essay if you have time remaining in this test period. Do not return the Language Arts, Writing booklet until you finish both Parts I and II of the Language Arts, Writing Test.

Writing, Part II

Topic E

All's fair in love and war.

In your essay, give an example of the suit making the man. Explain what this saying means in your view. Use your personal observations, experience, and knowledge to support your essay.

Part II is a test to determine how well you can use written language to explain your ideas.

In preparing your essay, you should take the following steps.

- Read the **DIRECTIONS** and the **TOPIC** carefully.
- Plan your essay before you write. Use the scratch paper provided to make any notes. These notes will be collected but not scored.
- Before you turn in your essay, reread what you have written and make any changes that will improve your essay.

Your essay should be long enough to develop the topic adequately.

END OF EXAMINATION

SOCIAL STUDIES

Tests of General Educational Development

Directions

The Social Studies Test consists of multiple-choice questions intended to measure understanding of general social studies concepts. The questions are based on short readings that often include a map, graph, chart, cartoon, or figure. Study the information given and then answer the question(s) following it. Refer to the information as often as necessary in answering the questions.

You should spend no more than 45 minutes answering the questions in this booklet. Work carefully, but do not spend too much time on any one question. Be sure you answer every question.

Do not mark in this test booklet. Record your answers on the separate answer sheet provided. Be sure that all requested information is properly recorded on the answer sheet.

To record your answers, mark the numbered space on the answer sheet beside the number that corresponds to the question in the test booklet.

FOR EXAMPLE:

Early colonists of North America looked for settlement sites with adequate water supplies and access by ship. For this reason, many early towns were built near

(1) mountains
(2) prairies
(3) rivers
(4) glaciers
(5) plateaus

The correct answer is "rivers"; therefore, answer space 3 would be marked on the answer sheet.

Do not rest the point of your pencil on the answer sheet while you are considering your answer. Make no stray or unnecessary marks. If you change an answer, erase your first mark completely. Mark only <u>one</u> answer space for each question; multiple answers will be scored as incorrect. Do not fold or crease your answer sheet. All test materials must be returned to the test administrator.

GO ON TO THE NEXT PAGE

Social Studies

Directions: Choose the one best answer to each question.

Questions 1 through 3 refer to the following graph.

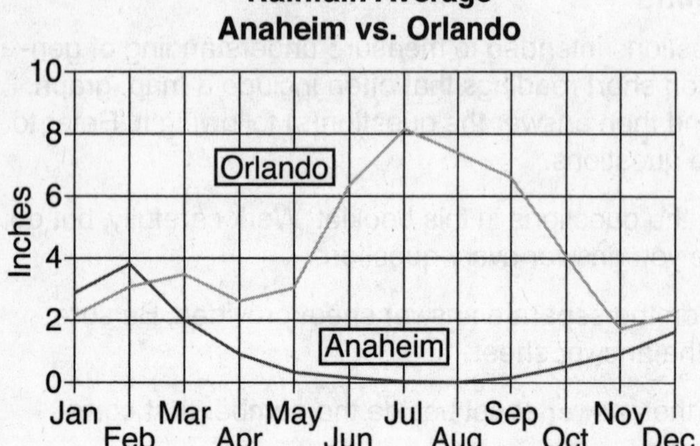

1. Based on the information in the graph, which statement best describes the relationship between rainfall in Anaheim and rainfall in Orlando?

   (1) Rainfall in Anaheim is caused by the rainfall in Orlando.
   (2) Whereas rainfall in Anaheim peaks during summer months, rainfall in Orlando drops.
   (3) Whereas rainfall in Orlando peaks in winter months, rainfall in Anaheim peaks in summer months.
   (4) In both Anaheim and Orlando, rainfall averages between 1 and 4 inches during winter months.
   (5) In both Anaheim and Orlando, rainfall averages between 4 and 8 inches during summer months.

2. Based on the graph, which season produces the most rainfall?

   (1) winter in Anaheim
   (2) winter in Orlando
   (3) spring in Anaheim
   (4) fall in Anaheim
   (5) summer in Orlando

3. Which sector of the economy would be most affected by unusually high amounts of rainfall?

   (1) the automobile industry
   (2) agriculture
   (3) international trade
   (4) the banking industry
   (5) the publishing industry

4. What is the period of tension and conflict between capitalist and communist nations from the mid-1940s to the early 1990s commonly known as?

   (1) the Cold War
   (2) World War II
   (3) the Korean War
   (4) the War on Terror
   (5) the Vietnam War

GO ON TO THE NEXT PAGE

Question 5 refers to the following political cartoon published by Thomas Nast about William "Boss" Tweed.

THE "BRAINS"

That achieved the Tammany Victory at the Rochester Democratic Convention.

5. Which statement best describes the main point of the cartoon?

(1) Wealthy people should not run for political office.
(2) Money cannot ensure victory in political contests.
(3) It was money, not "brains," that led to political victory.
(4) "Boss" Tweed has done a good job of raising funds for the government.
(5) "Brains" do not help win presidential elections.

6. All of the following are examples of major sources of fuel during the last century **EXCEPT**

(1) coal
(2) oil
(3) natural gas
(4) nuclear power
(5) hydrogen

Questions 7 through 9 refer to the following excerpt from President George Washington's "Farewell Address."

"I have already intimated to you the danger of parties in the state, with particular reference to the founding of them on geographical discriminations. Let me now take a more comprehensive view, and warn you in the most solemn manner against the baneful effects of the spirit of party, generally.

"...the common and continual mischiefs of the spirit of party are sufficient to make it the interest and duty of a wise people to discourage and restrain it."

7. Which statement best describes President Washington's main point in this excerpt?

(1) The United States should not enter into too many foreign alliances.
(2) The will of the people must be allowed through universal suffrage.
(3) Political parties are necessary and vital to democracy.
(4) The currency of the United States should not be based on a gold standard.
(5) Political parties are destructive to democracy.

GO ON TO THE NEXT PAGE

8. Based on the information in the excerpt, which development would have troubled President Washington the most?

   (1) the expansion of presidential powers in the twentieth century
   (2) the Treaty of Versailles
   (3) the power of lobbyists in Washington, DC
   (4) the development of competing political parties
   (5) long and expensive political campaigns

9. Why was President Washington concerned with the role of "geographical discriminations" in the political process?

   (1) Discrimination is morally wrong in all forms.
   (2) Geographical discriminations could lead to political division among northern and southern states.
   (3) Geographical discriminations would prevent westward expansion.
   (4) Geography made no difference in American politics before the twentieth century.
   (5) Geographical discriminations could make the United States vulnerable to military attack.

10. Monarchy is the system of government in which power is vested in a single ruler, a king or queen. Which nation has never had a monarchy?

    (1) the United States of America
    (2) the United Kingdom
    (3) France
    (4) Spain
    (5) Saudi Arabia

11. Which public figure was active in helping women to establish their right to vote?

    (1) Abigail Adams
    (2) Thomas Paine
    (3) Susan B. Anthony
    (4) Thomas Jefferson
    (5) Gloria Steinem

GO ON TO THE NEXT PAGE

Questions 12 and 13 refer to the following graph.

Unemployment Rate, 1890–1923

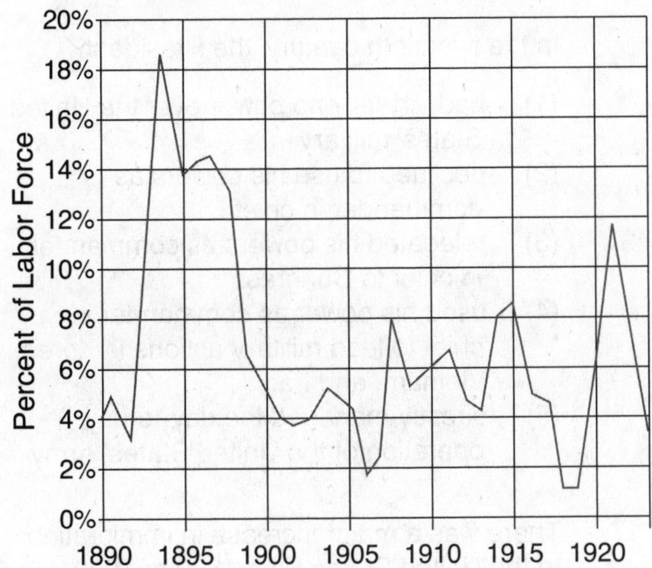

12. Which statement expresses an **OPINION,** rather than a fact, about the information presented in the graph?

(1) At no point between 1890 and 1923 did the unemployment rate exceed 25 percent.
(2) Ineffective and incompetent leadership led to increased unemployment during 1893 and 1894.
(3) The unemployment rate more than tripled between 1892 and 1895.
(4) The unemployment rate was below 10% between 1900 and 1910.
(5) The unemployment rate dropped significantly between 1895 and 1900.

13. Which statement best accounts for the decrease in the unemployment rate during 1917 and 1918?

The United States

(1) underwent a dramatic shift in economic policy during these years
(2) abolished slavery in every state
(3) entered World War I
(4) experienced major technological changes in manufacturing and agriculture
(5) suffered devastating losses in the financial markets

GO ON TO THE NEXT PAGE

Questions 14 through 16 refer to the following excerpt from the U.S. Constitution.

"The President shall be commander in chief of the Army and Navy of the United States, and of the militia of the several states, when called into the actual service of the United States; he may require the opinion, in writing, of the principal officer in each of the executive departments, upon any subject relating to the duties of their respective offices, and he shall have power to grant reprieves and pardons for offenses against the United States, except in cases of impeachment."

14. Which statement describes the presidential powers listed in this section of the Constitution?

The President is

(1) required to seek approval from Congress on numerous occasions, especially when issuing presidential pardons
(2) never allowed to commit a crime against the United States
(3) the chief diplomat of the United States and commander of the military
(4) required to be over the age of 35 and a natural-born citizen
(5) permitted to issue pardons and command the military

15. What is the purpose of "reprieves and pardons"?

Reprieves and pardons

(1) allow individuals to rewrite certain laws of the United States
(2) forgive individuals of crimes they have committed or are accused of
(3) require the deporting of guilty criminals to other countries
(4) only apply to death-penalty cases
(5) are serious limitations to presidential power

16. In the twentieth century, how important was the President's role as commander in chief in the actual management of the military?

In the twentieth century, the President

(1) had virtually no power over the United States' military
(2) declined to use his powers as commander in chief
(3) relegated his powers as commander in chief to Congress
(4) used his power as commander in chief to lead military actions in Korea, Vietnam, and Iraq
(5) directly managed the day-to-day operation of the United States' Army

17. There was a major increase in immigration to the United States from 1890 to 1920. Which statement best describes why so many Europeans left their home countries during this period?

European immigrants left Europe in order to

(1) escape poverty or persecution
(2) change American politics
(3) escape from military service at home
(4) enjoy better weather in the United States
(5) leave overcrowded European cities

GO ON TO THE NEXT PAGE

Questions 18 and 19 refer to the following map.

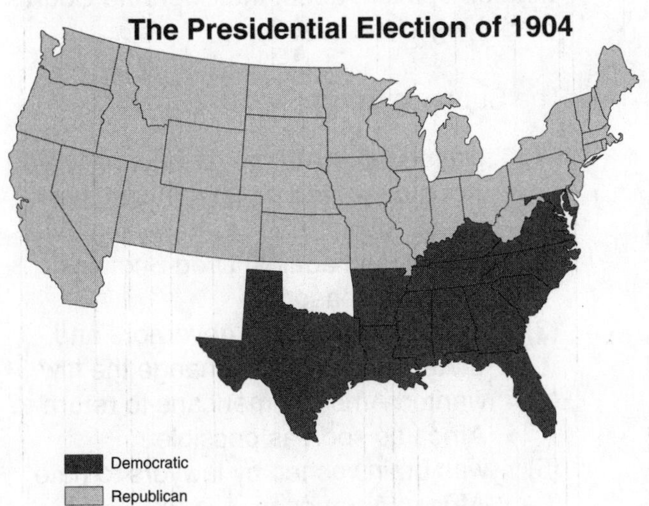

18. Which statement best describes why the breakdown of states is so important in presidential elections?

The breakdown of states is important because

(1) presidential elections are held only every four years
(2) presidents are elected by the Electoral College, not merely by popular vote
(3) individual states can veto a choice of president
(4) presidents need unanimous support from the states they win
(5) presidential campaigns are run on a state-by-state basis

19. The map verifies which claim about American politics?

(1) Southern states have always voted Democrat.
(2) Democrats and Republicans have never agreed about how to run government.
(3) Political parties tend to split along geographic boundaries.
(4) Theodore Roosevelt should never have been elected president.
(5) Western states tend to vote the same way as Southern states.

Questions 20 and 21 refer to the following map.

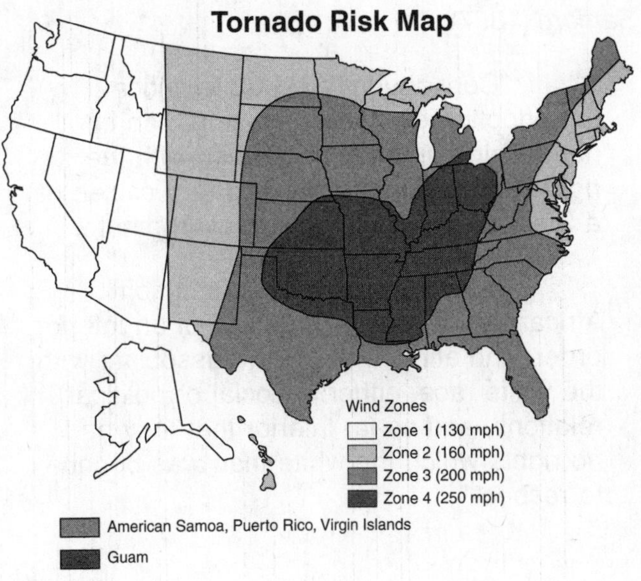

20. According to the map, which region is most in danger of tornadoes?

(1) the West Coast
(2) New England
(3) the Southeast
(4) the Midwest
(5) the Southwest

21. Which statement best describes why tornadoes are considered natural disasters?

(1) Tornadoes damage more area than do earthquakes and hurricanes.
(2) Tornadoes are often caused by natural fires.
(3) Tornadoes create extremely powerful winds that destroy personal property and threaten lives.
(4) Tornadoes pose little threat to individual safety.
(5) Tornadoes have destroyed several major American cities.

GO ON TO THE NEXT PAGE

Questions 22 and 23 refer to the following excerpt from the Supreme Court decision *Dred Scott v. Sanford* (1857).

> "Consequently, no State, since the adoption of the Constitution, can by naturalizing an alien invest him with the rights and privileges secured to a citizen of a State under the Federal Government...
>
> [According to the Constitution, African Americans are] beings of an inferior order, and altogether unfit to associate with the white race, either in social or political relations, and so far inferior that they had no rights which the white man was bound to respect."

22. What does this decision claim about American citizenship?

American citizens

(1) must be born in the continental United States
(2) cannot speak any language other than English at home
(3) have special rights that non-citizens cannot possess
(4) should be denied his rights and privileges if he violates the law
(5) can include members of any race

23. Which statement expresses a **FACT,** rather than an opinion, about the Supreme Court's reasoning in the case?

The Supreme Court

(1) claimed that African Americans were not guaranteed equal rights in the Constitution
(2) was biased against Dred Scott for personal reasons
(3) feared the power of governors and state legislatures to change the law
(4) wanted African Americans to return to Africa as soon as possible
(5) was brainwashed by lawyers to hate African Americans

GO ON TO THE NEXT PAGE

24. The North American Free Trade Agreement (NAFTA) was created to facilitate trade among Canada, the United States, and Mexico. Which of the following statements is true of NAFTA?

NAFTA

(1) unified all of the countries of the Western Hemisphere
(2) was a secret alliance formed against Communist nations
(3) had no impact on trade and development in the three countries
(4) faced no political controversy in the United States
(5) allowed for easier trade among the nations of North America

25. President John Adams once wrote that "the proposition that the people are the best keepers of their own liberties is not true. They are the worst conceivable, they are no keepers at all; they can neither judge, act, think, or will, as a political body." Which statement best describes his main point?

(1) There should be no governments.
(2) Governments are ineffective at controlling unruly people.
(3) People undermine their own freedoms and liberties.
(4) Liberty should not be given to all.
(5) People will always despise governments.

END OF EXAMINATION

DO NOT MARK OR WRITE ON THIS PAGE

SCIENCE

Tests of General Educational Development

Directions

The Science Test consists of multiple-choice questions intended to measure understanding of general concepts in science. The questions are based on short readings that often include a graph, chart, or figure. Study the information given and then answer the question(s) following it. Refer to the information as often as necessary in answering the questions.

You should spend no more than 53 minutes answering the questions in this booklet. Work carefully, but do not spend too much time on any one question. Be sure you answer every question.

Do not mark in this test booklet. Record your answers to the questions on the separate sheet provided. Be sure all requested information is properly recorded on the answer sheet.

To record your answers, mark the numbered space on the answer sheet beside the number that corresponds to the question in the test booklet.

FOR EXAMPLE:

Which of the following is the smallest unit in a living thing?

(1) tissue
(2) organ
(3) cell
(4) muscle
(5) capillary

The correct answer is "cell"; therefore, answer space 3 would be marked on the answer sheet.

Do not rest the point of your pencil on the answer sheet while you are considering your answer. Make no stray or unnecessary marks. If you change an answer, erase your first mark completely. Mark only <u>one</u> answer space for each question; multiple answers will be scored as incorrect. Do not fold or crease your answer sheet. All test materials must be returned to the test administrator.

GO ON TO THE NEXT PAGE

Directions: Choose the one best answer to each question.

1. A species is a group of organisms that can and do mate with each other to produce living, fertile offspring. Speciation is the formation of a new species. The process usually occurs as a result of evolution over many generations.

   Based on the information, which of the following is an example of speciation?

   (1) horses and donkeys mate to produce mules, which are sterile
   (2) scientists create hybrid vegetables that do not contain seeds
   (3) peaches and nectarines belong to the same species and grow on the same trees
   (4) a pet owner decides to get her cat spayed so that it can no longer reproduce
   (5) an earthquake splits a forest in half, and after 100 years, the squirrels on one side of the forest have changed so much that they can no longer mate with squirrels from the other side

2. Plants require nitrogen compounds in the soil in order to grow. Most plants drain the soil of nitrogen and over time will not be able to grow in the same area. However, legumes, such as peas, beans, alfalfa, and clover, have bacteria in their root nodules that release usable nitrogen back into the soil. If legumes are grown among other crops, the other crops with get the nitrogen they need and will survive for many seasons.

   The above information answers which of the following questions?

   (1) Which legumes provide the most nitrogen?
   (2) In which climates do legumes grow best?
   (3) What role do insecticides play in agriculture?
   (4) How does nitrogen help plants to grow?
   (5) Why do many farmers plant peas in the same fields as their other crops?

3. Which of the following observations about the universe is accurate?

   (1) Systems tend to become more ordered over time.
   (2) Collisions always result in molecules being split.
   (3) Inertia does not affect solid objects.
   (4) All liquids behave in the same manner.
   (5) Energy is never created or destroyed.

4. When white light, such as that from sunlight, contacts a surface, some of the light is reflected and some of the light energy is absorbed. The absorbed energy may be converted into other types of energy, such as heat, chemical energy, or electrical energy.

   Based on this information, why do many people in warm climates choose to wear light colors in the summer?

   Because light colors

   (1) attract energy
   (2) convert light into heat
   (3) convert light into chemical energy
   (4) reflect light
   (5) convert light into electricity

GO ON TO THE NEXT PAGE

5. Water is constantly being naturally recycled on Earth. Below is a picture of the water cycle, which depicts the natural processes that affect the flow of water.

Water Cycle

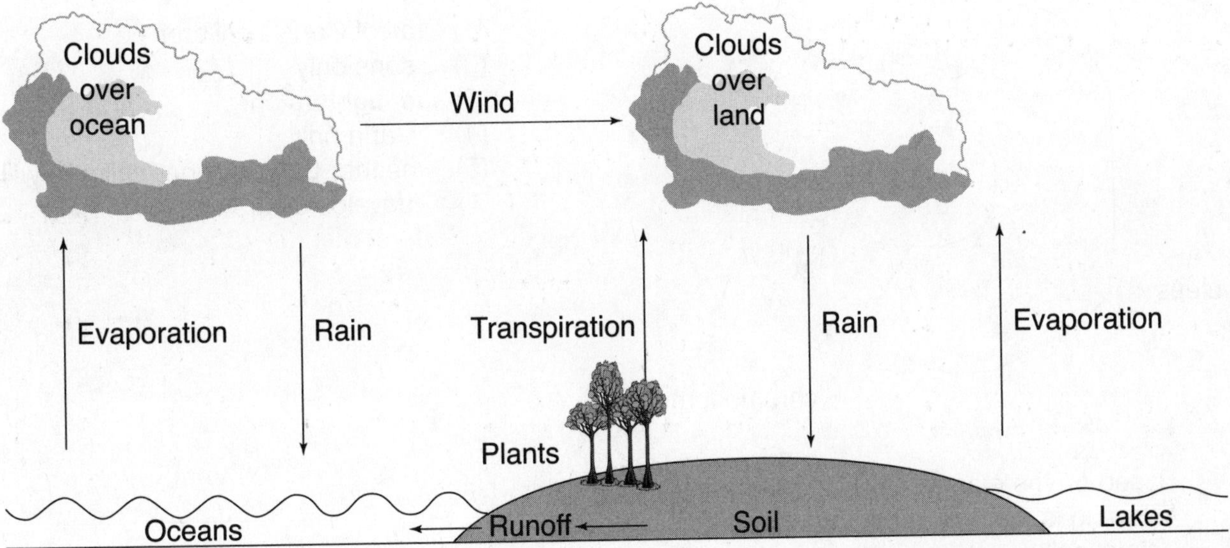

Based on the figure, which of the following processes deliver water to clouds?

(1) evaporation only
(2) evaporation and transpiration
(3) transpiration only
(4) precipitation only
(5) evaporation and precipitation

6. The figure below shows a man on a motorcycle driving through an inverted loop.

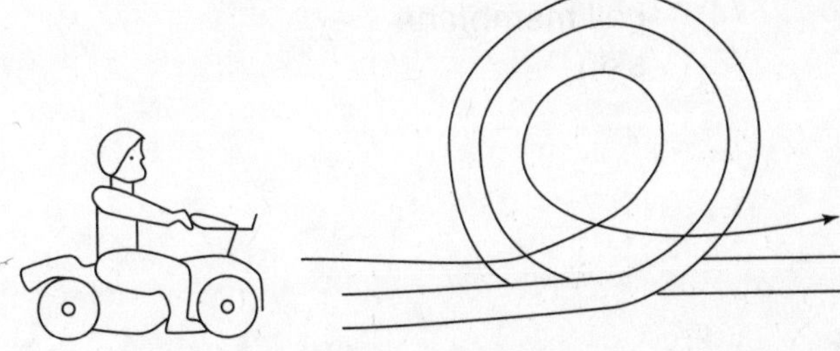

Which of the following factors allows the driver the ride upside-down without falling?

(1) gravity of the sun
(2) gravity of the earth
(3) centripetal acceleration
(4) heat
(5) magnetic attraction

GO ON TO THE NEXT PAGE

7. All living things are made up of cells. Below is a diagram representing an animal cell and some of the structures that make up the cell.

Animal Cell

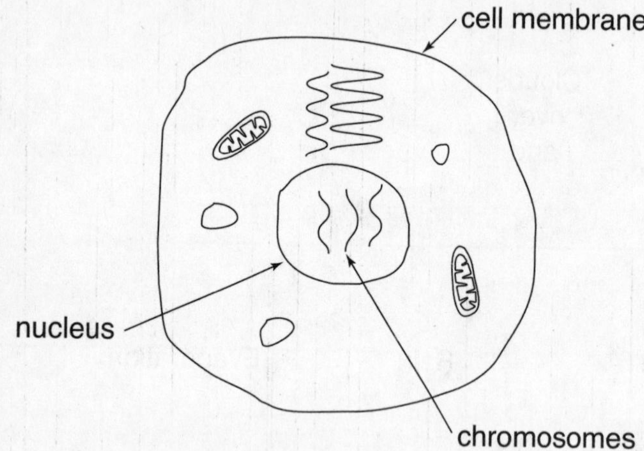

Based on the diagram, which of the following is the outermost structure of an animal cell?

(1) nucleus
(2) cell wall
(3) bacteria
(4) cell membrane
(5) skin

8. Carla carries a gene for a disease that can only affect males. Although Carla is not affected by the disease, her future children may be.

Which of Carla's future children might develop symptoms of this disease?

(1) all of Carla's children
(2) sons only
(3) daughters only
(4) Carla only
(5) neither Carla nor her children will develop symptoms

GO ON TO THE NEXT PAGE

Questions 9 and 10 refer to the following information.

Chromosomes come in pairs and contain genes, which code for inherited traits. If a gene is always expressed when present, it is called dominant and is represented by a capital letter. A dominant gene will be expressed whether an individual is pure and has two copies of the dominant gene or is hybrid and contains one dominant copy and one copy of another gene. In the case of hybrids, the dominant gene hides the expression the recessive gene. A recessive gene is only expressed when it is pure, and it is represented by a lowercase letter.

In pea plants, the gene for round pea shape is dominant and the gene for wrinkled pea shape is recessive. A plant that produces wrinkled peas must be pure for the wrinkled gene, meaning it must contain two copies of the wrinkled gene. A plant that produces round peas can either be pure for the round gene or be hybrid and have one gene for round shape and gene for wrinkled shape.

Punnett Squares are charts used to predict the odds of specific gene combinations in offspring. Below is a Punnet Square of a cross between a pea plant pure for wrinkled peas and a pea plant that produces round peas.

Punnett Square-Shape in Pea Plants

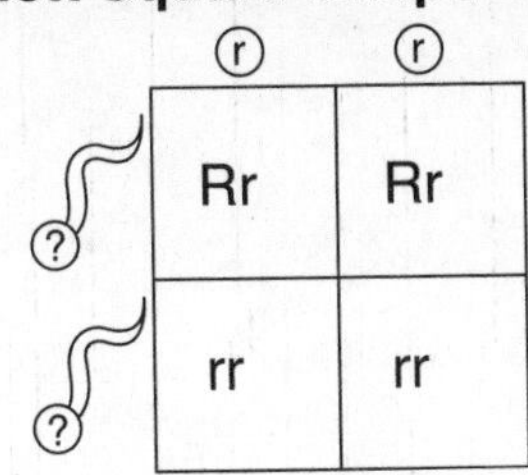

o	egg cell of female parent
∫	sperm cell of male parent
R	dominant round shape gene
r	recessive wrinkled shape gene
?	unknown gene

9. Based on the information and the Punnett Square, which of the following describes the plant that produces round peas?

(1) It is pure for the round gene.
(2) It is pure for the wrinkled gene.
(3) It is capable of producing both round and wrinkled peas
(4) It is hybrid and carries a hidden wrinkled gene
(5) It does not carry a hidden gene

10. Which of the following describes the offspring of this cross?

(1) $\frac{1}{2}$ produce round peas and $\frac{1}{2}$ produce wrinkled peas.
(2) All produce wrinkled peas.
(3) All produce round peas.
(4) $\frac{1}{2}$ produce wrinkled peas and $\frac{1}{2}$ produce both round and wrinkled peas.
(5) $\frac{1}{2}$ produce peas and $\frac{1}{2}$ do not produce peas

GO ON TO THE NEXT PAGE

11. Below is a figure of a closed container with a divider in the middle. Gas A is on the left side and Gas B is on the right.

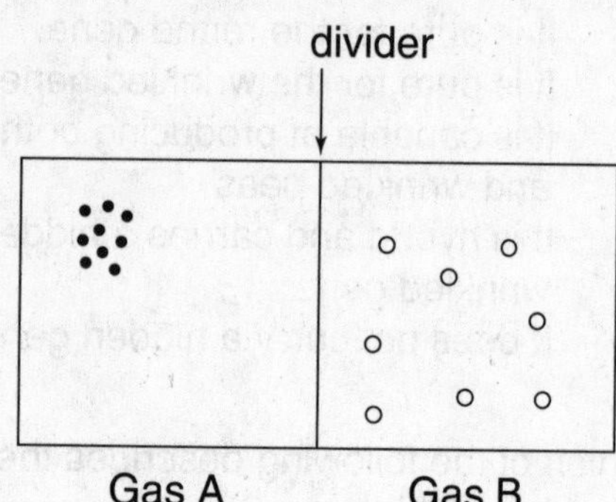

Which statement best describes the behavior of the gases after the divider is removed?

(1) Gas A will stay on the left and Bas B on the right.
(2) The gases will switch places.
(3) Gas A will evaporate, leaving only gas B.
(4) The gases will mix until they are evenly dispersed.
(5) Gas B will convert into Gas A.

12. Mass is a measure of the amount of matter in an object. Weight is determined by multiplying mass by downward forces on that object, such as gravity. The moon has less gravity than the earth. Based on the information, which of the following is true?

(1) A person would weigh the same on the moon as on Earth.
(2) A person would weigh more on Earth than on the moon.
(3) A person would weight more on the moon than on Earth.
(4) A person would have less mass on the moon than on Earth.
(5) A person would have less mass on Earth than on the moon.

13. Habituation is a type of learning in which an animal gets accustomed to a certain stimulus and over time ignores it. For example, worms usually curl up when poked, but if a worm is poked over and over again without being harmed, that worm will learn to ignore the poking and will not curl up.

Which of the following is an example of habituation?

(1) A girl studies hard in school because she likes to earn good grades.
(2) A cat is trained to use a litter box.
(3) A dolphin recognizes its reflection in a mirror.
(4) A man who moves near an airport initially wakes up when he hears a plane landing, but over time he is able to sleep through the noise without being disturbed.
(5) A young boy learns to behave well because he is placed in time-out when he misbehaves.

GO ON TO THE NEXT PAGE

14. The internal resistance of a fluid to flow is known as viscosity. For example, maple syrup is more viscous than water. The temperature affects the viscosity of the fluid. The graph below shows how temperature affects a certain liquid.

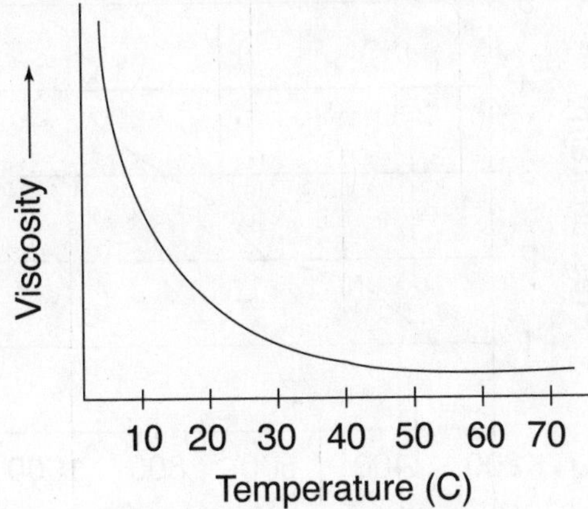

Under which condition will the viscosity of the liquid decrease?

(1) as its volume increases
(2) as its flow decreases
(3) as it is heated
(4) when it is stirred
(5) when it is in an enclosed container

15. Kinetic and potential represent all types of

(1) energy in the universe
(2) collisions in the universe
(3) inertia in the universe
(4) gravity in the universe
(5) matter in the universe

16. The figure below shows a bottle filled with equal amounts oil and water.

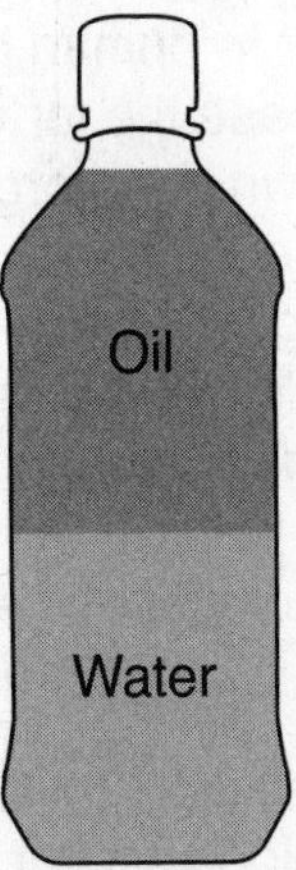

If this bottle is shaken and the contents are allowed to settle, which statement will best describe the content of the bottle?

(1) The oil will be on top and the water on bottom.
(2) The water will be on top and the oil on bottom.
(3) The water and oil will be side-by-side.
(4) The oil and water will be evenly mixed.
(5) The water will evaporate, leaving on the oil.

GO ON TO THE NEXT PAGE

17. Earthworms are very interesting creatures. They have both male and female reproductive systems, five hearts, and blood similar to human blood. Earthworms greatly increase the fertility of soil by breaking down dead organic matter and releasing useful compounds into the soil. By burrowing, earthworms also pull surface material underground and provide space underground for air and water to circulate.

Which characteristic of earthworms is most important in improving a farm environment?

(1) increase soil fertility
(2) have blood similar to human blood
(3) have male and female reproductive parts
(4) have five hearts
(5) eat insects that destroy plants

18. Gay-Lussac's law explains the behavior of gases when temperature is changed. That law states that, if volume remains constant, pressure will increase as temperature increases. Below is a graph illustrating Gay-Lussac's law for one gas.

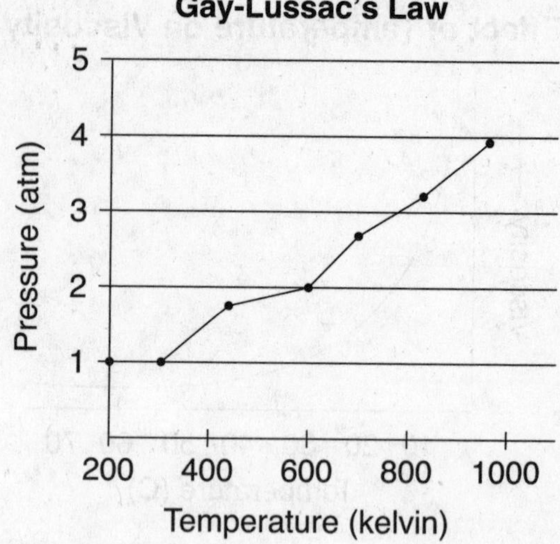

Which statement describes the behavior of the gas in the graph?

(1) As the temperature rises from 800 to 1000 Kelvin, the pressure rises from 3 to 4 atmospheres.
(2) Kelvin is a measure of the volume of the gas.
(3) If the trend in the graph continues, when the temperature reaches 1200 Kelvin the pressure will be near 1 atm.
(4) As the temperature rises, the pressure falls.
(5) As the temperature rises from 600 to 800 Kelvin, the pressure rises from 1 atmospheres to 3 atm.

GO ON TO THE NEXT PAGE

19. The periodic table lists information about all the known elements in the world. There are some trends with the properties of the elements. For example, atomic radius increases from right to left and from top to bottom. Atomic radius is a measure of the size of one atom. Below is a figure that shows this trend.

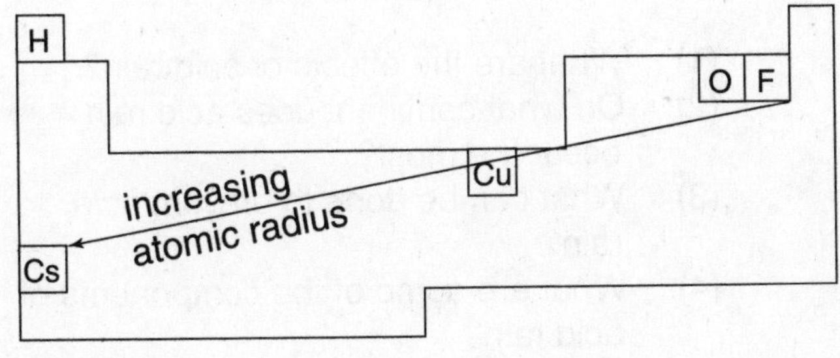

Cs Cesium
Cu Copper
F Flourine
H Hydrogen
O Oxygen

Based on the information and the figure, which of the following has the largest atomic radius?

(1) Cesium
(2) Copper
(3) Fluorine
(4) Hydrogen
(5) Oxygen

Questions 20 and 21

The three phases of matter are solid, liquid, and gas. A change from one to another is called a phase change. Below is a diagram showing the temperature and pressure for different phase changes for substance y.

Phase Change Diagram for Substance y

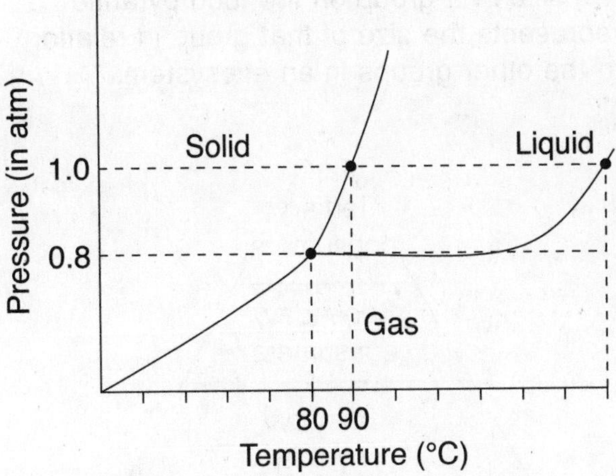

20. Which is a phase change that can happen at temperature of 90 degrees and pressure of 1 atm?

(1) condensation
(2) evaporation
(3) melting
(4) vaporization
(5) sublimation

21. At 1 atm and 100 degrees, substance y will be

(1) solid
(2) liquid
(3) gas
(4) evaporating
(5) freezing

GO ON TO THE NEXT PAGE

Questions 22 and 23

Different organisms get food from different sources. Producers make their own food, and primary consumers eat the producers. Secondary consumers eat the primary consumers and sometimes the producers as well, and tertiary consumers eat the secondary consumers. The picture below summarizes is called a food pyramid. The size of a group on the food pyramid represents the size of that group in relation to the other groups in an ecosystem.

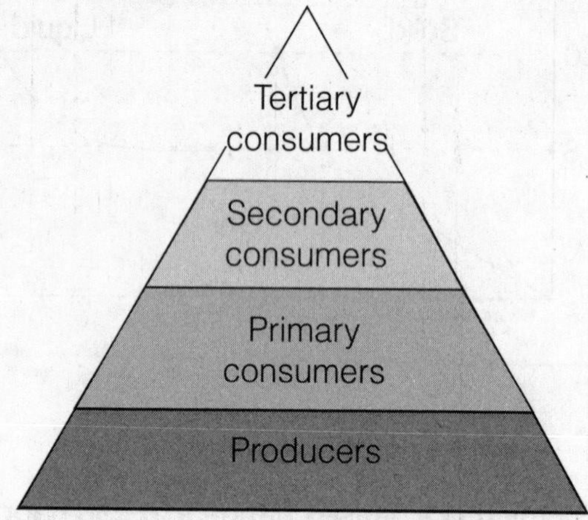

22. Which of the following would be present in the greatest numbers in an ecosystem?

(1) tertiary consumers
(2) secondary consumers
(3) primary consumers
(4) producers
(5) all are present in equal amounts.

23. Which of the following is most likely a producer?

(1) bird
(2) tree
(3) worm
(4) lion
(5) lizard

24. When coal and oil are burned, a chemical called sulfur dioxide is formed. Sulfur dioxide can interact with the ozone to form SO_3, which reacts with water to form sulfuric acid. The result of water contaminated with sulfuric acid is acid rain.

The information above answers which of the following questions?

(1) What are the effects of acid rain?
(2) On what continent does acid rain occur the most?
(3) What can be done to prevent acid rain?
(4) What are some of the components of acid rain?
(5) For how long has acid rain been a problem?

25. Properly digesting food has many steps, including chewing, swallowing, churning in the stomach, secretion of digestive enzymes, and absorption of nutrients. Which of the components of digested mentioned above are not under conscious control?

(1) chewing only
(2) churning in the stomach only
(3) absorption of nutrients only
(4) secretion of digestive enzymes only
(5) churning in the stomach, secretion of digestive enzymes, and absorption of nutrients

END OF EXAMINATION

LANGUAGE ARTS, READING

Tests of General Educational Development

Directions

The Language Arts, Reading Test consists of excerpts from fiction and nonfiction. Each excerpt is followed by multiple-choice questions about the reading material.

Read each excerpt first and then answer the questions following it. Refer back to the reading material as often as necessary in answering the questions.

Each excerpt is preceded by a "purpose question." The purpose question gives a reason for reading the material. Use these purpose questions to help focus your reading. You are not required to answer these purpose questions. They are given only to help you concentrate on the ideas presented in the reading material.

You should spend no more than 35 minutes answering the questions in this booklet. Work carefully, but do not spend too much time on any one question. Be sure you answer every question.

Do not mark in this test booklet. Record your answers on the separate answer sheet provided. Be sure that all requested information is properly recorded on the answer sheet.

To record your answers, mark the numbered space on the answer sheet beside the number that corresponds to the question in the test booklet.

FOR EXAMPLE:

It was Susan's dream machine. The metallic blue paint gleamed, and the sporty wheels were highly polished. Under the hood, the engine was no less carefully cleaned. Inside, flashy lights illuminated the instruments on the dashboard, and the seats were covered by rich leather upholstery.

The subject ("It") of this excerpt is most likely

(1) an airplane
(2) a stereo system
(3) an automobile
(4) a boat
(5) a motorcycle

The correct answer is "an automobile"; therefore, answer space 3 would be marked on the answer sheet.

Do not rest the point of your pencil on the answer sheet while you are considering your answer. Make no stray or unnecessary marks. If you change an answer, erase your first mark completely. Mark only <u>one</u> answer space for each question; multiple answers will be scored as incorrect. Do not fold or crease your answer sheet. All test materials must be returned to the test administrator.

GO ON TO THE NEXT PAGE

Questions 1 through 5 refer to the following excerpt.

WHAT DOES THE MANAGEMENT EXECUTIVE WANT FROM HIS ORGANIZATION?

Letter to the fans of the Saskatchewan Surfdogs

Building a championship team is everyone's job.

Winning the championship is the primary goal of every team in our baseball league. Within our organization, though, we are instituting many new policies and procedures in order to improve our odds toward that endeavor significantly. We feel that every small step we take toward unifying all employees in our quest for a championship will separate us from the other teams who believe that success only happens on the field of play and miss the opportunities to gain every possible advantage. Going forward, all employees of this organization will be expected to attend training meetings and educational forums about their jobs.

Retired superstar Joe Lippanelli, who played for the Surfdogs for 11 memorable years and now manages both the team and all minor league operations, has been promoting this idea since the day he took over management of the ballclub. He even discusses this in his memoir *The Team Made Me Great*. "I know that hard work and personal talent are inseparable from what we call success," he writes. "However, in this sport, as in life, it is pointless to think that you can succeed by only pursuing solitary goals without keeping the team in mind."

Joe's belief system that he has been pushing on all his players and coaches is now infiltrating the upper management system. We are now all unified toward the same goal—winning the ultimate trophy at the end of the year. It is no longer enough to have great players and coaches like Joe on the field; we now have this same level of detail and commitment to quality throughout the entire Saskatchewan Surfdogs organization, from the ballplayers to the ushers to the hot dog sellers to the parking attendants. This coming season will see all members of the Surfdogs family looking for every small opportunity to gain an edge on the competition.

We hope you come out to many games and enjoy the success we expect to have with this new company-wide commitment to winning. As Joe likes to say, "Just one mistake may lose the game, but it takes the whole team to win."

Sincerely,

Leonard Broadnax

Managing Executive Saskatchewan Surfdogs, Inc.

GO ON TO THE NEXT PAGE

Reading

1. Why has this organization decided to change its approach to its employees?
   (1) There has been criticism of the team that has not been properly handled by upper management.
   (2) The other teams are unwilling to communicate with the Surfdogs.
   (3) It has been 11 years since the organization last won a championship.
   (4) None of the current members of the staff are familiar with championship goals.
   (5) It is believe that a new approach will increase the chances of winning a championship.

2. It can be determined from the executive's letter that he believes small efforts will help the Surfdogs' chances because other teams
   (1) will be intimidated by their success
   (2) have never won a championship
   (3) are not as well organized with their marketing schemes
   (4) miss simple chances to improve their odds of winning
   (5) have been known to focus on the big picture

3. Mr. Broadnax most likely uses retired star Joe Lippanelli's comments and books in order to
   (1) provide reader with reference to an interesting and famous person
   (2) give information supporting the organization's plans for change
   (3) use a required baseball reference in a letter to baseball fans
   (4) use the opportunity to praise a once-great baseball player
   (5) ask readers to purchase a great baseball book

4. The basic premise of the organization's new plan is primarily: by forcing all employees to seek chances for improving, no matter in which part of the business they most often work, the organization as a whole will be able to
   (1) force underperforming employees to quit
   (2) figure out who the best employees are
   (3) earn an advantage over other baseball organizations
   (4) promote the manager, Joe Lippanelli
   (5) attract younger and more enthusiastic fans

5. Based on the information in the passage, it is possible to determine the attitude of the manager. He most likely values
   (1) education more than athleticism
   (2) business work more than baseball games
   (3) teammates more than coworkers
   (4) group success more than solo achievements
   (5) bravery more than intelligence

GO ON TO THE NEXT PAGE

Questions 6 through 11 refer to the following excerpt.

WHAT DOES THE SPEAKER OF THE PASSAGE ADVISE?

If you will cling to nature, to the simplest in Nature, to the little things that hardly anyone sees, and that can so unexpectedly become so big and beyond measuring; if you have this love of inconsiderable things and seek quite simply, as one who serves, to win the confidence of what seems poor: then everything will become easier, more coherent, and somehow more conciliatory for you, not in your intellect perhaps, which lags marveling behind, but in your consciousness, waking and cognizance. You are so young, so before all beginning, and I want to beg you, as much as I can, dear sir, to be patient toward all that is unsolved in your heart and try to love the questions themselves like locked rooms and like books that are written in a very foreign tongue. Do not now seek the answers, which cannot be given you because you would not be able to live them. And the point is, to live everything. Live the questions now. Perhaps you will then, gradually, without noticing it, live along some distant day into the answer. Perhaps you do carry within yourself the possibility of shaping and forming as a particularly happy way of living; train yourself to it—but take whatever comes with great trust, and if only it comes out of your own will, out of some need in your inmost being, take it upon yourself and hate nothing. Almost everything serious is difficult; and everything is serious.

6. This passage comes from a letter of advice written to a young man who is a writer. It comes from an older man who is also a writer. The speaker (the older man) probably wrote this letter in order to

(1) share the rules of writing that all writers follow
(2) introduce the young man to a new style of literature
(3) share information that was earned through a lifetime of writing
(4) prevent the young man from making the mistake of choosing a writing career
(5) warn the young man that questions are serious and trust is dangerous

7. The speaker in this passage refers to a "love of inconsiderable things" (line 5–6). This refers to his belief that

(1) the things usually considered small in life actually have great importance
(2) people should not consider the small things in life unless they can become famous
(3) people should spend most of their attention on people who are usually ignored
(4) though inconsiderate people may be rude, they still require love from others
(5) inconsiderable things are usually young things and need the most love

GO ON TO THE NEXT PAGE

8. The speaker suggests that the young man should "not now seek the answers" (lines 19–20) but instead should "live the questions now." (line 23). Why does the speaker suggest this?

The speaker thinks the young man should focus on

(1) answering new questions
(2) finding others who can help
(3) living and gradually learning
(4) breaking down the logic of internal ideas
(5) determining which are the most important questions

9. The speaker states that "books written in a very foreign tongue" (lines 18–19) are similar to which of the following?

(1) well-known riddles
(2) unanswered questions in the heart
(3) waking and cognizance
(4) confidence and intellectual ideas
(5) personal free will

10. In the last line, the speaker states that "Almost everything serious is difficult; and everything is serious." Which of the following is likely being suggested by the speaker?

The speaker wants the young man listening to realize that

(1) the advice being given may not be easy to follow
(2) some questions are too serious to be solved
(3) the best writers are dramatic writers
(4) humor is rare both in Nature and in writing
(5) none of the advice being given is dishonest

11. Which of the following best summarizes the primary piece of advice that is contained in the passage?

(1) Good writing should not be humorous.
(2) Many questions are best answered through experience.
(3) Big questions about life to not occur in young people.
(4) Answers to life's questions are found only through reading.
(5) Hatred is poisonous to the intellectual life of a writer.

GO ON TO THE NEXT PAGE

Questions 12 through 16 refer to the following excerpt.

WHAT DO THE WOMEN DISCOVER?

MRS. HALE: Mrs. Peters?

MRS. PETERS: Yes, Mrs. Hale?

MRS. HALE: What do you suppose Minnie was so nervous about?

MRS. PETERS: Oh—I don't know. I don't know as she was nervous. I sometimes sew awful queer when I'm just tired. (Mrs. Hale starts to say something and stops) Well I must get these things wrapped up. I wonder where I can find a piece of paper and string.

MRS. HALE: In that cupboard, maybe.

MRS. PETERS: (Looking in cupboard) Why, here's a bird-cage! Did she have a bird, Mrs. Hale?

MRS. HALE: Why, I don't know whether she did or not—I've not been here for so long. There was a man around last year selling canaries cheap, but I don't know as she took one; maybe she did. She used to sing real pretty herself.

MRS. PETERS: (Glancing around) Seems funny to think of a bird here. But she must have had one, or why should she have had a cage? I wonder what happened to it.

MRS. HALE: I suppose maybe the cat got it.

MRS. PETERS: No, she didn't have a cat. Cats made her nervous.

MRS. HALE: Hmm...

MRS. PETERS: (Examining cage) Why, look at this door. It's broke. One hinge is pulled apart.

MRS. HALE: (Looking too) Looks as if someone must have been rough with it.

MRS. PETERS: Why, yes. (Puts cage on table)

MRS. HALE: I don't like this place.

MRS. PETERS: But I'm awful glad you came with me.

MRS. HALE: It would be lonesome for me sitting here alone.

MRS. HALE: It would, wouldn't it? (Dropping sewing, voice falling) But I tell you what I do wish, Mrs. Peters. I wish I had come over some times when Minnie was here. I—(looking around the room)—wish I had.

MRS. PETERS: But of course you were awful busy, Mrs. Hale—your house and your children.

MRS. HALE: I could've come. I stayed away because it weren't cheerful—and that's why I ought to have come. I—I've never liked this place. I dunno what it is, but it's a lonesome place and always was. I wish I had come over to see Minnie Foster sometimes. I can see now—(shakes her head)

MRS. PETERS: Well, you mustn't reproach yourself, Mrs. Hale. Somehow we just don't see how it is with other folks until—something comes up.

MRS. HALE: Not having children makes less work and Mr. Wright out to work all day, and no company when he did come in. Did you know John Wright, Mrs. Peters?

GO ON TO THE NEXT PAGE

MRS. PETERS: Not to know him. I've seen him in town. They say he was a good man.

MRS. HALE: Yes—good; he didn't drink, and kept his word as well as most, I guess, and paid his debts. But he was a hard man, Mrs. Peters. Just to pass the time of day with him—(shivers) Like a raw wind that gets to the bone. (Pauses, her eye falling on the cage) I should think she would have wanted a bird. But what do you suppose went with it?

MRS. PETERS: I don't know, unless it got sick and died. (She reaches over and swings the broken door, swings it again, both women watch it)

MRS. HALE: Come to think of it, she was kind of like a bird herself—real sweet and pretty, but kind of timid and—fluttery. How she did change... (Then as if struck by a happy thought and relieved to get back to every day things) Tell you what, Mrs. Peters, why don't you take the quilt in with you when you see Minnie? It might help take up her mind.

MRS. PETERS: Why, I think that's a real nice idea, Mrs. Hale.

Susan Glaspell, TRIFLES, 1920

12. This excerpt is from a play (called Trifles) in which several characters in the play mock Mrs. Hale and Mrs. Peters for focusing on trifles—things that don't matter. Which of the following could best explain why the author chose this title?

The title gives more information because it

(1) highlights the insignificance of the life they lead
(2) emphasizes the idea that small things don't really matter
(3) reveals the most important theme of the play
(4) shows that the play is not a very important drama
(5) gives a clue as to who the least important characters are

13. It is likely that Mrs. Hale and Mrs. Peters are greatly concerned about Minnie because they

(1) have regularly been in touch with her
(2) have seen her around from time to time
(3) do not know where she is
(4) wish to find the bird that is missing
(5) realize there is much sewing to be done

GO ON TO THE NEXT PAGE

14. Which of the following things are explicitly compared in the passage above?
    (1) Mrs. Hale and Mrs. Peters
    (2) Mrs. Hale and Minnie
    (3) Minnie and her husband
    (4) Minnie and the bird
    (5) Mrs. Peters and the bird

15. It can be inferred from the passage that Minnie's husband, John Wright could best be described as
    (1) wealthy, yet uncharitable
    (2) honest, but unfriendly
    (3) hard-working, yet unintelligent
    (4) quiet and inspirational
    (5) shy and loyal

16. Based on the clues in the passage, what is the most likely explanation for the broken bird cage without a bird?
    (1) The cat caught it.
    (2) It flew away due to the broken cage.
    (3) Perhaps there never was any bird.
    (4) The bird is still flying in the house somewhere.
    (5) Someone may have intentionally injured the bird.

GO ON TO THE NEXT PAGE

Questions 17 through 21 refer to the following excerpt.

WHAT DOES THE SPEAKER THINK OF WAR?

The Man He Killed

Had he and I met
By some old ancient inn,
We should have sat us down to wet
Right many a nipperkin*

But ranged as infantry
And staring face to face
I shot at him, as he at me,
And killed him in his place.

I shot him dead because—
Because he was my foe,
Just so: my foe of course he was;
That's clear enough; although

He thought he'd enlist, perhaps,
Off-hand like—just as I—
Was out of work — had sold his traps—
No other reason why.

Yes, quaint and curious war is!
You shoot a fellow down
You'd treat, if met where any bar is,
Or help to half-a-crown

*a drink

Thomas Hardy, "The Man He Killed," 1902

17. The speaker of this poem is most likely

(1) a father
(2) a soldier
(3) a bartender
(4) a war protester
(5) a civilian

18. The poem suggests that combatants in a war might treat each other differently if instead of participating in a war, they had

(1) met instead in a different setting
(2) been soldiers in the same army
(3) known each other as children
(4) previously worked together
(5) helped each other financially

GO ON TO THE NEXT PAGE

19. The speaker describes war as "quaint and curious." This type of description could be described as

(1) a theory
(2) an exaggeration
(3) a puzzle
(4) an understatement
(5) an inquiry

20. Thomas Hardy, the author of this poem, often dealt with the theme of fate is his novels and poetry.

What aspect of the poem most strongly illustrates this theme?

(1) a man buying another man a drink
(2) a man losing his job
(3) two men shooting, but only one dying
(4) one man hating his enemy more than the other
(5) one man helping another with money

21. The speaker in the poem describes shooting another because "he was my foe." However, based on the tone of the poem, it more likely the case that the man was killed because the speaker

(1) was under oppressive attack in his own country
(2) was protecting the lives his family members
(3) became confused and panicked during a gunfight
(4) happened to encounter the other man during a war
(5) was fighting for a better cause than his opponent

END OF EXAMINATION

MATHEMATICS

Tests of General Educational Development

Directions

The Mathematics Test consists of questions intended to measure general mathematics skills and problem-solving ability. The questions are based on short readings that often include a graph, chart, or figure.

You should spend no more than 45 minutes answering the questions in this booklet. Work carefully, but do not spend too much time on any one question. Be sure you answer every question.

Formulas you may need are given on page 252. Only some of the questions will require you to use a formula. Not all the formulas given will be needed.

Some questions contain more information than you will need to solve the problem; other questions do not give enough information. If the question does not give enough information to solve the problem, the correct answer choice is "Not enough information is given."

The use of calculators is allowed only in Part I.

Do not mark in this test booklet. The test administrator will give you blank paper for your calculations. Record your answers on the separate answer sheet provided. Be sure that all requested information is properly recorded on the answer sheet.

To record your answers, fill in the numbered circle on the answer sheet beside the number that corresponds to the question in the test booklet.

FOR EXAMPLE:

If a grocery bill totaling $15.75 is paid with a $20.00 bill, how much change should be returned?

(1) $5.25
(2) $4.75
(3) $4.25
(4) $3.75
(5) $3.25

The correct answer is $4.25; therefore, answer space 3 would be marked on the answer sheet.

Do not rest the point of your pencil on the answer sheet while you are considering your answer. Make no stray or unnecessary marks. If you change an answer, erase your first mark completely. Mark only one answer space for each question; multiple answers will be scored as incorrect. Do not fold or crease your answer sheet. All test materials must be returned to the test administrator.

GO ON TO THE NEXT PAGE

Mathematics, Part I

FORMULAS

AREA (A) of a:	
square	$A = s^2$; where s = side
rectangle	$A = lw$; where l = length, w = width
parallelogram	$A = bh$; where b = base, h = height
trapezoid	$A = \frac{1}{2}(b_1 + b_2)h$; where b = base, h = height
triangle	$A = \frac{1}{2}bh$; where b = base, h = height
circle	$A = \pi r^2$; where $\pi = 3.14$, r = radius
PERIMETER (P) of a:	
square	$P = 4s$; where s = side
rectangle	$P = 2l + 2w$; where l = length, w = width
triangle	$P = a + b + c$; where a, b, and c are the sides
CIRCUMFERENCE (C) of a circle:	$C = \pi d$; where $\pi = 3.14$, d = diameter
VOLUME (V) of a:	
cube	$V = s^3$; where s = side
rectangular container	$V = lwh$; where l = length, w = width, h = height
square pyramid	$V = \frac{1}{3}(\text{base edge})^2 h$
cone	$V = \frac{1}{3}\pi r^2 h$
cylinder	$V = \pi r^2 h$; where $\pi = 3.14$, r = radius, h = height
PYTHAGOREAN RELATIONSHIP	$c^2 = a^2 + b^2$; where c = hypotenuse, a and b are legs of a right triangle
DISTANCE (d) BETWEEN TWO POINTS ON A PLANE	$d = \sqrt{(x_2 - x_1)^2 + (y_2 - y_1)^2}$; where (x_1, y_1) and (x_2, y_2) are two points in a plane
SLOPE OF A LINE (m)	$m = \frac{y_2 - y_1}{x_2 - x_1}$; where (x_1, y_1) and (x_2, y_2) are two points in a plane
MEAN	**mean** $= \frac{x_1 + x_2 + \ldots x_n}{n}$; where the x's = the values for which a mean is desired, and n = number of values in the series
MEDIAN	**median** = the point in an ordered set of numbers at which half of the numbers are above and half of the numbers are below this value
SIMPLE INTEREST (i)	$i = prt$; where p = principal, r = rate, t = time
DISTANCE (d) as function of rate and time	$d = rt$; where r = rate, t = time
TOTAL COST (c)	$c = nr$; where n = number of units, r = cost per unit

Mathematics, Part I

Directions: You will have 22 minutes to complete questions 1–13. You may use your calculator with these questions only. Choose the one best answer to each question.

1. At Lakeside Park restaurant, servers earn an average of $840 less per month than chefs. The restaurant employs 4 chefs and 18 servers. Let c represent the average monthly pay of a chef.

   Which of the following functions correctly shows the relationship between the monthly payroll (P) and the wages of these employees?

   (1) $P = 4c + 18(c - 840)$
   (2) $P = 4(c - 840) + 18c$
   (3) $P = 4(c - 840) + 18(c - 840)$
   (4) $P = 4 + c + 18 + (c - 840)$
   (5) $P = 4(c)(18)(c - 840)$

2. The scale on a map states that 0.5 inches = 20 miles. Maria wants to know the distance from her house to her grandmother's house. On the map, the distance between the two houses is 3 inches. What is the actual distance, in miles, between Maria's house and her grandmother's house?

   (1) 3 miles
   (2) 6 miles
   (3) 15 miles
   (4) 60 miles
   (5) 120 miles

Major	2008	2009
Urban Studies	24	31
Psychology	40	37
History	19	23
Chemistry	31	38
Business	28	24

3. According to the table above, what was the increase in the total number of graduates in these 5 departments from 2008 to 2009?

   (1) 9
   (2) 11
   (3) 20
   (4) 25
   (5) 295

4. Vijay invested $1000 at 4% annual interest. Yvette invested $500 less than Vijay, but her bank paid her 6% annual interest. After one year, what was the DIFFERENCE between the amount of interest Yvette had earned and the amount of interest Vijay had earned.

   (1) $10.00
   (2) $20.00
   (3) $30.00
   (4) $40.00
   (5) Not enough information is given.

GO ON TO THE NEXT PAGE

5. Each number below is a possible solution for $2x + 3 > 6$ EXCEPT:

(1) 9
(2) 6
(3) 3
(4) 2
(5) 0

6. The diameter of one bicycle wheel is 28 cm. The spokes attach from the hub (center) to the rim. The distance around the wheel of a different bicycle is 22π. What is the difference between the lengths of the spokes of the two bicycles, in cm.

(1) 3
(2) 3π
(3) 6
(4) 6π
(5) 9

7. Arthur is renting a skating rink for a party. The basic charge is $200 plus an additional $5 per person. If *n* people attend the party, which equation can be used to find *T*, the total cost of renting the rink?

(1) $T = 200n + 5$
(2) $T = (200 + 5)n$
(3) $T = \frac{200+5}{n}$
(4) $T = 5n + 200$
(5) $T = (200)(5n)$

8. For the triangle shown in the diagram below, angle *A* measures 100° and sides *AB* and *AC* have the same length. What is the measure of angle *C*?

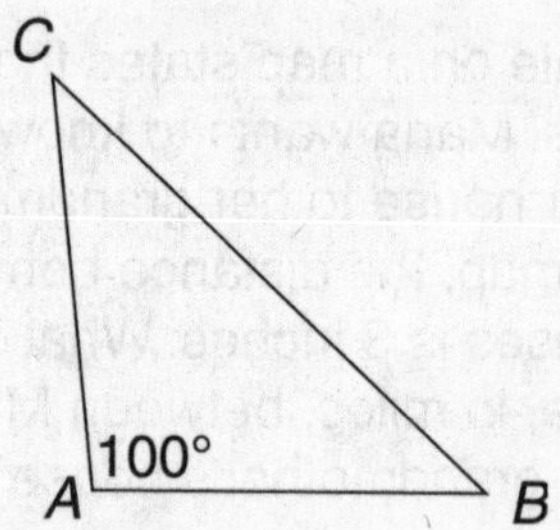

(1) 30°
(2) 40°
(3) 45°
(4) 140°
(5) 180°

GO ON TO THE NEXT PAGE

9. The town of Wynnewood offers billboard space along the highway. A 5 foot by 8 foot rectangular advertising space costs $120.

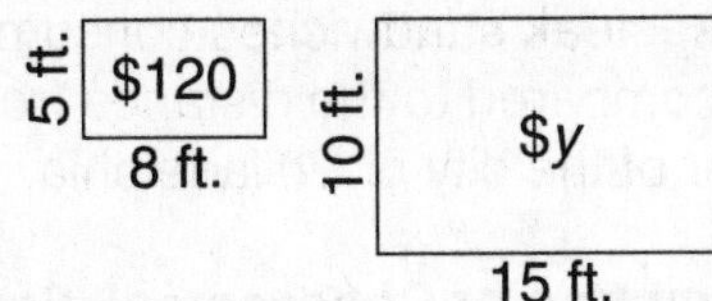

If the price (y) of a sign is proportional to its AREA, which of the following expressions correctly determines the price (y) of a 10 foot by 15 foot billboard?

(1) $\frac{120}{y} = \frac{150}{40}$

(2) $\frac{40}{120} = \frac{150}{y}$

(3) $\frac{40}{20} = \frac{150}{y}$

(4) $\frac{40}{y} = \frac{120}{150}$

(5) $\frac{26}{y} = \frac{50}{120}$

10. 184 people sign up for a bus tour of Washington, DC. If each bus can take 35 people, how many buses are needed?

PLEASE DO NOT WRITE IN THIS TEST BOOKLET.

Mark your answer in the circles in the grid on your answer sheet.

11. At a certain time of day a 3 foot tall pole casts a shadow 4 feet long. How tall is a pole that casts a shadow 12 feet long at the same time of day?

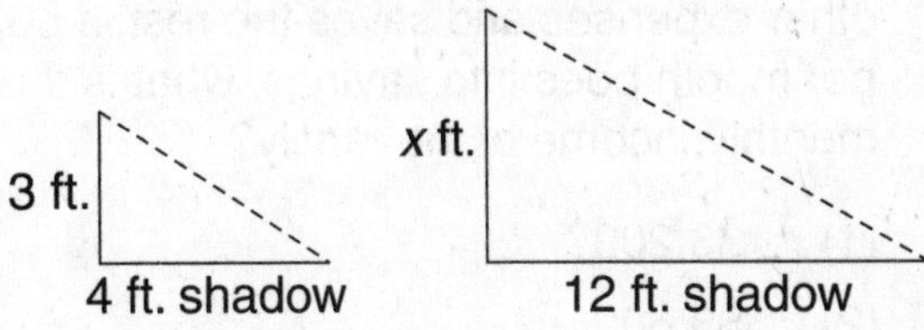

(1) 5 feet

(2) 6 feet

(3) 7 feet

(4) 9 feet

(5) 15 feet

12. Adam rents a car for $50 per day plus $0.20 per mile. If Adam uses the car for 2 days and drives a total of 180 miles, what is his total cost?

(1) $36

(2) $90

(3) $136

(4) $190

(5) $220

13. A rectangle and a triangle have equal areas. The rectangle is 12 x 8. The base of the triangle is 32. What is the height of the triangle?

(1) 3

(2) 4

(3) 6

(4) 16

(5) 24

END OF MATHEMATICS, PART I

Directions: You will have 22 minutes to complete questions 14–25. You may NOT use a calculator with these questions. Choose the one best answer to each question.

14. A family spends 25% of its monthly income on food, 23% on rent, 42% on other expenses and saves the rest. If $320 per month goes into savings, what is the monthly income of the family?

(1) $3,200
(2) $3,600
(3) $4,150
(4) $4,200
(5) $5,025

15. What is the slope of a line passing through coordinates (3,8) and (5,2) on the *x*,*y* coordinate plane?

(1) -3
(2) $-\frac{1}{3}$
(3) 0
(4) $\frac{1}{3}$
(5) 3

16. The graph below shows the number of cheesesteak sandwiches consumed per year compared to the distance from the center of the city of Philadelphia.

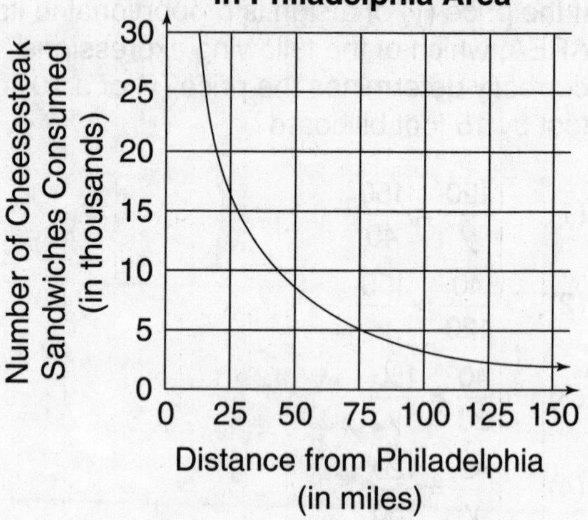

Based on the graph, what is the approximate number of cheesesteak sandwiches consumed annually 60 miles from the center of Philadelphia?

(1) 15,000
(2) 12,000
(3) 10,000
(4) 7,000
(5) 4,000

17. $3x - 1 = 11$. What is $x^2 + x$?

(1) 12
(2) 15
(3) 16
(4) 18
(5) 20

GO ON TO THE NEXT PAGE

18. A company's income of $120,000 is distributed in the following way:

Distribution of Expenses for Sales of $120,000 in a Clothing Company

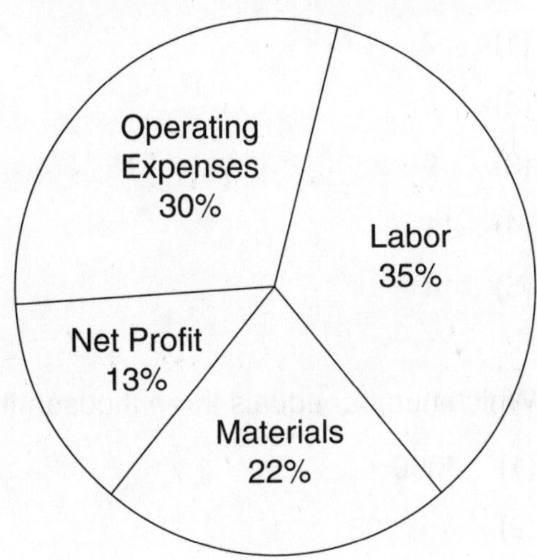

How much money is spent on Materials?

PLEASE DO NOT WRITE IN THIS TEST BOOKLET.

Mark your answer in the circles in the grid on your answer sheet.

19. A school has 18 classes with 35 students each. To reduce the class size to 30, how many new classes must be formed?

PLEASE DO NOT WRITE IN THIS TEST BOOKLET.

Mark your answer in the circles in the grid on your answer sheet.

20. Margo buys a new car for $17,900. The dealer gives her an instant rebate of $1350. She gives the dealer a down payment of $850. The terms of her payment plan are 0% interest for 60 months. Which of the following mathematical expressions gives her monthly payments?

(1) $\frac{17{,}900 + 850 + 1{,}350}{60}$

(2) $\frac{17{,}900}{60(850 + 1{,}350)}$

(3) $\frac{17{,}900 - (850 + 1{,}350)}{60}$

(4) $\frac{17{,}900 - 850 - 1{,}350}{60}$

(5) $\frac{17{,}900 + (850 - 1{,}350)}{60}$

GO ON TO THE NEXT PAGE

21. What is the area of the triangle below?

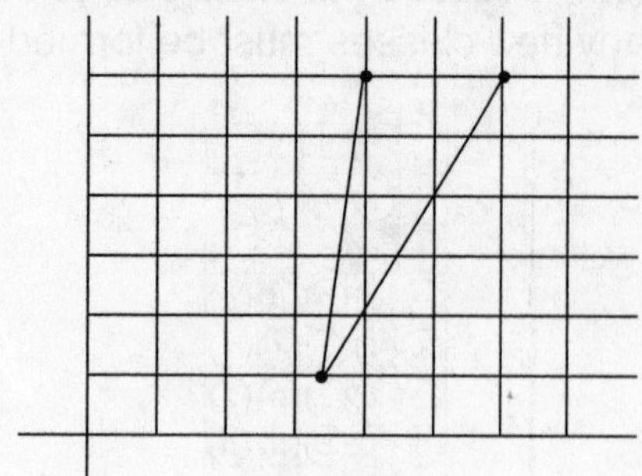

PLEASE DO NOT WRITE IN THIS TEST BOOKLET.

Mark your answer in the circles in the grid on your answer sheet.

22. A bell rings every 2 hours. A second bell rings every 3 hours. A third bell rings every 4 hours. If all three bells ring at 9:00 am, when will all three bells ring again?

(1) 12:00 pm
(2) 2:00 pm
(3) 6:00 pm
(4) 9:00 pm
(5) Not enough information given.

23. A team has won 20 of 30 games so far this season and has 15 more games scheduled to play. How many of the remaining games must be won in order to win 60% of the games of the season.

(1) 7
(2) 8
(3) 9
(4) 11
(5) 14

24. Which number equals three thousandths?

(1) 3000
(2) .03
(3) .3
(4) .3000
(5) .003

25. A driver drives x miles on the 1st day, y miles on the 2nd day and z miles on the 3rd day. The average miles per day is expressed as:

(1) $\frac{xyz}{3}$
(2) $\frac{xy+z}{3}$
(3) $x+y+z$
(4) $\frac{x+y+z}{3}$
(5) $3xyz$

END OF EXAMINATION

Answers and Explanations for Practice Test 3

WRITING

1. 3
2. 5
3. 3
4. 5
5. 2
6. 2
7. 4
8. 3
9. 1
10. 3
11. 4
12. 2
13. 5
14. 2
15. 1
16. 3
17. 2
18. 4
19. 3
20. 1
21. 1
22. 5
23. 2
24. 4
25. 1

SOCIAL STUDIES

1. 4
2. 5
3. 2
4. 1
5. 3
6. 5
7. 5
8. 4
9. 2
10. 1
11. 3
12. 2
13. 3
14. 5
15. 2
16. 4
17. 1
18. 2
19. 3
20. 4
21. 3
22. 3
23. 1
24. 5
25. 3

SCIENCE

1. 5
2. 5
3. 5
4. 4
5. 2
6. 3
7. 4
8. 2
9. 4
10. 1
11. 4
12. 2
13. 4
14. 3
15. 1
16. 1
17. 1
18. 1
19. 1
20. 3
21. 2
22. 4
23. 2
24. 4
25. 5

READING

1. 5
2. 4
3. 2
4. 3
5. 4
6. 3
7. 1
8. 3
9. 2
10. 1
11. 2
12. 3
13. 2
14. 4
15. 2
16. 5
17. 2
18. 1
19. 4
20. 3
21. 4

MATH

1. 1
2. 5
3. 2
4. 1
5. 5
6. 1
7. 4
8. 2
9. 2
10. 3
11. 4
12. 3
13. 3
14. 1
15. 1
16. 4
17. 5
18. 26,400
19. 3
20. 4
21. 5
22. 4
23. 1
24. 5
25. 4

EXPLANATIONS

Writing

1. 3 There is no comma necessary in the underlined portion of the sentence. A comma generally separates elements of a sentence, but there are no elements to separate here. For example, you wouldn't write, "He, hit the ball." You would write, "He hit the ball." This eliminates choices 1, 2, and 4. Choice 5 is in the present tense, while the rest of the sentence is in the past tense. This leaves 3 as the correct choice.

2. 5 In this sentence, the word *selector's* is a possessive noun, but it refers to only one selector when it is supposed to refer to both. The plural possessive (the selectors *possess* the V-time bank accounts) has the apostrophe *after* the last *s*. Choice 5 is correct.

3. 3 An investigation can't discover something. People can discover something by investigating, but an investigation can only *uncover* or *reveal* something. This leaves choice 3 as the correct answer.

4. 5 The phrase *discovered by Human Resources* is passive and could be written better. Beginning the sentence with *Human Resources* corrects this flaw. Nothing else needs to be changed, so that leaves choice 5 as the answer.

5. 2 The word *been* is always associated with either *has, have, have not* or *has not* or any contraction of these, so the original is incorrect. Choice 3 is technically correct but is awkward. In choices 4 and 5 the word *being* is unnecessary. Choice 2 is the correct answer.

6. 2 The word *definitely* is redundant and can be eliminated. Since none of the choices offer that option, you need to pick the answer that best addresses this. Choice 2 is the only one that addresses this issue and is correct because it makes the intent of the sentence clear.

7. 4 The hyphen in *work-off* makes it an adjective and what we're looking for is a verb. The warehousemen are *working off* their debt. Answer choice 4 is the only one that addresses this error.

8. 3 The author of the memo is asking for advice, and the sentence as written doesn't convey this. Choices 3 and 5 are the only ones that address this error. Choice 5 uses the noun *advice* when she is actually looking for a verb. *Advise*, as in choice 3, fits the bill.

9. 1 Choice 1 is correct because sentence 11 gives an example of why Charlie Sanderson's decision was flawed before it is even stated that his decision was flawed. Sentences 11 and 12 should be switched.

10. 3 This is a simple grammatical error, and if you catch it, you know that answer choice 3 is correct. All the other choices except 4 make the sentence grammatically incorrect, and choice 4 changes the intended meaning of the sentence.

11. 4 As in Question 1, there are no discrete elements of the sentence that need to be separated by a comma. Choice 4 is your answer.

12. 2 Use the word *less* when it's something you can measure, e.g., *less water*, and use the word *fewer* when describing something you can count, e.g., fewer *gallons* of water. Choice 2 is correct.

13. 5 The word *farther* is used when you're talking about distance. This eliminates choices 1 and 3. *Even compelling* in choice 2 doesn't make sense, and choice 4 doesn't work—you can say, "better evidence" or "more compelling evidence" but "better compelling evidence" doesn't make sense. Choice 5 addresses these issues and is the correct answer.

14. 2 The word *all* is in the sentence twice, referring to the same things. This is redundant and is addressed by choice 2.

15. 1 Every time you begin a sentence with the word *if,* you need a *then* part of the sentence (or its equivalent). Since this sentence doesn't have this, the sentence is a fragment.

16. 3 The only place this sentence makes sense is at the end of paragraph A, as this paragraph describes an event that caused mass extinctions. Choice 3 is your answer.

17. 2 As in Question 7, the hyphens turn these words into an adjective. Example: You can say, "it's a band-for-band match" or "they match band for band" but you can't say, "they match band-for-band."

18. 4 When you talk about an object, you refer to it as "something *that*..." and when you talk about people, you refer to them "someone *who*..." This leaves you with choices 3 and 4. Since the sentence says, "Have you ever..." it's in what's called the "present perfect" tense, which is a period of time that spans from some unspecified point in the past up to *and including* the present. Therefore, the phrase should be "advertisements that *say*..." Choice 4 is your answer.

19. 3 Here's a simple mistake. The definition isn't *quiet*—that doesn't make sense. So you're left with answer choices 3 and 4. *Simply* is an adverb, so that won't work. You're left with answer 3.

20. 1 This sentence is passive (something "done by" you as opposed to you "doing" something) and could be written better. The only active beginning is in choice 1.

21. 1 *Interest* is singular, so that knocks out choice 2. Choices 3 and 5 change the meaning of the sentence, so they're out. Choice 4 is clearly awkward. This leaves you with answer choice 1 which is written correctly.

22. 5 The problem here is the phrase "looking good." Answer 5 is the only choice that addresses this.

23. 2 This sentence doesn't make sense where it is because there's no big amount of money mentioned at this point that could go a long way for corporate executives. At the end of the article, however, is the big payoff. Thirty-three million dollars will go a long way for just about anybody, so sentence 18 should come after that. The correct choice is 2.

24. 4 Choice 1 changes *compounded*, which is an adjective, to a verb, and that changes the meaning of the sentence. The same thing applies to choice 2. Choice 3 doesn't make any sense, while choice 5 doesn't really change the sentence at all. Choice 4 puts things into the present tense where the sentence is supposed to be, and also makes more sense than the original. Choice 4 is the answer.

25. 1 There's just nothing wrong with this sentence, so choice 1 is your answer. But just to make sure, let's check the other answers. You "multiply," you don't "multiplies" so choice 2 is wrong. 3 doesn't make sense and besides, *percentages* is plural and *one-third* is singular. You can't say "10 *billions* dollars," so 4 is out. Choice 5—"If you multiplying"? You can say, "if you *are* multiplying" but "If you multiplying" is clearly wrong. Three cheers for answer choice 1!

Social Studies

1. 4 Be sure to eliminate answers that are obviously wrong. Rainfall in Anaheim cannot *cause* the rainfall in Orlando, so choice 1 is incorrect. Choices 2, 3, and 5 are all factually incorrect. Only choice 4 makes sense and is verifiable by the data from the graph.

2. 5 A way to rephrase the question is to ask, "Where is the graph at its highest?" The answer, of course, is during summer and the line that represents the highest value is for Orlando. Therefore, choice 5 is correct.

3. 2 Agriculture is an intellectual word for farming, which would logically be the most affected by "unusually high amounts of rainfall." Therefore, choice 2 is correct.

4. 1 The Cold War defined the second half of the twentieth century, whereas "The War on Terror" (choice 4) is a twenty-first century phenomenon and World War II (2), the Korean War (3), and the Vietnam War (5) lasted a few years each during the 1940s, 1950s, and 1960s, respectively.

5. 3 The cartoon indicates that "Boss" Tweed was able to buy his political victory, rather than earn it through brains or hard work. Thus, choice 3 is the correct answer. The other choices can be eliminated because they do not accurately describe the content of the picture.

6. 5 While hydrogen (choice 5) has long been considered a potential source of energy, it has not played the prominent role of fossil fuels, such as coal (1), oil (2), and natural gas (3). Nuclear power (4) has played a major role in the late twentieth century.

7. 5 According to the excerpt, Washington argued against the negative effects of political parties, so choice 3 is incorrect and 5 is correct. Choice 1 is a trap answer because Washington did argue against foreign alliances, but elsewhere in the "Farewell Address." Choices 2 and 4 are off-topic.

8. 4 Because Washington is most concerned with political parties, choice 4 is correct. Though Washington would likely have been troubled by all of these developments, notice that the question clearly states "based on the information in the excerpt."

9. 2 President Washington was concerned with the role of "geographical discriminations" in the political process because they could lead to precisely the sort of north-south division that led to the Civil War. For that reason, choice 2 is correct. Be wary of the extreme language in choices 1 and 4: "in all forms" and "made no difference."

10. 1 The United States of America has never had a king or queen, so choice 1 is the correct answer. The United Kingdom (choice 2) and Spain (4) are constitutional monarchies, which means the king or queen is more of a figurehead than a potent political force. Saudi Arabia (5) is ruled by a powerful (or absolute) monarch. France (3), though it did have monarchs for centuries, is longer ruled by kings or queens.

11. 3 Susan B. Anthony (choice 3) famously helped women earn the right to vote. While Abigail Adams, (1) the wife of President John Adams, did advocate for women's rights, she did not actively pursue legislation. Gloria Steinem (5), a prominent feminist of the twentieth century, was born into a world in which women could already vote.

12. 2 Do not be intimidated by questions with graphs. Just test the answer choices against the data presented in the graph. This question asks you for an opinion, rather than a fact, so eliminate the four answer choices that are verifiable facts.

13. 3 Traditionally, entering warfare decreases the unemployment rate as employees become soldiers and new manufacturing jobs are created. Choice 3 is therefore correct. Eliminate answers that are out of the time period, such as choice 2 (slavery ended in the 1860s) and choice 5 (the stock market crash happened more than a decade after 1917–1918.

14. 5 According to this excerpt from the Constitution, the President can issue pardons and command the military, so choice 5 is correct. The President is not required to seek approval from Congress for pardons (choice 1). Though choices 2, 3, and 4 are mostly accurate, they do not apply to this excerpt, so be careful as you read!

15. 2 The purpose of "reprieves and pardons" is to forgive individuals of crimes, so choice 2 is correct. Choice 1 is obviously wrong: no individual has the power to "rewrite" laws, not even the President. Choice 5 is the opposite of the truth because the ability to pardon is one of the President's most absolute powers.

16. 4 In the twentieth century, Presidents have used their power as commander-in-chief to begin military actions in Korea, Vietnam, and Iraq (choice 4). In none of these instances was a formal of declaration of war issued by Congress. Choices 1, 2, and 5 are too extreme to be likely. Is it even possible that the President could *manage the day-to-day operations* of the military, as choice 5 indicates?

17. 1 Many immigrants to the United States have sought to "escape poverty or persecution," so choice 1 is correct. While some immigrants have been motivated by the factors listed in choices 2 through 5, choice 1 was a primary motivation.

18. 2 It is more important to consider a map of the Electoral College than to merely look at total votes (the popular vote) because the President is elected indirectly by the Electoral College. In 1876 and 2000, for example, the losing candidates won the overall vote, but lost in the Electoral College. Therefore, choice 2 is correct. Eliminate choices 3 and 4 because they are implausible: how could a President ever win the *unanimous* support of an entire state? Choices 1 and 5, although factually correct, are not answers to this specific question.

19. 3 The map clearly shows that Southern states voted for Parker, whereas states in the North and West voted for Roosevelt. Consequently, answer choice 3 does the best job of explaining the data. Choice 1 is not verifiable by the map alone and contains extreme language ("always"). Choices 2 and 4 are opinions, not facts, about the topic.

20. 4 The map clearly indicates that the Midwest is most likely to experience a tornado. Choice 4 is thus the correct answer.

21. 3 Tornadoes often damage a smaller area than major earthquakes and hurricanes, so choice 1 is incorrect. Choices 2 and 4 are obviously wrong and choice 5 exaggerates the extent of damage caused by tornadoes.

22. 3 The infamous *Dred Scott* decision claimed that American citizens have exclusive rights, so choice 3 is correct. According to the decision, African Americans are "beings of an inferior order," choice 5 is incorrect. Choices 1, 2, and 4 are all irrelevant to the topic presented in the excerpt.

23. 1 The only fact listed among these opinions is found in choice 1. The exaggerated and highly value-laden claims of the other choices make them opinions. Pay close attention to the verbs used in these choices: "was biased," "feared," and "was brainwashed." These sorts of claims are very hard to prove as *facts*.

24. 5 NAFTA cannot have accomplished impossible goals, such as that listed in choice 1. Avoid conspiratorial language (choice 2) and extreme language (choices 3 and 4). Choice 5 is therefore the only reasonable answer.

25. 3 John Adams claimed that individuals were not very good at protecting their own freedom, so choice 3 is correct. Choice 1 is extreme and it is obvious that a President would never oppose all forms of government. Choices 4 and 5 twist the language of the quote to mean something else and are therefore incorrect.

Science

1. 5 The passage states that speciation is the formation of a new species, and that a species is a group of individuals that can interbreed to produce fertile offspring. Choice 1 is incorrect because the offspring are not fertile, and 2 is incorrect because no offspring can be produced if there are no seeds. Choice 3 is incorrect because the answer states that peaches and nectarines are the same species, and Choice 4 is incorrect because nothing new is created. Choice 5 is correct because it describes groups of animals that can no longer breed with each other and thus are new species.

2. 5 The passage discusses how legumes such as peas provide nitrogen for the soil. The passage does not mention the amounts of nitrogen or the climates, so choices 1 and 2 are incorrect. The passage is not about insecticides nor does it describe exactly how nitrogen helps plants, so answers 3 and 4 are incorrect. Choice 5 is correct because the passage implies that legumes such as peas are planted with other crops to provide nitrogen to fertilize those crops.

3. 5 This question requires the knowledge that energy is never created nor destroyed, so 5 is correct. All of the other statements are false.

4. 4 People wear light colors to stay as cool as possible. If the light were absorbed, it would be converted into energy such as heat, so that would not help a person to stay cool. Therefore, the light must be reflected, and 4 is correct.

5. 2 Upward arrows show water being delivered to clouds, and the upward arrows are labeled evaporation and transpiration so 2 is correct. Precipitation is represented by a downward arrow and shows water leaving the clouds.

6. 3 This questions requires the knowledge that centripetal acceleration allows for circular movement that appears to defy gravity, so 3 is correct. Gravity of the sun does not have a significant effect so 1 is correct, and gravity of earth would pull the cyclist downward so 2 is incorrect. Heat has nothing to do with this situation and there is no evidence of magnetism, so 4 and 5 are incorrect.

7. 4 The figure shows a labeled animal cell. The outermost structure is labeled as the cell membrane, so 4 is correct.

8. 2 The question states that Carla is not affected, so 4 is out. The passage also states that only males are affected so 1 and 3 are out since those choices include daughters. The passage does say that her future children may be affected, so answer 5 is out. Choice 2 is correct because Carla's sons may develop the disease.

9. 4 The Punnett Square shows that some of the offspring have only wrinkled genes and some have both round and wrinkled genes. Since half of the offspring only possess wrinkled genes, and since each offspring must receive a gene from each parent, the parent with round peas must have given wrinkled genes to some of the offspring. Therefore, the parent with round peas must also have a wrinkled gene and be hybrid, so 4 is correct.

10. 1 Half of the offspring possess only wrinkled genes and will therefore produce wrinkled peas. The offspring in the other half possess one wrinkled gene and one round gene. Since round is dominant over wrinkled, these offspring will produce round peas. Therefore, 1 is correct.

11. 4 This question requires the knowledge that gases spread out to fit the space of a container. If the divider were removed, both gases would spread out as much as possible and will mix with each other, so 4 is correct.

12. 2 If the moon has less gravity than the sun, then there would be less of a downward force on a person on the moon so a person would weight more on Earth than on the moon and 2 is correct. Since the mass does not change, 4 and 5 are incorrect.

13. 4 According to the passage, habituation occurs when an animal gets accustomed to a harmless stimulus and stops responding to that stimulus. Choice 4 is correct because the man gets accustomed to the sound of the airplanes landing and stops responding to the sound.

14. 3 The graph shows that as the temperature increases, the viscosity decreases. Since heating increases temperature, 3 is correct.

15. 1 This question requires the knowledge that kinetic and potential are types of energy, so 1 is correct.

16. 1 Oil is less dense than water, which is why it floats on top of the water as shown in the figure. If the bottle is shaken and the contents are allowed to settle, the water and oil will go back to the way they were before the bottle was shaken, so 1 is correct.

17. 1 This question asks which characteristic on worms improves a farm environment. While 2, 3, and 4 are true and mentioned in the passage, they have nothing to do with improving a farm environment. Choice 5 would benefit a farm but is not mentioned in the passage and is not something that worms do. Choice 1 is correct because worms do increase soil fertility and that does improve a farm environment.

18. 1 The graph shows that as the temperature rises, so too does the pressure, so 3 and 4 are incorrect. Kelvin is the unit for temperature, so 2 is incorrect. Careful examination of the graph shows that 1 is correct and 5 is not.

19. 1 The periodic table shows that atomic radius increases going down and to the left. Cs is the element that is farthest down and to the left, and the legend shows that Cs represents cesium, so 1 is correct.

20. 3 Based on the graph, at a temperature of 90 degrees and a pressure of 1 atm substance y can exist as solid or liquid. The changes that can occur between solids and liquids are freezing and melting. Only melting is listed, so 3 is correct.

21. 2 The graph shows that at 1 atm, anything above 90 degrees and below 150 degrees will be liquid. Since 100 degrees is in this range, substance y will be liquid and 2 is correct.

22. 4 The passage states that the space a group takes up on a food pyramid is proportional to the number of species in that group compared to the other groups. On the food pyramid, producers take up the most space, so they would be present in the greatest numbers in an ecosystem. Therefore, 4 is correct.

23. 2 The passage says producers make their own food. Birds, worms, lions, and lizards all consume food, so 1, 3, 4, and 5 are incorrect. Choice 2 is correct because trees are plants and plants make their own food.

24. 4 The passage does not mentioned the effects of acid rain, so 1 is wrong. Neither the location nor the history of acid rain is mentioned, so 2 and 5 are incorrect. The passage does not mention prevention, so 3 is wrong. Choice 4 is correct, because the passage states that sulfuric acid mixed with water becomes acid rain, so several components of acid rain are mentioned.

25. 5 The question asks which elements of digestion are not under conscious control, meaning which elements are done involuntarily. Of the mentioned functions, only chewing is voluntary, so the correct answer is 5 since it lists everything but chewing.

Reading

1. 5 The answer is 5 because in the first paragraph the writer states "winning championships is the primary goal of every team" and that the new policies are intended to "improve our odds toward that endeavor." There is no evidence in the letter of team criticism in 1 or communication with other teams in 2 or how long since they have won a championship. Choice 4 is extreme and cannot be supported.

2. 4 The answer is 4 because the writer states in the first paragraph that the other teams "miss the opportunities to gain every possible advantage." Choice 1 may be true, but is not stated in the letter. Choices 2 and 3 cannot be known by the information in the passage. Choice 5 may be true, but does not answer the question directly and is not as good an answer as 4.

3. 2 The answer is 2 because the quote follows the major point of the letter that team focus on details will be the key to success. Thus, the quote is given, as most quotes are, in order to support the position taken in the letter. The reference to the manager supports the overall argument. Choice 1 states that the manager is famous, but that is not why he was quoted. Choice 4 mentions the manager's fame, which is true but does not answer the question. The other answers are unsupported.

4. 3 The answer is 2 because the writer states in the third paragraph that all members of the organization will be "looking for every small opportunity to gain an edge on the competition." Choices 1 and 2 are an inference that goes beyond what is stated in the passage. Choices 4 and 5 are not mentioned in the letter.

5. 4 The answer is 4 because the manager is quoted as saying that he does not believe in succeeding personally "without keeping the team in mind." The title of his book also shows that he values the group over the individual. No mention is made of education in 1 or business work in 2 or bravery in 5. Teammates and coworkers are the same thing for a baseball player and they are not compared in the letter.

6. 3 The answer is 3 because the speaker in the passage says, "you are so young" and "I want to beg you, as much as I can, dear sir, to be patient." This is obviously from an older, experienced person full of advice for a younger writer. Choice 3 is most likely true. Choice 1 indicates that all writers follow the same rules, which is extreme. No new literature is mentioned, as in 2. Writing is what both speaker and listener do, so 4 contradicts the passage. Choice 5 is extreme, calling trust "dangerous."

7. 1 The answer is 1 because the speaker states that clinging to "the simplest in Nature" that "hardly anyone sees" it is possible to see things become "unexpectedly so big and beyond measuring." Thus, the little things can become large and important. Nothing is mentioned of fame, as in 2. Choice 4 talks about inconsiderate people, not inconsiderable things. Choices 3 and 5 are not supported by the passage.

8. 3 The answer is 3 because the speaker further goes on to state that answers may come gradually and that the listener may "live into the answer." He also suggests patience "toward all that is unsolved." All comments point toward slow living and learning. Choice 1 contradicts the passage. Choice 5 is close to the topic, but not explicitly stated. Choices 2 and 4 are not mentioned.

9. 2 The answer is 2 because the books are directly compared to "the questions themselves" The speaker also states "do not seek answers." Thus the two ideas are tied together and only 2 addressed this. Choices 1, 4, and 5 are not supported by information in the passage. Choice 3 is mentioned in the passage but does not answer the exact question asked.

10. 1 The answer is 1 because the speaker's comment follows much advice about how to write and live and learn. This final quote is to remind the listener that it will not be easy. The comment to "hate nothing" shows that there is much at stake. So, the future will not always be easy. Choice 2 discussed questions, which is on topic, but does not agree with the passage in saying serious questions cannot be solved. Choices 3 and 4 are extreme and nothing is known about great writers or humor from the passage. Choice 5 is also extreme.

11. 2 The answer is 2 because the entire passage discusses advice on how to live, answer internal questions and have patience in finding answers. Only 2 states this accurately. Choice 1 is never stated. Choice 3 is against common sense. Choice 4 says that "only" reading can answer questions, which is not clear from the passage. Choice 5 may be true but does not answer the question.

12. 3 The answer is 3 because it is in agreement with the theme and conversations that the two characters have regarding their neighbor. They discover a bird cage which seems insignificant initially, but eventually reveals many details about their friend. Such small things add up to illustrate the most important parts of the play. Only 3 addresses this. Choice 2 contradicts this theme. Choices 4 and 5 could not accurately describe the writer's opinion. Choice 1 cannot be known from the information given.

13. 2 The answer is 2 because evidence is given in several places in the conversation. Mrs. Hale says, "I wish I had come over sometimes" which implies that she lived close by. And later, Mrs. Hale says, "How she did change," which shows that she saw her occasionally. Choice 1 suggests that the women saw Minnie frequently, but that is contradicted by their conversation by how little they saw her. Choice 3 is not true as they mention bringing her a quilt. Choices 4 and 5 are not significant details or reason for great concern.

14. 4 The answer is 4 because Mrs. Hale states that Minnie was "kind of like a bird herself—real sweet and pretty." That is a direct comparison. No other answer correctly identifies a comparison from the passage. Answer 1 identifies the two main characters, but they are not compared. Answer 3 suggests that Minnie and her husband were compared, but they were only described individually. There is no support for answers 2 or 5.

15. 2 The answer is 2 because Mr. Wright is described as a man who didn't drink, paid his debts and kept his word. But he is also described as "a hard man" and like a "raw wind." Clearly, this means he is basically honest, but not very nice. Choice 3 may be half-right if he worked hard, but nothing is said of his intelligence. Nothing is said in the excerpt of the play of his wealth, in 1, his inspiration, seen in 4, or his loyalty, in 5.

16. 5 The answer is 5 because the evidence of the broken door on the cage with "one hinge pulled apart" and the comment from Mrs. Hale that it looked as if "someone must have been rough with it." This leads to the logical conclusion that something violent happened to the bird. Choice 1 contradicts the passage since there was no cat. Choices 2, 3, and 4 are all possible, but are not the most likely explanation given the information in the passage. Only 5 accounts for all the details.

17. 2 The answer is 2 because the speaker states that they both were "ranged as infantry and staring face to face" and that "he was my foe." The clearest explanation is that the speaker is a soldier. All other choices could possibly be true, but no evidence is given in the passage. Choice 2 is correct.

18. 1 The answer is 1 because the poem opens with the suggestion "had he and I but met by some old ancient inn" which considers a different meeting. The speaker further states that if they met differently "where any bar is," that he'd treat his foe to a drink. No mention in the poem is made of children, work or finances, as in 3, 4 and 5. Choice 2 mentions the soldiers being in the same army which is somewhat logically, but not stated in the poem, so it cannot be the correct answer.

19. 4 The answer is 4 because this description is rather mild. Calling something curious suggests a small puzzle or unusual event, not a war in which people are killed. Obviously, the speaker is commenting on

war in a negative way and wishes rather to drink with his foe than shoot at him. So, this statement is short of the strong language to be expected regarding war, or in other words, an understatement. Choice 2 is the opposite of understatement. Choice 3 is not as good as 4. The other answers are unsupported.

20. 3 The answer is 3 because it directly relates to both the basic plot of the poem and its theme of friends and foes and how they come to be. Fate involves destiny and chance which is captured in the idea of answer 3. Choice 1, buying a drink is mentioned, but is not a fateful thing. This is also true of 2 and 5. No mention is made of how much the combatants hate each other, 4.

21. 4 The answer is 4 because it restates the details in the poem. The speaker also states very simply that they were foes, but also wonders why the man may have enlisted and ends by stating, "no other reason why." This eliminates the idea that the two foes are schemers or that they perhaps fight due to love or hate of anyone or anything in particular. They shot at each other due to chance. No evidence exists of an attack, 1. Nothing is mentioned of family members, 2, or panic, 3. The poem mentions no cause for either man, 5.

Math

1. 1 There are 4 chefs, each of who average c per month. There are 18 servers, who each average $840 less than the chefs' wages (c). Subtract $840 from c and multiply that by 18 servers. Add the totals of the two groups to get the monthly payroll.

2. 5 The scale on a map states that 0.5 inches = 20 miles. Therefore, 1 inch = 40 miles. The distance between the houses on the map was 3 inches. 40 miles times 3 equals 120 miles.

3. 2 In 2007 there were a total of 142 graduates. In 2008, 153 students graduated. 153 – 142 = 11.

4. 1 The difference between the amounts of interest they earned is $10:

Vijay's interest after one year is $1000 × 0.04 = $40.

Yvette's interest after one year is $500 × 0.06 = $30

5. 5 Careful on "EXCEPT" questions because we are looking for the answer that does NOT work out. Expect 4 of the 5 answer choices to work and choose the only one that does not. Plug In each answer choice as x. All but the integer zero work (2)(0) + 3 = 3, which is NOT greater than 6.

6. 1 A bicycle wheel is like a circle. The rim represents the circumference, and each spoke represents the radius. If the diameter of the first bike is 28 cm, the radius is half of that (14 cm). With the second bike, we are told that the distance around the wheel (the circumference) is 22π. Remember that the circumference formula is πd. Therefore, the diameter of the second bike is 22, making its radius half of that (11 cm). The difference between the lengths of the spokes of the two bicycles is 14 cm – 11 cm = 3 cm.

7. 4 To rent the skating rink, Arthur must pay \$200 plus \$5 per person. Multiply the number of people at the party (*n*) by 5 and then ADD that to the basic charge of \$200.

8. 2 There are 180° in a triangle. If angle *A* measures 100°, the other two angles must total 80°. If sides AB and AC have equal lengths, their opposite angles (*B* and *C*) have equal measures. Therefore, both *B* and *C* have angles of 40° each.

9. 2 The area of the billboard is directly proportional to its price. As the area increases, the price increases. When setting up a proportion, make sure the units correspond correctly on either side of the equal sign: $\frac{40}{120}$ is equal to $\frac{150}{y}$.

10. 6 Divide the number of people on the tour, 184, by the number of people each bus can hold, 35. The answer is 5.26 buses. A sixth bus is needed to hold everyone.

11. 4 The triangles created by the two poles and their shadows are similar. The 3 foot pole's shadow is 4 feet long. The other pole's shadow is 12 feet long, 3 times longer than the other shadow. So the other pole is 3 times taller than the 3 foot pole, making it 9 feet tall.

12. 3 The base charge is \$100 (\$50 per day times 2 days). The cost for mileage is 180 × \$0.20 = \$36. Together they total \$136.

13. 3 Both the rectangle and triangle have areas of 96 or (12)(8). The formula for the area of a triangle is $A = \frac{bh}{2}$. So insert the numbers you know: $96 = \frac{32h}{2}$. Solving for *h* will give you 6.

14. 1 If you total the known percentages of food, rent and other expenses, you will get 90% (25 + 23 + 42 = 90). The remainder, 10%, goes into savings. If \$320 month is 10% of the total, the entire monthly income is \$3,200.

15. 1 The slope formula is $\frac{y_2 - y_1}{x_2 - x_1}$.

Using the points given, we get $\frac{8-2}{3-5} = \frac{6}{-3} = -3$.

16. 4 Find the point along the horizontal line that's roughly 60 miles. Move your pencil directly up to the curve. Now move your pencil directly to the left, to the horizontal axis. The number is roughly 7,000.

17. 5 Solve for *x*. If $3x - 1 = 11$, then $3x = 12$. Divide both sides by 3 to get *x* by itself: $x = 4$. Now use 4 in the other equation, $x^2 + x$: $4^2 + 4 = 16 + 4 = 20$.

18. 26,400

Materials represent 22% of the company's budget of \$120,000. Simply multiply 0.22 by \$120,000 to get \$26,400.

19. 3 Find out the total number of students in the school: Multiplying 18 classes by 35 students per class gives you 630 students. To find out how many new classes must be formed to reduce class size to 30, divide 630 by 30 students per class, equaling 21 classes. So you must form 3 new classes.

20. 4 Begin with the total price of the car, \$17,900. Subtract the rebate of \$1350 and the down payment of \$850. Then divide what's left by 60 to get the monthly payments $\frac{17900-850-1350}{60}$.

21. 5 Area of a triangle is $A = \frac{bh}{2}$. The base is 2. Remember to get the VERTICAL height by imagining a perpendicular line from the top of triangle down to the base. Draw a line with your pencil. The height is 3. Using the numbers you have: $A = \frac{(2)(5)}{2} = 5$.

22. 4 Write it out: Bell 1 rings every 2 hours. Beginning at 9 am it will ring again at 11 am, 1 pm, 3 pm, 5 pm, 7 pm and 9 pm. Bell 2 will ring every 3 hours: 9 am, 12 pm, 3 pm, 6 pm and 9 pm. Bell 3 rings every 4 hours: 9 am, 1 pm, 5 pm and 9 pm. So all 3 bells will ring again at 9 pm.

23. 1 Take the total number of games the team will play this season: 30 games so far, plus 15 more to play equals 45 games. Calculate the number of games it must win in order to win 60% of games for the season. (45)(0.6) = 27. The team has already won 20 games, so it only needs to win 7 more.

24. 5 Be careful when counting decimal places! "Three thousandths" is 0.003.

25. 4 To get an average (mean), add all 3 days of driving: $x + y + z$ and then divide that by 3, which looks like $\frac{x+y+z}{3}$.

Practice Test 4

Completely darken bubbles with a No. 2 pencil. If you make a mistake, be sure to erase mark completely. Erase all stray marks.

1

YOUR NAME: (Print) Last First M.I.

SIGNATURE: DATE: / /

HOME ADDRESS: (Print) Number and Street

City State Zip Code

PHONE NO.: (Print)

IMPORTANT: Please fill in these boxes exactly as shown on the back cover of your test book.

2. TEST FORM

3. TEST CODE

4. REGISTRATION NUMBER

5. YOUR NAME

First 4 letters of last name | FIRST INIT | MID INIT

6. DATE OF BIRTH

Month	Day	Year
JAN		
FEB		
MAR	0 0	0 0
APR	1 1	1 1
MAY	2 2	2 2
JUN	3 3	3 3
JUL	4	4 4
AUG	5	5 5
SEP	6	6 6
OCT	7	7 7
NOV	8	8 8
DEC	9	9 9

7. SEX

MALE

FEMALE

FORM NO. 00001-PR

Start with number 1 for each new section. If a section has fewer questions than answer spaces, leave the extra answer spaces blank. Be sure to erase any errors or stray marks completely.

WRITING

1 A B C D E	11 A B C D E	21 A B C D E	31 A B C D E
2 A B C D E	12 A B C D E	22 A B C D E	32 A B C D E
3 A B C D E	13 A B C D E	23 A B C D E	33 A B C D E
4 A B C D E	14 A B C D E	24 A B C D E	34 A B C D E
5 A B C D E	15 A B C D E	25 A B C D E	35 A B C D E
6 A B C D E	16 A B C D E	26 A B C D E	36 A B C D E
7 A B C D E	17 A B C D E	27 A B C D E	37 A B C D E
8 A B C D E	18 A B C D E	28 A B C D E	38 A B C D E
9 A B C D E	19 A B C D E	29 A B C D E	39 A B C D E
10 A B C D E	20 A B C D E	30 A B C D E	40 A B C D E

SOCIAL STUDIES

1 A B C D E	11 A B C D E	21 A B C D E	31 A B C D E
2 A B C D E	12 A B C D E	22 A B C D E	32 A B C D E
3 A B C D E	13 A B C D E	23 A B C D E	33 A B C D E
4 A B C D E	14 A B C D E	24 A B C D E	34 A B C D E
5 A B C D E	15 A B C D E	25 A B C D E	35 A B C D E
6 A B C D E	16 A B C D E	26 A B C D E	36 A B C D E
7 A B C D E	17 A B C D E	27 A B C D E	37 A B C D E
8 A B C D E	18 A B C D E	28 A B C D E	38 A B C D E
9 A B C D E	19 A B C D E	29 A B C D E	39 A B C D E
10 A B C D E	20 A B C D E	30 A B C D E	40 A B C D E

Start with number 1 for each new section. If a section has fewer questions than answer spaces, leave the extra answer spaces blank. Be sure to erase any errors or stray marks completely.

SCIENCE

1 A B C D E	11 A B C D E	21 A B C D E	31 A B C D E
2 A B C D E	12 A B C D E	22 A B C D E	32 A B C D E
3 A B C D E	13 A B C D E	23 A B C D E	33 A B C D E
4 A B C D E	14 A B C D E	24 A B C D E	34 A B C D E
5 A B C D E	15 A B C D E	25 A B C D E	35 A B C D E
6 A B C D E	16 A B C D E	26 A B C D E	36 A B C D E
7 A B C D E	17 A B C D E	27 A B C D E	37 A B C D E
8 A B C D E	18 A B C D E	28 A B C D E	38 A B C D E
9 A B C D E	19 A B C D E	29 A B C D E	39 A B C D E
10 A B C D E	20 A B C D E	30 A B C D E	40 A B C D E

READING

1 A B C D E	11 A B C D E	21 A B C D E	31 A B C D E
2 A B C D E	12 A B C D E	22 A B C D E	32 A B C D E
3 A B C D E	13 A B C D E	23 A B C D E	33 A B C D E
4 A B C D E	14 A B C D E	24 A B C D E	34 A B C D E
5 A B C D E	15 A B C D E	25 A B C D E	35 A B C D E
6 A B C D E	16 A B C D E	26 A B C D E	36 A B C D E
7 A B C D E	17 A B C D E	27 A B C D E	37 A B C D E
8 A B C D E	18 A B C D E	28 A B C D E	38 A B C D E
9 A B C D E	19 A B C D E	29 A B C D E	39 A B C D E
10 A B C D E	20 A B C D E	30 A B C D E	40 A B C D E

MATH

1 A B C D E	11 A B C D E	21 A B C D E	31 A B C D E
2 A B C D E	12 A B C D E	22 A B C D E	32 A B C D E
3 A B C D E	13 A B C D E	23 A B C D E	33 A B C D E
4 A B C D E	14 A B C D E	24 A B C D E	34 A B C D E
5 A B C D E	15 A B C D E	25 A B C D E	35 A B C D E
6 A B C D E	16 A B C D E	26 A B C D E	36 A B C D E
7 A B C D E	17 A B C D E	27 A B C D E	37 A B C D E
8 A B C D E	18 A B C D E	28 A B C D E	38 A B C D E
9 A B C D E	19 A B C D E	29 A B C D E	39 A B C D E
10 A B C D E	20 A B C D E	30 A B C D E	40 A B C D E

CAUTION Use the answer spaces in the grids below for Section 6 or Section 7 only if you are told to do so in your test book.

Student-Produced Responses ONLY ANSWERS ENTERED IN THE OVALS IN EACH GRID WILL BE SCORED. YOU WILL NOT RECEIVE CREDIT FOR ANYTHING WRITTEN IN THE BOXES ABOVE THE OVALS.

Grids 9, 10, 11, 12, 13 (each grid):

	/	/	
.	.	.	.
	0	0	0
1	1	1	1
2	2	2	2
3	3	3	3
4	4	4	4
5	5	5	5
6	6	6	6
7	7	7	7
8	8	8	8
9	9	9	9

PLEASE DO NOT WRITE IN THIS AREA

SERIAL #

[illegible] answer spaces blank. Be sure to erase any errors or stray marks completely.

Use the answer spaces in the grids below for Section [illegible] only if you are told to do so in your test book.

ONLY ANSWERS ENTERED IN THE CIRCLES IN EACH GRID WILL BE SCORED. YOU WILL NOT RECEIVE CREDIT FOR ANYTHING WRITTEN IN THE BOXES ABOVE THE CIRCLES.

LANGUAGE ARTS, WRITING

Tests of General Educational Development

Directions

The Language Arts, Writing Test is intended to measure your ability to use clear and effective English. This test includes both multiple-choice questions and an essay. These directions apply only to the multiple-choice section; a separate set of directions is given for the essay.

The multiple-choice section consists of paragraphs with lettered paragraphs and numbered sentences. Some of the sentences contain errors in sentence structure, usage, or mechanics (punctuation, and capitalization). After reading the numbered sentences, answer the multiple-choice questions that follow. Some questions refer to sentences that are correct as written. The best answer for these questions is the one that leaves the sentence as originally written. The best answer for some questions is the one that produces a sentence that is consistent with the verb tense and point of view used throughout the text. A document is often repeated in order to allow for additional questions on a second page. The repeated document is the same as the first

You should spend no more than 40 minutes on the multiple-choice questions and 45 minutes on your essay. Work carefully, but do not spend too much time on any one question. Be sure you answer every question. You may begin working on the essay part of this test as soon as you complete the multiple-choice section.

Do not mark in this test booklet. Record your answers on the separate answer sheet provided. Be sure that all requested information is properly recorded on the answer sheet.

To record your answers, mark one numbered space on the answer sheet beside the number that corresponds to the question in the test booklet.

FOR EXAMPLE:
Sentence 1: **We were honored to meet governor Phillips.**

Which correction should be made to sentence 1?

(1) insert a comma after honored
(2) change honored to honer
(3) change governor to Governor
(4) change were to was
(5) no correction is necessary

In this example, the word "governor" should be capitalized; therefore, answer space 3 would be marked on the answer sheet.

Do not rest the point of your pencil on the answer sheet while you are considering your answer. Make no stray or unnecessary marks. If you change an answer, erase your first mark completely. Mark only one answer space for each question; multiple answers will be scored as incorrect. Do not fold or crease your answer sheet. All test materials must be returned to the test administrator.

GO ON TO THE NEXT PAGE

Writing, Part I

Directions: Choose the one best answer to each question.

Questions 1 through 8 refer to the following informational article.

Subways

(A)

(1) If you have never been to a big city that has a subway you may not appreciate how complicated such a transit system can be. (2) Traveling on endless miles of underground track, without the endless train cars, large cities such as New York or Tokyo could not function. (3) As vital as they are, the modern subway is only about 100 years old.

(B)

(4) The first modern subways, the IRT, BMT, and IND lines in New York City, was built during the first few years of the twentieth century. (5) Although people had long wanted to make trains that could run underground in order to relieve traffic pressure in the streets above. (6) It was not until the advent of electricity that such a system was possible. (7) A precursor to the modern subway built in the late nineteenth century. (8) This early subway was propelled by air pressure in a pneumatic tube. (9) Largely forgotten, an abandoned tube stations were rediscovered during repairs of a modern subway station.

(C)

(10) Now subway systems can be found in cities throughout the world. (11) Subways were impossible before the advent of electricity because earlier trains were powered by coal and emitted dangerous smoke underground. (12) Today's subways are an efficient means of transporting millions of people quickly, they produce much less pollution than cars.

1. Sentence 1: **If you have never been to a big city that has a subway you may not appreciate how complicated such a transit system can be.**

   Which correction should be made to sentence 1?

   (1) change have to has
   (2) replace a big city with big cities
   (3) insert a comma after subway
   (4) replace you may not with one may not
   (5) replace such a with such

2. Sentence 2: **Traveling on endless miles of underground track, without the endless train cars, large cities such as New York or Tokyo could not function.**

   If you rewrote sentence 2 beginning with

   Large cities such as New York or Tokyo could not function

   the next words should be

   (1) traveling on endless miles
   (2) without the endless train cars
   (3) endlessly with train cars
   (4) without traveling on endless
   (5) without endless miles of underground

GO ON TO THE NEXT PAGE

3. Sentence 3: **As <u>vital as they are, the modern subway is</u> only about 100 years old.**

Which is the best way to write the underlined portion of the sentence? If the original is they best way, choose option (1)?

(1) vital as they are, the modern subway is
(2) they are vital, the modern subway is
(3) vitally, the modern subway is
(4) the modern subway, vitally, are
(5) vital as they are, modern subways are

4. Sentence 4: **The first modern subways, the IRT, BMT, and IND lines in New York City, was built during the first few years of the twentieth century.**

Which correction should be made to sentence 4?

(1) change <u>subways</u> to <u>subway</u>
(2) change <u>lines</u> to <u>line</u>
(3) remove the comma after <u>New York City</u>
(4) change <u>was built</u> to <u>were built</u>
(5) replace <u>of the</u> with <u>in the</u>

5. Sentence 5: **Although people had long wanted to make trains that could run underground in order to relieve traffic pressure in the streets above.**

Which correction should be made to sentence 5?

(1) replace <u>Although people</u> with <u>People</u>
(2) insert a comma after <u>wanted</u>
(3) change <u>trains that could</u> to <u>trains, which could</u>
(4) replace <u>in order to</u> with <u>for the purpose of</u>
(5) change <u>streets above</u> to <u>above streets</u>

6. Sentence 7: **A precursor to the modern subway built in the late nineteenth century.**

Which correction should be made to sentence 7?

(1) change <u>to</u> to <u>of</u>
(2) change <u>modern subway</u> to <u>the subway of today</u>
(3) insert <u>was</u> after <u>subway</u>
(4) replace <u>late</u> with <u>latter</u>
(5) no correction is necessary

7. Sentence 11: **Subways were impossible before the advent of electricity because earlier trains were powered by coal and emitted dangerous smoke underground.**

Which revision should be made to sentence 11?

(1) move sentence 11 to follow sentence 2
(2) move sentence 11 to the beginning of paragraph B
(3) move sentence 11 to the beginning of paragraph C
(4) move sentence 11 to follow sentence 6
(5) remove sentence 11

8. Sentence 12: **Today's subways are an efficient means of transporting millions of <u>people quickly, they produce</u> much less pollution than cars.**

Which is the best way to write the underlined portion of this sentence? If the original is the best way, choose option (1)?

(1) people quickly, they produce
(2) people quickly; they produce
(3) people quickly, but they produce
(4) people quickly, they produce
(5) quick people, producing

GO ON TO THE NEXT PAGE

Questions 9 through 17 refer to the following memorandum.

The Law Offices of Torani, Church, & Iris

98 East Third Ave
Suite 23
Stephensville, FL 21310
(923) 555-0643

MEMORANDUM

To: Marguerite Flowers, Office Manager
From: Fred Torani, Managing Partner, Torani, Church, & Iris
Subject: Merger with Josephs & Sullivan
Date: May 15, 2009

(A)

(1) The purpose of this memo is highlighting the most important issues that we will have to address in order to facilitate the coming merger. (2) While we believe the merger will go smoothly, there are a number of issues that must be resolved before it can begin.

(B)

(3) You will need to instruct your staff to create an inventory of our office equipment. (4) Such as printers and computers. (5) Also need to contact the office manager at Josephs & Sullivan to make sure that he conducts a similar inventory of his office. (6) The reason for the creation of this inventory is because we need to know what equipment we need and what we can sell.

(C)

(7) How many employees we have at our office and how many people work at Josephs & Sullivan is the next thing that needs to be determined by you. (8) We need to determine how much office space we will need. (9) You should estimate 40 square feet of office space per employee. (10) Next you should contact the Records managers at our office and at Josephs & Sullivan while finding out how many files each have. (11) The Records managers should be able to tell you how much space the files will occupy after we combine ours with theirs. (12) We will also need to figure out which employee positions is redundant or duplicative so that staff can be reassigned.

(D)

(13) This merger will be difficult and time-consuming, I am confident that we will be a stronger law firm afterwards. (14) Please get started with the merger planning as soon as you can. (15) If you need anything or if you are not sure whom to contact at Josephs & Sullivan, either call me or Lourdes Garcia, which is my counterpart at Josephs & Sullivan.

GO ON TO THE NEXT PAGE

9. Sentence 1: **The purpose of this memo is highlighting the most important issues that we will have to address in order to facilitate the coming merger.**

Which is the most effective revision of sentence 1?

(1) This memo's purpose is highlighting the most important issues that we will have to address in order to facilitate the coming merger.
(2) The purpose of this memo is to highlight the most important issues that we will have to address in order to facilitate the coming merger.
(3) The purpose of this memo is to highlight the more important issue that we will have to address in order to facilitate the coming merger.
(4) To facilitate the coming merger, this memo is to highlight with purpose the most important issues that we will have to address.
(5) The most important issues that we will have to address in order to facilitate the coming merger will purposefully be highlighted in this memo.

10. Sentences 3 and 4: **You will need to instruct your staff to create an inventory of <u>our office equipment</u>. <u>Such as printers</u> and computers.**

Which is the best way to write the underlined portions of these sentences? If the original is the best way, choose option (1).

(1) our office equipment. Such as printers
(2) our office equipment. For example printers
(3) our office equipment such a printers
(4) our office equipment, such as printers
(5) our office equipment for such printers

11. Sentence 5: **Also need to contact the office manager at Josephs & Sullivan to make sure that he conducts a similar inventory of his office.**

Which correction should be made to sentence 5?

(1) change <u>Also</u> to <u>You also</u>
(2) change <u>need</u> to <u>should</u>
(3) insert a comma after <u>Sullivan</u>
(4) change <u>conducts</u> to <u>is conducting</u>
(5) change <u>of</u> to <u>at</u>

12. Sentence 6: **<u>The reason for the creation of this inventory is because we need to</u> know what equipment we need and what we can sell.**

Which is the best way to write the underlined portion of this sentence? If the original is best, choose option (1)

(1) The reason for the creation of this inventory is because we need to
(2) The reason for creating this inventory is so that one may
(3) We are creating this inventory because we need to
(4) The creation of this inventory is in order to
(5) Because of our needs, this inventory is being created to know

GO ON TO THE NEXT PAGE

The memorandum is repeated for your use in answering the remaining questions.

The Law Offices of Torani, Church, & Iris

98 East Third Ave
Suite 23
Stephensville, FL 21310
(923) 555-0643

MEMORANDUM

To: Marguerite Flowers, Office Manager
From: Fred Torani, Managing Partner, Torani, Church, & Iris
Subject: Merger with Josephs & Sullivan
Date: May 15, 2009

(A)

(1) The purpose of this memo is highlighting the most important issues that we will have to address in order to facilitate the coming merger. (2) While we believe the merger will go smoothly, there are a number of issues that must be resolved before it can begin.

(B)

(3) You will need to instruct your staff to create an inventory of our office equipment. (4) Such as printers and computers. (5) Also need to contact the office manager at Josephs & Sullivan to make sure that he conducts a similar inventory of his office. (6) The reason for the creation of this inventory is because we need to know what equipment we need and what we can sell.

(C)

(7) How many employees we have at our office and how many people work at Josephs & Sullivan is the next thing that needs to be determined by you. (8) We need to determine how much office space we will need. (9) You should estimate 40 square feet of office space per employee. (10) Next you should contact the Records managers at our office and at Josephs & Sullivan while finding out how many files each have. (11) The Records managers should be able to tell you how much space the files will occupy after we combine ours with theirs. (12) We will also need to figure out which employee positions is redundant or duplicative so that staff can be reassigned.

(D)

(13) This merger will be difficult and time-consuming, I am confident that we will be a stronger law firm afterwards. (14) Please get started with the merger planning as soon as you can. (15) If you need anything or if you are not sure whom to contact at Josephs & Sullivan, either call me or Lourdes Garcia, which is my counterpart at Josephs & Sullivan.

GO ON TO THE NEXT PAGE

13. Sentence 7: **How many employees we have at our office and how many people work at Josephs & Sullivan is the next thing that needs to be determined by you.**

If you rewrote sentence 7 beginning with

The next thing that you

the next words should be

(1) should by our needs determine
(2) need to be determining
(3) be able to determine
(4) need to determine
(5) necessarily should determine

14. Sentence 10: **Next you should contact the Records managers at our office and at Josephs & Sullivan while finding out how many files each have.**

Which correction should be made to sentence 10?

(1) insert a comma after should
(2) replace contact with have contacted
(3) change our to hour
(4) insert also after and
(5) change while finding with to find

15. Which revision would improve the effectiveness of the memorandum?

(1) join paragraphs B and C
(2) move paragraph C to follow paragraph D
(3) remove paragraph D
(4) move sentence 3 to the end of paragraph A
(5) remove sentence 15

16. Sentence 12: **We will also need to figure out which employee positions is redundant or duplicative so that staff can be reassigned.**

Which correction should be made to sentence 12?

(1) change which to what
(2) change is to are
(3) insert a comma after redundant
(4) change staff to staffs
(5) replace can be to might have been

17. Sentence 13: **This merger will be difficult and time-consuming, I am confident that we will be a stronger law firm afterwards.**

Which is the best way to write the underlined portion of this sentence? If the original is the best way, choose option (1).

(1) time-consuming, I am confident that we will
(2) will be time-consuming, I am confident that we will
(3) time-consuming, but I am confident that we will
(4) time-consuming, and I am confident that we will
(5) will be time-consuming, I am confident that we

GO ON TO THE NEXT PAGE

Questions 18 through 25 refer to the following article.

Finding a Job

(A)

(1) A first time job applicant often is not certain how to begin searching fore a job. (2) If you are applying for a job at an office, you probably want to wear a suit to the interview. (3) A great place to begin your job search is an employment listing service. (4) Many of these employment services is available on the internet.

(B)

(5) Once you find a job that interests you, you should send in your application packet. (6) Your application packet should include a cover letter, a copy of your resume, and list references that your future employer can contact. (7) The cover letter should state why you are interested in the job and why you feel that you would be qualified for it. (8) Your resume should state and brief describe your education, past employment, and any relevant skills that you possess. (9) Your list of references include the names of a few people that know you well and could recommend you for the position.

(C)

(10) Once you get an interview. (11) You should think about how to present yourself to your future employer. (12) You should take some time to learn about your future employer; for example, take some time to research how it started and the nature of work it does. (13) While the interview is an important part of your future employer's decision of whether to hire you, you should do everything you can to make a good first impression.

18. Sentence 1: **A first time job applicant often is not certain how to begin searching fore a job.**

Which is the best way to write the underlined portion of this sentence? If the original is the best way, choose option (1).

(1) how to begin searching fore a job.
(2) how they should begin searching fore a job.
(3) whether to begin searching for jobs.
(4) how to begin searching four a job.
(5) how to begin searching for a job.

19. Sentence 2: **If you are applying for a job at an office, you probably want to wear a suit to the interview.**

Which revision should be made to the placement of sentence 2?

(1) move sentence 2 to follow sentence 5
(2) move sentence 2 to follow sentence 7
(3) remove sentence 2
(4) no revision is necessary
(5) move sentence 2 to follow sentence 11

GO ON TO THE NEXT PAGE

20. Sentence 4: **Many of these employment services is available on the internet.**

Which correction should be made to sentence 4?

(1) change Many to Most
(2) insert a comma after these
(3) replace is with are
(4) insert for viewing after is
(5) change on to at

21. Sentence 6: **Your application packet should include a cover letter, a copy of your resume, and list references that your future employer can contact.**

Which correction should be made to sentence 6?

(1) insert a comma after packet
(2) replace a copy with and a copy
(3) change your resume to you're resume
(4) change list to a list of
(5) replace can with should

22. Sentence 8: **Your resume should state and brief describe your education, past employment, and any relevant skills that you possess.**

Which is the best way to write the underlined portions of this sentence? If the original is the best way, choose option (1).

(1) and brief describe your education, past employment, and
(2) and briefly describe your education, past employment, and
(3) while brief describe your education, past employment, and
(4) and brief description of your education, past employment, or
(5) or briefly describe your education, passed employment, and

23. Sentence 9: **Your list of references include the names of a few people that know you well and could recommend you for the position.**

Which correction should be made to sentence 9?

(1) insert should after references
(2) insert a comma after list
(3) replace know with no
(4) change and to or
(5) replace the with that

24. Sentences 10 and 11: **Once you get an interview. You should think about how to present yourself to your future employer.**

Which is the best way to write the underlined portions of these sentences? If the original is the best way, choose option (1).

(1) get an interview. You should think
(2) obtain an interview. And you should think
(3) get an interview, one should be thinking
(4) get an interview, you should think
(5) obtain an interview, but you have thought

25. Sentence 13: **While the interview is an important part of your future employer's decision of whether to hire you, you should do everything you can to make a good first impression.**

The most effective revision of sentence 13 would begin with which group of words?

(1) As the interview is an important
(2) Everything should be done by you
(3) Even though an interview is
(4) While the interview can be
(5) Despite the importance of the interview

GO ON TO LANGUAGE ARTS, WRITING, PART II

DO NOT MARK OR WRITE ON THIS PAGE

LANGUAGE ARTS, WRITING, PART II

Tests of General Educational Development

Essay Directions and Topic

Look at the box on page 290. In the box are your assigned topic and the letter of that topic.

You must write on the assigned topic ONLY.

Mark the letter of your assigned topic in the appropriate space on your answer sheet booklet. Be certain that all other requested information is properly recorded in your answer sheet booklet.

You will have 45 minutes to write on your assigned essay topic. You may return to the multiple-choice section after you complete your essay if you have time remaining in this test period. Do not return the Language Arts, Writing booklet until you finish both Parts I and II of the Language Arts, Writing Test.

Two evaluators will score your essay according to its overall effectiveness. Their evaluation will be based on the following features:

- Well-focused main points
- Clear organization
- Specific development of your ideas
- Control of sentence structure, punctuation, grammar, word choice, and spelling

REMEMBER, YOU MUST COMPLETE BOTH THE MULTIPLE-CHOICE QUESTIONS (PART I) and THE ESSAY (PART II) TO RECEIVE A SCORE ON THE LANGUAGE ARTS, WRITING TEST. To avoid having to repeat both parts of the test, be sure to observe the following rules.

- Do not leave the pages blank.
- Write legibly in ink so that the evaluators will be able to read your writing.
- Write on the assigned topic. If you write on a topic other than the one assigned, you will not receive a score for the Language Arts, Writing Test.
- Write your essay on the lined pages of the separate answer sheet booklet. Only the writing on theses pages will be scored.

IMPORTANT:
You may return to the multiple-choice section after you complete your essay if you have time remaining in this test period. Do not return the Language Arts, Writing booklet until you finish both Parts I and II of the Language Arts, Writing Test.

GO ON TO THE NEXT PAGE

Writing, Part II

Topic E

What skill do you possess that has been particularly helpful in your life?

In your essay, identify that skill and explain how it has helped you. Use your personal observations, experience, and knowledge to support your essay.

Part II is a test to determine how well you can use written language to explain your ideas.

In preparing your essay, you should take the following steps.

- Read the **DIRECTIONS** and the **TOPIC** carefully.
- Plan your essay before you write. Use the scratch paper provided to make any notes. These notes will be collected but not scored.
- Before you turn in your essay, reread what you have written and make any changes that will improve your essay.

Your essay should be long enough to develop the topic adequately.

END OF EXAMINATION

SOCIAL STUDIES

Tests of General Educational Development

Directions

The Social Studies Test consists of multiple-choice questions intended to measure understanding of general social studies concepts. The questions are based on short readings that often include a map, graph, chart, cartoon, or figure. Study the information given and then answer the question(s) following it. Refer to the information as often as necessary in answering the questions.

You should spend no more than 45 minutes answering the questions in this booklet. Work carefully, but do not spend too much time on any one question. Be sure you answer every question.

Do not mark in this test booklet. Record your answers on the separate answer sheet provided. Be sure that all requested information is properly recorded on the answer sheet.

To record your answers, mark the numbered space on the answer sheet beside the number that corresponds to the question in the test booklet.

FOR EXAMPLE:

Early colonists of North America looked for settlement sites with adequate water supplies and
access by ship. For this reason, many early towns were built near

(1) mountains
(2) prairies
(3) rivers
(4) glaciers
(5) plateaus

The correct answer is "rivers"; therefore, answer space 3 would be marked on the answer sheet.

Do not rest the point of your pencil on the answer sheet while you are considering your answer. Make no stray or unnecessary marks. If you change an answer, erase your first mark completely. Mark only <u>one</u> answer space for each question; multiple answers will be scored as incorrect. Do not fold or crease your answer sheet. All test materials must be returned to the test administrator.

GO ON TO THE NEXT PAGE

1. The Twenty-second Amendment to the Constitution states that "No person shall be elected to the office of the President more than twice, and no person who has held the office of President, or acted as President, for more than two years of a term to which some other person was elected President shall be elected to the office of the President more than once..." In which situation would this amendment apply?

    (1) A president is elected from a state that was not part of the original thirteen colonies.
    (2) A president attempts to run for a third term of office.
    (3) The United States military refuses to accept the president as commander-in-chief.
    (4) The president dies before his first term in office is complete.
    (5) The president is impeached and removed from office during his first term.

Questions 2 and 3 refer to the following graph and information.

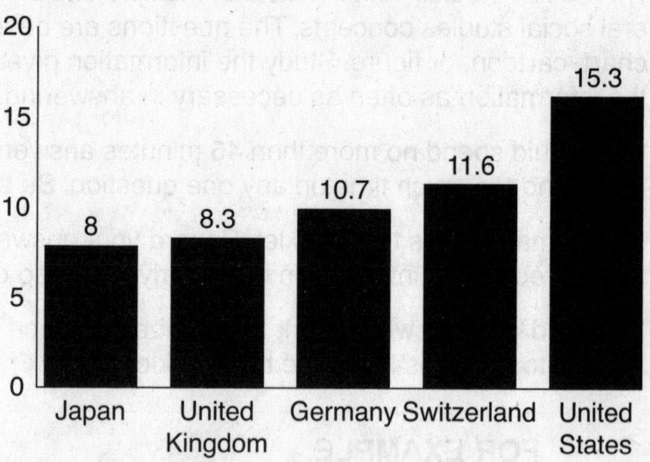

The gross domestic product (GDP) is the total value of the goods and services produced by a country in a given year. This graph depicts the percentage of the GDP spent on healthcare every year.

2. Which statement is a **FACT,** not an opinion, of the information in the graph?

    (1) The quality of healthcare in the United States is declining.
    (2) Japan and Switzerland both have inefficient and wasteful government spending programs.
    (3) The United States spends too much money on healthcare.
    (4) The United States expends a larger proportion of its GDP on healthcare than does Japan or Switzerland.
    (5) The Japanese healthcare system is the best in the world.

GO ON TO THE NEXT PAGE

3. Which nation spent the smallest proportion of its GDP on healthcare?

(1) Japan
(2) United Kingdom
(3) Germany
(4) Switzerland
(5) the United States

4. Urbanization is the process by which rural or natural lands become urban through immigration and the building of infrastructure. In which natural environment has urbanization most frequently occurred?

(1) mountainous regions
(2) deserts
(3) river valleys
(4) wetlands
(5) arctic tundras

5. During the late 18th and early 19th centuries, Great Britain experienced major changes in manufacturing, agriculture, mining, and transportation.

What is this era called?

(1) the Age of Mechanization
(2) Reconstruction
(3) the Great Depression
(4) World War I
(5) the Industrial Revolution

6. In 1803 Thomas Jefferson facilitated the purchase of a French territory from New Orleans to present-day Montana. The acquisition of these lands nearly doubled the size of the United States overnight.

What is this transaction called?

(1) the Gadsden Purchase
(2) the Louisiana Purchase
(3) the French and Indian War
(4) the Treaty of Versailles
(5) the Mexican Cession

GO ON TO THE NEXT PAGE

Questions 7 through 9 refer to the following excerpt from *Miranda v. Arizona,* a Supreme Court decision from 1966.

> "The person in custody must, prior to interrogation, be clearly informed that he has the right to remain silent, and that anything he says will be used against him in the court of law; he must be clearly informed that he has the right to consult with a lawyer and to have the lawyer with him during interrogation, and that, if he is indigent, a lawyer will be appointed to represent him...
>
> ...If the individual indicates in any manner, at any time prior to or during questioning, that he wishes to remain silent, the interrogation must cease... If the individual states that he wants an attorney, the interrogation must cease until an attorney is present. At that time, the individual must have an opportunity to confer with the attorney and to have him present during any subsequent questioning."

7. Which statement best describes the main point of Supreme Court's decision according to this excerpt?

   (1) Interrogations must cease whenever attorneys are present.
   (2) The United States must protect the rights of non-citizen residents.
   (3) Individuals must know their rights before they are interrogated by the police.
   (4) Individuals should not be arrested by police officers under any circumstances.
   (5) The police can never work with attorneys during interrogations.

8. According to this excerpt, under what circumstances must an interrogation stop?

   Interrogations must stop when

   (1) a police officer uses brutality and violence against a person
   (2) a person requests to go home
   (3) a police officer is caught bribing an attorney
   (4) a person requests to remain silent or have an attorney present
   (5) a police officer requests that an attorney be present for the interrogation

9. Which statement best describes the impact of *Miranda v. Arizona* on the American criminal justice system?

   The decision

   (1) has had virtually no affect on the criminal justice system since it was first handed down
   (2) has destroyed the constitutional rights of arrested individuals, especially the protections of the First and Fourth Amendments
   (3) has required police officers to inform individuals of their right to remain silent and their right to an attorney
   (4) has undermined the ability of attorneys to defend their clients
   (5) was overturned several years after it was handed down

GO ON TO THE NEXT PAGE

Questions 10 and 11 refer to the following cartoon of President Theodore Roosevelt.

THE LION-TAMER

10. Which statement best describes the main point of this cartoon about President Theodore Roosevelt?

    President Roosevelt is

    (1) a victim of the trusts that run Washington, DC and Wall Street
    (2) limited by the Constitution to act in economic affairs
    (3) guilty of crimes and misdemeanors in the business world and should be impeached
    (4) controlling the excesses of big business and Wall Street
    (5) a competent diplomat and commander in chief of the armed forces

11. President Theodore Roosevelt is also famous for preserving millions of acres of forestland, animal habitats, and natural resources. What is this practice called?

    (1) Partisan politics
    (2) Conservationism
    (3) Global warming
    (4) Environmental alarmism
    (5) Biodiversity

12. The Cuban Missile Crisis was a confrontation between the Soviet Union, the United States, and Cuba during the early 1960s. What larger conflict was the Cuban Missile Crisis a part of?

    (1) the Cold War
    (2) the Spanish-American War
    (3) World War II
    (4) the Civil War
    (5) the Vietnam War

GO ON TO THE NEXT PAGE

Questions 13 and 14 refer to the following graph and information.

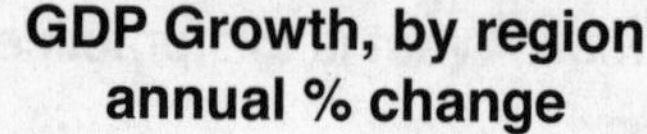

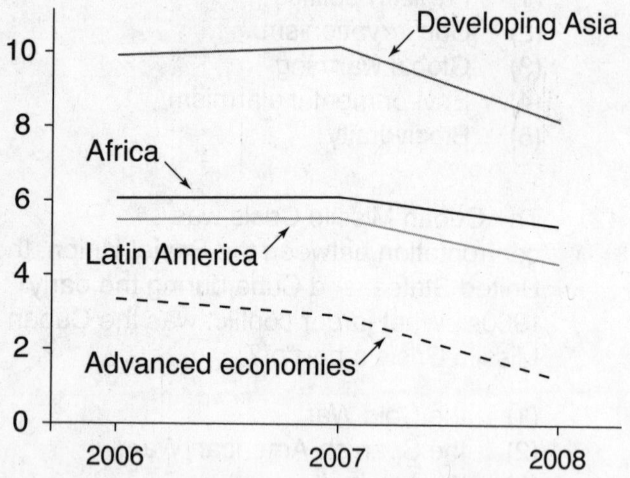

The gross domestic product (GDP) is the total value of the goods and services produced by a country in a given year.

13. Which observation is confirmed by the data from the graph?

(1) The United States is declining in importance.
(2) The GDP's of nations in Developing Asia are growing faster than those of Latin America and the Caribbean.
(3) The economies of African nations are in ruins and cannot be fixed.
(4) Caribbean nations are poorer than African nations.
(5) The growth rate of GDP's has increased exponentially in recent years.

14. Which factors have played most important role in encouraging growth in "developing" Asian nations?

(1) industrialization, manufacturing, and exports
(2) gold-based currency, agriculture, and socialism
(3) population decline, environmental disasters, and plague
(4) education, cultural production, and the arts
(5) technology, gold-based currency, and population decline

15. In *Democracy in America,* Alexis de Tocqueville wrote that "Americans combine the notions of religion and liberty so intimately in their minds that it is impossible to make them conceive of one without the other." Which statement best describes Tocqueville's main point?

Tocqueville believed that

(1) Americans understood freedom in terms of religion and religion in terms of freedom
(2) Americans had no conception of freedom
(3) American religion could not coexist with constitutionally-protected freedoms
(4) Americans had created a system of politics inferior to those of France and other European countries
(5) Americans understood religion only as a liberating force in the world

GO ON TO THE NEXT PAGE

Questions 16 and 17 refer to the following map.

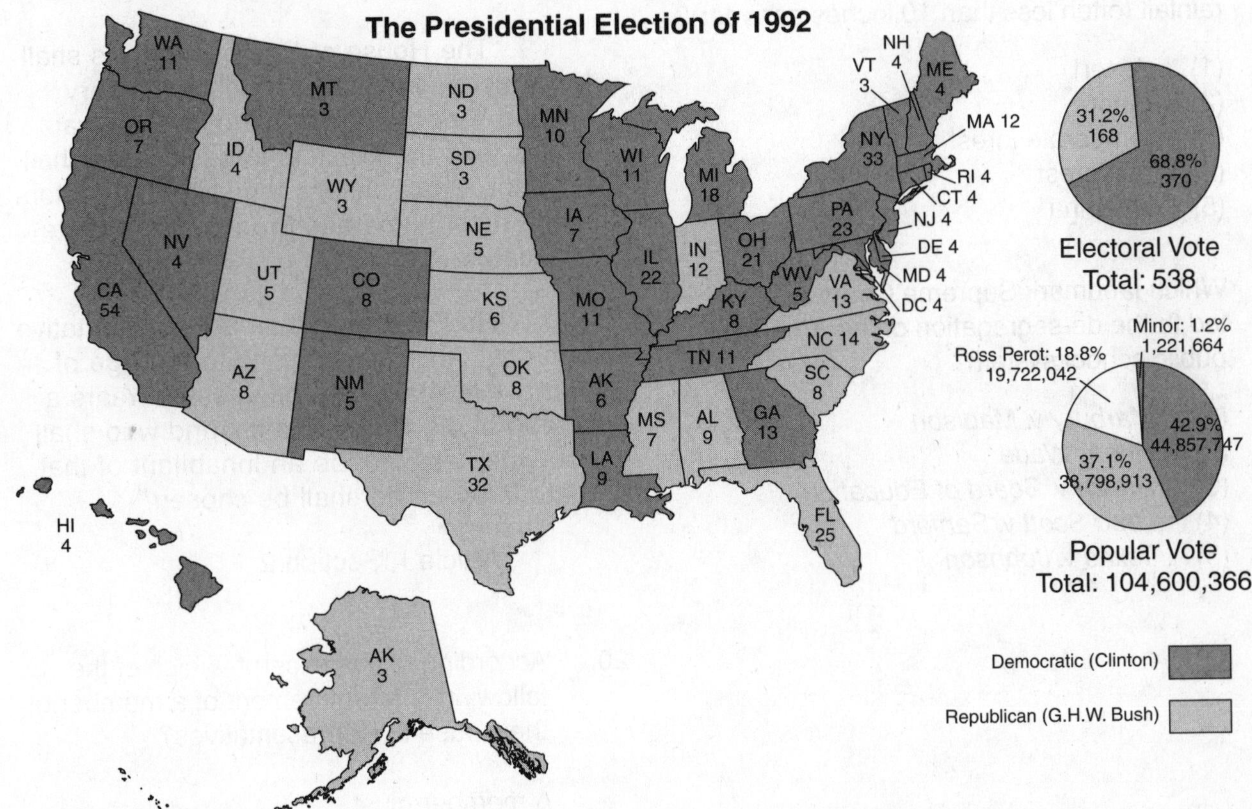

16. According to the map, which statement is true?

Presidential elections

(1) almost never end with a clear winner
(2) are an ineffective way to choose a leader even though they are required by the Constitution
(3) have never involved third-party candidates
(4) do not produce identical results for the popular vote and the Electoral College
(5) are based only on the popular vote

17. Why do some states, such as California, Texas, and New York have so many electoral votes in the Electoral College?

These states

(1) are larger than many other states
(2) are less financially stable than other states
(3) are closely aligned to the federal government
(4) are among the wealthiest states
(5) have some of the largest state populations

GO ON TO THE NEXT PAGE

18. Which term describes a landscape or region that receives an extremely low rainfall (often less than 10 inches per year)?

(1) desert
(2) tundra
(3) temperate forest
(4) rainforest
(5) savanna

19. Which landmark Supreme Court decision led to the de-segregation of the American public school system?

(1) *Marbury v. Madison*
(2) *Roe v. Wade*
(3) *Brown v. Board of Education*
(4) *Dred Scott v. Sanford*
(5) *Texas v. Johnson*

Questions 20 through 22 refer to the following excerpt from the Constitution.

"The House of Representatives shall be composed of Members chosen every second Year by the People of the several States, and the Electors in each State shall have the Qualifications requisite for Electors of the most numerous Branch of the State Legislature.

No Person shall be a Representative who shall not have attained to the Age of twenty five Years, and been seven Years a Citizen of the United States, and who shall not, when elected, be an Inhabitant of that State in which he shall be chosen."

Article I, Section 2

20. According to this excerpt, which of the following is a requirement of a member of the House of Representatives?

A member must

(1) be a resident of the state he or she represents
(2) be at least 35 years old
(3) pass a background check to ensure no recent violations of the law
(4) have experience in state legislatures
(5) have spent his or her entire life within the continental United States

GO ON TO THE NEXT PAGE

21. According to the excerpt, what is distinctive about the House of Representatives?

The House of Representatives is

(1) less important than the Senate
(2) larger than the Senate
(3) given the same powers as the Senate
(4) under the direct supervision of the President
(5) elected every 4 years

22. The House of Representatives is part of which branch of government?

(1) the Executive Branch
(2) the Treasury Branch
(3) the Judicial Branch
(4) the Diplomatic Branch
(5) the Legislative Branch

23. Globalization is the transformation of local or regional phenomena into global ones. Which situation is an example of globalization?

(1) a border dispute between two Asian nations that leads to the deaths of hundreds of people
(2) the destruction of the rainforest by the Brazilian government
(3) subsistence farming in southern African nations
(4) the use of solar energy instead of fossil-fuel based energy
(5) increasingly powerful international organizations help to intervene in local disputes

GO ON TO THE NEXT PAGE

Questions 24 and 25 refer to the following graph.

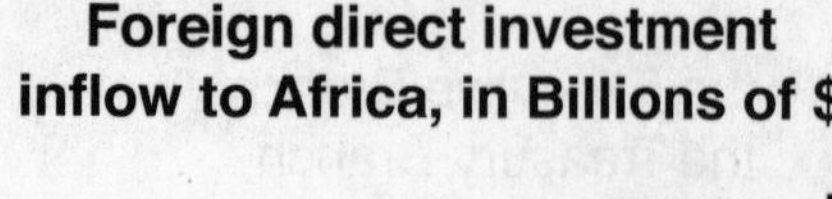

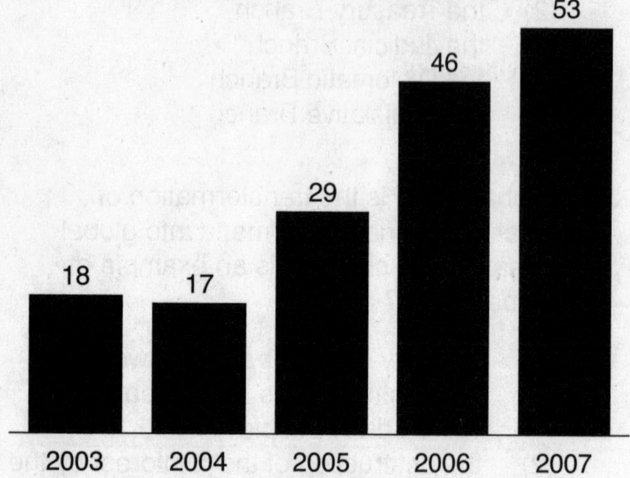

Source: UN Africa Renewal, from data in UNCTAD, World Investment Report 2006, 2008

24. The graph indicates recent direct investment in African nations. Why do some foreign companies invest in African nations?

Companies invest in Africa because

(1) African nations have some of the world's strongest economies
(2) African political leaders are closely involved in European economic problems
(3) African economies are mostly oriented toward international trade and technology
(4) African nations provide mining resources and some manufacturing
(5) African culture requires tribute from other nations' companies

25. Which statement describes an **OPINION,** not a fact, about foreign investment in Africa?

Foreign investment

(1) has increased in recent years
(2) has more than doubled from 2003 to 2007
(3) is wasteful because African nations will never have strong economies
(4) is the result of coordinated international efforts to help African economies
(5) has bolstered the economies of some African nations

END OF EXAMINATION

SCIENCE

Tests of General Educational Development

Directions

The Science Test consists of multiple-choice questions intended to measure understanding of general concepts in science. The questions are based on short readings that often include a graph, chart, or figure. Study the information given and then answer the question(s) following it. Refer to the information as often as necessary in answering the questions.

You should spend no more than 53 minutes answering the questions in this booklet. Work carefully, but do not spend too much time on any one question. Be sure you answer every question.

Do not mark in this test booklet. Record your answers to the questions on the separate sheet provided. Be sure all requested information is properly recorded on the answer sheet.

To record your answers, mark the numbered space on the answer sheet beside the number that corresponds to the question in the test booklet.

FOR EXAMPLE:

Which of the following is the smallest unit in a living thing?

(1) tissue
(2) organ
(3) cell
(4) muscle
(5) capillary

The correct answer is "cell"; therefore, answer space 3 would be marked on the answer sheet.

Do not rest the point of your pencil on the answer sheet while you are considering your answer. Make no stray or unnecessary marks. If you change an answer, erase your first mark completely. Mark only one answer space for each question; multiple answers will be scored as incorrect. Do not fold or crease your answer sheet. All test materials must be returned to the test administrator.

GO ON TO THE NEXT PAGE

Directions: Choose the one best answer to each question.

1. Sometimes animals from different species adapt in similar ways to their environments. Sometimes, this results in the animals having body parts that do the same function, even though the structures evolved separately and might look nothing alike. These body parts are called analogous structures.

   Based on the information above, which of the following is a pair of analogous structures?

   (1) the wing of a bird and the wing of a mosquito
   (2) the gill slit of a fish and the tail of a fish
   (3) the mouth of a tiger and the stomach of a lion
   (4) the hand of a baby and the hand of an adult
   (5) the nest of a bird and the burrow of a rabbit

2. Groundwater often seeps into underground caverns. As the water drips from the ceiling of the cavern, some minerals may be deposited in the water. The mineral water drips to the floor. After the water evaporates, the minerals are left behind and build up over time, forming stalagmites.

   The information above provides the answer to which of the following questions?

   (1) What types of minerals are found in groundwater?
   (2) What causes the formation of underground caverns?
   (3) What is the difference between stalagmites and stalactites?
   (4) How tall can stalagmites grow to be?
   (5) How are stalagmites formed?

3. Below is a table showing the percentage of total blood volume for several components of human blood.

Percent Composition of Human Blood	
Dissolved Gases	1%
Nutrients	3%
Red Blood Cells	43%
Water	51%
White Blood Cells	2%

   What percentage of human blood is not made up of cells?

   (1) 1
   (2) 9
   (3) 45
   (4) 55
   (5) 57

GO ON TO THE NEXT PAGE

4. A solution has two parts, a solute, which is dissolved, and a solvent, commonly water, which the solute is dissolved in. Osmosis is the flow of water from an area of high solute concentration to an area with low solute concentration.

In the experiment below, a beaker with a semi permeable membrane is filled with equal amounts of water at time 1. Different amounts of solute molecules are added to each side. The picture labeled Time 2 shows the same beaker after 10 minutes have passed. Which of the following best explains the results?

(1) The solute particles passed through the semi permeable membrane.
(2) Gravity lowered the water level on the right side of the beaker.
(3) Since the left side of the beaker had more solute than the right, water moved to the left through osmosis.
(4) The molecules on the left interacted with the water and caused it to expand.
(5) Some of the water on the right side evaporated.

5. Below is a diagram of a celestial event known as a lunar eclipse.

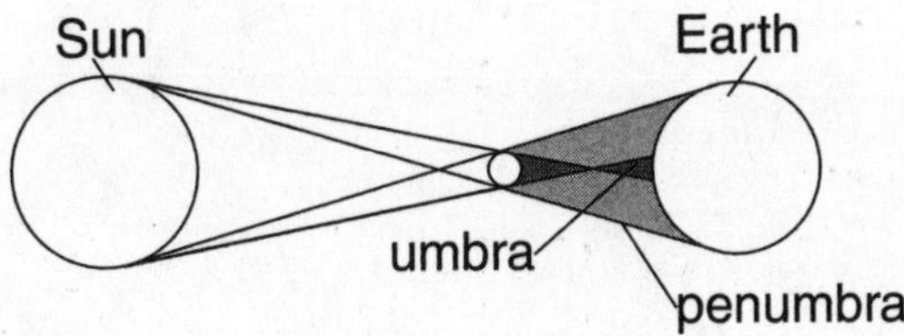

What is the unlabeled spherical object?

(1) star
(2) moon
(3) cloud
(4) satellite
(5) planet

6. While handling strong acids, a chemist wears safety goggles. Which of the following is the best reason for this?

(1) to see the acids better
(2) to keep long hair away from the acids
(3) to protect the eyes from possible acid splashes
(4) to reduce glare
(5) to magnify the chemicals

7. Radio waves travel extremely far through air but are unable to travel well under water.

Based on this information, which of the following vehicle is least likely to have a radio receiver?

(1) submarine
(2) car
(3) train
(4) airplane
(5) sailboat

8. Two brown-eyed parents have a child with blue eyes. Which of the following statements is the most likely explanation for this?

(1) The child's eyes mutated.
(2) The child's eyes were diseased.
(3) Both parents carried a hidden gene for blue eyes.
(4) One parent carried a hidden gene for blue eyes.
(5) The child was born with brown eyes that later turned blue.

GO ON TO THE NEXT PAGE

Questions 9 and 10 refer to the following information.

Blood type in humans is determined by proteins on the surface of red blood cells. The genes that code for these proteins are located on chromosomes, which come in pairs. Dominant genes are those that are always expressed when present. A recessive gene is only expressed if it is pure, meaning if both genes in the pair code for the recessive trait. The gene for type A blood and the gene for type B blood are both dominant, while the gene for type O blood is recessive. Type AB blood occurs when an individual is hybrid and has one type A gene and one type B gene. Since these genes are co dominant, a hybrid expresses both A and B proteins.

Below is a table listing the gene combinations and the resulting blood types.

Genes and Blood Type

Genes	Blood Type
I^AI^A or I^A	A
I^BI^B or I^B	B
I^AI^B	AB
	O

The chart below is called a Punnett Square and is used to determine the odds of the occurrence of different gene pairs. This Punnett Square shows the results when two hybrid parents with type AB blood have children.

Punnett Square: Blood Type in Humans

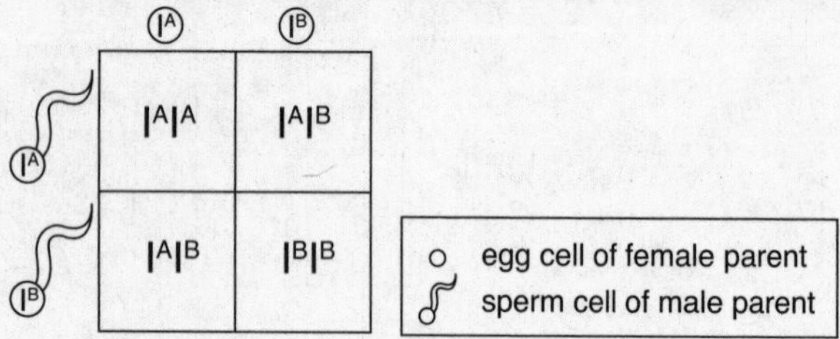

9. Which of the following are possible blood types of offspring of two parents with type AB blood?
   (1) A, B, AB, and O
   (2) A, B, and AB only
   (3) A and B only
   (4) AB only
   (5) only

10. Based on the information and the table, which is must be true of a woman with type O blood?
    (1) She is pure for a recessive gene.
    (2) She is hybrid.
    (3) She had parents with type AB blood.
    (4) Her blood does not clot properly.
    (5) She has exactly one copy of the gene for type O blood.

GO ON TO THE NEXT PAGE

Questions 11 and 12 are based on the following information and graph.

To make a solution, a substance, called the solute, is dissolved in another substance, called the solvent. Solubility is the maximum amount of solute that can be dissolved under certain conditions. Solubility is usually given as grams of solute in grams of solvent.

Solubility of Gases in Temperature

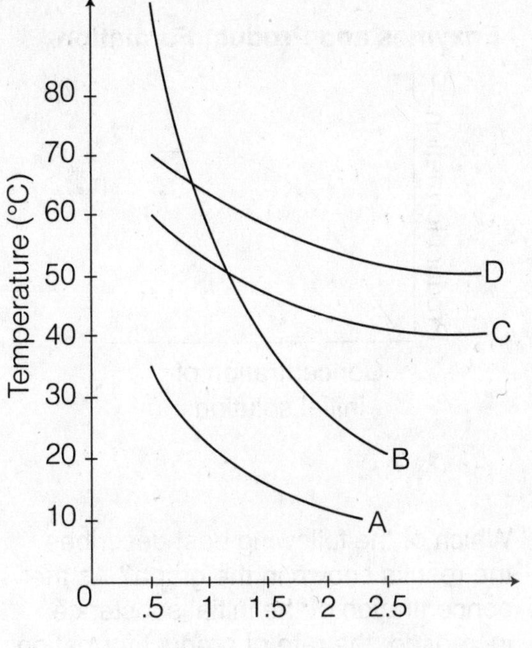

11. Which statement is most supported by the information and graph above?

(1) Pressure has no effect on the solubility of a gas.
(2) The solubility of most gases increases as temperature increases.
(3) Temperature has no effect on the solubility of a gas.
(4) Most gases dissolve at the same rate.
(5) The solubility of most gases decreases as temperature increases.

12. At 40°C, how many grams of Gas B would dissolve per 100 grams of water?

(1) 0
(2) 1
(3) 1.5
(4) 2
(5) 2.5

13. A parasite is an organism that relies on another organism, called a host, to survive. A parasite always harms its host.

Based on the information, which of the following is an example of a parasite?

(1) bacteria that live in a human intestine and produce vitamin K for the human
(2) a tapeworm that lives in a dog's stomach and prevents the dog from absorbing nutrients from food
(3) a cat that relies on its owner to provide it food
(4) bees that drink nectar from flowers and help spread pollen from one flower to another
(5) a male wolf that fights another male wolf to become the leader of the pack

GO ON TO THE NEXT PAGE

14. The periodic table lists information about all the known elements in the world. There are some trends with the properties of the elements. For example, ionization energy increases from left to right and from bottom to top. Ionization energy is the energy required to pull an electron off an atom. The figure below shows this trend.

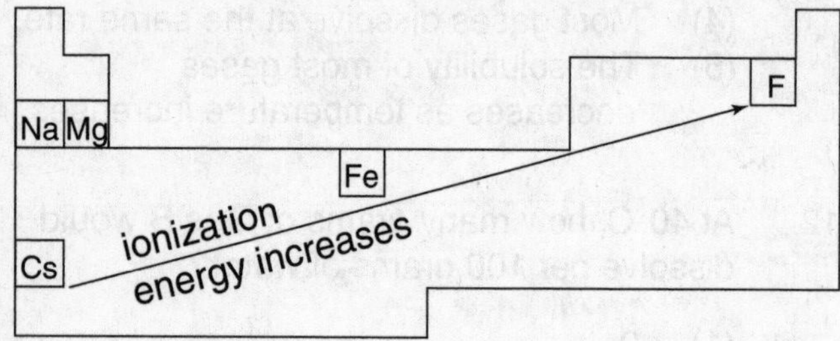

Cs Cesium
F Fluorine
Fe Iron
Na Sodium
Mg Magnesium

Based on the information and figure, which of the following elements has the highest ionization energy?

(1) Cesium
(2) Fluorine
(3) Iron
(4) Sodium
(5) Magnesium

An enzyme speeds up a chemical reaction by interacting with the initial substance and making it easier to form a product. In most cases, an enzyme can only interact with one molecule of the initial substance at a time.

The graph below shows the results of an experiment that measured the rate of product formation as the concentration of the initial substance is increased. A limited amount of enzyme was present during this experiment.

Enzymes and Product Formation

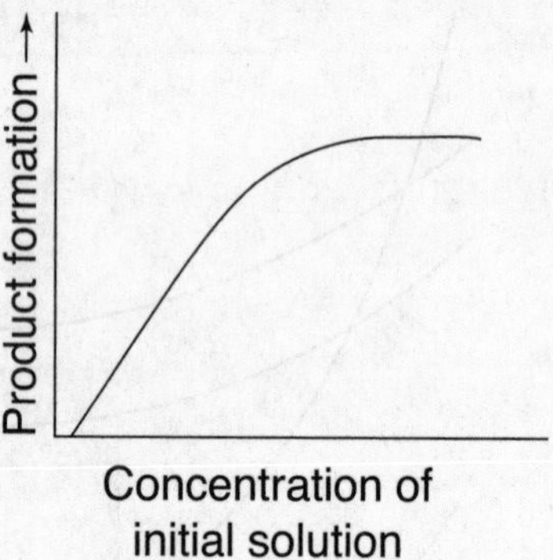

15. Which of the following best describes the results shown in the graph? As the concentration of the initial substance increased, the rate of product formation

(1) increased continually
(2) increased and then leveled off
(3) increased and then decreased
(4) decreased continually
(5) remained constant

GO ON TO THE NEXT PAGE

16. Which of the following is a simple machine?

(1) car
(2) computer
(3) horse
(4) paper
(5) pulley

17. Below is a graph recording the distance traveled by a turtle within an 8 minute period.

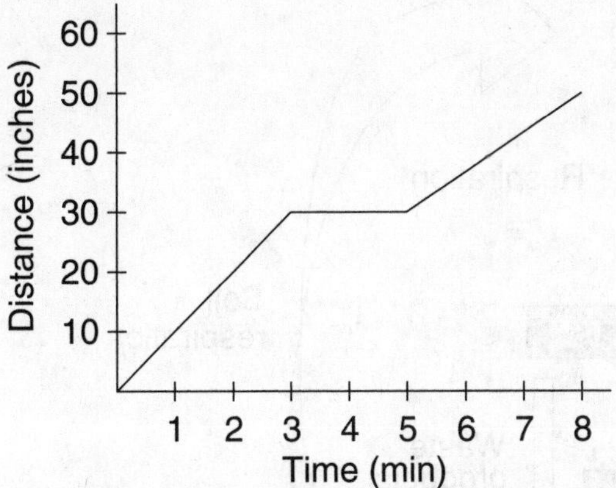

Which of the following best describes the behavior of the turtle as shown in the graph?

(1) The turtle walks at a steady pace for 8 minutes.
(2) The turtle does not move during the 8 minute period.
(3) The turtle travels a total distance of 30 inches in 8 minutes.
(4) The turtle walks for 3 minutes, rests for 2 minutes, and then walks another 3 minutes.
(5) The turtle walks a total of 8 inches.

18. Jet stream is a strong current of air high above land. Airplanes often take advantage of jet streams, since the air will push the plane and reduce the amount of fuel needed. The figure below shows jet stream across the United States.

Jet Stream in United States

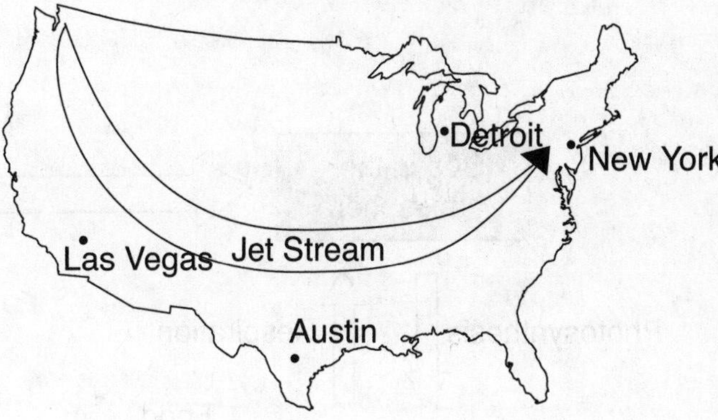

Jet stream would most benefit a flight from

(1) New York to Austin
(2) New York to Las Vegas
(3) Austin to Las Vegas
(4) Detroit to New York
(5) New York to Detroit

GO ON TO THE NEXT PAGE

19. Carbon dioxide is a very important molecule. The carbon in it is used by plants to make food, and that food is consumed by animals and eventually returned to the soil or atmosphere. The diagram below shows the carbon cycle.

The Carbon Cycle

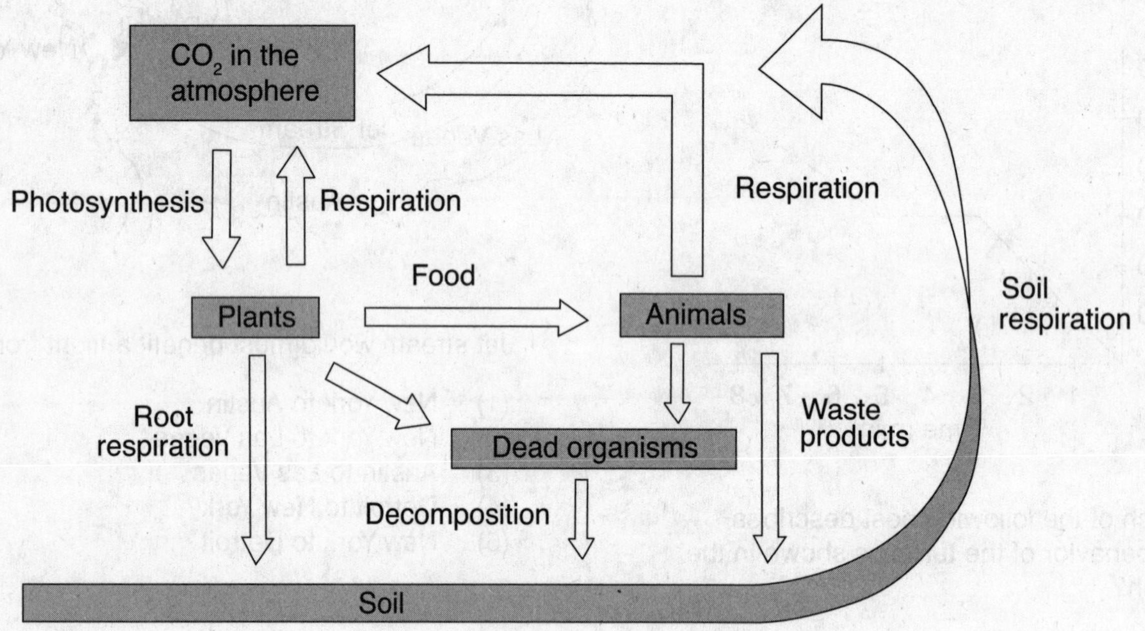

According to the diagram, which of the following deposit carbon into soil?

(1) plants, animals, and dead organisms
(2) dead organisms only
(3) plants only
(4) animals and dead organisms only
(5) the atmosphere only

GO ON TO THE NEXT PAGE

20. In most environments, there is a limited amount of nutrients. As a result, living organisms must compete for food and resources. In the experiment below, a type of single celled organism called an amoeba was cultured alone and with a mixture of other single celled organisms. The same amounts of nutrients were provided in each culture.

Amoeba Population Growth

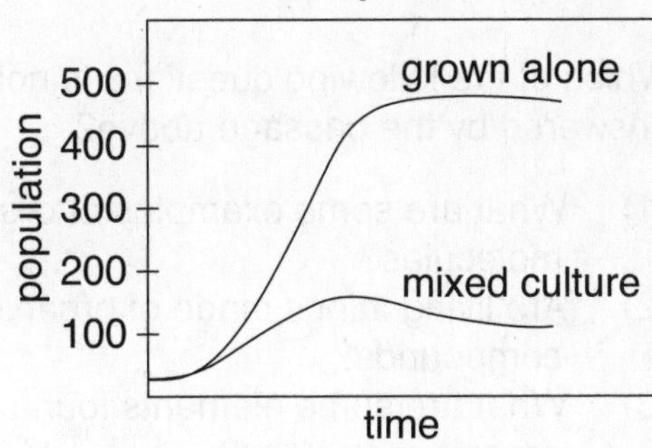

Which of the following conclusions can be drawn from this graph?

(1) Amoebas are more evolved than the organisms in the mixed culture.
(2) Amoebas reproduce more rapidly when cultured alone.
(3) This species of amoeba does not survive well alone.
(4) Amoebas reproduce more rapidly in a mixed culture.
(5) Amoebas reproduce at the same rate as every other single celled organism.

21. In a chemical reaction, chemicals known as reactants undergo some sort of a change and the resulting chemicals are called products. Below is a graphical representation of the amount of potential energy stored in the chemical bonds at various stages of a specific chemical reaction.

Energy of a Reaction

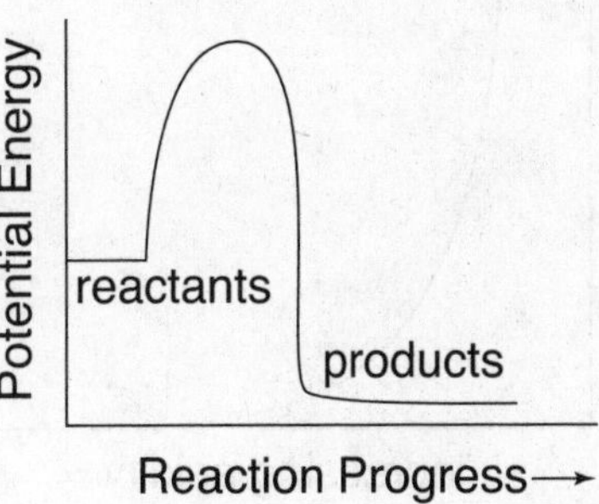

Which of the following statements correctly interprets the graph?

(1) The products have more potential energy than the reactants.
(2) The reactants have more potential energy than the products.
(3) There is no net change in potential energy.
(4) The amount of kinetic energy starts very high.
(5) The amount of potential energy drops midway through the reaction and rises again.

GO ON TO THE NEXT PAGE

22. Toxins and pollutants contaminating water supplies can lead to acid rain, which can be devastating to animals and plants. The graph below shows the effects of acid rain on a population of eels living in a contaminated river.

Effect of Acid Rain on Eel Size

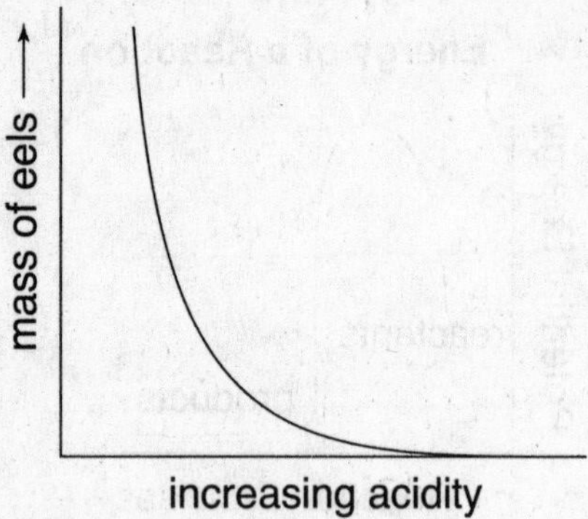

Based on the graph, which of the following statements is most accurate?

(1) As the water becomes more acidic, the eels decrease in mass and eventually die.
(2) Acid rain appears to have no effect on eels.
(3) Acid rain causes the eels to mutate and become deformed.
(4) As the water becomes more acidic, the eels become larger.
(5) The eels are able to adapt well to an acidic environment.

23. Organic compounds are carbon-based substances found in all living things. Carbohydrates, fats, and proteins are all made of organic molecules. Organic molecules are made primarily of carbon and hydrogen, but other elements such as oxygen and nitrogen are also present as well. Because organic molecules are chemicals that are found in life, both chemists and biologists study organic compounds.

Which of the following questions is not answered by the passage above?

(1) What are some examples of organic molecules?
(2) Are living things made of organic compounds?
(3) What are some elements found in organic molecules?
(4) What types of bonds hold organic molecules together?
(5) What types of scientists study organic compounds?

GO ON TO THE NEXT PAGE

24. Scientists study fossils to learn the conditions of earth during certain periods of time. These fossils are found buried in rock layers. According to geological studies, rock layers develop chronologically, so older rocks are found deeper underground than newer rocks. Below is a cross section of rock layers currently being studied by geologists.

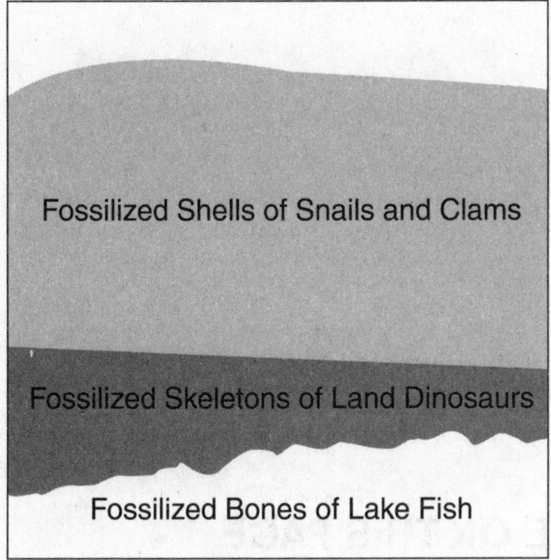

Based on the figure above, which of the following best describes the location from which this geological cross section was taken?

(1) This area has always been a desert.
(2) This area has always been covered by water.
(3) This area first was covered by an ocean, then was above sea level, then was under a freshwater source.
(4) This area first was under an ocean, then above sea level, then under an ocean again.
(5) This area was first under a freshwater source, then above water level, and then under an ocean.

25. Imprinting is a type of learning in which animals learn a piece of information during a critical phase. The most studied form of imprinting is called filial imprinting, which is when a young animal, usually a baby bird, learns to recognize its parent. Typically, whatever object or animal that young animal is exposed to during the critical time will be recognized as that young animal's mother.

Based on the information above, which of the following is most likely to learn through filial imprinting?

(1) young spider
(2) young tree
(3) young goldfish
(4) young goose
(5) young earthworm

END OF EXAMINATION

DO NOT MARK OR WRITE ON THIS PAGE

3. 3 The answer is 3 because the writer states that he wants the zoning board to "take action" in the first paragraph and that "there are too many things going on without the involvement of local residents" in the last paragraph. Choices 1, 2 and 5 are somewhat mentioned, but they are all extreme answers and not clearly part of his proposal. Nothing is stated about residents building their own homes as in 4.

4. 4 The answer is 4 because the writer states that there are accepted negative aspects of development and that the community is experiencing "radical changes" that are worrisome. Clearly, the community and the writer like some aspects of the changes and not others. The obvious danger to growth is the presence of problems that are not acceptable. Choices 1 and 5 mention construction companies that are only briefly mentioned. Choice 2 is not mentioned. Choice 3 is extreme.

5. 1 The answer is 1 because only answer 1 is not mentioned in the letter. Choices 4, "careless redevelopment of Main Street," and 5, "if we are to keep our peaceful environment," are addressed in the first paragraph. Choices 2 and 3 are mentioned in the second paragraph as examples of acceptable changes during growth.

6. 1 The answer is 1 because the first line of the passage states, "As doctors often do I took a trial shot…" He also relates the entire story of trying to help a sick girl. He is obviously a doctor. No other answer is supported.

7. 4 The answer is 4 because the speaker is a doctor and thus likely has a health reason to check the child's condition. Also, the last paragraph states that he is there to look at her throat for diphtheria and that she might "possibly die of it." So, he must check her throat for illness. Choice 2 indicates medicine, which might be necessary but is not stated in the passage. None of the remaining answers is supported by the passage details.

8. 3 The answer is 3 because he states in the passage that he knows there is something serious at stake—an illness. His last comment in the passage is "shall we have to open it for you?" a suggestion that he will have to be forceful and not "nice." There is no indication that he dislikes children, 1, or plans to be cruel, 5. He may be a little angry for his damaged glasses, but that is not why he states he dislikes being called nice. There is no evidence to support 4.

9. 1 The answer is 1 because the child shows resistance and does not speak or answer any questions. She is obviously against the doctor looking at her throat and does all she can to stop it, including trying to hit him. Choice 2 is incorrect since the doctor did not hurt her and there is nothing stating that he gave her medicine, 3. Choice 4 may be partly true if she is sick, but fever is not stated in the passage. Choice 5 does not answer the question of why Mathilda attacked and knocked the glasses away.

10. 4 The answer is 4 because the excerpt reveals that something important is at stake. The parents and the visiting doctor want to look in the child's throat for evidence of illness, but she does not want to reveal it. The doctor knows how serious it is and is annoyed both with the child and the parents. Thus, the next step is likely that he forcefully, for her own good and with her parents help, looks

down her throat for the illness. Because there were cases "in the school" recently and the child will not show, it is reasonable to conclude that she is actually ill and the doctor will find it. No other answer can be supported with information from the passage.

11. 1 The answer is 1 because the doctor understands that the child is trying to protect herself, though she does not understand that the doctor will help. She is likely frightened and has already resisted her parents successfully. So, the doctor somewhat admires the strength of the child for resisting, even though she could be preventing the help she needs. He is annoyed with the parents for not pushing her harder to see her throat, given the seriousness of the potential illness and their weakness and comments about being "nice" influence his opinion of them. Choice 2 is extreme and discusses raising children which is not within the scope of the passage. Choice 3 cannot be claimed since the child's intelligence is not in question. The doctor was not puzzled, 4, and did not think the parents "strong and intelligent," as in 5.

12. 3 The answer is 3 because Tesh directly states that he values having a job and eating. Working as an actress is possible, but can begin with "going to see a play occasionally." Choice 3 states this most clearly. Choice 1 is not stated, and answer 2 contradicts what he is generally indicating by his comments. Choice 4 is not supported by the passage as Tesh appears to be speaking honestly. Choice 5 does not have any support in the passage.

13. 3 The answer is 3 because Rigley states that "church people do not usually associate the two institutions," referring to church and theater. Tesh states that he thinks "they should be associated." This is their disagreement—the comparison of church people and theater people. Choice 1 is incorrect since Rigley gives one comment about the girl as an actress. Choice 2 confuses the comparison by discussing what is acted on stage. Choice 4 is half-right since they only discuss how papers portray theater, not religion. Choice 5 is not possible but not stated.

14. 2 The answer is 2 because the comment follows Rigley's statement that "one doesn't see much of the best sense of the theater nowadays." Tesh's comment is directly made to answer that criticism. Tesh thus believes that Rigley's statement is made without personal experience. Choice 1 cannot be known and is extreme. Choice 3 incorrectly discusses performances rather than the theater or theater people. Choice 4 does not properly address Tesh's opinion. Literature is not mentioned, 5.

15. 1 The answer is 1 because Tesh understands that Rigley would object to the close comparison of church (which Rigley supports) and theater (which Rigley does not) being "in the same profession," so he stops Rigley first and explains his intended meaning. Tesh states that he meant them "in their best sense," thus clarifying what he meant about church and church people. Choice 2 is unlikely just based on a gesture and not further supported by information from the passage. The conversation is about theater, but is not intended for Tesh to show his acting ability, 3. Tesh is not trying to impress Mrs. Zooker, 4, and the conversation goes on, so 5 is wrong.

16. 1 The answer is 1 because Rigley is clearly positive about religion and negative about theater. Though he may be biased, his opinion is clear. He does not state an opinion about Mrs. Zooker's daughter, as in 2 and 5. Choice 3 is extreme and not stated. Choice 4 might be true, but nothing in the passage indicates this.

17. 1 The answer is 1 because the entire passage discusses Spring and directly addresses April as if the month were a person. The details are often positive with "the smell of the earth is good" and "there is no death." But they are also negative, highlighting the dead "brains of men," "maggots," and "life in itself is nothing." This is all a very cynical view of a beautiful time. Choice 3 is incorrect since the details are not specifically scientific even though they mention earth and flowers. The best answer must be negative. Only 1 is accurate.

18. 4 The answer is 4 because the main theme of the poem is that the speaker thinks the earth is beautiful, but that there are other negative things in the world that outweigh it and cannot be forgotten no matter how beautiful spring may seem. Choice 1 contradicts the poem. Choice 2 is not stated and hot temperatures can be good or bad. Choice 3 is almost correct since the earth is said to smell good, but it is not compared in smell to flowers. Choice 5 misses the positive points made in the poem. Only 4 includes the idea that spring is beautiful, just not enough.

19. 3 The answer is 3 because both life and death are directly mentioned in the passage. The first half of the poem describes new things such as "little leaves" and "the spikes of the crocus" and the second half of the poem describes dead and dying things such as "maggots," "life in itself is nothing, an empty cup." No other answer is supported by the passage as a comparison.

20. 1 The answer is 1 because this addresses the difference between the beauty of April and the negative parts of life. The speaker seems to think that April and its beautiful displays of nature are designed to "quiet" the viewer from seeing the harder parts of life. Choice 1 addresses this most clearly. Choice 2 may be true, but does not answer the question. Choice 3 is not supported by the passage. Choice 4 is never stated. Choice 5 does not explain what would be "quieting" about these things if they are so negative.

21. 3 The answer is 3 because the speaker acknowledges the beauty of nature as described in the first half of the poem, but refuses to ignore the worse parts of nature. Thus, the phrase "I know what I know" is an insistence to remember the bad parts of life and nature that might otherwise be forgotten when overwhelmed by beauty and nature. Nothing in the poem shows the speaker to be a biologist (1). Choice 2 may be true, but is not as good an answer as 3. Choice 4 is too literal and specific without answering the question. Choice 5 is extreme and unstated in the passage.

Math

1. 4 To get a perimeter, simply add the lengths of all sides: 11 + 15 + 3 + 6 + 3 + 2 + 15 = 55

2. 5 Multiply \$49.95 by 0.06 = 2.997. Rounding to the nearest penny means to have only two digits to the right of the decimal point. Since the digit to the right of 2.99 is bigger than 50, you must round up. So the 2.99 becomes 3.00.

3. 1 Multiply the number of households, 13,500 by the number of mobile phones, 3. 7, to get 49,950.

4. 3 Follow the order of operations. $5^2 + 3$ gives us 28 in the parentheses. Divide 28 by 4 to get 7. Finally, subtract the 2 to get 5.

5. 1.25 To find the empty space, find the volume of the entire cooler by multiplying the three dimensions (height, width, depth): $2 \times 3 \times 1 = 6$ cubic feet. Then subtract the amount of food, 4.75 cubic feet, to get 1.25 cubic feet of empty space.

6. 1 Divide the number of clients he meets, 192, by 6. 192 / 6 = 32.

7. 3 To find the circumference of the wheel, you must get a diameter. Remember that a diameter is twice the radius, which, for this wheel, is 9. So the diameter is 18. Formula for circumference is $C = \pi d$. Using 18 for d, we get $C = 18\pi$. The wheel rotates 50 times. So $18\pi \times 50 = 900\pi$.

8. 2 Add the prices of the paintings to get the total: 85 + 110 + 135 = 330. She put down 40% of the total: $330 \times 0.4 = 132$. She still owes \$330 – \$132 = \$198. Divide \$198 by 6 payments to get \$33 per payment.

9. 4 Plug In a number for x. If $x = 5$ gallons, then a proportion can be set up: 2 cups of sugar make 1 gallon of iced tea, so 10 cups of sugar make 5 gallons of iced tea. Our target number is 10. Only $2x$ gives us 10.

10. 1 After Michelle paid the deductible of \$500, there was \$350 remaining. The insurance company paid 80% of that, so \$350 × 0.8 = \$280. Michelle had to pay the remaining \$70 (\$350 – \$280 = \$70).

11. 1 Volume of a cylinder is $\pi r^2 h$. Remember that radius is half the diameter. Volume of Cylinder L is $\pi \times 4^2 \times 20 = 320\pi$. Volume of Cylinder R is $\pi \times 10^2 \times 8 = 800\pi$. Only 1 is true.

12. 5 Adding just the x's gives $8x$, adding just the y's gives $3y$, and $7z$. The x's, y's and z cannot be combined, so the solution is $8x + 3y + 7z$.

13. 2 Multiply 75 minutes by 5 days to get 375 minutes of commuting per week. Then divide 375 minutes by 60 minutes in an hour to get 6.25 hours. 6.25 hours is 6 ¼ hours, which is 6 hours, 15 minutes.

14. **3** Median is the middle value. To find the middle, arrange the numbers from small to large in order to find the middle one. Since there are six numbers, you will have two middle ones, so the average of these two will be the median. The average of 3 ft. 2 in. and 3 ft. 4 in. is 3 ft. 3 in.

15. **94,750** 325 passengers – 30 First Class (FC) = 295 Coach seats.

30 FC × \$700 per ticket = \$21,000.

295 Coach × \$250 = \$73,750

\$21,000 + \$73,750 = <u>\$94,750</u> gross revenue for a full flight.

16. **3** Convert the improper fraction, $-\frac{7}{3}$, into a mixed number, $-2\frac{1}{3}$. It is located between negative 3 and negative 4 at point C.

17. **4** Replace every x with –4 and solve the equation. Remember that when squaring a negative number, it becomes positive. Thus, $(-4^2) = 16$.

$$\frac{16-3(-4)+2}{16-6}=\frac{16-(-12)+2}{10}=\frac{16+12+2}{10}=\frac{30}{10}=\frac{3}{1}=3$$

18. **7.5** Remember to compare similar parts of the triangles in similar triangle problems. Two possible proportions to find the value of y are $\frac{8}{10}=\frac{6}{y}$ or $\frac{8}{6}=\frac{10}{y}$. Either way, when you cross-multiply, you get $60 = 8y$, and $y = 7.5$.

19. **1** The slope formula is $\frac{y_2-y_1}{x_2-x_1}$

Using the points given, we get $\frac{-7-2}{2-(-1)}=\frac{-9}{-3}=-3$

20. **10** Count 'em up! On Monday he takes 2 tablets: one at 2 pm then one 8 hours later at 10 pm. On Tuesday and Wednesday he takes 3 tablets a day, at 6 am, 2 pm, and 10 pm. On Thursday he takes 2 tablets: one at 6 am and the last one at 2 pm. 2 + 3 + 3 + 2 = 10 tablets.

21. **2** Multiply \$1,000 by 1.05. The answer is \$1,050.

22. **5** \$75 × 3 days = \$225. Donna's personal use was 15% = 0.15. Multiply \$225 by 0.15 = \$33.75.

23. **5** Since Line AB is a diameter with length 8, the center of the circle will be halfway between points A and B, at (2, 7). The radius is 4 (half the diameter). The distance from the center of the circle (2, 7) to point C (x, 7) must be 4, as it is also a radius. So $x = 6$.

24. **4** First, convert 4 feet into inches by multiplying 4 by 12 = 48 inches. Then divide 48 by 2.5 = 19.2. The question asked how many strips could be cut, so it's 19 strips, with 0.2 to discard.

25. **1** The number of combinations is found by multiplying the variety of choices together. 3 × 8 × 5 = 120.

Practice Test 5

Completely darken bubbles with a No. 2 pencil. If you make a mistake, be sure to erase mark completely. Erase all stray marks.

1

YOUR NAME: ______________________ (Print) Last First M.I.

SIGNATURE: ______________________ DATE: / /

HOME ADDRESS: ______________________ (Print) Number and Street

______________________ City State Zip Code

PHONE NO.: ______________________ (Print)

IMPORTANT: Please fill in these boxes exactly as shown on the back cover of your test book.

2. TEST FORM

3. TEST CODE

0	A	0	0	0
1	B	1	1	1
2	C	2	2	2
3	D	3	3	3
4	E	4	4	4
5	F	5	5	5
6	G	6	6	6
7		7	7	7
8		8	8	8
9		9	9	9

4. REGISTRATION NUMBER

0	0	0	0	0	0
1	1	1	1	1	1
2	2	2	2	2	2
3	3	3	3	3	3
4	4	4	4	4	4
5	5	5	5	5	5
6	6	6	6	6	6
7	7	7	7	7	7
8	8	8	8	8	8
9	9	9	9	9	9

5. YOUR NAME

First 4 letters of last name					FIRST INIT	MID INIT
A	A	A	A		A	A
B	B	B	B		B	B
C	C	C	C		C	C
D	D	D	D		D	D
E	E	E	E		E	E
F	F	F	F		F	F
G	G	G	G		G	G
H	H	H	H		H	H
I	I	I	I		I	I
J	J	J	J		J	J
K	K	K	K		K	K
L	L	L	L		L	L
M	M	M	M		M	M
N	N	N	N		N	N
O	O	O	O		O	O
P	P	P	P		P	P
Q	Q	Q	Q		Q	Q
R	R	R	R		R	R
S	S	S	S		S	S
T	T	T	T		T	T
U	U	U	U		U	U
V	V	V	V		V	V
W	W	W	W		W	W
X	X	X	X		X	X
Y	Y	Y	Y		Y	Y
Z	Z	Z	Z		Z	Z

6. DATE OF BIRTH

Month	Day		Year	
JAN				
FEB				
MAR	0	0	0	0
APR	1	1	1	1
MAY	2	2	2	2
JUN	3	3	3	3
JUL		4	4	4
AUG		5	5	5
SEP		6	6	6
OCT		7	7	7
NOV		8	8	8
DEC		9	9	9

7. SEX

MALE

FEMALE

The Princeton Review

FORM NO. 00001-PR

Start with number 1 for each new section. If a section has fewer questions than answer spaces, leave the extra answer spaces blank. Be sure to erase any errors or stray marks completely.

WRITING

1 Ⓐ Ⓑ Ⓒ Ⓓ Ⓔ	11 Ⓐ Ⓑ Ⓒ Ⓓ Ⓔ	21 Ⓐ Ⓑ Ⓒ Ⓓ Ⓔ	31 Ⓐ Ⓑ Ⓒ Ⓓ Ⓔ
2 Ⓐ Ⓑ Ⓒ Ⓓ Ⓔ	12 Ⓐ Ⓑ Ⓒ Ⓓ Ⓔ	22 Ⓐ Ⓑ Ⓒ Ⓓ Ⓔ	32 Ⓐ Ⓑ Ⓒ Ⓓ Ⓔ
3 Ⓐ Ⓑ Ⓒ Ⓓ Ⓔ	13 Ⓐ Ⓑ Ⓒ Ⓓ Ⓔ	23 Ⓐ Ⓑ Ⓒ Ⓓ Ⓔ	33 Ⓐ Ⓑ Ⓒ Ⓓ Ⓔ
4 Ⓐ Ⓑ Ⓒ Ⓓ Ⓔ	14 Ⓐ Ⓑ Ⓒ Ⓓ Ⓔ	24 Ⓐ Ⓑ Ⓒ Ⓓ Ⓔ	34 Ⓐ Ⓑ Ⓒ Ⓓ Ⓔ
5 Ⓐ Ⓑ Ⓒ Ⓓ Ⓔ	15 Ⓐ Ⓑ Ⓒ Ⓓ Ⓔ	25 Ⓐ Ⓑ Ⓒ Ⓓ Ⓔ	35 Ⓐ Ⓑ Ⓒ Ⓓ Ⓔ
6 Ⓐ Ⓑ Ⓒ Ⓓ Ⓔ	16 Ⓐ Ⓑ Ⓒ Ⓓ Ⓔ	26 Ⓐ Ⓑ Ⓒ Ⓓ Ⓔ	36 Ⓐ Ⓑ Ⓒ Ⓓ Ⓔ
7 Ⓐ Ⓑ Ⓒ Ⓓ Ⓔ	17 Ⓐ Ⓑ Ⓒ Ⓓ Ⓔ	27 Ⓐ Ⓑ Ⓒ Ⓓ Ⓔ	37 Ⓐ Ⓑ Ⓒ Ⓓ Ⓔ
8 Ⓐ Ⓑ Ⓒ Ⓓ Ⓔ	18 Ⓐ Ⓑ Ⓒ Ⓓ Ⓔ	28 Ⓐ Ⓑ Ⓒ Ⓓ Ⓔ	38 Ⓐ Ⓑ Ⓒ Ⓓ Ⓔ
9 Ⓐ Ⓑ Ⓒ Ⓓ Ⓔ	19 Ⓐ Ⓑ Ⓒ Ⓓ Ⓔ	29 Ⓐ Ⓑ Ⓒ Ⓓ Ⓔ	39 Ⓐ Ⓑ Ⓒ Ⓓ Ⓔ
10 Ⓐ Ⓑ Ⓒ Ⓓ Ⓔ	20 Ⓐ Ⓑ Ⓒ Ⓓ Ⓔ	30 Ⓐ Ⓑ Ⓒ Ⓓ Ⓔ	40 Ⓐ Ⓑ Ⓒ Ⓓ Ⓔ

SOCIAL STUDIES

1 Ⓐ Ⓑ Ⓒ Ⓓ Ⓔ	11 Ⓐ Ⓑ Ⓒ Ⓓ Ⓔ	21 Ⓐ Ⓑ Ⓒ Ⓓ Ⓔ	31 Ⓐ Ⓑ Ⓒ Ⓓ Ⓔ
2 Ⓐ Ⓑ Ⓒ Ⓓ Ⓔ	12 Ⓐ Ⓑ Ⓒ Ⓓ Ⓔ	22 Ⓐ Ⓑ Ⓒ Ⓓ Ⓔ	32 Ⓐ Ⓑ Ⓒ Ⓓ Ⓔ
3 Ⓐ Ⓑ Ⓒ Ⓓ Ⓔ	13 Ⓐ Ⓑ Ⓒ Ⓓ Ⓔ	23 Ⓐ Ⓑ Ⓒ Ⓓ Ⓔ	33 Ⓐ Ⓑ Ⓒ Ⓓ Ⓔ
4 Ⓐ Ⓑ Ⓒ Ⓓ Ⓔ	14 Ⓐ Ⓑ Ⓒ Ⓓ Ⓔ	24 Ⓐ Ⓑ Ⓒ Ⓓ Ⓔ	34 Ⓐ Ⓑ Ⓒ Ⓓ Ⓔ
5 Ⓐ Ⓑ Ⓒ Ⓓ Ⓔ	15 Ⓐ Ⓑ Ⓒ Ⓓ Ⓔ	25 Ⓐ Ⓑ Ⓒ Ⓓ Ⓔ	35 Ⓐ Ⓑ Ⓒ Ⓓ Ⓔ
6 Ⓐ Ⓑ Ⓒ Ⓓ Ⓔ	16 Ⓐ Ⓑ Ⓒ Ⓓ Ⓔ	26 Ⓐ Ⓑ Ⓒ Ⓓ Ⓔ	36 Ⓐ Ⓑ Ⓒ Ⓓ Ⓔ
7 Ⓐ Ⓑ Ⓒ Ⓓ Ⓔ	17 Ⓐ Ⓑ Ⓒ Ⓓ Ⓔ	27 Ⓐ Ⓑ Ⓒ Ⓓ Ⓔ	37 Ⓐ Ⓑ Ⓒ Ⓓ Ⓔ
8 Ⓐ Ⓑ Ⓒ Ⓓ Ⓔ	18 Ⓐ Ⓑ Ⓒ Ⓓ Ⓔ	28 Ⓐ Ⓑ Ⓒ Ⓓ Ⓔ	38 Ⓐ Ⓑ Ⓒ Ⓓ Ⓔ
9 Ⓐ Ⓑ Ⓒ Ⓓ Ⓔ	19 Ⓐ Ⓑ Ⓒ Ⓓ Ⓔ	29 Ⓐ Ⓑ Ⓒ Ⓓ Ⓔ	39 Ⓐ Ⓑ Ⓒ Ⓓ Ⓔ
10 Ⓐ Ⓑ Ⓒ Ⓓ Ⓔ	20 Ⓐ Ⓑ Ⓒ Ⓓ Ⓔ	30 Ⓐ Ⓑ Ⓒ Ⓓ Ⓔ	40 Ⓐ Ⓑ Ⓒ Ⓓ Ⓔ

Start with number 1 for each new section. If a section has fewer questions than answer spaces, leave the extra answer spaces blank. Be sure to erase any errors or stray marks completely.

SCIENCE

1 Ⓐ Ⓑ Ⓒ Ⓓ Ⓔ	11 Ⓐ Ⓑ Ⓒ Ⓓ Ⓔ	21 Ⓐ Ⓑ Ⓒ Ⓓ Ⓔ	31 Ⓐ Ⓑ Ⓒ Ⓓ Ⓔ
2 Ⓐ Ⓑ Ⓒ Ⓓ Ⓔ	12 Ⓐ Ⓑ Ⓒ Ⓓ Ⓔ	22 Ⓐ Ⓑ Ⓒ Ⓓ Ⓔ	32 Ⓐ Ⓑ Ⓒ Ⓓ Ⓔ
3 Ⓐ Ⓑ Ⓒ Ⓓ Ⓔ	13 Ⓐ Ⓑ Ⓒ Ⓓ Ⓔ	23 Ⓐ Ⓑ Ⓒ Ⓓ Ⓔ	33 Ⓐ Ⓑ Ⓒ Ⓓ Ⓔ
4 Ⓐ Ⓑ Ⓒ Ⓓ Ⓔ	14 Ⓐ Ⓑ Ⓒ Ⓓ Ⓔ	24 Ⓐ Ⓑ Ⓒ Ⓓ Ⓔ	34 Ⓐ Ⓑ Ⓒ Ⓓ Ⓔ
5 Ⓐ Ⓑ Ⓒ Ⓓ Ⓔ	15 Ⓐ Ⓑ Ⓒ Ⓓ Ⓔ	25 Ⓐ Ⓑ Ⓒ Ⓓ Ⓔ	35 Ⓐ Ⓑ Ⓒ Ⓓ Ⓔ
6 Ⓐ Ⓑ Ⓒ Ⓓ Ⓔ	16 Ⓐ Ⓑ Ⓒ Ⓓ Ⓔ	26 Ⓐ Ⓑ Ⓒ Ⓓ Ⓔ	36 Ⓐ Ⓑ Ⓒ Ⓓ Ⓔ
7 Ⓐ Ⓑ Ⓒ Ⓓ Ⓔ	17 Ⓐ Ⓑ Ⓒ Ⓓ Ⓔ	27 Ⓐ Ⓑ Ⓒ Ⓓ Ⓔ	37 Ⓐ Ⓑ Ⓒ Ⓓ Ⓔ
8 Ⓐ Ⓑ Ⓒ Ⓓ Ⓔ	18 Ⓐ Ⓑ Ⓒ Ⓓ Ⓔ	28 Ⓐ Ⓑ Ⓒ Ⓓ Ⓔ	38 Ⓐ Ⓑ Ⓒ Ⓓ Ⓔ
9 Ⓐ Ⓑ Ⓒ Ⓓ Ⓔ	19 Ⓐ Ⓑ Ⓒ Ⓓ Ⓔ	29 Ⓐ Ⓑ Ⓒ Ⓓ Ⓔ	39 Ⓐ Ⓑ Ⓒ Ⓓ Ⓔ
10 Ⓐ Ⓑ Ⓒ Ⓓ Ⓔ	20 Ⓐ Ⓑ Ⓒ Ⓓ Ⓔ	30 Ⓐ Ⓑ Ⓒ Ⓓ Ⓔ	40 Ⓐ Ⓑ Ⓒ Ⓓ Ⓔ

READING

1 Ⓐ Ⓑ Ⓒ Ⓓ Ⓔ	11 Ⓐ Ⓑ Ⓒ Ⓓ Ⓔ	21 Ⓐ Ⓑ Ⓒ Ⓓ Ⓔ	31 Ⓐ Ⓑ Ⓒ Ⓓ Ⓔ
2 Ⓐ Ⓑ Ⓒ Ⓓ Ⓔ	12 Ⓐ Ⓑ Ⓒ Ⓓ Ⓔ	22 Ⓐ Ⓑ Ⓒ Ⓓ Ⓔ	32 Ⓐ Ⓑ Ⓒ Ⓓ Ⓔ
3 Ⓐ Ⓑ Ⓒ Ⓓ Ⓔ	13 Ⓐ Ⓑ Ⓒ Ⓓ Ⓔ	23 Ⓐ Ⓑ Ⓒ Ⓓ Ⓔ	33 Ⓐ Ⓑ Ⓒ Ⓓ Ⓔ
4 Ⓐ Ⓑ Ⓒ Ⓓ Ⓔ	14 Ⓐ Ⓑ Ⓒ Ⓓ Ⓔ	24 Ⓐ Ⓑ Ⓒ Ⓓ Ⓔ	34 Ⓐ Ⓑ Ⓒ Ⓓ Ⓔ
5 Ⓐ Ⓑ Ⓒ Ⓓ Ⓔ	15 Ⓐ Ⓑ Ⓒ Ⓓ Ⓔ	25 Ⓐ Ⓑ Ⓒ Ⓓ Ⓔ	35 Ⓐ Ⓑ Ⓒ Ⓓ Ⓔ
6 Ⓐ Ⓑ Ⓒ Ⓓ Ⓔ	16 Ⓐ Ⓑ Ⓒ Ⓓ Ⓔ	26 Ⓐ Ⓑ Ⓒ Ⓓ Ⓔ	36 Ⓐ Ⓑ Ⓒ Ⓓ Ⓔ
7 Ⓐ Ⓑ Ⓒ Ⓓ Ⓔ	17 Ⓐ Ⓑ Ⓒ Ⓓ Ⓔ	27 Ⓐ Ⓑ Ⓒ Ⓓ Ⓔ	37 Ⓐ Ⓑ Ⓒ Ⓓ Ⓔ
8 Ⓐ Ⓑ Ⓒ Ⓓ Ⓔ	18 Ⓐ Ⓑ Ⓒ Ⓓ Ⓔ	28 Ⓐ Ⓑ Ⓒ Ⓓ Ⓔ	38 Ⓐ Ⓑ Ⓒ Ⓓ Ⓔ
9 Ⓐ Ⓑ Ⓒ Ⓓ Ⓔ	19 Ⓐ Ⓑ Ⓒ Ⓓ Ⓔ	29 Ⓐ Ⓑ Ⓒ Ⓓ Ⓔ	39 Ⓐ Ⓑ Ⓒ Ⓓ Ⓔ
10 Ⓐ Ⓑ Ⓒ Ⓓ Ⓔ	20 Ⓐ Ⓑ Ⓒ Ⓓ Ⓔ	30 Ⓐ Ⓑ Ⓒ Ⓓ Ⓔ	40 Ⓐ Ⓑ Ⓒ Ⓓ Ⓔ

MATH

1 Ⓐ Ⓑ Ⓒ Ⓓ Ⓔ	11 Ⓐ Ⓑ Ⓒ Ⓓ Ⓔ	21 Ⓐ Ⓑ Ⓒ Ⓓ Ⓔ	31 Ⓐ Ⓑ Ⓒ Ⓓ Ⓔ
2 Ⓐ Ⓑ Ⓒ Ⓓ Ⓔ	12 Ⓐ Ⓑ Ⓒ Ⓓ Ⓔ	22 Ⓐ Ⓑ Ⓒ Ⓓ Ⓔ	32 Ⓐ Ⓑ Ⓒ Ⓓ Ⓔ
3 Ⓐ Ⓑ Ⓒ Ⓓ Ⓔ	13 Ⓐ Ⓑ Ⓒ Ⓓ Ⓔ	23 Ⓐ Ⓑ Ⓒ Ⓓ Ⓔ	33 Ⓐ Ⓑ Ⓒ Ⓓ Ⓔ
4 Ⓐ Ⓑ Ⓒ Ⓓ Ⓔ	14 Ⓐ Ⓑ Ⓒ Ⓓ Ⓔ	24 Ⓐ Ⓑ Ⓒ Ⓓ Ⓔ	34 Ⓐ Ⓑ Ⓒ Ⓓ Ⓔ
5 Ⓐ Ⓑ Ⓒ Ⓓ Ⓔ	15 Ⓐ Ⓑ Ⓒ Ⓓ Ⓔ	25 Ⓐ Ⓑ Ⓒ Ⓓ Ⓔ	35 Ⓐ Ⓑ Ⓒ Ⓓ Ⓔ
6 Ⓐ Ⓑ Ⓒ Ⓓ Ⓔ	16 Ⓐ Ⓑ Ⓒ Ⓓ Ⓔ	26 Ⓐ Ⓑ Ⓒ Ⓓ Ⓔ	36 Ⓐ Ⓑ Ⓒ Ⓓ Ⓔ
7 Ⓐ Ⓑ Ⓒ Ⓓ Ⓔ	17 Ⓐ Ⓑ Ⓒ Ⓓ Ⓔ	27 Ⓐ Ⓑ Ⓒ Ⓓ Ⓔ	37 Ⓐ Ⓑ Ⓒ Ⓓ Ⓔ
8 Ⓐ Ⓑ Ⓒ Ⓓ Ⓔ	18 Ⓐ Ⓑ Ⓒ Ⓓ Ⓔ	28 Ⓐ Ⓑ Ⓒ Ⓓ Ⓔ	38 Ⓐ Ⓑ Ⓒ Ⓓ Ⓔ
9 Ⓐ Ⓑ Ⓒ Ⓓ Ⓔ	19 Ⓐ Ⓑ Ⓒ Ⓓ Ⓔ	29 Ⓐ Ⓑ Ⓒ Ⓓ Ⓔ	39 Ⓐ Ⓑ Ⓒ Ⓓ Ⓔ
10 Ⓐ Ⓑ Ⓒ Ⓓ Ⓔ	20 Ⓐ Ⓑ Ⓒ Ⓓ Ⓔ	30 Ⓐ Ⓑ Ⓒ Ⓓ Ⓔ	40 Ⓐ Ⓑ Ⓒ Ⓓ Ⓔ

CAUTION Use the answer spaces in the grids below for Section 6 or Section 7 only if you are told to do so in your test book.

Student-Produced Responses

ONLY ANSWERS ENTERED IN THE OVALS IN EACH GRID WILL BE SCORED. YOU WILL NOT RECEIVE CREDIT FOR ANYTHING WRITTEN IN THE BOXES ABOVE THE OVALS.

Grids 9, 10, 11, 12, 13 (each identical):

	/	/	
.	.	.	.
	0	0	0
1	1	1	1
2	2	2	2
3	3	3	3
4	4	4	4
5	5	5	5
6	6	6	6
7	7	7	7
8	8	8	8
9	9	9	9

PLEASE DO NOT WRITE IN THIS AREA

SERIAL #

LANGUAGE ARTS, WRITING

Tests of General Educational Development

Directions

The Language Arts, Writing Test is intended to measure your ability to use clear and effective English. This test includes both multiple-choice questions and an essay. These directions apply only to the multiple-choice section; a separate set of directions is given for the essay.

The multiple-choice section consists of paragraphs with lettered paragraphs and numbered sentences. Some of the sentences contain errors in sentence structure, usage, or mechanics (punctuation, and capitalization). After reading the numbered sentences, answer the multiple-choice questions that follow. Some questions refer to sentences that are correct as written. The best answer for these questions is the one that leaves the sentence as originally written. The best answer for some questions is the one that produces a sentence that is consistent with the verb tense and point of view used throughout the text. A document is often repeated in order to allow for additional questions on a second page. The repeated document is the same as the first.

You should spend no more than 40 minutes on the multiple-choice questions and 45 minutes on your essay. Work carefully, but do not spend too much time on any one question. Be sure you answer every question. You may begin working on the essay part of this test as soon as you complete the multiple-choice section.

Do not mark in this test booklet. Record your answers on the separate answer sheet provided. Be sure that all requested information is properly recorded on the answer sheet.

To record your answers, mark one numbered space on the answer sheet beside the number that corresponds to the question in the test booklet.

FOR EXAMPLE:
Sentence 1: **We were honored to meet governor Phillips.**

Which correction should be made to sentence 1?

(1) insert a comma after <u>honored</u>
(2) change <u>honored</u> to <u>honer</u>
(3) change <u>governor</u> to <u>Governor</u>
(4) change <u>were</u> to <u>was</u>
(5) no correction is necessary

In this example, the word "governor" should be capitalized; therefore, answer space 3 would be marked on the answer sheet.

Do not rest the point of your pencil on the answer sheet while you are considering your answer. Make no stray or unnecessary marks. If you change an answer, erase your first mark completely. Mark only one answer space for each question; multiple answers will be scored as incorrect. Do not fold or crease your answer sheet. All test materials must be returned to the test administrator.

GO ON TO THE NEXT PAGE

Directions: Choose the one best answer to each question.

Questions 1 through 9 refer to the following memorandum.

Hamilton Products Corp.

259 Apple Ring Rd.
Terra Fina, NM 89210
(783) 555-3498

MEMORANDUM

To: Department Heads Working Group; Bob Tisch, VP for Strategy and Planning; New Day Planning Team

From: Joseph Kahlo, CEO

Subject: Summary New Day Strategies

Date: August 14, 2009

(A)

(1) The purpose of this memo is to provide a summary of the key strategies developed by the New Day Planning Team that the marketing, operations, and human resources departments will implement in the coming fiscal quarter. (2) Beginning during the second quarter of 2003, our company's market share began to decline compared to historical averages, our market share has remained low since then. (3) The management team developing a new set of strategies in order to regain our former position as the industry leader.

(B)

(4) The Marketing department will work with the outside firm of Fridman & Piñon to update our brand and create more consistency in our marketing materials. (5) The Operations department will conduct an internal audit to identify inefficiencies and working to eliminate it when they can.

(C)

(6) The Human Resources department will conduct a review of employees to determine redundant positions and brainstorm how to attract outside talent. (7) In the New Day binders these strategies are all been outlined. (8) The binders will be distributed at the New Day workshop at the National Conference that will be held from July 23–25, 2009 at the Hotel Bloggs in Saint Louis. (9) Hotel reservations at www.hotelbloggsstlouis.com.

(D)

(10) As head of your department. (11) One should communicate these strategies to your subordinates. (12) Everyone who reports to you should be aware of what is expected of them and they should understand what roles they will be expected to play. (13) The success of the New Day plan depends upon prompt and effective implementation of its strategies at every level of our organization. (14) Make sure to hold conversation meetings with your team so that you can be sure that they can raise any questions about the New Day Plan. (15) Bring your team's questions with you when you attend the conference. (16) If you have any urgent questions before then, contact Bob Tisch. (17) See you in St. Louis.

GO ON TO THE NEXT PAGE

Writing, Part I

1. Sentence 2: **Beginning during the second quarter of 2003, our company's market share began to decline compared to historical <u>averages, our market share has remained</u> low since then.**

   Which is the best way to write the underlined portion of this sentence? If the original is best, choose option (1)

   (1) averages, our market share has remained
   (2) averages, and our market share remained
   (3) averages our market share remained
   (4) averages, our market share remaining
   (5) averages and our market share has remained

2. Sentence 3: **The management team developing a new set of strategies in order to regain our former position as the industry leader.**

   Which correction should be made to sentence 3?

   (1) change <u>management team</u> to <u>team that manages</u>
   (2) insert <u>are</u> after <u>team</u>
   (3) change <u>developing</u> to <u>has developed</u>
   (4) change <u>in order to</u> to <u>for the purpose of</u>
   (5) insert <u>which was</u> after <u>position</u>

3. Sentence 5: **The Operations department will conduct an internal audit to identify inefficiencies and working to eliminate it when they can.**

   Which is the most effective revision of sentence 5?

   (1) The Operations department will conduct an internal audit to identify inefficiencies and working to eliminate them where they can.
   (2) The Operations department will be conducting an internal audit to identify and working to eliminate inefficiencies when they can.
   (3) The Operations department will conduct an internal audit to identify inefficiencies and working to eliminate them where it can.
   (4) The Operations department will conduct an internal audit to identify and work to eliminate inefficiencies where possible.
   (5) The Operations department will audit inefficiencies internally and working to eliminate it when they can.

4. Sentence 7: **In the New Day binders these strategies are all been outlined.**

   If you rewrote sentence 7 beginning with <u>These strategies are</u>

   the next words should be

   (1) in outline form
   (2) being completely outlined
   (3) all in the
   (4) all outlined in
   (5) all been outlined

GO ON TO THE NEXT PAGE

The memorandum is repeated for your use in answering the remaining questions.

Hamilton Products Corp.

259 Apple Ring Rd.
Terra Fina, NM 89210
(783) 555-3498

MEMORANDUM

To: Department Heads Working Group; Bob Tisch, VP for Strategy and Planning; New Day Planning Team
From: Joseph Kahlo, CEO
Subject: Summary New Day Strategies
Date: August 14, 2009

(A)

(1) The purpose of this memo is to provide a summary of the key strategies developed by the New Day Planning Team that the marketing, operations, and human resources departments will implement in the coming fiscal quarter. (2) Beginning during the second quarter of 2003, our company's market share began to decline compared to historical averages, our market share has remained low since then. (3) The management team developing a new set of strategies in order to regain our former position as the industry leader.

(B)

(4) The Marketing department will work with the outside firm of Fridman & Piñon to update our brand and create more consistency in our marketing materials. (5) The Operations department will conduct an internal audit to identify inefficiencies and working to eliminate it when they can.

(C)

(6) The Human Resources department will conduct a review of employees to determine redundant positions and brainstorm how to attract outside talent. (7) In the New Day binders these strategies are all been outlined. (8) The binders will be distributed at the New Day workshop at the National Conference that will be held from July 23–25, 2009 at the Hotel Bloggs in Saint Louis. (9) Hotel reservations at www.hotelbloggsstlouis.com.

(D)

(10) As head of your department. (11) One should communicate these strategies to your subordinates. (12) Everyone who reports to you should be aware of what is expected of them and they should understand what roles they will be expected to play. (13) The success of the New Day plan depends upon prompt and effective implementation of its strategies at every level of our organization. (14) Make sure to hold conversation meetings with your team so that you can be sure that they can raise any questions about the New Day Plan. (15) Bring your team's questions with you when you attend the conference. (16) If you have any urgent questions before then, contact Bob Tisch. (17) See you in St. Louis.

GO ON TO THE NEXT PAGE

5. Sentence 9: **Hotel reservations at www.hotelbloggsstlouis.com.**

   Which is the most effective revision of sentence 9?

   (1) Hotel reservations are available to be made at www.hotelbloggsstlouis.com.
   (2) Hotel reservations are able to be made for you at www.hotelbloggsstlouis.com.
   (3) Make your hotel reservations at www.hotelbloggsstlouis.com.
   (4) At www.hotelbloggsstlouis.com hotel reservations are available.
   (5) Reservations for hotels, available at www.hotelbloggsstlouis.com

6. Sentences 10 and 11: **As head of your <u>department</u>. <u>One</u> should communicate these strategies to your subordinates.**

   Which is the best way to write the underlined portions of these sentences? If the original is the best way, choose option (1).

   (1) department One
   (2) department. You
   (3) department, and you
   (4) department, one
   (5) department, you

7. Sentence 12: **Everyone who reports to you should be aware of what is expected of them and they should understand what roles they will be expected to play.**

   Which correction should be made to sentence 12?

   (1) change <u>Everyone who reports</u> to <u>Those who report</u>
   (2) change <u>should be aware</u> to <u>should be made aware</u>
   (3) insert <u>also</u> after <u>and</u>
   (4) replace <u>should understand</u> with <u>should be made to understand</u>
   (5) change <u>roles</u> to <u>role</u>

8. Sentence 13: **The success of the New Day plan depends upon <u>prompt and effective implementation of its strategies at every</u> level of our organization.**

   Which is the best way to write the underlined portion of this sentence? If the original is the best way, choose option (1).

   (1) prompt and effective implementation of its strategies at every
   (2) promptness and effectively implementing it's strategies at every
   (3) promptly and effectiveness in the implementation of its strategies at every
   (4) promptness and effectiveness in the implementing of the strategies at every
   (5) implementation of prompt and effective strategies at every

9. Which revision would improve the effectiveness of the memorandum?

   (1) remove paragraph A
   (2) move sentence 6 to the end of paragraph B
   (3) join paragraphs B and C
   (4) remove paragraph C
   (5) remove sentence 2

GO ON TO THE NEXT PAGE

Questions 10 through 17 refer to the following article.

Buying Your First Car

(A)

(1) Buying your first car can be one of the most difficult decisions that you make as a young adult. (2) Their are so many factors that you have to consider. (3) For example, do you want a big car or a small car? (4) Many people don't even know where to start.

(B)

(5) One thing that first-time car buyers often do not consider is fuel efficiency. (6) Cars built in the last decade use less fuel than the past. (7) Even though an older car might be less expensive. (8) You might end up paying allot more in the long run at the fuel pump. (9) Smaller cars often use less fuel than trucks or vans.

(C)

(10) The cost of maintenance is another thing that should be considered by you before you buy a car. (11) A car that is initially inexpensive can turn out to be no bargain, if you have to take it into the mechanic every other month to get repaired. (12) Also foreign cars sometimes has expensive parts. (13) However, even small sports cars can be fuel inefficient due to their more powerful engines.

(D)

(14) Because there are so many things to consider, if you do your research and think carefully about what you actually need in a car. (15) You'll make the right decision for you.

10. Sentence 2: **<u>Their are so many</u> factors that you have to consider.**

Which is the best way to write the underlined portion of this sentence? If the original is the best way, choose option (1).

(1) Their are so many
(2) They're is so many
(3) They're are so many
(4) There are so many
(5) Their is so many

11. Sentence 6: **Cars built in the last decade use less fuel than the past.**

The most effective revision of sentence 6 would include which group of words?

(1) Cars that were built
(2) during the last decade
(3) use fewer fuels
(4) than they did in the past
(5) than those built in the past

GO ON TO THE NEXT PAGE

12. Sentences 7 and 8: **Even though an older car might be less expensive. You might end up paying allot more in the long run at the fuel pump.**

Which is the best way to write the underlined portions of these sentences? If the original is the best way, choose option (1).

(1) be less expensive. You might
(2) have been less expensive. You might
(3) have been less in expense, you might
(4) be less expensive, you might
(5) have been less in expense, you may

13. Sentence 8: **You might end up paying allot more in the long run at the fuel pump.**

Which correction should be made to sentence 8?

(1) replace might with may
(2) insert a comma after paying
(3) replace allot with a lot
(4) change the long run to the end
(5) replace at the with at a

14. Sentence 10: **The cost of maintenance is another thing that should be considered by you before you buy a car.**

Which is the best way to write the underlined portions of this sentence? If the original is the best way, choose option (1).

(1) is another thing that should be considered by you before
(2) is another thing that you should consider before
(3) was another thing that should be considered by you when
(4) is something that should be considered before
(5) is what you must consider before

15. Sentence 12: **Also foreign cars sometimes has expensive parts.**

Which correction should be made to sentence 12?

(1) change Also to As well
(2) change sometimes to often
(3) replace has with have
(4) insert a comma after has
(5) change expensive parts to parts, that are expensive

16. Sentence 13: **However, even small sports cars can be fuel inefficient due to their more powerful engines.**

Which revision should be made to the placement of sentence 13?

(1) move sentence 13 to follow sentence 3
(2) move sentence 13 to follow sentence 9
(3) remove sentence 13
(4) move sentence 13 to the beginning of paragraph C
(5) move sentence 13 to follow sentence 14

17. Sentence 14: **Because there are so many things to consider, if you do your research and think carefully about what you actually need in a car.**

The most effective revision of sentence 14 would begin with which group of words?

(1) While there are so many
(2) Since many things to consider
(3) If you do your research
(4) While considering many things
(5) Thinking carefully about what

GO ON TO THE NEXT PAGE

Questions 18 through 25 refer to the following informational article.

Coffee

(A)

(1) Next time you walk by a coffee shop, you should stop, and consider the history of the humble coffee bean. (2) Coffee is prepared by brewing coffee beans after it has been roasted. (3) Coffee has been consumed since the 9th century, it is native to Ethiopia.

(B)

(4) During World War II, coffee shortages caused many European countries to develop alternative drinks, which did not contain coffee beans. (5) Coffee was first introduce to Europe in the 16th and 17th centuries. (6) By the late 17th century, people all over Europe were enjoying a hot cup of coffee. (7) On the other hand, people in the Middle East and Africa. (8) Had been drinking coffee for hundreds of years before the Europeans started.

(C)

(9) Now people all over the world drink coffee. (10) Today coffee being one of the most traded agricultural products in the entire world.

18. Sentence 1: **Next time you walk by a coffee shop, you should stop, and consider the history of the humble coffee bean.**

    Which correction should be made to sentence 1?

    (1) change you walk to one walks
    (2) replace by a with by an
    (3) remove the comma after stop
    (4) replace and consider with while considering
    (5) change the humble to a humble

19. Sentence 2: **Coffee is prepared by brewing coffee beans after it has been roasted.**

    Which correction should be made to sentence 2?

    (1) change is to was
    (2) insert a comma after prepared
    (3) change beans to bean's
    (4) replace it has with they have
    (5) change been to bean

GO ON TO THE NEXT PAGE

20. Sentence 3: **Coffee has been consumed since the 9th century, it is native to Ethiopia.**

If you rewrote sentence 3 beginning with

Native to Ethiopia,

the next words should be

(1) people have consumed
(2) coffee has been consumed
(3) the 9th century is when
(4) it is the consumption of
(5) coffee has consumed since

21. Sentence 4: **During World War II, coffee shortages caused many European countries to develop alternative drinks, which did not contain coffee beans.**

Which revision should be made to sentence 4?

(1) move sentence 4 to follow sentence 1
(2) move sentence 4 to follow sentence 6
(3) move sentence 4 to the beginning of paragraph C
(4) move sentence 4 to follow sentence 10
(5) remove sentence 4

22. Sentence 5: **Coffee was first introduce to Europe in the 16th and 17th centuries.**

Which correction should be made to sentence 5?

(1) change was first to was at first
(2) change introduce to introduced
(3) replace to Europe with in European countries
(4) change and to or
(5) replace centuries with century

23. Sentence 6: **By the late 17th century, people all over Europe were enjoying a hot cup of coffee.**

Which is the best way to write the underlined portion of the sentence? If the original is they best way, choose option (1)?

(1) people all over Europe were enjoying
(2) all over Europe, the people enjoy
(3) people were all over Europe enjoying
(4) in Europe the people enjoyed
(5) people were enjoying all over Europe

24. Sentences 7 and 8: **On the other hand, people in the Middle East and Africa. Drinking coffee for hundreds of years before the Europeans started.**

Which is the best way to write the underlined portions of these sentences? If the original is the best way, choose option (1)?

(1) Middle East and Africa. Drinking coffee
(2) Middle East and Africa, while drinking coffee
(3) Middle East and Africa, coffee was drunk
(4) Middle East and Africa. Drank coffee
(5) Middle East and Africa had been drinking coffee

25. Sentence 10: **Today coffee being one of the most traded agricultural products in the entire world.**

Which correction should be made to sentence 10?

(1) change being to is
(2) insert a comma after one
(3) change most to more
(4) replace in with of
(5) no correction is necessary

GO ON TO LANGUAGE ARTS, WRITING, PART II

DO NOT MARK OR WRITE ON THIS PAGE

LANGUAGE ARTS, WRITING, PART II

Tests of General Educational Development

Essay Directions and Topic

Look at the box on page 362. In the box are your assigned topic and the letter of that topic.

You must write on the assigned topic **ONLY**.

Mark the letter of your assigned topic in the appropriate space on your answer sheet booklet. Be certain that all other requested information is properly recorded in your answer sheet booklet.

You will have 45 minutes to write on your assigned essay topic. You may return to the multiple-choice section after you complete your essay if you have time remaining in this test period. Do not return the Language Arts, Writing booklet until you finish both Parts I and II of the Language Arts, Writing Test.

Two evaluators will score your essay according to its overall effectiveness. Their evaluation will be based on the following features:

- Well-focused main points
- Clear organization
- Specific development of your ideas
- Control of sentence structure, punctuation, grammar, word choice, and spelling

REMEMBER, YOU MUST COMPLETE BOTH THE MULTIPLE-CHOICE QUESTIONS (PART I) and THE ESSAY (PART II) TO RECEIVE A SCORE ON THE LANGUAGE ARTS, WRITING TEST. To avoid having to repeat both parts of the test, be sure to observe the following rules.

- Do not leave the pages blank.
- Write legibly in ink so that the evaluators will be able to read your writing.
- Write on the assigned topic. If you write on a topic other than the one assigned, you will not receive a score for the Language Arts, Writing Test.
- Write your essay on the lined pages of the separate answer sheet booklet. Only the writing on these pages will be scored.

IMPORTANT:
You may return to the multiple-choice section after you complete your essay if you have time remaining in this test period. Do not return the Language Arts, Writing booklet until you finish both Parts I and II of the Language Arts, Writing Test.

GO ON TO THE NEXT PAGE

Topic F

Support can arrive in many different ways, from many different sources.

In your essay, identify a time in which you received support when you needed it. Explain how that support helped you. Use your personal observations, experience, and knowledge to support your essay.

Part II is a test to determine how well you can use written language to explain your ideas.

In preparing your essay, you should take the following steps.

- Read the **DIRECTIONS** and the **TOPIC** carefully.
- Plan your essay before you write. Use the scratch paper provided to make any notes. These notes will be collected but not scored.
- Before you turn in your essay, reread what you have written and make any changes that will improve your essay.

Your essay should be long enough to develop the topic adequately.

END OF EXAMINATION

SOCIAL STUDIES

Tests of General Educational Development

Directions

The Social Studies Test consists of multiple-choice questions intended to measure understanding of general social studies concepts. The questions are based on short readings that often include a map, graph, chart, cartoon, or figure. Study the information given and then answer the question(s) following it. Refer to the information as often as necessary in answering the questions.

You should spend no more than 45 minutes answering the questions in this booklet. Work carefully, but do not spend too much time on any one question. Be sure you answer every question.

Do not mark in this test booklet. Record your answers on the separate answer sheet provided. Be sure that all requested information is properly recorded on the answer sheet.

To record your answers, mark the numbered space on the answer sheet beside the number that corresponds to the question in the test booklet.

FOR EXAMPLE:

Early colonists of North America looked for settlement sites with adequate water supplies and access by ship. For this reason, many early towns were built near

(1) mountains
(2) prairies
(3) rivers
(4) glaciers
(5) plateaus

The correct answer is "rivers"; therefore, answer space 3 would be marked on the answer sheet.

Do not rest the point of your pencil on the answer sheet while you are considering your answer. Make no stray or unnecessary marks. If you change an answer, erase your first mark completely. Mark only <u>one</u> answer space for each question; multiple answers will be scored as incorrect. Do not fold or crease your answer sheet. All test materials must be returned to the test administrator.

GO ON TO THE NEXT PAGE

Directions: Choose the one best answer to each question.

Questions 1 through 3 refer to the following map.

New World

1. According to the map, which nation controlled the largest amount of territory in the New World?

   (1) Portugal
   (2) France
   (3) Great Britain
   (4) Spain
   (5) The Netherlands

2. What caused many European nations to leave their colonies in the New World?

   European nations left the New World because they

   (1) decided it was more profitable to create colonies elsewhere
   (2) were forced out by rebellions, revolutions, and warfare
   (3) were forced out by natural disasters, plague, and famine
   (4) objected to absolutist monarchies
   (5) had consumed all of the natural resources of the region

GO ON TO THE NEXT PAGE

3. Which languages are most commonly spoken in North and South America today?

(1) French, Dutch, and Russian
(2) English, French, and Dutch
(3) Spanish, Portuguese, and German
(4) German, Spanish, and French
(5) Spanish, English, and Portuguese

4. The Secretary of State is the chief diplomat of the United States and a high-profile figure in the federal government. Through what branch of the federal government does the Secretary of State work?

(1) the Legislative Branch
(2) the Diplomatic Branch
(3) the Executive Branch
(4) the Judicial Branch
(5) the Constitutional Branch

Questions 5 and 6 refer to the following cartoon and information.

This cartoon depicts President Theodore Roosevelt before the building of the Panama Canal.

5. Which statement best describes the main point of the cartoon?

(1) President Roosevelt was the victim of Colombian aggression and was a weak leader of the United States.
(2) Colombia had bribed the United States into a building a canal in its territory.
(3) President Roosevelt was pressured by the Congress to build the canal.
(4) President Roosevelt was pressuring Colombia with money.
(5) Colombia should buy the canal from the United States.

GO ON TO THE NEXT PAGE

6. Why is the building of the Panama Canal significant in world history?

The Panama Canal

(1) allowed for trade to flow much more easily between the Atlantic and Pacific Oceans
(2) nearly destroyed the United States' economy
(3) undermined the independence of the United States
(4) improved relations between the United States and Colombia
(5) improved the quality of American exports

7. Alexander Hamilton once said that "Constitutions should consist only of general provisions; the reason is that they must necessarily be permanent, and that they cannot calculate for the possible change of things."

How does the United States Constitution "calculate for the possible change of things"?

The United States Constitution

(1) contains no specific provisions
(2) excludes any discussion of the legislative branch
(3) allows for amendments to be made
(4) protects the autonomy of the Supreme Court
(5) undermines immigration policies

GO ON TO THE NEXT PAGE

Questions 8 through 11 refer to this excerpt of Martin Luther King Jr.'s famous "I Have a Dream" speech from the March on Washington in 1963.

"We must forever conduct our struggle on the high plane of dignity and discipline. We must not allow our creative protest to degenerate into physical violence. Again and again we must rise to the majestic heights of meeting physical force with soul force. The marvelous new militancy which has engulfed the Negro community must not lead us to distrust of all white people, for many of our white brothers, as evidenced by their presence here today, have come to realize that their destiny is tied up with our destiny and their freedom is inextricably bound to our freedom. We cannot walk alone.

And as we walk, we must make the pledge that we shall march ahead. We cannot turn back. There are those who are asking the devotees of civil rights, "When will you be satisfied?" We can never be satisfied as long as our bodies, heavy with the fatigue of travel, cannot gain lodging in the motels of the highways and the hotels of the cities. We cannot be satisfied as long as the Negro's basic mobility is from a smaller ghetto to a larger one. We can never be satisfied as long as a Negro in Mississippi cannot vote and a Negro in New York believes he has nothing for which to vote. No, no, we are not satisfied, and we will not be satisfied until justice rolls down like waters and righteousness like a mighty stream."

8. Martin Luther King Jr. led many protests for civil rights. What does the term "civil rights" mean in this context?

Civil rights are

(1) the rights and freedoms not guaranteed by the Bill of Rights
(2) the rights and freedoms required by state law, not federal law
(3) only for African Americans
(4) the rights and freedoms that assure everyone's ability to participate in political and social life
(5) the rights and freedoms that every citizen has always had equally

9. Martin Luther King Jr. says to the audience that "We can never be satisfied as long as a Negro in Mississippi cannot vote and a Negro in New York believes he has nothing for which to vote." In what way was the situation in Mississippi different from that in New York?

(1) Unlike African Americans in New York, African Americans in Mississippi were being denied the right to vote.
(2) Mississippi was still only a territory, whereas New York was a state.
(3) African Americans in Mississippi had already achieved total equality.
(4) African Americans in Mississippi were much poorer than those in New York.
(5) The situation was not different.

GO ON TO THE NEXT PAGE

10. According to the excerpt, what must civil rights protesters avoid?

    Protesters must avoid

    (1) having too many unreasonable political goals
    (2) full membership in political organizations and parties
    (3) violence and racism against white people
    (4) religious organizations and churches
    (5) trusting in the Constitution to protect them

11. Martin Luther King Jr. fought to end racial segregation. Which statement best describes racial segregation?

    Racial segregation is

    (1) a scientific theory that supports racism
    (2) a belief that the United States' Constitution does not apply to all areas of life
    (3) when the government ensures that racial minorities do not have the right to vote
    (4) the separation of different racial groups in daily life and public institutions
    (5) the system whereby racial minorities are included in political life

GO ON TO THE NEXT PAGE

Questions 12 through 14 refer to the following chart and information.

Year	Urban	Rural
1800	6%	94%
1810	7%	93%
1820	7%	93%
1830	9%	91%
1840	11%	89%
1850	15%	85%
1860	20%	80%
1870	26%	74%
1880	28%	72%
1890	35%	65%
1900	40%	60%
1910	46%	54%
1920	51%	49%
1930	56%	44%
1940	57%	43%
1950	60%	40%
1960	63%	37%
1970	74%	26%
1980	74%	26%
1990	75%	25%

Source: U.S. Census Bureau

This graph compares the proportion of the United States' population living in urban areas to that living in rural areas. It is based on data from the U.S. Census Bureau.

12. According to the chart, what was the first year that the United States had a larger urban population than a rural one?

(1) 1800
(2) 1820
(3) 1860
(4) 1900
(5) 1920

13. The data from this chart comes from the United States Census Bureau. What is a census?

A census is a(n)

(1) unconstitutional procedure that taxes goods
(2) information about a population collected every ten years
(3) tax on all American citizens administered every ten years
(4) measure of corporate wealth production conducted on an annual basis
(5) calculation based on environmental changes

14. What is one result of the changes shown in the graph?

(1) Urban centers have become unimportant in recent years.
(2) Rural areas have become densely populated and wealthy.
(3) Rural areas now contain a smaller percentage of the U.S. population.
(4) Agriculture became increasingly important to the U.S. economy during the twentieth century.
(5) Urban centers have become less populous.

GO ON TO THE NEXT PAGE

Questions 15 and 16 refer to the following excerpt from the Supreme Court decision *Schenck v. United States* (1919).

"The question in every case is whether the words used are used in such circumstances and are of such a nature as to create a clear and present danger that they will bring about the substantive evils that the United States Congress has a right to prevent. It is a question of proximity and degree. When a nation is at war, many things that might be said in time of peace are such a hindrance to its effort that their utterance will not be endured so long as men fight, and that no Court could regard them as protected by any constitutional right."

15. The Supreme Court decided that there were limits to free speech in some circumstances. Under what circumstances was free speech limited?

Free speech was limited when

(1) the United States was at war and individual speech a "clear and present danger" to national security
(2) the United States presented a "clear and present danger" to the rights of individuals
(3) "substantive evils" threatened the rights of the First Amendment
(4) the United States military was presented with a "clear and present danger" from a foreign, hostile enemy
(5) "substantive evils" threaten the religious and moral well-being of society

16. The legal right to free speech is protected by what important legal document?

The legal right to free speech is protected by

(1) the Stamp Act of 1765
(2) the Emancipation Proclamation
(3) the Federalist Papers
(4) the Bill of Rights
(5) the Articles of Confederation

17. During the period from 1919 to 1933, the sale, manufacture, and transportation of alcohol for consumption was illegal. What was this era called?

(1) World War I
(2) Prohibition
(3) the Great Depression
(4) World War II
(5) the Cold War

18. Laissez-faire capitalism is a system in which the government does not intervene in the marketplace and allows economic events to take their own course. Which statement expresses an **OPINION,** not a fact, about laissez-faire capitalism?

(1) Many politicians express a belief in laissez-faire capitalism.
(2) Laissez-faire capitalism is not an official legal doctrine.
(3) Laissez-faire capitalism does not involve the ownership of all major industries by the government.
(4) Many Communist nations reject the beliefs of laissez-faire capitalism.
(5) Laissez-faire capitalism is irresponsible and should not play a role in the development of law.

GO ON TO THE NEXT PAGE

Questions 19 through 21 refer to the following excerpt from Rachel Carson's *Silent Spring* (1962).

"It is an extraordinary fact that the deliberate introduction of poisons into a reservoir is becoming a fairly common practice. The purpose is usually to promote recreational uses, even though the water must be treated at some expense to make it fit for its intended use as drinking water. When sportsmen of an area want to "improve" fishing in a reservoir, they prevail on authorities to dump quantities of poison into it to kill the undesired fish, which are then replaced with hatchery fish more suited to the sportsmen's taste. The procedure has a strange Alice-in-Wonderland quality. The reservoir was created as a public water supply, yet the community, probably unconsulted about the sportsmen's project, is forced either to drink water containing poisonous residues or to pay our tax money for treatment of the water to remove the poisons—treatments that are by no means foolproof."

19. Which statement best describes a claim made in this excerpt?

(1) Pesticides are destroying American crops.
(2) The pharmaceutical industry has capitalized on an uneducated populace.
(3) Many natural habitats naturally contain pesticides.
(4) Some people are deliberately poisoning water supplies to kill fish and replace them with other fish.
(5) Fish secrete poisons into the public's drinking supply.

20. According to the excerpt, what is one negative effect of the "introduction of poisons into a reservoir"?

(1) It undermines federally-funded conservation efforts.
(2) It has the potential to poison the drinking water of humans.
(3) It helps sustain a vibrant ecosystem.
(4) It participates in a larger process of globalization.
(5) It adversely affects the climate of a region.

21. Which major political movement was most influenced by Rachel Carson's *Silent Spring*?

(1) the feminist movement
(2) the civil rights movement
(3) the abolitionist movement
(4) the sexual revolution
(5) the environmental movement

22. Fossil fuels are sources of energy based on carbons and hydrocarbons found in the earth's crust. Common fossil fuels are oil, coal, and natural gas. Which statement expresses a **FACT,** not an opinion, about fossil fuels?

(1) Fossil fuels are wasteful and should be replaced with better types of fuels.
(2) Environmentalists are afraid of fossil fuels because they do not understand their true impact on the environment.
(3) Fossil fuels are destroying the moral character of the United States.
(4) Many nations are dependent on fossil fuels as a major source of energy.
(5) There are many better and newer forms of energy than fossil fuels and the United States should be using these new forms of energy.

GO ON TO THE NEXT PAGE

Questions 23 and 24 refer to the following graph.

Estimated Native American Population of Mexico, 1518–1593

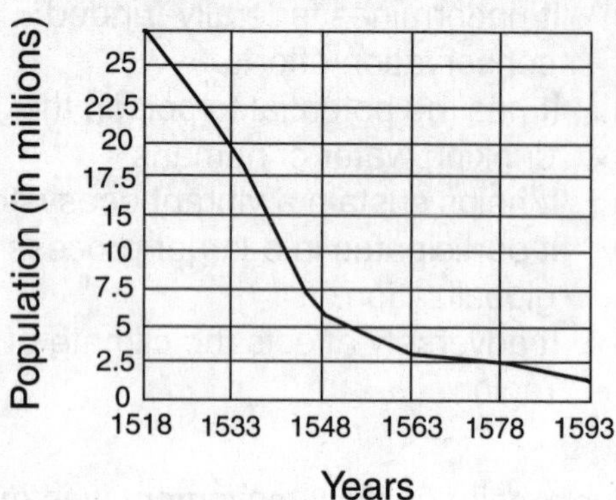

23. According to the information in the graph, which statement is true?

(1) The population of Native Americans fluctuated wildly during the sixteenth century.
(2) Almost 20 million Native Americans died between 1518 and 1548.
(3) More Native Americans died in the period from 1548 to 1578 than in the period from 1518 to 1548.
(4) Many Native Americans immigrated into Mexico during the sixteenth century.
(5) The Spanish conquistadors were more interested in Peru than in Mexico.

24. The populations of Native Americans in North and South America declined sharply in the sixteenth century. What was the primary factor that led to this decline?

The population declined because

(1) many Native Americans fled to Europe
(2) many Native Americans could not feed themselves
(3) disease killed the vast majority of the Native American population
(4) the Spanish conquistadors executed more than 90 percent of the population
(5) the Native American tribes declared war on each other

GO ON TO THE NEXT PAGE

<u>Question 25</u> refers to the preamble to the Constitution.

> "We the People of the United States, in Order to form a more perfect Union, establish Justice, insure domestic Tranquility, provide for the common defence, promote the general Welfare, and secure the Blessings of Liberty to ourselves and our Posterity, do ordain and establish this Constitution for the United States of America."

25. Which statement is true of the preamble to the Constitution?

    The preamble

    (1) states the purpose of the Constitution
    (2) rejects the belief that human rights are universal
    (3) contains the entire text of the Constitution
    (4) rejects the Articles of Confederation and the Bill of Rights
    (5) recreates the Declaration of Independence

END OF EXAMINATION

DO NOT MARK OR WRITE ON THIS PAGE

SCIENCE

Tests of General Educational Development

Directions

The Science Test consists of multiple-choice questions intended to measure understanding of general concepts in science. The questions are based on short readings that often include a graph, chart, or figure. Study the information given and then answer the question(s) following it. Refer to the information as often as necessary in answering the questions.

You should spend no more than 53 minutes answering the questions in this booklet. Work carefully, but do not spend too much time on any one question. Be sure you answer every question.

Do not mark in this test booklet. Record your answers to the questions on the separate sheet provided. Be sure all requested information is properly recorded on the answer sheet.

To record your answers, mark the numbered space on the answer sheet beside the number that corresponds to the question in the test booklet.

FOR EXAMPLE:

Which of the following is the smallest unit in a living thing?

(1) tissue
(2) organ
(3) cell
(4) muscle
(5) capillary

The correct answer is "cell"; therefore, answer space 3 would be marked on the answer sheet.

Do not rest the point of your pencil on the answer sheet while you are considering your answer. Make no stray or unnecessary marks. If you change an answer, erase your first mark completely. Mark only <u>one</u> answer space for each question; multiple answers will be scored as incorrect. Do not fold or crease your answer sheet. All test materials must be returned to the test administrator.

GO ON TO THE NEXT PAGE

Science

Directions: Choose the one best answer to each question.

1. Evolutionary fitness is determined by how much an organism contributes to the next generation's gene pool. The more living offspring an organism produces, the more fit that organism is.

   According to the above definition, which of the following individuals is currently the most evolutionarily fit?

   (1) a 3 year old child who has never had a cold
   (2) a 25 year old childless man who works out daily and eats healthfully
   (3) a 30 year old woman who has had 5 miscarriages and 6 healthy children
   (4) a sick 97 year old woman with three healthy children
   (5) a healthy 100 year old man with one healthy child

Questions 2 and 3 are based on the following information and table:

The table below shows a partial analysis of the composition of soil taken from a canyon in the desert.

Material	Percent Composition
Silt	25%
Clay	15%
Sedimentary Rock	12%
Metamorphic Rock	10%

2. Which of the following scientists would probably be most interested in these results?

   (1) geologist
   (2) medical researcher
   (3) astronomer
   (4) zoologist
   (5) botanist

3. What percent of the sample consists of rock?

   (1) 10
   (2) 12
   (3) 15
   (4) 22
   (5) 25

GO ON TO THE NEXT PAGE

Questions 4 and 5

The graph below shows the amount of rainfall during the spring and summer months in the city of Mayfair.

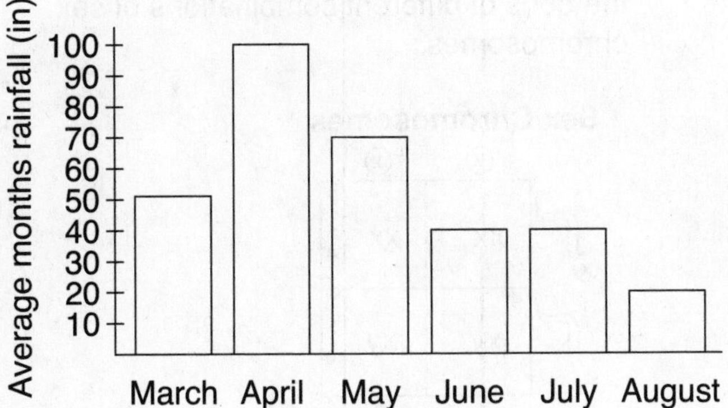

4. Between which two months was the increase in average monthly rainfall the greatest?

   (1) March and April
   (2) April and May
   (3) May and June
   (4) June and July
   (5) July and August

5. Which of the following questions can be answered based on the information in the chart?

   (1) Which is the driest of the four seasons?
   (2) How much rain falls in November?
   (3) What types of clouds produce rain?
   (4) Which is the rainiest spring or summer month?
   (5) What is the average temperature of the spring and summer months?

6. A child swings a bucket of water in circles several times, but the water does not spill from the bucket.

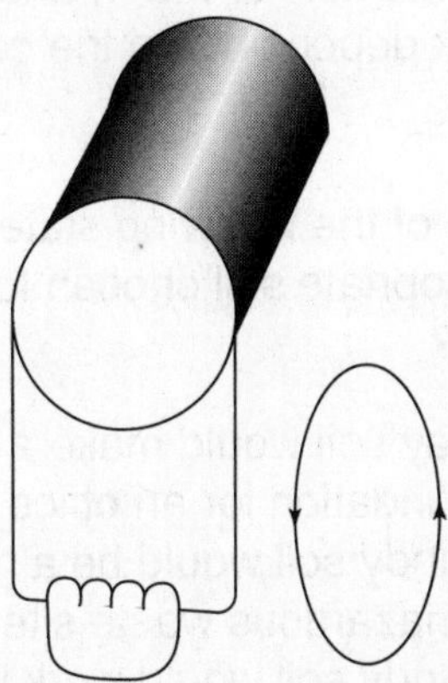

Which is the best explanation for this?

   (1) The force of gravity prevents the water from spilling.
   (2) The centripetal force directed inward prevents the water from spilling while the bucket is rotated slowly.
   (3) The centripetal force directed inward prevents the water from spilling while the bucket is rotated quickly.
   (4) The water has frozen inside the bucket.
   (5) Intermolecular forces between water molecules prevent water from spilling out of the bucket.

GO ON TO THE NEXT PAGE

7. Sandy soil allows the flow of water and maintains its shape regardless of the water content. In contrast, clay soil forms a barrier against the flow of water, and tends to swell or shrink depending on the content of the water.

In which of the following statements is the appropriate soil chosen for the given location?

(1) Clay soil would make a good foundation for an office building.
(2) Sandy soil would be a good base for a hazardous waste site.
(3) Sandy soil would work well in a drain field.
(4) Sandy soil would prevent water from seeping out of a pond.
(5) Clay soil would allow the roots of plants to absorb the most rainwater.

8. Gender is determined by a pair of chromosomes known as the sex chromosomes. Women have two X chromosomes, while males have one X and one Y. A child inherits and X chromosome from its mom and either an X or a Y from its dad. The Punnett Square below shows the odds of different combinations of sex chromosomes.

Sex Chromosomes

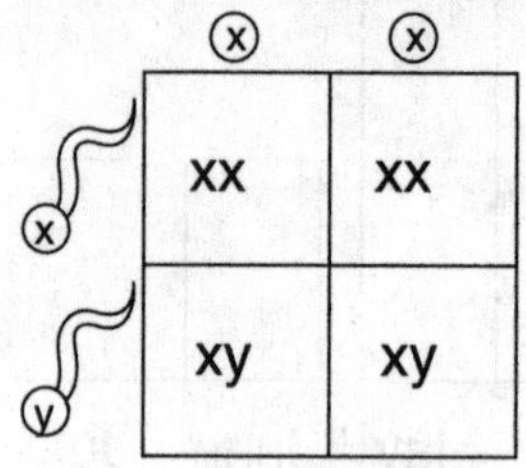

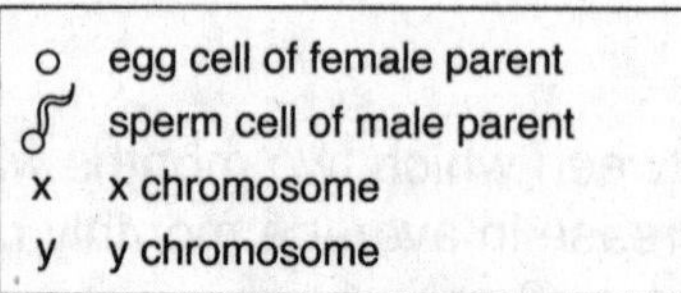

Based on the information and chart, what percentage of children are expected to be male?

(1) 100%
(2) 75%
(3) 50%
(4) 25%
(5) 0%

GO ON TO THE NEXT PAGE

9. Genes determine many of the traits that an organism has. Genes are located on chromosomes, and both are found in pairs. Some genes are dominant, meaning they are always expressed when present. Dominant genes can hide recessive genes, which are only expressed when both genes in a pair are recessive. In hybrids, which have one dominant gene and one recessive gene, the dominant trait is expressed.

In rabbits, the gene for black fur is dominant and represented by the capital letter B. The gene for brown fur is recessive and represented by the lowercase letter b. The chart below is a Punnett Square, which predicts the ratios of different combinations of genes in offspring. The cross below is between a black rabbit and a brown rabbit. Each is pure for its trait, which means each has two copies of the same gene.

If the Punnett were properly completed, the offspring from this cross would all be

(1) black
(2) brown
(3) black with brown spots
(4) brown with black spots
(5) white

10. The graph below shows John's distance from home as he travels on his bicycle.

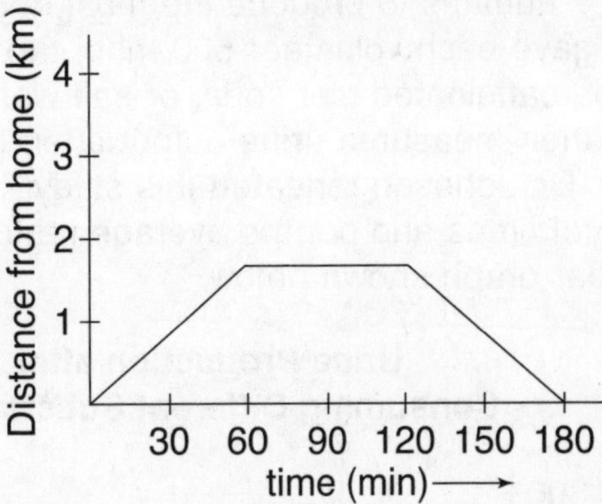

Which of the following bike trips could this graph represent?

(1) John rides 2 kilometers to the park, stops for lunch, and rides 2 more kilometers to the zoo.
(2) John rides in a 6 kilometer race and does not take a break.
(3) John rides 2 kilometers to his grandmother's house, stays for one hour, and then rides back home.
(4) John rides his bike nonstop for 4 hours.
(5) John rides to the park and back without stopping.

GO ON TO THE NEXT PAGE

Questions 11 and 12

Dr. Johnson performed a medical experiment to determine which substances cause humans to produce the most urine. She gave each volunteer 500 ml of tap water, caffeinated diet soda, or salt water. She then measured urine output after 1 hour. Dr. Johnson repeated this study several times and put the average results in the bar graph shown below.

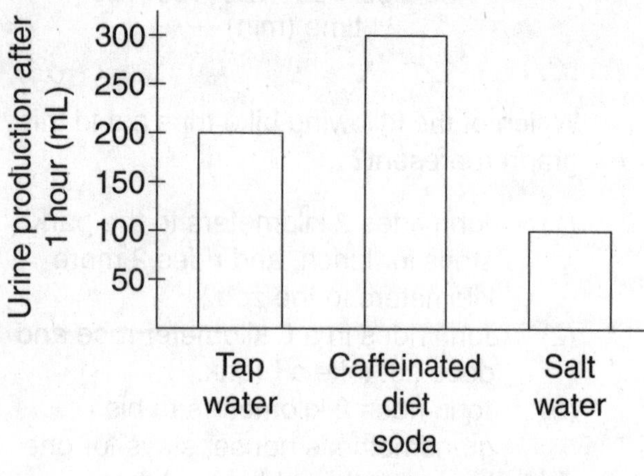

11. Which conclusion best supports the data in the graph?

(1) All liquids cause humans to produce the same amount of urine.
(2) Caffeine decreases the amount of urine produced.
(3) Salt increases the amount of urine produced.
(4) The amount of urine produced is always greater than the amount of fluid ingested.
(5) Salt causes a person to retain water and produce less urine.

12. Which question cannot be answered based on Dr. Johnson's research?

(1) Which substance causes a person to produce more urine: caffeine or water?
(2) Do caffeine and salt have the same effects on human urine production?
(3) Which substance causes a person to produce less urine: water or soda?
(4) Does drinking a larger volume of water cause a human to produce more urine?
(5) What is the average amount of urine produced one hour after a person consumes 500ml of salt water?

13. Classical conditioning is a type of learning in which an animal responds to something neutral because the animal associates it with something that produces a response. For example, scientist Ivan Pavlov discovered that feeding his dog made the dog salivate. Pavlov began to ring a bell just before feeding his dog, and over time his dog began to salivate upon hearing the bell, even if no food was present.

Which of the following is an example of classical conditioning?

(1) a squirrel that stores nuts in the fall to prepare for the winter
(2) a student who usually eats lunch after math class feels hungry during math class even when his schedule is changed
(3) a duckling that decides the first moving thing it sees is its mother
(4) a chef who memorizes his recipes
(5) a boy who studies for his history exam and passes

GO ON TO THE NEXT PAGE

14. Chemicals can be classified as acidic, neutral, or basic. This classification is based on a measurement called pH. A pH below 7 means a substance is acidic, a pH of 7 means a substance is neutral, and a pH above 7 means a substance is basic. An indicator is something that changes color based on the pH of the solution to which it is added. For example, cabbage juice is an indicator that turns blue when added to a base.

The table below shows pH value for several liquids.

liquid	**pH**
apple juice	3
water	7
acid rain	5
ammonia	11

Based on the information and the table, in which of the following substances would cabbage juice turn blue?

(1) ammonia only
(2) water only
(3) both ammonia and water
(4) apple juice only
(5) both water and acid rain

15. A plastic ball is dropped from the top of a building as shown below.

Free Fall of Ball

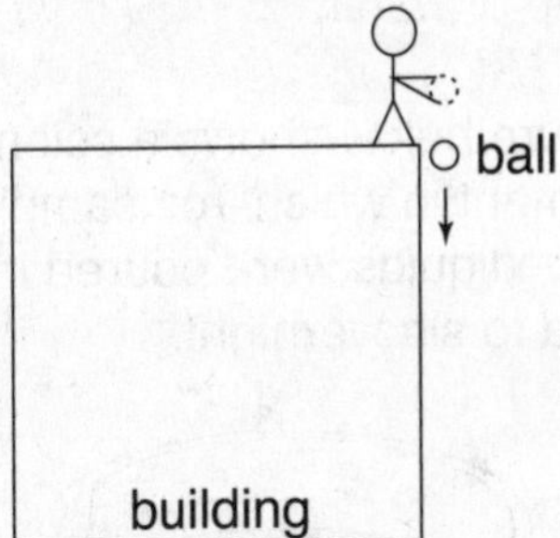

Which of the following is most likely to reduce the acceleration of the falling ball?

(1) gravity
(2) air resistance
(3) magnetic forces
(4) friction against the top of the building
(5) centripetal forces from within the ball

GO ON TO THE NEXT PAGE

16. Density is a measure of the mass of a substance per unit of volume. For example, maple syrup is more dense than water, so one cup of maple syrup weighs more than one cup of water.

The figure below shows a science experiment in which 1oz samples of several common liquids were poured into a cup and allowed to sit overnight.

Based on the information and figure, which of the following statements is most accurate?

(1) Baby oil has the highest density of the five liquids.
(2) Honey has the highest density of the five liquids.
(3) All of the liquids have the same density.
(4) Water is the least dense of the five liquids.
(5) Eventually all five liquids will mix together.

17. Pesticides are often used to kill insects that destroy crops. However, commercial pesticides also destroy beneficial insects and release toxins into the soil. To prevent the negative side effects, some farmers use natural methods to control destructive garden insects.

Ladybugs are considered helpful insects to have in the garden because they consume many smaller insects, such as aphids, that would otherwise destroy plants. Like most insects, ladybugs reproduce rapidly and thrive best in warm climates.

Why would a gardener release ladybugs into his or her garden?

Because ladybugs

(1) destroy plants
(2) transfer their bright color pigments to flowers
(3) feed on weeds
(4) feed on insects that are pollinators
(5) feed on insect pests

GO ON TO THE NEXT PAGE

18. Charles's law describes the behavior of gases as temperature is increased and pressure is kept constant. Below is a graph illustrating Charles's law.

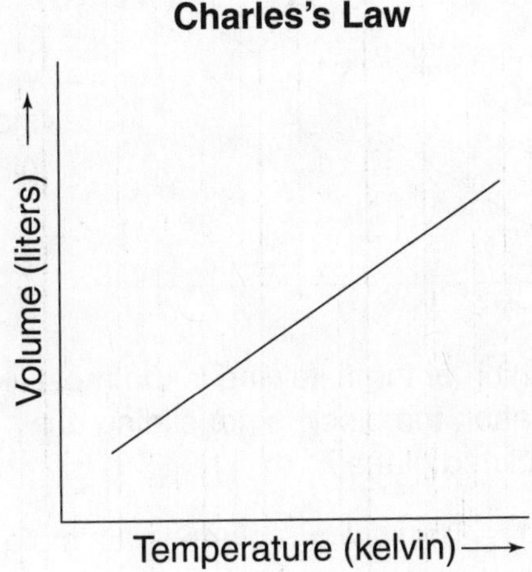

Based on the information and graph, which statement represents Charles's law?

(1) As temperature increases, volume decreases.
(2) As temperature increases, pressure decreases.
(3) As temperature increases, volume remains unchanged.
(4) As temperature decreases, volume increases.
(5) As temperature increases, volume increases.

19. The partial pressure of a gas is related to the amount of that gas in a container. The total pressure within the container is found by adding together the partial pressures of all the gases within that container. Below is a figure of a closed container filled with two gases. The partial pressure of Gas A is 200 Torr and the partial pressure of Gas B is 500 Torr.

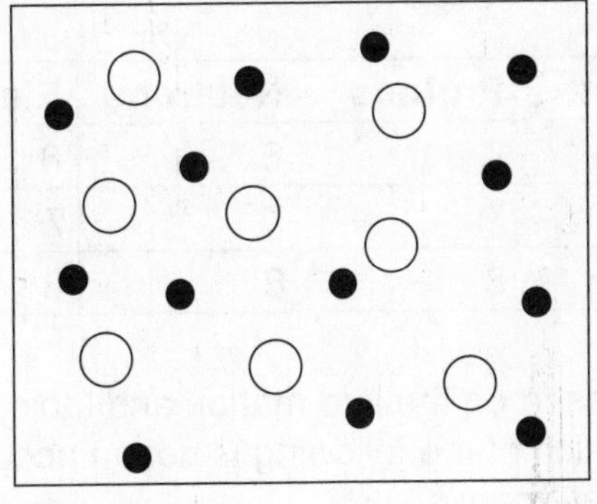

○ = Gas A

● = Gas B

Based on the information and diagram, which of the statements is accurate?

(1) The total pressure in the container is 700 Torr.
(2) The total pressure in the container is 300 Torr.
(3) The total pressure in the container is 200 Torr.
(4) The total pressure in the container is 500 Torr.
(5) Torr is a measure of temperature.

GO ON TO THE NEXT PAGE

20. An atom is the smallest particle an element can be broken into. It contains neutrons, protons, and electrons. The atomic number of an element is the number of protons in one atom of the element, and the atomic weight is determined by adding the number of neutrons and number of protons. Below is a chart listing the number of atomic particles found in one atom of three common elements.

Element	Protons	Neutrons	Electrons
Carbon	6	6	6
Nitrogen	7	7	7
Oxygen	8	8	8

Based on the information and table, which of the following is not an accurate statement?

(1) The atomic number of carbon is 6.
(2) The atomic weight of nitrogen is 14.
(3) The atomic number of oxygen is 8.
(4) The atomic weight of carbon is 12.
(5) The atomic weight of oxygen is 24.

21. The figure below shows a wooden block on top of a wooden inclined plane.

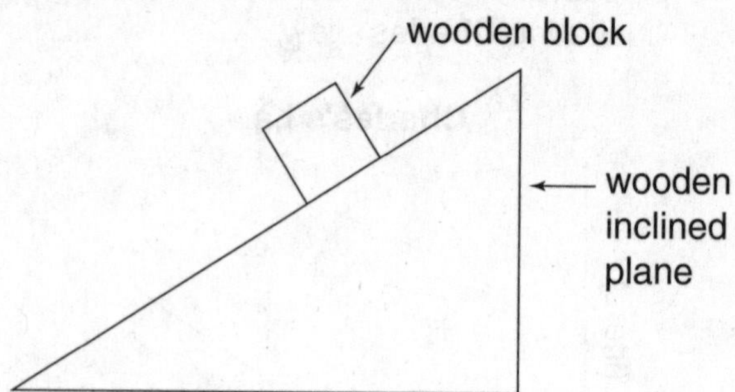

Which of the following is the most likely reason the block is not sliding down the inclined plane?

(1) The inclined plane is a simple machine.
(2) The block is magnetically attracted to the inclined plane.
(3) Gravity is pulling the block down the inclined plane.
(4) Static friction between the inclined plane and the block is preventing the block from sliding.
(5) A strong wind is blowing the block up the inclined plane.

GO ON TO THE NEXT PAGE

22. Igneous rock is formed when melted rock cools and hardens. Melted rock under the Earth's surface is called magma, while melted rock above the Earth's surface is called lava. Igneous rock is formed underground when magma cools in small pockets. Igneous rock is also formed above ground when a volcano erupts and spews lava that cools and hardens into igneous rock.

The passage above provides an answer to which of the following questions?

(1) How do volcanoes form?
(2) How deep under the Earth's surface does magma cool?
(3) What is the difference between magma and lava?
(4) Is igneous rock harder than metamorphic rock?
(5) How long does lava take to cool?

23. A teacher designed an experiment to test his student's knowledge of buoyancy. He placed a small fiberglass canister on the bottom of an empty barrel. The students were instructed to lift the canister to the surface of the barrel without touching the canister. The students were given water, oil, and funnels. Which of the following techniques would successfully lift the canister to the surface of the barrel?

(1) fill the barrel with water
(2) fill the canister with water
(3) fill the canister with water and the barrel with water
(4) fill the canister with oil
(5) fill the barrel with funnels

GO ON TO THE NEXT PAGE

Questions 24 and 25

The Richter Scale is used to measure seismic activity, which is energy released as heat and vibrations during earthquakes. The chart below shows the classifications and effects of earthquakes with different measurements on the Richter Scale.

Richter Magnitude	Classification	Effects
less than 2.0	micro	not felt
2.0–3.9	minor	may be felt
4.0–4.9	light	noticeable shaking but damages are unlikely
5.0–5.9	moderate	may cause damage to unstable structures
6.0–6.9	strong	can cause damages in areas up to 100 miles
7.0–7.9	major	can cause damages in areas several hundred miles large
8.0–9.9	great	can cause damages in areas several thousand miles large

24. The chart above would be most helpful to a scientist studying

(1) volcanoes
(2) hurricanes
(3) tornadoes
(4) fires
(5) earthquakes

25. According to the chart and information above, seismic activity measuring 7.5 on the Richter Scale would most likely

(1) not be felt
(2) cause no damage
(3) damage areas up to 100 miles large
(4) damage areas several hundred miles large
(5) damage areas several thousand miles large

END OF EXAMINATION

LANGUAGE ARTS, READING

Tests of General Educational Development

Directions

The Language Arts, Reading Test consists of excerpts from fiction and nonfiction. Each excerpt is followed by multiple-choice questions about the reading material.

Read each excerpt first and then answer the questions following it. Refer back to the reading material as often as necessary in answering the questions.

Each excerpt is preceded by a "purpose question." The purpose question gives a reason for reading the material. Use these purpose questions to help focus your reading. You are not required to answer these purpose questions. They are given only to help you concentrate on the ideas presented in the reading material.

You should spend no more than 35 minutes answering the questions in this booklet. Work carefully, but do not spend too much time on any one question. Be sure you answer every question.

Do not mark in this test booklet. Record your answers on the separate answer sheet provided. Be sure that all requested information is properly recorded on the answer sheet.

To record your answers, mark the numbered space on the answer sheet beside the number that corresponds to the question in the test booklet.

FOR EXAMPLE:

It was Susan's dream machine. The metallic blue paint gleamed, and the sporty wheels were highly polished. Under the hood, the engine was no less carefully cleaned. Inside, flashy lights illuminated the instruments on the dashboard, and the seats were covered by rich leather upholstery.

The subject ("It") of this excerpt is most likely

(1) an airplane
(2) a stereo system
(3) an automobile
(4) a boat
(5) a motorcycle

The correct answer is "an automobile"; therefore, answer space 3 would be marked on the answer sheet.

Do not rest the point of your pencil on the answer sheet while you are considering your answer. Make no stray or unnecessary marks. If you change an answer, erase your first mark completely. Mark only one answer space for each question; multiple answers will be scored as incorrect. Do not fold or crease your answer sheet. All test materials must be returned to the test administrator.

GO ON TO THE NEXT PAGE

Directions: Choose the one best answer to each question.

Questions 1 through 5 refer to the following excerpt.

WHAT DOES THIS STUDENT WANT HER SCHOOL TO DO?

Letter to the school board of Ewell Hish School.

The teachers make the school.

Though I am soon to graduate and leave Ewell High School forever, I feel it is my duty to do all I can to preserve the excellent academic tradition here. I do not want to see my school, a few years from now, in a situation where we continue to make decisions on the side of the policy-makers and not on the side of the students. It is very possible that if the school board and Ewell H.S. administrators—and there seem to be so very many of them—choose the path of eliminating teachers whenever there is a budget crisis, we will eventual lead ourselves into a very weak academic program or to no school at all. It would be a terrible outcome if future Ewell H.S. students do not get the same tremendous opportunities that I have had.

Personally, I cannot imagine what my high school experience would have been like without Mr. Hileman and his Classics course. The Latin, Greek, and history lessons that I learned with my fellow classmates in his room were unforgettable. I became a better student in his classroom. In short, I learned the most important lesson—how to learn on my own. So, I am taking many memories and many academic skills with me when I graduate. I worry that future students will never even experience these great lessons. How can the loss of all these things, including the termination of a very good Classics course, possibly be the best solution for the school's financial woes? There are other options.

There are other ways the school can maintain its financial standing without damaging its academic programs. We must explore all of them, as the current plan is clearly a move that will damage us, no matter the monetary implications. Recall that in September during his annual speech to returning students, Principal Jeffries said to all of us, "Be sure to take advantage of what makes Ewell H.S. so great—we may not have the prettiest lawns outside or the largest gymnasium, but we have the best teachers you can find." If Mr. Hileman goes, this will no longer be true. We must find an alternative solution.

Sincerely,

Joanna Lang

Joanna Lang

Ewell H.S. Senior

GO ON TO THE NEXT PAGE

Reading

1. The letter writer quotes the principal of the school's annual address to students (lines 27–30) primarily in order to

   (1) show her passion for the school
   (2) reveal her insight into the plans of the administration
   (3) admit that she knows the principal well
   (4) expose a deceitful practice of the school's leader
   (5) give further support to her argument

2. It can be inferred from the letter, that at Ewell H.S. the administration has apparently recently decided to

   (1) remove a popular teacher for financial reasons
   (2) reduce the budget for sports and beautification
   (3) have the principal address the full student body
   (4) change policy on the importance of studying foreign languages
   (5) include input from the student body when making policy decision

3. Which of the following is a weakness of the opinion expressed in the letter?

   (1) Additional funds could be saved by spending less on the gymnasium and campus grounds.
   (2) Budget difficulties within a school system are usually the result of improper management.
   (3) Some students in the future may not like Mr. Hileman.
   (4) A graduating Senior cannot influence the future policies of the school.
   (5) No alternative solutions are given to address the reasons for Mr. Hileman's departure.

4. The letter writer suggests several possible negative results after the departure of Mr. Hileman. Which of the following is NOT mentioned as one of these potential future problems?

   (1) weakened academic programs at Ewell H.S.
   (2) additional loss of teachers for financial reasons
   (3) an inferior experience for future students
   (4) more dangerous school environment
   (5) termination of the Classics program

5. The letter writer indicates that the most crucial thing she learned in Mr. Hileman's classroom was

   (1) history
   (2) Greek
   (3) how to learn
   (4) a sense of humor
   (5) Latin

GO ON TO THE NEXT PAGE

Questions 6 through 11 refer to the following excerpt.

WHAT IS HOLMES' OPINION OF WATSON'S OBSERVATIONS?

[The following is an excerpt from a Sherlock Holmes mystery featuring the great detective Sherlock Holmes and his long-time assistant Watson.]

Watson had been watching his companion intently ever since he had sat down to the breakfast table. Holmes happened to look up and catch his eye.

"Well, Watson, what are you thinking about?" he asked.

"About you."

"Me?"

"Yes, Holmes. I was thinking how superficial are these tricks of yours and how wonderful is it is that the public should continue to show interest in them.

"I quite agree," said Holmes. "In fact, I have a recollection that I have myself made a similar remark."

"Your methods," said Watson severely, "are really easily acquired."

"No doubt," Holmes answered with a smile. "Perhaps you will yourself give and example of this method of reasoning."

"With pleasure," said Watson. "I am able to say that you were greatly preoccupied when you got up this morning."

"Excellent!" said Holmes. "How could you possibly know that?"

"Because you are usually a very tidy man and yet you have forgotten to shave."

"Dear me! How very clever!" said Holmes, "I had no idea, Watson, that you were so apt a pupil. Has your eagle eye detected anything more?"

"Yes, Holmes. You have a client named Barlow, and you have not been successful in his case."

"Dear me, how could you know that?"

"I saw the name outside his envelope. When you opened it you have a groan and thrust it into your pocket with a frown on your face."

"Admirable! You are indeed observant. Any other points?"

"I fear Holmes, that you have taken to financial speculation."

"How *could* you tell that, Watson?"

"You opened the paper, turned to the financial page, and gave a loud exclamation of interest."

"Well, that is very clever of you Watson. Any more?"

"Yes, Holmes, you have put on your black coat, instead of your dressing gown, which proves that you are expecting some important visitor at once."

"Anything more?"

"I have no doubt that I could find other points, Holmes, but I only give you these few, in order to show you that there are other people in the world who can be as clever as you."

"And some not so clever," said Holmes. "I admit that they are few, but I am afraid, my dear Watson, that I must count you among them."

"What do you mean Holmes?"

GO ON TO THE NEXT PAGE

"Well, my dear fellow, I fear your deductions have not been as happy as I should have wished."

"You mean that I was mistaken."

"Just a little that way, I fear. Let us take the points in their order: I did not shave because I have sent my razor to be sharpened. I put on my coat because I have, worse luck, an early meeting with my dentist. His name is Barlow, and the letter was to confirm the appointment. The cricket* page is beside the financial one, and I turned to it to find if Surrey was holding its own against Kent. But go on, Watson, go on. It's a very superficial trick and no doubt you will soon acquire it."

*a sporting game, somewhat similar to baseball

Arthur Conan Doyle, HOW WATSON LEARNED THE TRICK, 1922

6. The word "happy," in line 66, could be replaced with which of the following

(1) accurate
(2) elated
(3) joyous
(4) friendly
(5) regular

7. The word *could* is italicized in line 44 most likely because Holmes

(1) is shouting at Watson
(2) is whispering so no one else hears
(3) is emphasizing the word
(4) needs more information
(5) is unsure of how best to make his comment

GO ON TO THE NEXT PAGE

8. Holmes says "Excellent" and "Dear Me! and "Admirable!" in response to several of Watson's apparently insightful comments. Holmes attitude when making these comments could best be described as

(1) genuinely alarmed
(2) completely amazed
(3) consistently facetious
(4) utterly confused
(5) somewhat disagreeable

9. Holmes says that "I admit that they are few, but I am afraid, my dear Watson, that I must count you among them" in lines 61–63. Who is Holmes referring to when saying "they" and "them"?

(1) the people Holmes has appointments with
(2) Holmes' enemies
(3) people who are as clever as Holmes
(4) people who are not as clever as Holmes
(5) the visitors that the men are expecting

10. Following this conversation, what is likely now Watson's opinion regarding observations?

Watson now believes that

(1) he can accurately imitate Holmes' success in observation
(2) Holmes opinion is biased and flawed
(3) no one can reproduce the level of accuracy in detection that Holmes achieves
(4) it is not quite as easy as he had previously thought
(5) no one should consider Holmes to be a clever man

11. The phrase "holding its own" (line 78) could best be replaced with which of the following without changing the meaning of the paragraph?

(1) preparing for departure
(2) competing well
(3) recovering from a contest
(4) practicing quickly
(5) participating erratically

GO ON TO THE NEXT PAGE

Questions 12 through 16 refer to the following excerpt.

WHAT DO THE TWO MEN THINK ABOUT ART?

MR. WENTWORTH: Of course, I don't pretend to be an artist myself, but I have always studied and loved pictures, and when you say "learning how to paint"—

JOE: That's exactly what it is. Learning how to paint. Learning what art is. Getting life into it instead of abstract ideas.

MR. WENTWORTH: Art? But art is beauty! Eternal beauty. You can't change art over night, like a fashion!

JOE: Art changes as life changes. Art has always changed. If it didn't, why isn't your Japanese art just like Greek art? And Greek art like the Italian?

MR. WENTWORTH: Oh, in that way, of course. But all the great masters obey the eternal laws of beauty!

JOE: There aren't any eternal laws of beauty! There's only the eternal impulse to create. Every artist has to express himself in his own way. What you call the "eternal laws" are merely the particular expressions your own favorite painters happened to work out in their time. If they had lived in another time—

MR. WENTWORTH: A master would always be a master. There's no change possible in the vision of the soul.

JOE: The painter with an original vision is always opposed by the schools. That is, at first. But when he wins out, then the schools merely take over his technique and use it as a club to put down the next creator. And so it goes.

MR. WENTWORTH: Naturally, the great artist suffers hardship. But if we once admit there are no laws, where are we? Anarchy!

JOE: The laws are contained in the impulses themselves. They come with the vision, not before it! If any one thinks this modern art is just an easy way of painting—

MR. WENTWORTH: But the Louvre! All those beautiful pictures, those priceless treasures! What about the Louvre?

JOE: The Louvre? It's a museum.

MR. WENTWORTH: What do you mean by "it's a museum"?

JOE: I mean that it's the place to put pictures in when they are dead.

MR. WENTWORTH: Dead? A great masterpiece dead?

JOE: Of course. No man lives forever. Nobody that was ever born was useful enough to live forever. The bigger a man is the longer his influence is creative, in art and everything else, but the time always comes when his value is spent. When the world needs a new influence.

MR. WENTWORTH: But see here, young man, you wouldn't do away with the Louvre, would you? Why, what would happen if these ideas were carried out....

GO ON TO THE NEXT PAGE

JOE: No, I wouldn't do away with it. Why should I? If to burn it down would wake people up to life, I'd do it in a minute. But it wouldn't. They would only sanctify the superstition and make it immortal. No, leave the Louvre as it is. It's really quite useful.

MR. WENTWORTH: But good gracious! Useful?

JOE: Yes. Like history. To do away with the Louvre would be to destroy a part of history. There's no good doing that. We need history—it cranks up life—but we've got to recognize that after all it is only history, not life itself—not art.

MR. WENTWORTH: But what is art, if the Louvre isn't?

Horace Holley, PICTURES, 1916

12. Joe describes his impression of what often happens to painters with "an original vision" (line 32). He believes that original artists are always

(1) better than previous artists
(2) unaware of their place in history
(3) initially resisted by established art experts
(4) those found in museums
(5) modern artists

13. The passage makes it clear that within the world of art, Mr. Wentworth highly values

(1) established rules
(2) photography
(3) oil painting
(4) Greek art
(5) Japanese art

14. Joe states "No man lives forever" (line 58) in order to illustrate what larger point about art?

No matter how accomplished or skillful any artist may become, the world always

(1) remembers dead pictures
(2) needs new artists
(3) values great museums
(4) determines the best art critics
(5) desires abstract ideas

15. Based on what Joe states about art, it is likely that he gets many of his ideas about art

(1) from art school
(2) from Mr. Wentworth
(3) while painting
(4) while in the Louvre
(5) from art books

16. Joe states both that he would burn the Louvre down if it would "wake people up to life" (line 73). What does the Louvre represent to him?

(1) bad art
(2) death
(3) work
(4) modern art
(5) passion

GO ON TO THE NEXT PAGE

Questions 17 through 21 refer to the following excerpt.

WHAT IS THE SPEAKER'S OPINION OF HIS FATHER?

Sundays too my father got up early
and put his clothes on in the blueblack cold,
then with cracked hands that ached
from labor in the weekday weather made
banked fires blaze. No one even thanked him.

I'd wake and hear the cold splintering, breaking.
When the rooms were warm, he'd call,
and slowly I would rise and dress,
fearing the chronic angers of that house,

Speaking indifferently to him,
who had driven out the cold,
and polished my good shoes as well.
What did I know, what did I know
of love's austere and lonely offices?

Robert Hayden, "Those Winter Sundays"

17. If given the chance to go back in time and live this moment again, the speaker would most likely wish to do all of the following EXCEPT:

    (1) speak more warmly to the father
    (2) offer gratitude for the polished shoes
    (3) offer gratitude for the warm house
    (4) stay out of the cold and in bed
    (5) offer to help the father make the fire

18. This poem describes a scene from the speaker's past with the father. The speaker's feelings for the father have seemingly changed over time. That change has been

    (1) from childlike to lonely
    (2) from positive to negative
    (3) from cold to warm
    (4) from emotional to serious
    (5) from thankful to indifferent

GO ON TO THE NEXT PAGE

19. What is suggested by the speaker's fear of "the chronic angers of that house"?

    (1) there was reason to be afraid of the unknown parts of the house
    (2) there were many arguments in the household among the family members.
    (3) it was cold every morning in the house
    (4) no one liked to speak first thing in the morning
    (5) the house creaked and shifted frequently as old houses do

20. Based on the poem, which of the following is most likely true about the speaker's father?

    (1) He works in an office building.
    (2) He is often angry.
    (3) He gets up early every day.
    (4) He does not like to be thanked.
    (5) He is unmarried.

21. The last two lines of the poem convey a feeling of

    (1) investigation
    (2) regret
    (3) resentment
    (4) forgetfulness
    (5) joy

END OF EXAMINATION

MATHEMATICS

Tests of General Educational Development

Directions

The Mathematics Test consists of questions intended to measure general mathematics skills and problem-solving ability. The questions are based on short readings that often include a graph, chart, or figure.

You should spend no more than 45 minutes answering the questions in this booklet. Work carefully, but do not spend too much time on any one question. Be sure you answer every question.

Formulas you may need are given on page 398. Only some of the questions will require you to use a formula. Not all the formulas given will be needed.

Some questions contain more information than you will need to solve the problem; other questions do not give enough information. If the question does not give enough information to solve the problem, the correct answer choice is "Not enough information is given."

The use of calculators is allowed only in Part I.

Do not mark in this test booklet. The test administrator will give you blank paper for your calculations. Record your answers on the separate answer sheet provided. Be sure that all requested information is properly recorded on the answer sheet.

To record your answers, fill in the numbered circle on the answer sheet beside the number that corresponds to the question in the test booklet.

FOR EXAMPLE:

If a grocery bill totaling $15.75 is paid with a $20.00 bill, how much change should be returned?

(1) $5.25

(2) $4.75

(3) $4.25

(4) $3.75

(5) $3.25

The correct answer is $4.25; therefore, answer space (3) would be marked on the answer sheet.

Do not rest the point of your pencil on the answer sheet while you are considering your answer. Make no stray or unnecessary marks. If you change an answer, erase your first mark completely. Mark only <u>one</u> answer space for each question; multiple answers will be scored as incorrect. Do not fold or crease your answer sheet. All test materials must be returned to the test administrator.

GO ON TO THE NEXT PAGE

Mathematics, Part I

FORMULAS

AREA (A) of a:	
square	$A = s^2$; where s = side
rectangle	$A = lw$; where l = length, w = width
parallelogram	$A = bh$; where b = base, h = height
trapezoid	$A = \frac{1}{2}(b_1 + b_2)h$; where b = base, h = height
triangle	$A = \frac{1}{2}bh$; where b = base, h = height
circle	$A = \pi r^2$; where $\pi = 3.14$, r = radius
PERIMETER (P) of a:	
square	$P = 4s$; where s = side
rectangle	$P = 2l + 2w$; where l = length, w = width
triangle	$P = a + b + c$; where a, b, and c are the sides
CIRCUMFERENCE (C) of a circle:	$C = \pi d$; where $\pi = 3.14$, d = diameter
VOLUME (V) of a:	
cube	$V = s^3$; where s = side
rectangular container	$V = lwh$; where l = length, w = width, h = height
square pyramid	$V = \frac{1}{3}(\text{base edge})^2h$
cone	$V = \frac{1}{3}\pi r^2h$
cylinder	$V = \pi r^2h$; where $\pi = 3.14$, r = radius, h = height
PYTHAGOREAN RELATIONSHIP	$c^2 = a^2 + b^2$; where c = hypotenuse, a and b are legs of a right triangle
DISTANCE (d) BETWEEN TWO POINTS ON A PLANE	$d = \sqrt{(x_2 - x_1)^2 + (y_2 - y_1)^2}$; where (x_1,y_1) and (x_2,y_2) are two points in a plane
SLOPE OF A LINE (m)	$m = \frac{y_2 - y_1}{x_2 - x_1}$; where (x_1,y_1) and (x_2,y_2) are two points in a plane
MEAN	**mean** $= \frac{x_1 + x_2 + \ldots x_n}{n}$; where the x's = the values for which a mean is desired, and n = number of values in the series
MEDIAN	**median** = the point in an <u>ordered</u> set of numbers at which half of the numbers are above and half of the numbers are below this value
SIMPLE INTEREST (i)	$i = prt$; where p = principal, r = rate, t = time
DISTANCE (d) as function of rate and time	$d = rt$; where r = rate, t = time
TOTAL COST (c)	$c = nr$; where n = number of units, r = cost per unit

Mathematics, Part I

<u>Directions</u>: You will have 22 minutes to complete questions 1–13. You may use your calculator with these questions only. Choose the one best answer to each question.

1. Leslie's cookie recipe calls for $\frac{3}{4}$ cup of brown sugar to make 3 dozen cookies.

   If she has 3 cups of brown sugar but sufficient amounts of the other ingredients, how many cookies can she make?

   (1) $\frac{3}{4}$ dozen

   (2) 2.25 dozen

   (3) 6 dozen

   (4) 8 dozen

   (5) 12 dozen

2. A teacher is taking his 15 students to the aquarium. The usual entry fee is $6.75. Group rates on admission are $6.25 for the first 12 students, and $5.50 for each additional student. Group leaders pay $5.00. What is the total fee for the entire group?

   (1) $75.00

   (2) $96.50

   (3) $97.50

   (4) $98.75

   (5) $102.50

3. How many calories would a 180-pound man use by biking for 20 minutes? Use the data in the chart below.

Activity	Calories used per hour, per pound of weight
Sleeping	2.6
Sitting	3.5
Walking	5.1
Bicycling	10.3

   (1) $\frac{(180 \times 10.3)}{20}$

   (2) $\frac{(180 \times 3)}{10.3}$

   (3) $\frac{(180 \times 10.3)}{3}$

   (4) $\frac{(180 \times 20)}{10.3}$

   (5) $\frac{(10.3 \times 3)}{180}$

4. How many degrees is the innermost angle of a slice of pizza if there are 8 equal slices in a pizza pie?

   (1) 360

   (2) 180

   (3) 90

   (4) 50

   (5) 45

GO ON TO THE NEXT PAGE

5. Razeeka worked 7 hours, 15 minutes on Monday, 9 hours, 25 minutes on Tuesday, 5 hours 10 minutes on Wednesday, and 8 hours, 40 minutes on Thursday. How many more hours and minutes must she work on Friday in order to have a 40-hour work week?

(1) 7 hours, 50 minutes
(2) 8 hours, 30 minutes
(3) 8 hours, 50 minutes
(4) 9 hours, 30 minutes
(5) 10 hours, 10 minutes

6. Kendra needs to put a fence around the perimeter of her backyard to contain her new puppy. How many feet of fence must she purchase?

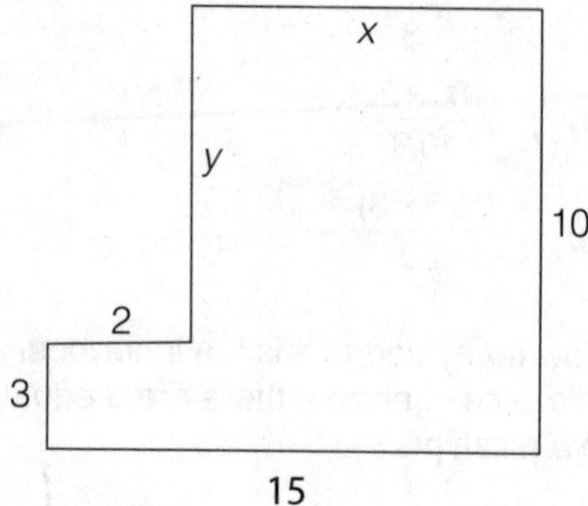

(1) 29
(2) 37
(3) 50
(4) 82
(5) 90

7. Which number equals 9 hundredths?

(1) .09
(2) .009
(3) .9
(4) .900
(5) .90

8. A newspaper charges advertisers in its classified section a total of $2.25 for the first ten words and $0.80 for each additional word. What is the cost of a 23-word ad?

(1) $3.05
(2) $5.30
(3) $12.65
(4) $18.40
(5) $23.30

9. Victor worked 3 days at his job as a server. He made $42.00 in tips the first day, $37.50 the second day and $51.00 on the third day. What was his average tip earnings per day?

(1) $43.33
(2) $43.50
(3) $43.85
(4) $130.50
(5) $130.75

GO ON TO THE NEXT PAGE

10. What is the radius of a circle with area 36π?

PLEASE DO NOT WRITE IN THIS TEST BOOKLET.

Mark your answer in the circles in the grid on your answer sheet.

11. What is the median of the following set of numbers, if $y = 2$?

$\{4y, 3 + y, \frac{12}{y}, 7 - y, \frac{20}{y}\}$

(1) $\frac{12}{y}$

(2) $\frac{20}{y}$

(3) $4y$

(4) $7 - y$

(5) $3 + y$

12. The temperature at 6:00 am is –8°F. At 9:00 A.M. the temperature is 6°F. If the temperature rises at a constant rate, what will the temperature be at 3:00 pm?

(1) 14°F

(2) 20°F

(3) 24°F

(4) 29°F

(5) 34°F

13. If a shoe store is having a 20% off sale and you pay $48 for a pair of shoes, how much was the original price of the shoes? (Disregard the $ sign when gridding your answer.)

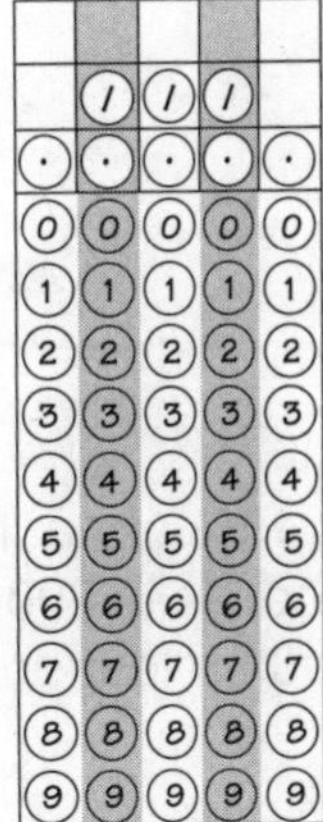

PLEASE DO NOT WRITE IN THIS TEST BOOKLET.

Mark your answer in the circles in the grid on your answer sheet.

END OF MATHEMATICS, PART 1

Directions: You will have 22 minutes to complete questions 14–25. You may NOT use a calculator with these questions. Choose the one best answer to each question.

14. In the figure below, the area of the triangle is 60. What is the value of h?

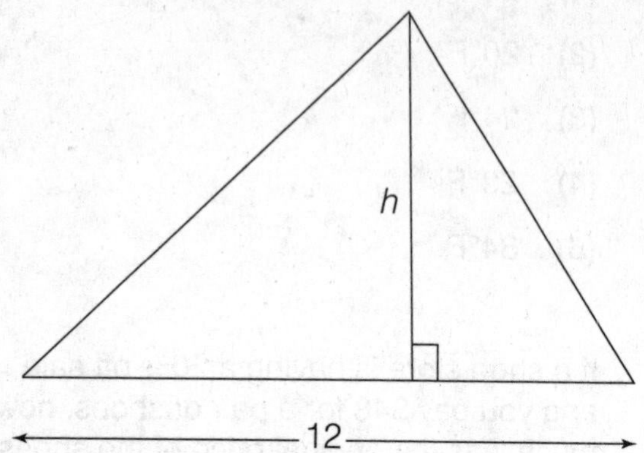

(1) 12
(2) 10
(3) 8
(4) 6
(5) 5

15. Marisol uses 15% of her house as a home office. If her house is 2000 square feet, how many square feet does she use as an office?

(1) 120
(2) 133.3
(3) 150
(4) 300
(5) 333

16. The speed of sound is 330 meters per second. If you see a flash of lightning and it takes 10 seconds to hear the thunder, how many kilometers away is it?

(1) $\frac{(10)(330)}{100}$
(2) $\frac{(10)(330)}{1000}$
(3) (10)(330)(100)
(4) (10)(330)(1,000)
(5) (10)(330)

17. On the ruler in the diagram below, which letter corresponds to $\frac{5}{8}$ inches?

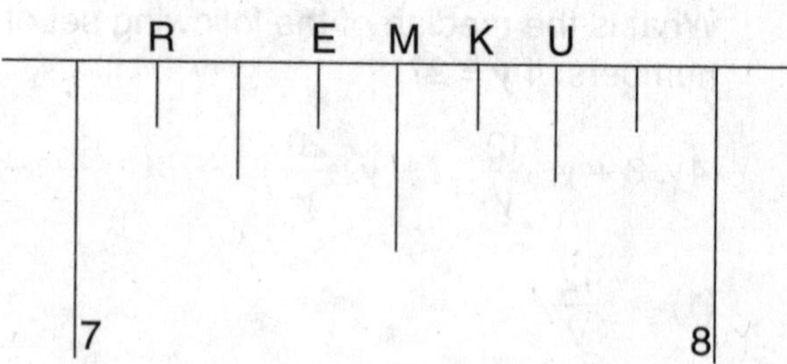

(1) K
(2) R
(3) E
(4) M
(5) U

GO ON TO THE NEXT PAGE

18. The scale of a certain real car to a toy model of that car is 15 to 1. What is the diameter of the steering wheel (in inches) of the full size car if the model's steering wheel is 2.5 inches?

PLEASE DO NOT WRITE IN THIS TEST BOOKLET.

Mark your answer in the circles in the grid on your answer sheet.

19. What is the slope of a line passing through coordinates (2,7) and (–1,2) on the *x,y* plane?

(1) $-\frac{5}{3}$

(2) $-\frac{1}{9}$

(3) $\frac{3}{5}$

(4) -9

(5) $\frac{5}{3}$

20. What is the batting average for the following five players, whose individual batting averages are 0.340, 0.390, 0.370, 0.330 and 0.350?

PLEASE DO NOT WRITE IN THIS TEST BOOKLET.

Mark your answer in the circles in the grid on your answer sheet.

GO ON TO THE NEXT PAGE

21. What is the graph below describing?

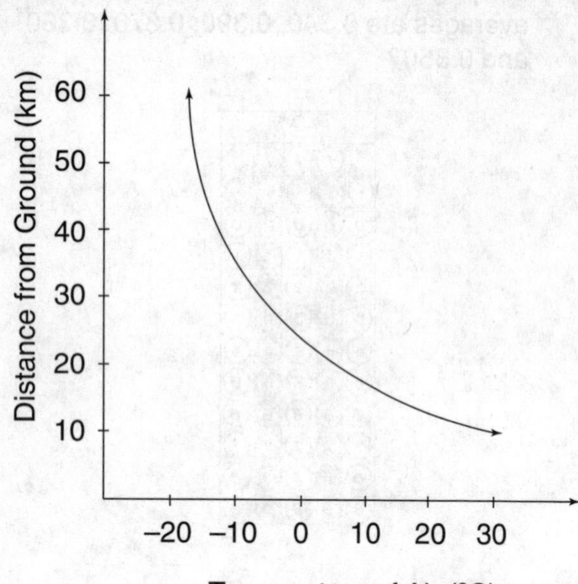

(1) As the distance from the ground increases, the air temperature remains the same.
(2) As the distance from the ground increases, the air temperature increases.
(3) As the distance from the ground increases, the air temperature decreases.
(4) As the distance from the ground increases, the air temperature fluctuates.
(5) Not enough information given to determine an answer.

22. If $x = 4$ and $y = 5$. What is $x^2 + 3y$?

(1) 13
(2) 16
(3) 25
(4) 31
(5) 37

23. If Sonia's net (take-home) pay is $2700 per month and her mortgage is one-third of that, how much money does she have remaining for other expenses?

(1) $1,800
(2) $1,500
(3) $1,200
(4) $925
(5) $900

GO ON TO THE NEXT PAGE

24. What is the best way to determine the area of the shaded portion of the diagram?

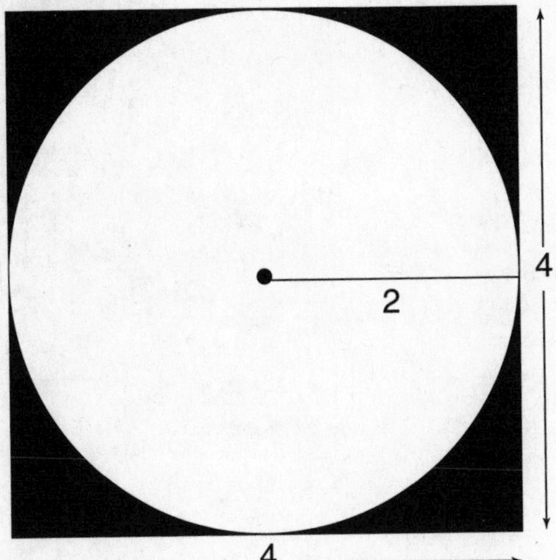

(1) $16 - 8\pi$

(2) $16 - 4\pi$

(3) $16 + 8\pi$

(4) $16 + 4\pi$

(5) $16 - 2\pi$

25. If there are 475 milligrams of a certain component in a 1.25 gram capsule, how many milligrams of other components are there in the rest of the capsule?

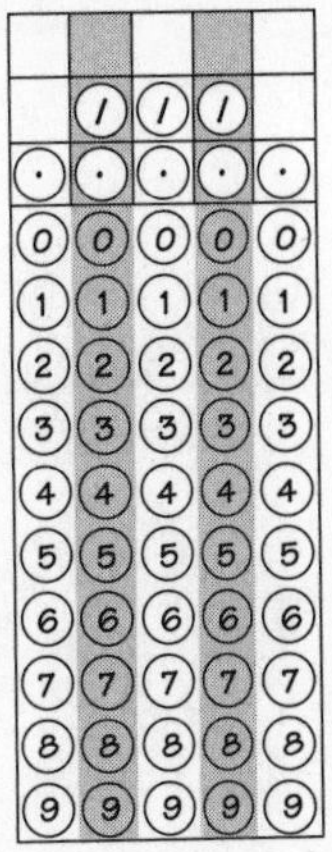

PLEASE DO NOT WRITE IN THIS TEST BOOKLET.

Mark your answer in the circles in the grid on your answer sheet.

END OF EXAMINATION

DO NOT MARK OR WRITE ON THIS PAGE

Answers and Explanations for Practice Test 5

WRITING

1. 5
2. 3
3. 4
4. 4
5. 3
6. 5
7. 1
8. 1
9. 2
10. 4
11. 5
12. 4
13. 3
14. 2
15. 3
16. 2
17. 1
18. 3
19. 4
20. 2
21. 5
22. 2
23. 1
24. 5
25. 1

SOCIAL STUDIES

1. 4
2. 2
3. 5
4. 3
5. 4
6. 1
7. 3
8. 4
9. 1
10. 3
11. 4
12. 5
13. 2
14. 3
15. 1
16. 4
17. 2
18. 5
19. 4
20. 2
21. 5
22. 4
23. 2
24. 3
25. 1

SCIENCE

1. 3
2. 1
3. 4
4. 1
5. 4
6. 3
7. 3
8. 3
9. 1
10. 3
11. 5
12. 4
13. 2
14. 1
15. 2
16. 2
17. 5
18. 5
19. 1
20. 5
21. 4
22. 3
23. 1
24. 5
25. 4

READING

1. 5
2. 1
3. 5
4. 4
5. 3
6. 1
7. 3
8. 3
9. 4
10. 4
11. 2
12. 3
13. 1
14. 2
15. 3
16. 2
17. 4
18. 3
19. 3
20. 3
21. 2

MATH

1. 5
2. 2
3. 3
4. 5
5. 4
6. 3
7. 1
8. 3
9. 2
10. 6
11. 1
12. 5
13. 60
14. 2
15. 4
16. 2
17. 1
18. 37.5
19. 5
20. 0.356
21. 3
22. 4
23. 1
24. 2
25. 775

EXPLANATIONS

Writing

1. 5 The answer is 5 because sentence 2, as written, joins together two complete sentences with a comma; only choices 3 and 5 fix this. Choice 3 is wrong because it lacks a conjunction.

2. 3 The answer is 3 because *developing* is the wrong verb form; only 3 corrects this.

3. 4 The answer is 4 because in the original sentence, the verbs *identify* and *working to eliminate* are not parallel; only 4 corrects this. Choice 5 changes the meaning of sentence 5.

4. 4 The answer is 4 because it best maintains the meaning of sentence 7. Choice 1 changes the verb outline into a noun. Choice 2 changes the meaning. Choice 3 lacks the verb *outline.* Choice 5 uses the wrong verb form.

5. 3 The answer is 3. Choices 1, 2, and 4 are passive. Choice 5 lacks a verb.

6. 5 The answer is 5 because sentence 10 is a fragment and thus needs to be joined to sentence 11. Choice 3 adds an unneeded conjunction while choice 4 uses the wrong pronoun.

7. 1 The answer is 1 because the pronoun should be plural to agree with the rest of sentence 12. No other choices fix this.

8. 1 The answer is 1 because sentence 13 is correct as written.

9. 2 The answer is 2 because sentence 6 discusses the strategy for one of the departments and thus belongs in paragraph B. Choice 3 is wrong because paragraphs B and C discuss different things.

10. 4 The answer is 4 because the correct word is *There* and the other choices use the wrong word. *Their* is the possessive pronoun. *They're* is a contraction for "they are."

11. 5 The answer is 5 because the cars built recently are being compared to other earlier cars and only choice 5 makes the proper comparison. Choice 4 actually compares cars built recently with themselves.

12. 4 The answer is 4 because sentence 7 on its own is a fragment and choices 3 and 5 use the wrong verb form.

13. 3 The answer is 3 because the correct word is *a lot* and only choice 3 fixes this. The word *allot* means "give to someone as a share."

14. 2 The answer is 2 because choices 1, 3, and 4 are in the passive voice and choice 5 changes the meaning.

15. 3 The answer is 3 because the verb *has* is singular and therefore does not agree with the noun *foreign cars* and only choice 3 fixes this. Choice 2 changes the meaning.

16. 2 The answer is 2 because sentence 13 discusses fuel efficiency, which is discussed in paragraph B.

17. 1 The answer is 1 because the conjunction *because* suggests that the two parts of sentence 14 are similar in meaning when they are in fact they are divergent in meaning. Only choices 1 and 4 fix this, but 4 changes the meaning.

18. 3 The answer is 3 because the comma after *stop* is incorrect and only choice 3 fixes this. Choice 1 uses the wrong pronoun. Choices 2 and 5 use the wrong articles.

19. 4 The answer is 4 because sentence 2 suggests that *coffee beans* are what are being roasted and thus needs a plural pronoun. Choice 1 incorrectly changes the tense.

20. 2 The answer is 2 because the phrase *Native to Ethiopia* lacks a subject and only choices 2 and 5 correctly place coffee after the comma. Choice 5 changes the meaning.

21. 5 The answer is 5 because sentence 4 does not belong anywhere in the passage as it discusses non-coffee drinks while the rest of the passage discusses coffee.

22. 2 The answer is 2 because the verb *introduce* is plural while the subject *Coffee* is singular; the word should be *introduced.*

23. 1 The answer is 1 because sentence 6 is correct as written.

24. 5 The answer is 5 because neither sentence 7 nor 8 is complete on its own. Choice 2 changes the meaning and choice 3 uses the wrong verb form.

25. 1 The answer is 1 because as written, sentence 10 is incomplete: it lacks a verb. Only choice 1 fixes this.

Social Studies

1. 4 The largest empire at the time of the map was Spain, which controlled nearly all of Latin America. Therefore, choice 4 is correct.

2. 2 European nations left the New World because they could not sustain their empires, in either military or economic terms, against revolutions and warfare. Thus choice 2 is correct. Choices 1, 3, and 5 are all factually incorrect and choice 4 would have been impossible in those empires that were themselves absolutist monarchies.

3. 5 Some of the languages listed among the choices are not commonly spoken in the Western Hemisphere, especially Russian, Dutch, and German. This means that choices 1, 2, 3, and 4 are all incorrect.

4. 3 The Secretary of State is a member of the President's Cabinet, which is his group of chief advisers. Therefore, the Secretary of State works in the Executive Branch and choice 3 is correct. Because there is no such thing as the "Diplomatic Branch" (choice 2) or the "Constitutional Branch" 4, these choices should be eliminated.

5. 4 The cartoon indicates that President Roosevelt pressured the Colombian government with financial bribes, so choice 4 is correct. Because Roosevelt was not being portrayed as a victim, choices 1, 2, and 3 are incorrect. Choice 5 conveys the opposite meaning of the transaction depicted in the image.

6. 1 The Panama Canal opened a trade route directly between the Atlantic and Pacific Oceans conveniently located between North and South America. This opened up dramatic new possibilities for international trade in the Western Hemisphere. None of the other answer choices are factually correct.

7. 3 The Constitution allows for amendments, or changes, to its text. There have been twenty-seven such amendments since the ratification of the Constitution in 1787. The first ten amendments are known as the Bill of Rights. Eliminate answer choices that make no sense, such as choice 1, which makes the impossible claim that there are no specific provisions in the Constitution. Similarly, choice 2 makes the ridiculous claim that the Constitution says nothing about the Legislative Branch. Choices 4 and 5 are also incorrect and irrelevant to the quote.

8. 4 Civil rights are the "rights and freedoms that assure everyone's ability to participate in national political life" (choice 4). Some of these rights are indeed protected in the Bill of Rights, so choices 1 and 2 are incorrect. Because not everyone has had these rights equally, choices 3 and 5 are also incorrect.

9. 1 Eliminate incorrect answers. Mississippi and New York were both states, so choice 2 is incorrect. The extreme language of choices 3 and 5 ("total equality" and "not different") indicate that they are unlikely as correct answers. Only choice 1 is logically possible: during the 1960s African Americans in Mississippi were being denied the right to vote.

10. 3 Martin Luther King Jr. argued for non-violent forms of protest: "We must not allow our creative protest to degenerate into physical violence." Therefore, choice 3 is correct. Each of the other choices is either factually incorrect or off-topic.

11. 4 Racial segregation is best defined in choice 4: "the separation of different racial groups in daily life and public institutions" because segregation is fancy word for separation. Choices 2, 3, and 5 address different topics.

12. 5 Whenever you see a chart or graph, remember to take your time reading any titles, captions, or labels that can help you understand the material. According to this chart, it was not until 1920 that a majority of the American population lived in urban areas.

13. 2 A census is the information that is gathered every ten years by the federal government, so choice 2 is correct. It is mandated by the Constitution in order to determine representation in Congress and the Electoral College.

14. 3 Eliminate answers that are obviously incorrect, such as choice 1. The majority of Americans now live in urban centers. Because rural areas are, by definition, *not* densely populated, choice 2 is also incorrect. Both choices 4 and 5 describe the opposite of historical reality.

15. 1 Though the language of the Court's ruling may be difficult to get through, it is clear that free speech is limited when people present a "clear and present danger" to the United States. Therefore, choice 1 is correct. Each of the other choices twists the language of the prompt.

16. 4 The First Amendment is one of ten included in the Bill of Rights. It protects five essential freedoms of American citizens: freedom of speech, religion, press, assembly, and petition. The Stamp Act of 1765 (1) was passed by the British government as a tax on the American colonies. The Emancipation Proclamation 2 was the document that prohibited slavery in some states in 1863. The Federalist Papers 3 were a collection of articles mean to promote the Constitution before its ratification. The Articles of Confederation 5 was an early constitution of the newly formed United States.

17. 2 "Prohibition" (2) describes the period from 1919 to 1933, when the sale, manufacture, and transportation of alcohol for consumption was illegal. While the events described in each of the other answer choices also occurred in the twentieth century, they had little to do with the prohibition of alcohol.

18. 5 Choice 5 is the only option that includes an opinion subject to dispute. Words like "irresponsible" and "should not..." are red flags that this choice is an opinion, not a verifiable and objective fact.

19. 4 Only choice 4 accurately describes the information presented in the passage. The practice of deliberately poisoning water supplies (4) is clearly stated in the passage, whereas the other answer choices refer to irrelevant or factually incorrect information.

20. 2 Carson was clearly concerned about the effect of pesticides on drinking water for humans (2). Some of the choices should be eliminated immediately because they express ideas that violate common sense. For example, Carson was not arguing that "one negative effect of the 'introduction of poisons into a reservoir'" was that it "helps sustain a vibrant ecosystem" (3). This is not a "negative effect" and no one would ever argue that poisons ultimately help the environment.

21. 5 The excerpt is discussing environmental movement (5), not the feminist movement 1, which was concerned with women's rights. The text is also not about civil rights 2 or about abolition 3, which was the movement to end slavery. The sexual revolution of the 1960s and 1970s 4 is also off-topic.

22. 4 Pay close attention to the wording of the answer choices. Highly critical and negative language is often a clue that you are looking at an opinion, not a fact. Examples include "wasteful" (1), "afraid... they do not understand..." (2), "destroying the moral character" (3) and "better" (5). Notice that both choices 1 and 5 make recommendations about what "should" happen and are therefore opinions, not facts.

23. 2 The graph does not indicate fluctuation in population (1), immigration (4), or Spanish interest (5). It simply conveys that many Native Americans died in the period. Therefore, choice 2 is correct, since 3 is disproved by the graph.

24. 3 The populations of Native Americans declined dramatically because of disease brought from the European conquerors, so choice 3 is correct. Some of the choices should be eliminated because they are obviously wrong. Choices 1 and 2, for example, describe highly unlikely situations. Choice 4 would have been pragmatically impossible and against the primary goals of the Spanish conquest; indeed, many sought to conquer, not destroy.

25. 1 The preamble is a clear statement of the purpose of the document and comes before the main body. Of course, it does not reject a notion of human rights (2) and does not contain the "entire text" of the Constitution (3). It also makes no claim to reject the Bill of Rights (4) or to "recreate" the Declaration of Independence (5).

Science

1. 3 The passage states that evolutionary fitness is determined by an organism's contribution to the next generation's gene pool. The individual with the most living children is the most fit by this definition, so 3 is correct. The individuals in 1 and 2 have not contributed to the next generation's gene pool, while the people in 4 and 5 have fewer children than the woman in 3 and so are less fit.

2. 1 The chart provides information about soil and rock. A geologist studies soil and rock so 1 is best.

3. 4 Sedimentary rock is 12% and metamorphic rock is 10%. Since 12% + 10% = 22%, 4 is correct.

4. 1 This question requires careful examination of the graph. From March to April the average inches of rainfall increases by 50. In all the following months, the rainfall decreases. Therefore, 1 is correct.

5. 4 This graph only shows spring and summer months, so there is no information provided for all for seasons or for November so 1 and 2 are incorrect. Types of clouds and temperatures are not mentioned, so 3 and 5 are incorrect. The chart shows that April is the rainiest spring or summer month in the city of Mayfair, so 4 is correct.

6. **3** This question requires that centripetal force is felt during rapid circular motion. Choice 1 is wrong because gravity would pull the water down, and 2 is incorrect because the bucket must be rotated quickly. Choice 3 correctly describes centripetal force. There is no reason to believe the water has frozen, so 4 is incorrect, and if answer 5 were correct then water would never spill from any container, so 5 is incorrect.

7. **3** Choice 1 is incorrect because clay changes size and this would not provide a stable foundation for a building. Choice 2 is incorrect because sandy soil provides drainage and hazardous waste should not drain out of its disposal site. Choice 3 is correct because sandy soil allows for drainage, but 4 is incorrect because sandy soil would not contain water in a pond. Choice 5 is incorrect because clay soil would prevent water from reaching the roots.

8. **3** In the chart shown, half of the offspring have one X and one Y and are males and half have two X chromosomes and are female. Therefore, 50% are expected to be male and 3 is correct.

9. **1** Each parent must give one gene to each offspring. Since the brown rabbit only has brown genes, each child will inherit one brown gene. Since the black rabbit only has black genes, each child must inherit one black gene. Therefore, each child will be hybrid, with one black gene and one brown gene. Since the passage states black is dominant over brown, black will be expressed, so 1 is correct.

10. **3** At the beginning, John is 0 km from home. Then, he rides 2 km from home, and for a period of time John's distance from home remains 2 km. This indicates that he stopped. Finally, John's distance from home decreases back to 0, indicating that John rode back home. Choice 3 supports this data.

11. **5** The graph shows that the average urine output after drinking caffeinated diet soda was larger than the urine production after drinking tap water, which was larger than the urine production after drinking salt water. Only 5 draws an accurate conclusion based on these results so 5 is correct.

12. **4** Choices 1, 2, 3, and 5 represent questions that can be answered based on the graph shown. Choice 4 asks about urine production for different volumes of water. Since only 500 ml of water was given, there is no way to know from this experiment whether larger volumes of water would result in more urine production, so 4 is correct.

13. **2** The passage states that classical conditioning is a process in which an animal responds to something neutral because the animal associates it with something else. Choice 2 is correct because the student associates math with lunch and so responds to math by feeling hungry even when math is not before lunch.

14. **1** The passage states that bases turn blue in cabbage juice and that bases have a ph above 7. Only ammonia has a ph above 7, so 1 is correct because only ammonia will turn blue.

15. 2 Gravity would pull the ball down, so 1 is incorrect. Choice 2 is correct because air resistance would push against the ball and reduce its acceleration. The ball is plastic so there are no magnetic forces and 3 is incorrect. The ball is not touching the building so 4 is incorrect. The ball is not moving in a circle so there is no centripetal force, and 5 is incorrect.

16. 2 The densest liquid will have the most mass per volume and will sink to the bottom. Since honey sank, it has the highest density so 2 is correct and 1 is incorrect. Water is not on top so it does not have the least density, so 4 is incorrect. The liquids are not mixed so they have different densities and 3 and 5 are incorrect.

17. 5 The passage states that ladybugs are helpful insects because they consume many smaller insects that would otherwise destroy plants. Therefore, 5 is correct.

18. 5 This graph shows a line increasing as it goes up and to the right. Therefore, as temperature increases, volume increases, and 5 is correct.

19. 1 The passage states that total pressure is determined by adding partial pressures of all the gases in a container. The total pressure in this container would be the partial pressure of Gas A plus the partial pressure of Gas B, which is 20 + 500 = 700. Choice 1 is correct.

20. 5 The passage states that atomic number is the number of protons and atomic weight is the sum of protons and neutrons. The question asks which statement is not accurate. Choices 1–4 are accurate so they are incorrect. Choice 5 is correct because the atomic weight of oxygen should be the sum of the protons and neutrons. Since 8 + 8 = 16, the atomic weight of oxygen is 16, not 24.

21. 4 Static friction is the force that prevents objects from sliding, so 4 is correct. Since the block is not moving, 3 and 5 are incorrect. While an inclined plane is a simple machine, this does not answer the question so 1 is incorrect. Wood is not magnetically attracted, so 2 is incorrect.

22. 3 The passage states that magma is melted rock underground and lava is melted rock above ground, so 3 is correct. The passage does not mention how volcanoes are formed, so 1 is incorrect. Metamorphic rocks are never mentioned, so 4 is incorrect, and the depth and amount of time required for melted rock to cool are not mentioned so 2 and 5 are incorrect.

23. 1 The students need to make the canister float. Filling only the canister will not make it float, so 2 and 4 are incorrect. Filling the barrel with funnels would not help, so 5 is incorrect. Since oil is less dense than water, filling the canister with water and the barrel with oil would make the canister sink, so answer 3 is incorrect. Choice 1 is correct because if the barrel is filled with water, the fiberglass canister will float to the surface.

24. 5 The chart describes the effects of seismic activity, and the passage mentions that seismic activity is a measure of vibrations such as those associated with earthquakes, so 5 is correct.

25. 4 Seismic activity that measures 7.5 on the Richter Scale fits into the 7.0–7.9 range. The chart states that earthquakes ion this range damage areas several hundred miles large, so 4 is correct.

Reading

1. **5** The answer is 5 because the writer quotes the principal as an authority while making the point that teachers are the most important piece of the high schools success. Frequently, quotes used by authors are used to further develop and support an opinion. Choice 1 may be true but does not answer the question. The rest of the choices are not supported by the passage.

2. **1** The answer is 1 because the writer implies that the administrators are choosing "the path of eliminating teachers whenever there is a budget crisis." Choice 2 is half-right, mentioning the budget but for the wrong reason. Choice 5 may be a solution for the future, but is not what the administration has recently done. The rest of the choices are not supported by the passage.

3. **5** The answer is 5 because, of the five choices given, it is the only one supported by the information of the passage. The writer never suggests what should be done instead of firing Mr. Hileman, only that it shouldn't happen. Choices 1 may be true, but does not address the author's weakness. Choices 2 and 4 are not mentioned in the passage and cannot be verified. Choice 3 would not change the writer's opinion that Mr. Hileman is currently a good teacher.

4. **4** The author mentions all choices listed here except 4. In the third paragraph 1 is seen in "damaging its academic programs." Choice 2 is mentioned in "eliminating teachers" in the first paragraph. Choice 3 is seen in the first paragraph with students who may not "get the same tremendous opportunities." Choice 5 is mentioned in the second paragraph with the "termination of a very good Classics course."

5. **3** The answer is 3 because the writer indicates "I learned the most important lesson – how to learn" in the second paragraph. The other choices were all mentioned in the passage but do not answer the question.

6. **1** The best way to solve a question such as this is to treat the word in the passage as a blank within the sentence so that it can be replaced. Thus, the sentence is basically, "…your deductions have not been as _____ as I should have wished." Of the choices listed, only *accurate* is appropriate. Notice that the other choices are possible definitions of the word "happy", but not here in the way it is used. Frequently, words in context will test an unusual usage of the word.

7. **3** In the passage, the comment by Holmes is "How *could* you tell that, Watson?" In general, italics, when not used for titles are used for emphasis. That is the case here as Holmes understands that Watson is making a mistake and so is asking questions with great emphasis and in a humorous manner so as to urge Watson along into more mistakes. There is no indication that Holmes is shouting or whispering, as in 1 and 2. Though he is asking a question, 4 is wrong as it does not answer the question. Choice 5 is unsupported.

8. **3** The answer is 3 because Holmes knows that Watson is making mistakes (as he shows at the end of the passage) but he continues to respond enthusiastically to Watson as he makes those mistakes. Tone question about characters or authors must be supported with words and phrases in the passage. Here, Holmes is fooling around, so his answers are facetious and joking. Choice 1 is a literal interpretation and misses the truth of the conversation. No other choices have evidence in the passage.

9. **4** The answer is 4 because Watson states that some others in the world could perform clever tricks which Holmes answers by stating that there are also some others who are not as clever. This less-clever group is the one that Holmes is comparing Watson to, saying that he is one of them, a member of the group of people who are not clever. Only choice 4 is supported by the passage.

10. **4** The answer is 4 based on the entire story as revealed in the passage. In summary, Watson believes he is clever and can replicate Holmes' mental tricks. In reality, Watson gets everything very wrong. The obvious result of this is that Watson clearly cannot do what he thought he could and thus, it is not as simple and easy as he thought. Only 4 states this. Choice 1 has just been shown to be false. Choice 2 is unsupported. Choices 3 and 5 are extreme and cannot be known with certainty.

11. **2** The answer is 2 because it maintains the meaning of the sentence. To answer this question, treat the sentence as if it had a blank: "I turned to it to find if Surrey was _____ [holding its own] against Kent." The passage indicates that this is in reference to a game, so only 2, *competing well*, is appropriate.

12. **3** The answer is 3 because Joe directly states that "the painter with an original vision is always opposed by the schools." It cannot be verified if the artists in question were "better" or "unaware" as stated in 1 and 2. Choices 4 and 5 are not stated in the passage.

13. **1** The answer is 3 because Mr. Wentworth mentions that great masters "obey the eternal laws" and "if we once admit there are no laws, where are we? Anarchy!" This shows that his emphasis is on rules, unlike Joe's emphasis on life and new art. Greek and Japanese art are mentioned, as in 4 and 5, but are not clearly valued by Mr. Wentworth. The other choices are unsupported.

14. **2** The answer is 2 because Joe makes a large point regarding how relevant art is. He believes that new art is vital and that older art, though nice, does not last forever. He also states that "the time comes when his value is spent. When the world needs a new influence." This new influence obviously must be new artists. Choice 3 might be true but is not on the topic of Joe's comment. The other choices cannot be confirmed and are not supported directly in the passage.

15. **3** The answer is 3 because Joe states that the laws about painting are "contained in the impulses themselves, not before it!" In other words, Joe believes that what eventually become "laws" are things that artists began doing while creating. Joe does not believe that art comes after rules about art are established, but before the rules, while that artist is in action.

16. 2 The answer is 2. Throughout the passage, Joe states his desire to see new art and his lack of respect for older art that does not live forever. He also refers to the Louvre as a place to put pictures "when they are dead". This is contrasted to his desire to "wake people to life" and his belief that new art and new life are basically the same. To him, the Louvre represents death. Choice 1 is not supported since Joe understand the art in the Louvre may be good and was once relevant when it was made, but it's just now old. Choices 4 and 5 contradicts details about Joe in the passage.

17. 4 The answer is 2 because the poem mentions regret and late understanding of the father's actions. Thus, if given a chance to go back, the speaker would clearly want to appreciate what the father had done. That means that the speaker would clearly desire to perform the actions mentioned in 1, 2, 3 and 5.

18. 3 The answer is 3 because the poem as a whole describes the speaker at a younger age "speaking indifferently" to his father and that "no one even thanked him." It is clear that the father was doing kind things that were unappreciated. But the speaker is writing at a later age at a time in which he now does appreciate it. Thus his feelings have gone from a youth of indifference to a later age of appreciation. Only 3 is a close approximation of that change. All other choices are unsupported.

19. 2 The answer is 2 because it is the only choice given that can be supported. Choices 1 and 3 are unknown and cannot be assumed. Choice 4 might be true but is never stated in the passage and cannot be guessed with certainty. Choice 5 might also be true, but we must keep our interpretation to details in the passage with no outside information.

20. 3 The answer, 3, is clearly stated in the passage in the beginning of the passage with "Sundays too my father got up early." The word *too* implies that this was not the only day that his father did this. There must have been other days, likely every day. There is no indication that the father works anywhere in particular, as in 1, or if he is married, as in 5. Nothing is stated about the father's attitude, as in 2 and 4.

21. 2 The answer is 2 because the entire passage gives clues that the speaker is looking backwards to a prior time in his life. The details reveal that he now appreciates what his father did, even though at the time he did not thank him and "slowly would rise and dress" after his father had already made the house warm in preparation. The entire tone is one of looking back and seeing things differently. The final repeated.question "What did I know?" emphasizes this idea of regret.

Math

1. 5 Calculate how many times $\frac{3}{4}$ of a cup will go into 3 cups by dividing 3 cups by $\frac{3}{4}$ = 4. Therefore she can make 4 times the 3 dozen, which is 12 dozen.

2. 2 Multiply the first 12 students by \$6.25 = \$75.00. The next 3 students pay \$5.50 each, so \$5.50 × 3 = \$16.50. The teacher pays \$5.00. Therefore, \$75.00 + \$16.50 + \$5.00 = \$96.50 total.

3. 3 The 10.3 is per pound, so you must multiply by 180 lbs to get the number of calories the man will burn in an hour. 20 minutes is an hour divided by 3. So you must divide 10.3 × 180 by 3.

4. 5 There are 360° in a circle. If there are 8 equal slices in a circular pizza pie, divide 360 by 8 = 45°.

5. 4 Get the hours she has worked so far. One way is to add all the full hours (7 + 9 + 5 + 8 = 29 hours) and then add the minutes (15 + 25 + 10 + 40 = 90 minutes). 29 hours + 90 minutes = 30 hours, 30 minutes. She must work another 9.5 hours, or 9 hours, 30 minutes, to get to 40 hours.

6. 3 To get a perimeter, add all the sides. The two missing sides are 15 – 2 = 13, and 10 – 3 = 7. So 15 + 10 + 13 + 7 + 2 + 3 = 50.

7. 1 In decimals, the first digit to the right of the decimal point is the "tenths" digit, the next one to the right is the "hundredth" digit. So nine hundredths = 0.09.

8. 3 Out of 23 words, the first 10 words are a total of \$2.25. The remainder of the words, 13 words, are \$0.80 each = \$10.40. So \$2.25 + \$10.40 = \$12.65.

9. 2 To get an average, total all the things and then divide by the number of things. So 42.00 + \$37.50 + \$51.00 = \$130.50. Divide 130.50 by 3 to get \$43.50.

10. 6 Area of a circle = πr^2. If the area is 36π, then the radius is 6.

11. 1 To find the median, arrange the numbers from lowest to highest and select the middle number. In this problem, you must first replace each y with a 2 and then solve each equation. So $4y$ = **8**; $3 + y$ =5; $12/y$ = **6**; $7 - y$ = 5 and $20/y$ = **10**. Now arrange 8, 5, 6, 5 and 10 from lowest to highest: {5, 5, 6, 8, 10}. 6 is the median.

12. 5 The differences between the temperatures at 6 am and 9 am is 14°F. Therefore, the temperature rises by 14°F every 3 hours and will be 34°F at 3 pm.

13. 60 If \$48 represents 80% of the full price, divide 48 by 0.8 to get the original price of \$60. In other words, if x is the original price, solve for x: $48 = 0.8\,x$, so $\frac{48}{0.8} = x$ and $x = 60$.

14. 2 Area of a triangle = $\frac{1}{2}bh$. So, $60 = \frac{1}{2}(12)h$. $60 = 6h$. $10 = h$.

15. 4 15% of ,2000 sq feet can be expressed as 0.15 × 2,000 = 300 sq feet.

16. 2 Distance = rate × time, so Distance = 330m/s 10s = 3,300 meters. Divide meters by 1,000 to convert to kilometers.

17. 1 Examine the ruler to see that there are eight tick marks between the 7 and 8 inch marks, each representing an eighth of an inch. Count 5 tick marks past the 7 to get to $7\frac{5}{8}$.

18. 37.5 Multiply the length of the model's steering wheel, 2.5 inches, by 15. The answer is 37.5 inches.

19. 5 The slope formula is $\frac{y_2 - y_1}{x_2 - x_1}$

Using the points given, we get $\frac{7-2}{2-(-1)} = \frac{5}{2+1} = \frac{5}{3}$

20. **0.356** To find the average, add the five individual numbers and divide that total (1.78) by the number of batters 5 to give you 0.356

21. 3 Notice on the graph that as the distance from the ground, represented by the vertical (y) axis increases, the air temperature, represented by the horizontal (x) axis, decreases.

22. 4 Replace the x and y in the equation with $x = 4$ and $y = 5$, So $x^2 + 3y$ becomes $4^2 + 35 = 16 + 15 = 31$.

23. 1 Her mortgage is one-third of $2,700, which is $900. That leaves $1,800 for her other expenses.

24. 2 The shaded area is the whole square minus the circle. The area of the square is $4 \times 4 = 16$. The area of the circle is $\pi \times r^2$. So it's $\pi \times 2^2 = \pi 4$ or 4π. Subtract the circle from the square to get the shaded area: $16 - 4\pi$.

25. 775 If the capsule is 1.25 grams, it is 1,250 milligrams (mg). 1,250 mg – 475 mg = 775 mg.

NOTES

NOTES

NOTES